RORSCHACH
PSYCHOLOGY

John Wiley & Sons, Inc., New York · London · Sydney

edited by   **MARIA A. RICKERS-OVSIANKINA**
University of Connecticut

RORSCHACH
PSYCHOLOGY

THIRD PRINTING, DECEMBER, 1965

TO FRANK W. RICKERS

PREFACE

The function envisioned for this book might best be expressed by stating first what it is not. The book is not planned to furnish another instructional manual on the use of the Rorschach method. It does not intend to teach the standard mechanics of administering, scoring, and interpreting the test. Rather, it is directed to theory-minded readers from the ranks of clinicians and general psychologists alike.

It is no exaggeration to say that the majority of contemporary clinicians would find it difficult even to contemplate their field of specialization without Rorschach's contribution to it. In fact, for no small number, personality assessment and the Rorschach are practically synonymous. And yet, paradoxically enough, despite the prominence accorded to the Rorschach test in their daily work, these psychologists would be hard pressed if asked to spell out the place of their method within the theoretical framework of psychology at large and within the psychology of personality in particular. Conversely, many general psychologists, active in the area of personality, motivation, emotion, and cognition, are rarely aware of what a mine of wealth for their own domain can be found within the diversified pattern of a Rorschach protocol.

This surprising lack of contact between two groups equally devoted to the study of personality problems becomes at least partially understandable when the nature of the test and its history are considered. In the spirit of traditional faculty-symptom-oriented psychology and psychiatry of the second decade of our century, Hermann Rorschach set out to devise a method for the measurement of a particular psychological function, one that in its extreme manifestations serves as a differential symptom in psychiatric classification: the function of imagination. The choice of ink blots for such a purpose also has its precedent. However, in the course of his experimentations, with conventional methods on a conventional topic, clinical insight, supported by the then very new ideas of Freudian-Jungian psychoanalysis, soon extended the scope of his research beyond the traditions of his time. Keenly cognizant of the individuality of the particular person in whom he was observing the imaginative processes, Rorschach became impressed with the evidence that the subject's perceptual reactions, while yielding information about the imagination, were at the same time telling a great deal more about the person. He began to see the imaginative processes as closly interacting with other psychological functions. Recognition of this interaction, in turn, meant orientation to a fundamental principle of personality organization, and with this step he found himself right in the midst of the broad and complex problems of total-personality functioning.

We are told that grasping the inner workings of man was a lifelong concern of Rorschach's. It is understandable, therefore, how exciting the prospect must have been to him that his experimentations with ink blots might provide a workable method for attaining this goal. Inspired by such perspectives, he threw his full efforts into the task: the skills of artist and of scientist blended by the zeal of a sensitive, highly gifted man. The result, as we all know, was both a comprehensive schema for the representation of the total personality and a concrete procedure for measuring individual differences among personalities. Rorschach thus discovered a fundamental organismic principle independently and in advance of his scientific milieu, and, in addition, laid the groundwork for the quantitative study of these intricate patterns of personality organization.

It is hardly surprising that a revolutionary achievement of such magnitude and singularity could not be readily incorporated into the conventional psychology of his time. Although Rorschach's discovery remained apart from the main stream of academic psychology over the following decades, this did not mean stagnation. The exceptional usefulness of the method for personality assessment was soon recognized and realized in clinical settings. From this basic field of application it has been spreading rapidly into an ever-widening circle of psychodiagnostic investigations.

The extensive and varied use of the method has resulted in the accumulation of a vast amount of information about it. The bulk of this material is in the form of statistical studies on a broad range of populations tested for every conceivable purpose. The chief value of this impressive storehouse of empirical data lies in providing not only confirmation but also some modifications and extensions to the clinical validity of Rorschach's original interpretative hypotheses.

In addition to this dominant, primarily solidifying type of development, some noteworthy inroads are being made along frankly exploratory and qualitative rather than quantitative lines. The challenge of probing for further and further understanding of a person's personality, so characteristic of intensive clinical work, is particularly stimulated by test material as complex in nature as the Rorschach. In this manner, over the years, a good many new ways of looking at one aspect or another of the test have been evolved by perceptive clinicians, explicitly or implicitly guided by theoretical assumptions and principles inherent in their particular philosophy of psychopathology.

Finally, there are the relative newcomers, the system-oriented Rorschach workers. Centering their interest on the theoretical underpinnings of the instrument, these researchers attempt to relate the psychological interpretation of the test variables to ideas and findings from other areas of psychology, to evolve hypotheses around these relationships, and to subject them to experimental scrutiny.

This book was prompted by the feeling that the time was ripe for sorting out and formulating systematically from among these different sources the material that appeared promising for fostering our understanding of the psychological foundations of the method. Guided by these considerations, Rorschach issues that have stimulated basic research were selected for exploration in individual chapters. Each chapter is handled by an author for whom the particular topic constitutes a major research interest. An introductory chapter supplies a brief over-all view of the method and assigns the place of every chapter topic within the over-all frame.

Although intended primarily as contributions toward a theoretical basis for the Rorschach, these presentations are not shaped to conform to one specific theoretical model. In his writings, Rorschach left us neither a complete nor a neat or consistent theory for the conceptualization of the problems involved in his instrument. He was quite emphatic, however, in stressing certain basic premises that are absolutely indispensable for the comprehension of the psychological essence of his method: the utilization of primarily formal features of the test responses as indicators of personality dimensions and the adherence to the principle of interaction among the test variables. These general premises would seem to provide a favorable climate for present-day attempts to re-evaluate theoretically its major psychological properties. It is in the nature of formally conceived variables to be adaptable to the schemes of varying theoretical models. Without essential changes in the diagnostic procedure of the test, its theoretical foundation is, hence, capable of effectively participating in the growth process of contemporary psychological thinking.

Psychology of personality has hardly reached a level of scientific maturity that would permit meaningful conceptualization within one tight unitary system. At the same time it is evident that during the last decades some common trends have become dominant in the broad area of personality theory: a realization that, in order to contribute fruitfully to this branch of inquiry, the conceptual system employed must operate within a holistic, "molar" frame of thinking and, furthermore, must gear its hypothetical constructs to formal or functional categories. Consequently, in this book, a variety of holistically oriented modes of theorizing (including some European work) will be given expression, each author choosing the conceptual system that in his eyes holds the greatest promise for enriching insight into the Rorschach issues under consideration in his chapter. Although the level of generality of the constructs utilized in these presentations naturally will vary, the orientation is toward greater formalization than heretofore common in the Rorschach literature.

Similarly, the aim of this book also led to considerable freedom in choice of method for dealing with the assigned topic. Thus some authors depend heavily on experimental data, others base their reasoning primarily on clinical evidence. Some emphasize coverage of available research, others subordinate research citation to theory building. Some favor discursive speculation, others dwell on matters as concrete as the inauguration of a new scoring schema. Whatever the methodological approach and whatever the conceptual tools, the main criterion of selection remains throughout usability for a systematic formulation in the particular branch of inquiry. Occasional discrepancies in hypotheses advanced by different authors may then not only be expected but should actually be welcomed for throwing the issue into sharper focus. By the same token, scattered spots of overlap from chapter to chapter were allowed to stay lest the cogency within an author's message might suffer.

It is hoped that this collation will have the effect of enhancing the conceptual precision of the basic test variables, of detecting and delineating gaps in our knowledge, and of pointing up pertinent research areas. The groundwork then would have been laid for further fruitful interaction between theory and practice in the complex task of developing this most challenging field of Rorschach psychology.

ACKNOWLEDGMENTS

I wish to thank first of all the authors of the chapters for their willingness to adjust their contributions to the over-all framework of this book and for their acceptance of suggestions for modifications of the script. I am especially grateful to my colleague Jesse G. Harris, Jr., for preparing his chapter at a very short notice. Thanks are also due Drs. Samuel Beck, Marguerite Hertz, Bruno Klopfer, Zygmunt Piotrowski, and Roy Schafer, who checked the Appendix for accuracy of presentation of their respective systems.

The epigrams to Chapters 4, 7, 8, 10, 11, and 12 were provided by the respective authors of the chapters; the remaining eight epigrams were chosen by the editor.

Many more persons have contributed to the completion of this book. Special mention should be made of the competent and very conscientious efforts of Allan Warrern in translating Chapter 8, and of Hilde Bernstein and Alexander Nemeth in translating Chapter 11. The ultimate responsibility for the translations, however, is my own. Both translations were authorized by the authors. Besides assuming the major share of work in the construction of the Appendix, Laura Toomey handled the Index and helped in the stylistic polishing of parts of the manuscript; the latter task she shared with Elizabeth Ormsby. Marian Rollin and Mary Davis handled the preparation of the final copy with skill and circumspection.

Thanks are due to the following authors and publishers for permission to use the materials indicated:

1. Grune and Stratton copyright: Quotations from S. J. Beck's *Rorschach's test, Vol. I. Basic processes* (end ed. revised), 1949.

2. Hans Huber copyright: (*a*) Roland Kuhn's article on "Grundlegende statistische und psychologische Aspekte des Rorschachschen Formdeutversuches," *Zeitschrift für diagnostische Psychologie*, 1. Jahrgang, Heft 4, 1953 (abbreviated, modified, and translated). (*b*) Ewald Bohm's article "Das Binder'sche Helldunkelsystem," *Rorschachiana*, Vol. V, 1959 (modified and translated). (*c*) One poem by Albin

Zollinger from a collection of Swiss poetry.   (*d*) Short passages from H. Rorschach's *Psychodiagnostics*.

3. Society of Projective Techniques and Rorschach Institute, Inc., copyright: R. R. Holt's article on "Gauging primary and secondary processes in Rorschach responses," *J. proj. Tech.*, 20, 1956 (in modified and expanded form).

4. The Macmillan Company copyright: Passages from Z. Piotrowski's *Perceptanalysis*, 1957.

5. University of Chicago copyright: Short quotations from C. W. Morris' *Foundations of the theory of signs*, University of Chicago Press, 1955.

6. Year Book Publishers copyright: Passages from Rapaport et al., *Diagnostic psychological testing*, 1946.

MARIA A. RICKERS-OVSIANKINA

Storrs, Connecticut
July 1960

CONTRIBUTORS

EWALD BOHM, Ph.D.
Clinical Psychologist
Copenhagen, Denmark

CHARLES P. FONDA, Ph.D.
Director of Psychological Services
Mansfield Training School

JESSE G. HARRIS, JR., Ph.D.
Assistant Professor of Psychology
University of Connecticut

JOAN HAVEL, Ph.D.
Research Associate
Cornell University Medical College

LAURENCE HEMMENDINGER, Ph.D.
Chief Clinical Psychologist
Bridgeport Veterans Administration
Mental Hygiene Clinic

MARGUERITE R. HERTZ, Ph.D.
Clinical Professor
Western Reserve University

ROBERT R. HOLT, Ph.D.
Professor and Director
Research Center for Mental Health
New York University

JULES D. HOLZBERG, Ph.D.
Director Psychological Laboratories
Connecticut State Hospital

SHELDON J. KORCHIN, Ph.D.
Director Psychological Laboratories
Michael Reese Hospital

ROLAND KUHN, M.D.
Kantonale Heil-und-Pflegeanstalt, Münsterlingen

GARDNER MURPHY, Ph.D.
Director of Research
Menninger Foundation

LOIS B. MURPHY, Ph.D.
Research Consultant
Department of Child Psychology
Menninger Foundation

ZYGMUNT A. PIOTROWSKI, Ph.D.
Professor Clinical Psychology
Jefferson Medical College

MARIA A. RICKERS-OVSIANKINA, Ph.D.
Professor and Director of Graduate Program in
Clinical Psychology, University of Connecticut

DAVID SHAPIRO, Ph.D.
Chief Clinical Psychologist
Austen Riggs Center, Inc.

JEROME L. SINGER, Ph.D.
Lecturer
Teachers College
Columbia University

LAURA C. TOOMEY, M.A.
Clinical Psychologist
Community Child Guidance Clinic
Manchester

CONTENTS

INTRODUCTION

> To proceed beyond the limitations of a given
> level of knowledge the researcher, as a rule,
> has to break down *methodological taboos*
> which condemn as "unscientific" or "illogi-
> cal" the very methods or concepts which
> later on prove to be basic for the next ma-
> jor progress.
>
> KURT LEWIN

1 | *by M. A. Rickers-Ovsiankina*

SYNOPSIS OF PSYCHOLOGICAL PREMISES
UNDERLYING THE RORSCHACH

To engage profitably in explorations of the theoretical and research
potential of the Rorschach method, it is essential to keep in mind the
psychological tenets inherent in this highly valued, yet inadequately
understood, diagnostic instrument. In this chapter these issues are
put into focus by reviewing briefly the Rorschach's chief working principles, and by examining these principles in the light of contemporary
psychological knowledge.

The most outstanding virtue of the Rorschach method is generally
recognized to lie in its power for providing an integrated pattern of
the total personality, and for at once articulating this pattern in specific quantitative ways into a manifold of personality dimensions. This
accomplishment, still unique among assessment procedures, was made
possible to a considerable degree by the way in which Rorschach defined his task from a systematic point of view. His primary interest
was in getting at the nature of the basic modes of functioning, underlying all of an individual's psychic activity. He was quite explicit in
emphasizing that his goal was to uncover *how,* rather than *what,* the
person experiences. This meant looking, e.g., not so much for the particular content of a subject's preoccupations, hopes, and fears as for the
modes by which these psychic events come about: whether they are

3

experienced as impulsive upsurges, as all pervading emotional states, as lively resonances to the surrounding atmosphere, or as rationally controlled reactions. The concern is more with the formal or functional than with the contentual, substantive aspects of the personality.

It was Rorschach's conviction that a person's perceptual responses to the ink blots were capable of serving as clues to such basic tendencies so long as the responses were viewed consistently in the frame of this systematic orientation. Accordingly, when abstracting from the complex test performance certain components for analysis, he concentrated primarily on formal categories and only secondarily on content categories. With the formal test dimensions thus providing the basic structure or scaffolding of the equally formal personality configuration, the actual content of day-to-day experiences then, but only then, becomes important in lending individuality and concreteness to the formal representation. The outcome is a formalized, yet alive, picture of the complete personality.

Besides Rorschach's choice of categories of analysis, his manner of employing these variables is of equal importance for a full appreciation of what Rorschach has given psychology with his instrument. While taking full advantage of the amenability of these categories of analysis to precise identification and measurement, he never interpreted any one of the categories by itself, but always as dependent upon the others, thus adhering to his basic principle of interaction among psychological functions right at the level of their correlates within the test data.

Over and over again Rorschach impresses upon the reader the importance of observing this principle. Each scoring category is viewed in relation to the other extant categories—whether the numerical pattern of the whole protocol or a single test response is under consideration. An individual response acquires its true meaning only when perceived against the background of the total cross-sectional psychogram, and when considered in terms of its place in the longitudinal sequence of the test performance. It is a matter of wholes and sub-wholes of a horizontal-structural and of a temporal nature. This emphasis on the pattern or configuration, however, never leads to vague globality, since each component scoring category is given a great deal of attention *per se*, each being recorded and evaluated in careful and very specific detail. The Rorschach worker has to be constantly attuned to handling the subunits now as dependent parts and now as gestalten in their own right.   In other words, the test as envisioned by its founder constitutes a true *unitas multiplex*.

For an understanding of how such unified, formalized, yet richly individual personality pictures derive from a set of responses to ink blots, we must turn our attention to the psychological meaning of the test components, both singly and in their interplay.   Inasmuch as these components constitute the cornerstones of the method, it is only through an illumination of their respective roles in the test pattern that this pattern in its deeper personality implications will acquire full significance.   The manner in which Rorschach relates specific aspects of percepts, represented by the scoring categories, to those basic personality dimensions that were of major concern to him, reflects well the origin of the test; empirical generalizations, rational deductions, artistic intuition, hunches, and flashes of ideas intermingle in providing the foundation for this multifaceted system of interrelated functioning.   Unraveling this isomorphism of percept and personality is complicated by the fact that the correspondences do not constitute simple one-to-one equivalents.   Every category of test performance taps more than one psychological function and, conversely, a psychological characteristic is derived from a combination of several test categories.

In the following chapters, these links will be recast by utilizing contemporary theories, relevant research data, and accumulated clinical experience to explore, first, the major test categories individually and then, in the last four chapters, the method in its totality.   For purposes of unity in this multiauthored endeavor, the problems involved in the various chapter topics are here anticipated by means of a bird's eye view of the Rorschach procedure and its basic psychological postulates.

CATEGORIES OF ANALYSIS

A response to the ink blots is classified under four major headings:

Location refers to the area of the plate chosen, to whether the area is whole or part, and to what kind of part.

Determinant comprises the specific properties of the blot that according to the testee prompted the response, such as the form of the blot, its color, shading, kinesthetic features.

Content identifies the subject matter of the response in broad categories; e.g., human, animal, landscape.

Popularity-originality represents the opposite poles of frequency in the identification of a certain blot area with a certain content.

Under each of these four major classes Rorschach employed a set of differential scoring categories. In essence, his classification system is still followed in contemporary practice. Since the test has been used so widely, a considerable number of modifications have naturally evolved around certain aspects of the scoring system, resulting in additional scores, in subdivisions, and in reformulations. Inasmuch as these particularities of scoring lie outside the focal orientation of this book, they will not be discussed in the present synopsis. For the convenience of the reader, however, the Appendix contains in tabular form a schematic comparison of the main scoring systems appearing in English language publications.

Location

The location scores deal with such configurational properties of a percept as extension, connectedness, and segregation in visual space. The main distinctions derived from these features rest on the question as to whether the response pertains to the whole blot (W), to a readily isolated, frequently apprehended blot detail (D), to a less obvious blot detail (Dd), or whether the subject reverses figure and ground, selecting the white space for an interpretation (S). Within these classifications a good deal of attention is paid to such qualitative considerations as to whether a certain whole response is aimed at embracing the totality of the given material to the neglect of details, or whether the response constitutes an effort to combine into a meaningful whole as many of the details as possible.

The numerical constellation of location scores, supplemented by these kinds of qualitative elaborations, is considered to reveal the fundamental orientation of a person's mental functioning. This orientation refers to the relative weight of organization versus articulation, of synthesis versus analysis in the subject's cognitive activities, and to the degree of generality, complexity, and specificity that characterizes these activities. Although primarily indicative of such variations in intellectual ability, the psychological significance of the location scores is not limited to the cognitive area. In a way typical of Rorschach's thinking, the location measures reflect also some volitional factors of effort or intent toward cognitive display.

Here, then, essential psychological functions are identified effectively for diagnostic purposes on the basis of structural characteristics of a person's perceptual behavior. Quite independently, such properties of the perceptual process have been studied and conceptualized by the laboratory psychologist. The challenge of following up this parallel between the Rorschach and perception psychology is close at hand. It has been met in this book along several lines.

Chapter 2 reviews the work that has grown up around an interest in isolating numerically the organizational activity in Rorschach responses through a statistically established score. By citing norms for this "organization score," relating it to standard Rorschach factors, correlating it with functionally corresponding variables from other psychological tests, and comparing clinical groups on this measure, an empirical foundation for the psychological significance of the "organization score" is mapped out.

In Chapter 3, Werner's (25, 26) developmental sensory-tonic theory is utilized as a model for subdividing the location scores in terms of the type of organizational activity involved. According to this experimentally and genetically-observationally grounded theory, differences in perceptual behavior are to be viewed as indicative of differences in organismic levels of development. By applying the major criteria that differentiate such levels to the varieties of perceptual structuring observable among the location scores, it becomes possible to order the various types of perceptual structuring into a logical continuum. A quantifiable means is thus supplied for relating a certain aspect of test behavior to a broader orbit of theoretically founded conceptions regarding differences in mental functioning.

Chapter 4 is devoted to the problem of figure-ground reversal, a gestalt phenomenon that has intrigued the laboratory worker for some time, and that has been much investigated with respect to general laws governing its occurrence. It is through the Rorschach test, however, that research interest has turned to individual differences in this form of perceptual behavior, known in the context of the test as the space response (S). The emphasis here is not just on a subject's tendency for perceptual structuring, but on restructuring, i.e., on the shifting from the initially conceived configuration to the production of a new one and, moreover, achieving this by means of a figural reversal. Since ease and efficiency of restructuring is, nowadays, understood to be based on some very fundamental forces in a person's psychological make-up, the diagnostic implications of restructuring through figure-ground reversal would appear to be of particular significance. These implications are highlighted by employing contemporary personality theory for closer integration of the space response into the broader Rorschach pattern than heretofore customary. While lending to the space response greater clarity and weight as a test factor *per se,* such theoretical reformulation brings, in turn, new perspectives and new cohesion to the over-all potential of the Rorschach.

Determinants

The test is introduced by the examiner's question, "What might this be?" The subject's task is thus formulated as one of recognition. We know from psychology of memory that the occurrence of an experience of recognition presupposes the existence of a certain degree of similarity between the incoming stimulus complex and a system of memory traces left behind by an earlier perceptual process. According to gestalt theory (10) this correspondence does not imply absolute similarity, or similarity based on identity of elements, but rather similarity of gestalt character.

Instruction to the subjects to draw their percepts results in a considerable range of variations in apparently the same responses to the same blot or blot detail (11). As Brosin has pointed out, a response like "bat" is given with high frequency to several of the cards, which are neither identical in their perceptual features, nor does any one of them represent an accurate image of a real bat. What seems to elicit this response is that "these cards have a batlike character, . . . the gestalt quality of a bat" (4, p. 4). The question arises as to what it is that conveys to one subject a batlike character in a certain ink blot, or that makes another subject see the same blot as a crouching giant?

In Rorschach's thinking these problems occupy a central position. In the analysis of a person's perceptual performance he considers them under a separate classificational grouping called *determinants,* subdivided into *form, color, chiaroscuro (shading), movement.* In the following, these categories will be identified, first, in terms of the perceptual processes involved in each determinant and, second, in terms of the psychodiagnostic implications accorded to a determinant within the test procedure.

Perceptual processes. The description of the perceptual processes underlying the respective determinant will begin with the autochthonous properties of these processes and will then evolve from these properties the type of person-environment interplay and the activity level characteristic of the particular perceptual process.

Form (*F*). When the interpretation given by the subject is based primarily on the shape or form of the chosen blot area, as "bat" or "aeroplane" for all of card I, the determinant is indicated by the *Form* score (*F*). The perceptual process involved in this type of reaction can be readily represented as an instance of proficiency in perceptual organization. Structural gestalt principles as symmetry, contour, and closure operate in producing the figural quality that is perceived by the testee as a certain object. Individual parts are utilized according to their place within the over-all percept. The emerging gestalt character of the perceived figure is viewed in relation to another organized pattern, that of a memory trace complex; or, to state it a little differently, a "hypothesis" is checked against the input information (5). The more accurately these organizational principles are applied in bringing about the particular interpretation, i.e., the greater the figural "goodness" or the *prägnanz* of the percept, the higher, in Rorschach terminology, the form level of the subject's functioning.

In achieving such a *prägnant* percept, the subject has to exert a certain amount of effort. We know from the psychology of perception that the activation of organizational processes consumes energy. In establishing gestalt similarity between the visual figure before him and an appropriate memory image, the person has to apply himself actively and deliberately. He has to select, weigh, and evaluate. His reactions are controlled and guided by objective features of the given material. They are stimulusbound. In keeping with this nature of the task, the observer's activity level may be characterized as relatively high, and the prevailing subject-environment relation as object-determined, detached, and impersonal.

Movement (*M*). There is a type of response in which the gestalt character does not follow strictly from the forms of the two-dimensional card but implies, as it were, a third dimension. This occurs when the perceived configuration is no longer static for the subject, as in form-determined responses, but has a dynamic character, direction, figural incompleteness, tension. As Arnheim has demonstrated, "gradients of perceptual qualities . . . oblique forms, shadings" are apt to create the impression of movement (1, p. 271). On the Rorschach test such dynamic effect, when apprehended by a person, usually leads to an interpretation of a human or animal figure seen in motion. Accordingly, the determinant for this group of reactions is designated as *Movement* or *kinesthetic response*. Rorschach maintained that some kind of kinesthetic element actually enters into the experience of a genuine movement percept. From a theoretical point of view, this assumption is noteworthy since it anticipates in an interesting way present-day organismic models of perception (8, 27).

In the movement response we have, then, a situation where the subject manipulates the structural features of the stimulus manifold freely and autonomously in the course of his perceptual production. He is less stimulusbound and less closely dependent on the objectively given than in the case of a form response. In contrast to the latter, when bringing about the relatively complex movement response, the testee puts more of himself into the task, drawing on broader and deeper personal resources. Correspondingly the subject-environment relation is no longer detached and object-controlled, but is marked by spontaneity and ego involvement, while the activity level of the observer remains as high as in form perception.

COLOR (*C*). When the gestalt character of the percept is evoked either solely or in conjunction with form by the hue of the blot ("flowers, fire") the determinant of *Color* (*C*) is used in the scoring of the respective response. Whereas, with both form and movement interpretations, the subject is actively at work on an organizational process consuming energy, when color serves as the carrier of the gestalt character the situation is quite different in this respect. As the author has pointed out elsewhere (19), apart from the circumstance that color differences might demarcate different regions within the visual field and thereby bring into play the factor of form with its organizational properties, color perception as such does not involve complex processes of articulation and organization. Characteristically, the experience of color is of undifferentiated nature. It is a much more direct sense datum than is either form or movement. The person becomes aware of color at once, without an intermediate step of reflecting, organizing, or evaluating processes. Colors, particularly the warm or hard hues, impress themselves in an immediate, one might say personal, manner. They affect us, speak to us, in a simple, rather primitive, fashion. This impact is rarely experienced as neutral. Colors strike us as pleasing, displeasing, exciting, or soothing. They attract or repel us. Because of this vivid, emotionally toned quality, the author has referred to color experience as physiognomic (19). Similarly, Bash (3) has recently pointed out that color perception fits Metzger's identification of an entity's gestalt character in terms of its intrinsic nature or essence (*Wesen*).[1]

---

[1] Metzger (17) differentiates the following three modes by which the gestalt character of an entity may become apparent: (a) Structure (*Struktur*) or organi-

The object's physiognomy or essence is thrust upon the observer in a specific, individualized fashion. The direction of the action goes from object to subject. This latter aspect of the interplay, together with its immediacy and forcefulness has led to characterizing the subject's position in color perception as receptive, passive (21, 22), or as a state of surrender (8). The perceptual process that underlies the color determinant, then, may be characterized as a state of passivity regarding the activity level, and as a condition of being subjectively affected by the essence of a particular outside object with respect to the person-environment relation.

CHIAROSCURO (*Ch.*) Akin to the color is the *Chiaroscuro* or *shading* determinant. It is used when the gestalt character of the percept is brought about exclusively, or in combination with form, by transitions within the achromatic light-dark continuum. Unlike the chromatic response, however, the chiaroscuro interpretation is not evoked by single colors. A shading reaction is rather produced by a diffuse total impression of the manifold of lightness nuances blurring into each other. The darkness, or haziness, or fluffiness of this impression typically leads to percepts of a synesthetic nature, such as "fur," "storm clouds," "rocks." Following Bash's application of Metzger's classifications one might, therefore, identify the gestalt character of the chiaroscuro determinant as based chiefly on the substance or fabric of the perceived material (see footnote 1), or one might say with Koffka (10) and Gibson (7) that the response derives from the microstructure (grain, texture) of the stimulus constellation. Although the subject is in the case of the shading response equally, if not more than in the case of the color response, at the mercy of the environment, the components of the interaction stand out less, no part of the field acquires figure character, there is only ground. The situation is not experienced as one of being affected by the essence of an individual object in the environment, but rather as a generalized state of finding oneself in the atmosphere or the mood emanated by the material substance of the environmental setting. The diffuseness and lack of clearcut articulation within the setting has an overpowering, frequently disquieting or threatening, effect upon the observer. Because of the pervading quality of this effect, the subject feels submerged, enveloped by its atmosphere. Similarly to color experience, the person feels

---

zation (*Gefüge*), referring to all types of spatial-temporal formation and patterning; (b) global quality (*Ganzqualität*) or substance (*Ganzbeschaffenheit*), comprising all characteristics of material or fabric; (c) essence or intrinsic nature (*Wesen*), including all expressive, physiognomic features.

passively affected, acted upon by the environment, with the important difference, however, that now there is no one particular environmental object affecting the observer. Instead, there is a general blurring of boundaries, not only in the visual field but also in the person-versus-environment differentiation.

Psychodiagnostic implications. By thinking of the response determinants in the light of the perceptual processes underlying these determinants, it becomes psychologically meaningful, if not actually compelling, how these determinants can be understood as being functionally dependent on certain personality characteristics.

FORM. Rorschach saw in the form level not only a measure of the directly observable ability for appropriate structuring of visual stimulus material but, moreover, an index of the person's total rational equipment for comprehending and grasping relations. Such a generalization should make sense to those students of psychology who view all modes of cognitive functioning as governed by the same fundamental organizational laws, and who consider precision and versatility in structuring a crucial factor in evaluating any intellectual performance.

When, furthermore, the subject-environment relation described above for the F determinant is taken into consideration, it becomes clear that possession of a certain level of intellectual ability is not likely by itself to result in a corresponding level of form perception on the test. To adhere to the given reality of the test material throughout the examination, there has to be not only ability for accurate perception but also the power to apply oneself consistently to the task in a critical and objective manner. The exercising of such a power requires control over interference from internal pressures of an emotional-motivational nature, a constellation of forces dynamically referred to as ego strength. In Chapter 5 the role of the F determinant will be discussed within this broader framework of personality, rather than of mental ability alone.

MOVEMENT. Rorschach contended that the ability to employ the movement factor in interpreting the ink-blots implies mental productivity, a creative potential and, in a more extended sense, a tendency toward inner living. Viewing M as an indicator of creativity falls in line with gestalt psychological principles since structuring activity that depends for its completion on components not explicitly given (the type of structuring found in the movement response) is in gestalt literature equated cognitively with creativity and inventiveness rather than with mere comprehension (9). If, in addition, we accept the organismic dictum that no cognitive behavior is without supporting conative-emotional components (23), then it is to be expected that these components would be particularly evident in as complex a cognitive process as the movement response; and the spontaneous, ego-involving character of the subject-environment relation, prevailing in the "creating" of an M response, will further the participation of relatively central inner-personal regions. It is, then, inherent in the specific fashion by which the M determinant comes about that the study of such responses should be capable of providing clues not only regarding the subject's creative potential but also of supplying insights into the general realm of his inner living. In Chapter 6 the implications that follow from this role of the M determinant are examined, interpreted, and developed further from the position of *Percept-analysis* (18).

COLOR. In Rorschach practice the color determinant is related specifically to the emotional sphere and, more generally, to a person's environmental reactivity. The isomorphism of chromatic color perception and emotionality has been forecast by our earlier description of the perceptual properties of the color determinant. In a situation where an environmental object impresses its physiognomy or essence upon the observer in an immediate and impelling fashion, allowing for no emancipative distance, there can be no place for active reflection or sober evaluation, so fundamental in the exercise of purely intellectual functions of the human mind; the behavior will tend rather toward receptive and relatively primitive forms. If, furthermore, one wanted to identify these forms of behavior in terms of a conventional psychological function, the dimension of emotionality naturally suggests itself. As pointed out above, chromatic colors affect us with quite individualized, directed, and provocative qualities, and we know from general psychology that the experience of being affected in such ways by an environmental event is considered by authorities on the subject (2) to be equivalent to experiencing emotion.

Although matters of person-environment interaction play a cardinal role in most field-theoretical personality systems, Lewin's (12) treatment of the problem seems most appropriate to this discussion. In his conceptual model, both the extent of accessibility of inner personal regions to outside influences and the facility of outward expression of these regions depend on the degree of permeability of the individual's outside boundary. The greater the functional permeability of the outer boundary, the freer the interplay between the person and his

immediate environment. Applying this line of thinking to our discussion of color perception, one could say that the freedom of interplay is manifested equally in the subject's being easily impressed, affected, provoked by the essence of outside objects, and in his reacting to such "intrusions" in a spontaneous, immediate, and more or
less uncontrolled fashion. Among the latter reactions, emotionality
is but one mode, yet the clearest. From this point of view, color
responses on the Rorschach become indicators of a very basic personality variable—the degree of permeability of the subject's outside
boundary.

It would thus appear that the diagnostic role assigned by Rorschach
to the color determinant readily lends itself to fruitful treatment within
more contemporary theoretical frames. In Chapter 7 an attempt of
this kind is offered in the form of a set of formulations on the psychology of color perception that has been stimulated by Freudian ideas on
capacity for delay of tension discharge, and that is based on a scrutiny
of developmental and clinical Rorschach and non-Rorschach research
data.

CHIAROSCURO. The diffuse total impression of shading on the Rorschach finds its laboratory parallel in the total homogeneous field.
The latter, when produced under controlled "pure" conditions, is experienced phenomenologically as moving toward the subject and as
oppressing him (16). This finding corresponds well to the earlier
cited observations, emphasizing the depressive, discomfort- and anx-
iety-arousing states that seem to overpower the perceiver of the achromatic light-dark continuum. Psychiatrically, the emotional state of
anxiety has been frequently likened to a condition of being lost in a
world that has no discernible organization or, in a phrase of the exis-
tentialists, that engulfs the person by its nothingness. Correspondingly it has become Rorschach practice to interpret the chiaroscuro
responses on the test as signs of generalized emotional states or moods
(chiefly of a dysphoric nature) in contradistinction to the specifically
object-oriented emotions that are associated with the chromatic color
determinants.

In his original volume Rorschach did not consider the shading of
the ink blots as a separate test variable, and in his posthumous publication he merely introduced one score for it. Here was, then, a natural area for further development. In view of the extensive usage of
the test, it is not surprising that such developments have proceeded
through the years along a diversity of lines, both in classificational cri-

ause, in addition to constituting the least novel aspect
psychodiagnostic method, it has failed to stimulate a
t of either research or theoretical speculation.

PATTERN

ntation of the psychological tenets of the Rorschach
es now to a higher level of generality by focusing on the
rn that results from the interplay of the test components.
tset of this chapter, emphasis was placed on the point
interpretation involves a complex process of integration,
the part processes at times as relatively independent units
r contexts as dependent parts. An idea of how these in-
principles operate in reality can be gleaned from the
s of the M and the C determinants, when considered sep-
l when viewed within the experience type. As described
virtue of the particular perceptual features underlying each
eterminants, their individual roles as representatives of cer-
nality dimensions are accrued to them. The treatment,
er hand, of the same determinants as juxtaposed in the ex-
ype cogently brings out the power of organizational prin-
the Rorschach.

servation that the respective weights of either M or C are
lly accentuated, dampened, or blocked reflects the principle
ependence of subwholes within a larger whole. The fact that
whole—the experience type—carries new, broader psycho-
mplications than either of its constituent components did by
ves, illustrates the principle that the whole is greater than the
its parts. Finally, the circumstance that this integrated whole
xperience type—emerges as the catalytic factor of the super-
e whole—the total personality configuration—impressively ex-
es the principle of organization of a larger whole around a
r subunit or strong part, to use a gestalt term.

appreciation of how this complex method of interpretation
back and forth from one level of organization to another would
ps best be conveyed by following a Rorschach worker through
aborate procedure of studying a test record on all levels and in
tail: Viewing the combination of scores on an individual response
unit in its own right; analyzing the temporal pattern of these
nses in the sequence of the entire record and in relation to ac-

teria applied to the shading element and in the interpretative significance coordinated to these criteria.

For purposes of this book, rather than survey all of the scoring
systems, it seemed more appropriate to concentrate on one system,
of which the research and theoretical potentialities are relatively unknown in the United States: the method of Hans Binder, a student
and co-worker of Rorschach (Chapter 8). The distinguishing feature of this classificational system lies in the fact that it is consistently
based on the methodological principles of psychological phenomenology, and that it is linked to a theory of emotions, also phenomenological.[2]

Binder's treatment of the shading determinant shows the phenomenological procedure on two levels. Through painstaking qualitative analysis of a large number of subjects' responses and introspec-
tions to the shaded areas of the blots, he endeavored to discern the intrinsic personal meanings inherent in this material. After casting the
salient trends of his analysis into a set of classificational categories, he
was able to spell out the diagnostic significance of the different categories by relating them to the concepts of the Munich phenomenological theory of emotions. In addition to providing a demonstration
of psychological phenomenology in Rorschach usage, the exposition of
Binder's ideas on the chiaroscuro determinant acquaints the reader
with a scheme for conceptualizing emotive phenomena in a somewhat
more differentiated and subtle manner than is habitual in standard
clinical practice.

American commentaries on the phenomenological approach in psychology (14) usually point to the desirability for phenomenology to
parallel its contributions to the cognitive field by similar accomplishments in the emotional-motivational realm, and to the advisability of
strengthening its scientific respectability by some form of quantifica-
tion. It is the writer's opinion that Binder's chiaroscuro system constitutes a positive step in both these directions, particularly since

[2] Phenomenology is an orientation that emphasizes less the conceptualization
of data than a way of approaching them. It stresses the importance of viewing
psychological phenomena at their own face value. When dealing with new material, the psychologist is urged to cast aside any previously acquired frame of
reference and to contemplate his task with a fresh and unbiased attitude. By
observing carefully and recording with meticulous accuracy what is before him,
he is taking the first, indispensable step toward his ultimate goal of discovering
the intrinsic psychological nature of the phenomenon under consideration. "It
[phenomenology] reveals meaning as the very stuff of experience, and it invites
the psychologist to turn his attention to the meaningful aspects of the world"

some of his hypotheses would appear quite amenable to experimental manipulation.

EXPERIENCE TYPE ($M:C$). Besides the interpretative significance accorded the M and the C determinants separately, even greater significance is ascribed to their interrelationship. This interrelationship is represented by a variable, called the experience type (*Erlebnistypus*). It is expressed numerically as the ratio of the M to the sum C scores. When viewed in the frame of this configuration, the impact of the two determinants, their qualitative nuances, and, primarily, their broader personality implications, all undergo reciprocal modifications. Since M and C represent opposite forms of the subject-environment relation, Rorschach looked upon their numerical constellation as an expression of the fundamental polarity of an individual's stance to his surrounding world: his inwardly determined strivings versus his outwardly stimulated reactions. Depending on whether the balance in the ratio is tipped toward the movement or toward the color side, the experience type is designated as "introversive" or "extratensive" respectively. When the two sides approximate each other, either in abundance or in impoverishment, the experience type becomes "dilated" in the first place and "coartated" in the second. Considering how many intermediary combinations are possible, it is clear that this schema provides for a wide range of individualized patterns of basic orientations.

For Rorschach these patterns do not correspond to mutually exclusive personality types. Their poles are universal psychological functions, present in varying degrees in every person. He felt that the totality of a person's enduring features is most pertinently conceived when organized around this nuclear pattern, "the inmost, intimate capacity of resonance to life experiences" (6, p. 203), as Ellenberger has aptly defined the experience type. In evolving the ultimate personality picture from the test, all other variables are viewed in the light of this catalytic factor, or the "axis" as Rorschach liked to call it.

Because of the psychologically challenging problems that are entailed in the far-reaching significance attached to the experience type, a good deal of thinking has revolved around it. In Chapter 9 these activities are reviewed, emphasizing research findings, and culminating in some tentative theoretical prepositions that draw eclectically on several contemporary personality models.

(14, p. 228). The approach has been developed most fruitfully in Western continental Europe where its application to the cognitive areas of thinking and perception has yielded rich and penetrating descriptive insights.

Content

The last category of ana[...] ideational content of the su[...] ing categories, which deriv[...] process. As noted earlier, R[...] formal features the primary[...] actual content of the interp[...] secondarily" (20, p. 181), and [...] little indication as to the cont[...] in relation to the psychogram"[...] These two quotations convey suc[...] unquestionably subordinated to [...] factor plays an integral role, p[...] embedded into the total test anal[...]

In spite of the usual recognitic[...] account both the formal (functic[...] aspects in personality representatio[...] relatively unsuccessful in attaining[...] conceptually divergent avenues of [...] trast, Rorschach's psychodiagnosis st[...] both approaches, not in the loosely ad[...] but in a sense that takes seriously th[...] at every level of test interpretation. [...] vidual response always incorporates a[...] istics the respective content as an essen[...] fied in its significance by the formal ca[...] influence the meaning of these categorie[...] the color determinant is interpreted q[...] whether it serves as basis for the conte[...]

The actual procedures of adhering to [...] handling of the content variable may be e[...] zation through the inauguration of a rece[...] classifying content. This method, presente[...] to enhance the formalization of the content[...] system that grew out of the psychoanalyti[...] mary and secondary process.

The location, determinant, and content [...] far in this chapter and taken up in detail in [...] the book, cover Rorschach's major test com[...] tion of the popularity-originality dimension. T[...]

companying behavioral data; scrutinizing the cross-sectional config-uration (psychogram) of all the scoring categories; and, after all this sorting, weighing, relating, arranging, and rearranging has been done, observing the evolution of the final *unitas multiplex* of the Rorschach personality picture.

As important as it is for a proper understanding of the nature of the Rorschach method to witness this multifaceted process of test interpretation concretely and in full, no such demonstration will be attempted here. There are numerous publications which very ade-quately meet this need. Instead, it would appear closer to the intent of this book to concentrate on a few proposals for treating some com-plex issues of test interpretation.

In Chapter 11, the phenomenological-existential approach [3] is brought to bear, first, upon an analysis of the pattern of change among three temporally spaced protocols of the same subject, and then upon a re-examination of the conventional meaning of certain test categories. Chapter 12 is devoted to a cardinal problem of the Rorschach, the conceptualization of organization within the over-all personality con-stellation. A theoretical model of levels and interdependencies is pro-posed, and its applicability to Rorschach's implicit conceptual frame of reference is indicated.

PROBLEMS OF SCIENTIFIC APPRAISAL

An enterprise dealing with the place of the Rorschach within the broader orbit of psychology would be incomplete without considera-

---

[3] Phenomenological existentialism, presently exerting a profound influence upon European psychology and psychiatry, is an extension and adaptation of phenome-nology (see footnote 2). In its major objectives this movement may be likened, in the United States, to the systems of ideas centering around the concept of "self" (becoming, growth, self-actualization). Applied to a clinical setting phe-nomenological existentialism emphasizes that, "Knowing means knowing in the context of the same world. The world of this particular patient must be grasped from the inside, be known and seen so far as possible from the angle of the one who exists in it" (15, p. 56). "This phenomenal universe is the totality of 'evalu-ated' people and things which play potential or actual roles in his [the patient's] existence" (24, p. 12). Inasmuch as existence is a dynamic process of becoming, the understanding of a person in an existential sense is aided by directing the clinician's attention to crucial events in the individual's life, as crises, decisions, encounters of tragedy, and by attempting to grasp the extent and character of the person's consciousness of his own self, of fulfillment of his existence, and of finality of his life.

tion of an issue that recently has aroused a vast amount of argumentation: the dependability and trustworthiness of the Rorschach method as a diagnostic tool. The problem itself is certainly a legitimate one, recognized by every serious psychologist with respect for scientific standards. The controversy centers not around the need for such demonstration of worth, but around the question as to just what means of demonstration may be accepted as scientifically irreproachable.

Psychometric practice, influenced in its basic philosophy by behavioristic tradition, relies for such purposes on the two time-honored indicators—reliability and validity. For the readily isolatable and accurately measurable variables of psychometric assessment, these indicators constitute an entirely appropriate means of establishing in correspondingly dissective and quantitative fashion the respectability of a test. As the reader realizes by now, the Rorschach, and for that matter any projective technique, having grown up in a distinctly different theoretical climate has very little in common with psychometric tests either in objectives or in actual test composition, or in underlying premises. It hardly can be surprising, therefore, that its organismically integrated configuration of variables does not yield smoothly to evaluation by the traditional procedures of reliability-validity probing.

The recognition of this difficulty, however, should in no sense be interpreted as denial of the problem. The implication is rather a quest for recasting the criteria for establishment of the scientific worth of a projective method in a way that is syntonic to the intrinsic nature of the diagnostic tool. To the same extent to which a truly scientific spirit requires us to stand ready constantly to revise our knowledge, so this spirit compels us to modify correspondingly our means of evaluating the growing and changing body of knowledge. One might say that what should remain unquestioned with projective as with any other assessment techniques is the genotype of scientific standards, whereas the phenotype of carrying out these standards through the conventional psychometric procedures of reliability-validity testing constitutes a social lag in need of revision.

Accordingly, in Chapters 13 and 14, the ways and means of revising the phenotype are subjected to a scrutiny that begins from the ground up by identifying the issues in detail, examining various standard and newer approaches to them, and leading up to directions for further research.

BIBLIOGRAPHY

1. Arnheim, R. Perceptual and aesthetic aspects of the movement response. *J. Personal.*, 1951, **19**, 265–281.
2. Arnold, Magda. The status of emotion in contemporary psychology. In: A. A. Roback (ed.). *Present-day-psychology.* New York: Philosophical Library, 1955.
3. Bash, K. W. Ganzeigenschaften als Determinantenträger im Rorschach Versuch. *Schw. Z. f. Psychol. und ihre Anw.*, 1957, **16**, No. 2, 121–126.
4. Brosin, H. W., and Fromm, E. Some principles of gestalt psychology in the Rorschach experiment. *Rorschach Res. Exch.*, 1942, **6**, 1–15.
5. Bruner, J. S. Personality and the process of perceiving. In: R. R. Blake and G. V. Ramsey (eds.). *Perception—an approach to personality.* New York: Ronald Press, 1951.
6. Ellenberger, H. Hermann Rorschach, M.D., 1884–1922: A biographical study. *Bull. Menn. Clin.*, 1954, **18**, 173–219.
7. Gibson, J. J. The perception of visual surfaces. *Amer. J. Psychol.*, 1950, **63**, 367–384.
8. Goldstein, K. *The organism.* New York: Am. Book Co., 1939.
9. Koehler, W. Das Wesen der Intelligenz. In: A. Keller (ed.). *Kind und Umwelt, Anlage und Erziehung.* Leipzig: Deuticke, 1930.
10. Koffka, K. *Principles of gestalt psychology.* New York: Harcourt Brace, 1935.
11. Levine, K. and Grassi, J. The relation between blot and concept in graphic Rorschach responses. *Rorschach Res. Exch.*, 1942, **6**, 71–73.
12. Lewin, K. *Principles of topological psychology.* New York and London: McGraw-Hill, 1936.
13. Macleod, R. B. Some new tasks for psychological phenomenology. *Proceedings, 15th Intern. Congress Psychol.*, Brussels, 1957.
14. Macleod, R. B. The place of phenomenological analysis in social psychological theory. In: J. H. Rohrer and M. Sherif (eds.). *Social psychology at the crossroads.* New York: Harper, 1951.
15. May, R., Angel, E., Ellenberger, H. F. (eds.). *Existence: A new dimension in psychiatry and psychology.* New York: Basic Books, 1958.
16. Metzger, W. Optische Untersuchungen am Ganzfeld. II. Zur Phänomenologie des homogenen Ganzfelds. *Psych. Forsch.*, 1930, **13**, 6–29.
17. Metzger, W. *Psychologie.* 2nd ed. Darmstadt: Steinkopf, 1954.
18. Piotrowski, Z. *Perceptanalysis.* New York: Macmillan, 1957.
19. Rickers-Ovsiankina, Maria. Some theoretical considerations regarding the Rorschach method. *Rorschach Res. Exch.*, 1943, **7**, 41–53.
20. Rorschach, H. *Psychodiagnostics* (5th ed.). Bern: Huber, 1951.
21. Schachtel, E. On color and affect. Contributions to an understanding of Rorschach's test. II. *Psychiatry*, 1943, **6**, 393–409.
22. Shapiro, D. Color-response and perceptual passivity. *J. proj. Tech.*, 1956, **20**, 52–69.
23. Sheerer, M. Personality functioning and cognitive psychology. *J. Personal.*, 1953, **22**, 1–16.

24. van Kaam, A. L.   The third force in European psychology: its expression in a theory of psychotherapy.   Lecture before the staff of the V.A. Hospital, Lebanon, Pa., Mar. 13, 1958.
25. Werner, H., and Wapner, S.   The non-projective aspects of the Rorschach experiment: II. Organismic theory and perceptual response.   *J. soc. Psychol.*, 1956, **44**, 193–198.
26. Werner, H.   *Comparative psychology of mental development.*   Chicago: Follett, 1948.
27. Werner, H.   Motion and motion perception: a study on vicarious functioning. *J. Psychol.*, 1945, **19**, 317–327.

CATEGORIES OF ANALYSIS: LOCATION

They (atoms) move in the void and catching each other up jostle together, and some recoil in any direction that may chance, and others become entangled with one another in various degrees according to the symmetry of their shapes and sizes and positions and order, and they remain together and thus the coming into being of composite things is effected.

FLORUET SIMPLICIUS

2

by Marguerite R. Hertz

THE

ORGANIZATION ACTIVITY

Rorschach (28) did not refer directly to organizational activity as such in his original monograph. He considered it indirectly, however, in reference to the whole factor or W.[1] This factor represented for Rorschach the capacity of the individual to combine, abstract, and generalize. It also reflected organization drive. It indicated, as he said, "a conscious or unconscious 'willing' in the direction of achieving complicated performances, such as abstraction or combination in the interpretations" (28, p. 59). In addition, for Rorschach, the W was one of the components of intelligence.

Rorschach recognized that the capacity reflected by the whole response may likewise hold where all the elements of the blot were not included. Thus a response to the black areas in card III was considered a whole response even though the red details were not included. He also recognized the fact that only some whole responses represented complicated intellectual performance. Some, like the popular whole responses, were relatively easy and ordinary.

Rorschach then suggested that some W reflect organizational activ-

---

[1] For explanation of scoring symbols, see Appendix, pp. 441 ff. [Editor].

ity, that such activity depends on the mental set of the individual and his drive toward complicated performance, and that W is to be included in the battery of factors which reflect level of intellectual functioning.

RECENT APPROACHES TO EVALUATING ORGANIZATIONAL ACTIVITY

In the course of the years, it was recognized that the ease with which W's are achieved varies in the respective blots, that the capacity to combine and organize is revealed in varying degrees in the W factor, and that this capacity must be considered also in response to other areas of the blot besides the whole, and in relation to other aspects of the response. Vernon (40), for example, utilized a g which he combined with location categories (Wg, Dg) to reflect combinatory and integrative capacity. Guirdham (11) identified "incorporation responses" in the attempt to evaluate capacity for abstractive organization. Ford (8) worked with organizational links or $O L$ representing the number of logical connections within a response. An organizational factor called Z was systematically developed by Beck (2). Hertz (13) experimented with a similar organizational factor called g.

Approaching the problem from another point of view, Janoff (18) constructed a form-level rating scale which permits evaluation of organizational activity among other qualities. Klopfer et al. (20, 21) also consider the factor of organization in conjunction with the scoring of form responses, distinguishing accuracy, specification, and organization, all of which furnish the basis for a quantifiable evaluation of the form level of each Rorschach response. This is dealt with in a separate chapter on the F factor (p. 109).

Rapaport (27) was one of the first to sense the need for a more systematic approach to the qualitative differentiations of the combinatory, abstracting, and integrating abilities reflected in the Rorschach response. His work and influence are discernible in the subsequent developments with the location categories as evolved at Clark University by Friedman (9), Hemmendinger (12), Peña (25), Rosenblatt and Solomon (29), and Siegel (33). These are discussed in detail by Phillips and Smith (26), and are dealt with in the chapter on the genetic score of location (p. 58).

Indeed, most Rorschach workers have felt the need to develop some score or some means of evaluating the degree and kind of organizational activity reflected in the Rorschach response.

Beck's Z Score

Beck's (2) approach to the problem of organization is among the best known. He analyzed the various ways in which a group of 39 superior adults combined the figure into larger units. He identified six kinds of organization: (a) Wholes; (b) adjacent details seen in relation to each other; (c) distant details seen in combination; (d) white space organized with filled-in elements; (e) analysis-synthesis process; and (f) striving toward a whole. He computed frequency of occurrence of each of these "organizing acts," and considered frequency as an index of difficulty. He computed the sigma values of each kind of organizational activity in each card, transforming them into Z weights. "The varying conditions represented by the several figures are reflected in the different values that any one kind of organization attains in the several figures" (3, p. 60). Because of infrequency, the last two types of organizing acts which he set out to study were dropped.

A table of Z weights is presented giving the numerical values, ranging from 1–6, which he assigned to each kind of Z in each figure (3, p. 212). According to Beck, "A response is scored organization or Z when two or more portions of the figures are seen in relation to one another, and when the meaning perceived in the combination, or in any of the component portions, obtains only from the fact of this organization" (3, p. 59). Although all W are Z, any two or more component elements of the figure, i.e., two or more D, D with Dr, S or s, or any combination of these, may be organized into a relationship. All Z occur in responses determined at least in part by form. Where responses are determined entirely by color or shading, no Z value is possible.

In the Beck scheme, each response in a record is scrutinized and, where organization has taken place, the kind of organization is identified; after consultation with the table, the appropriate Z value is introduced in the scoring formula. Thus a response to card I—"Two witches flying on brooms" for the side figures—receives a weight of 4.0 according to the table because this is the value given to adjacent details in combination for this card. Again, a response to card II—"Dogs facing about to fight"—is weighted 5.5 because this Z value is given to the organization of distant details in card II. In summary, an organization score is computed for each individual consisting of the sum of all the Z values.

According to Beck, Z is "an index of the intellectual energy as such . . . the intellectual functioning per se" (4, p. 12). It reveals the power to grasp relations. It is the index to thinking power. It varies directly with intelligence.

Again, comparing W and Z within the normal range for a person's age group, both show the extent to which he is synthesizing. W tells more of his conceptual activity; Z of his grasp of relations between stimuli in his perceptual field (5, p. 23). The higher the sum Z, the more able is the individual to perform work which requires difficult and complex intellectual effort.

Like every other factor in the Rorschach, the interpretation of Z varies with the total personality picture. Evaluation of the Z score of an individual must be made in terms of his "mental well-being or illness generally, the affective influences, the attitude to reality, the fantasy living" (4, p. 12–13). Thus Z is discussed for the most part in terms of other factors and patterns. Z with W, R, and content reflects the ego's initiative and energy (5, p. 19). The Z score in compulsive characters may be high. "This is not only because of their intellectual drive, but also because the command forces them to look for connections. . . ." It may be low because "the frantic search for the minute . . . actually prevents their grasping relations of which they are capable. . . . The Z total can be reduced also as a direct consequence of the rigorous reaction pattern, the defense which constricts the functioning along all dimensions of the personality" (5, p. 30). Again, high Z with $F-$ and emphasis on S represent a cluster suggesting the sick paranoid (5, p. 22).

Since Beck's original study, extensive use has been made of the Z factor. Norms have been reported for children, high school students, "normal" adults, college students, feeble-minded individuals, neurotic, schizophrenic, and brain-injured patients. Table 2.1 summarizes the norms in some of these studies.

The Organization Category of g

An organization factor termed g (the g taken from the word "organization") was identified and developed at the Brush Foundation in conjunction with analyses of other Rorschach factors (13). It was felt that organization should be studied where it takes place in different details of the blots as well as in the whole areas. Furthermore it was thought that some means should be devised to study organiza-

TABLE 2.1.   Weighted Z Values

INVESTIGATOR	GROUP	N	MEAN	S. D.	MEDIAN
Beck (4)	Adults, "normal"		31.10	26.44	
Beck et al. (6)	Adults, employees of Spiegel Mail Order House	157	22.48	14.91	
	Vocational Group I *	36	28.60	15.70	
	″ ″ II	49	24.70	13.66	
	″ ″ III	48	20.60	14.00	
	″ ″ IV	24	16.20	15.40	
Beck (7)	Adults	60	18.90		
	High school students	48	25.54	19.60	
Thetford et al. (37)	Children				
	6–9 yrs.	69	7.15	7.40	4.88
	10–13 ″	62	8.45	10.10	5.61
	14–17 ″	24	28.90	23.00	24.50
	Total	155	11.05	14.45	6.10
Sisson and Taulbee (34)	Adults, "normal," 20–52 yrs.	60	24.03	18.32	
	Children, "normal," 8–18 yrs.	70	23.22	19.40	
Varvel (39)	College students	144	43.10		25.60
	Constricted subjects	20	20.70		10.26
Jolles (19) †	Children, feeble-minded	65	19.09	15.24	
Wishner (42)	Adults, "neurotic"	42	21.31	15.39	
Sisson and Taulbee (34)	Neurotics, 20–46 yrs.	35	26.87	19.59	
Beck (6)	Neurotics	50	20.30		
	Neurotics	60	24.90		
	Schizophrenics	60	20.65		
Sisson and Taulbee (34)	Schizophrenics, 20–46 yrs.	60	27.38	17.30	
	Organics, 19–44 yrs.	10	27.50	15.11	

* Refers to vocational groups described, p. 39.
† As reported by Kropp (22).

tional activity qualitatively. It is important to identify and assess organizational activity *per se*. It is even more important to evaluate that activity qualitatively to determine the accuracy and the complexity of the forms seen in relationship and the extent to which the combinations themselves are adequately realistic and constructive, or irrealistic, arbitrary, and far-fetched.

An organization score was therefore developed which takes into consideration the accuracy of fit of the form or forms seen in relationship (Rorschach determinants involving $F+$), vagueness (v), popularity (P), and originality (O), and the appropriateness of the relationships themselves. Organization was defined in approximately the same manner in which Beck defined his Z activity. Organization is said to take place where: (a) a blot area is analyzed into one or more component parts; (b) different forms are projected into those parts; (c) these are seen in relation to each other; and (d) the response given to the combination depends entirely on the fact of their being seen in combination.

Scoring scale. After considerable experimentation with various schemes of weighting in order to evaluate qualitative differentiations of this score, a simple scale was devised for weighting organization. This scheme is used today.

1. A score of 1.5 is assigned when the forms seen in relationship are accurate ($F+$) and original ($O+$).

2. A score of 1.0 is assigned when the forms seen in combination are accurate ($F+$) but neither original, popular, nor vague.

3. A weighting of .5 is assigned where forms seen in combination are either vague (v) or popular (P) or inaccurate ($F-$).

In our procedure of scoring, accuracy of fit is determined by consultation with published frequency tables (15) which serve as guides. These frequency tables are based on frequency of occurrence of forms in normal adolescents, supplemented by subjective judgments of three to five experienced judges where infrequent responses occurred. The lists in the frequency tables serve as guides for the scoring of form level. Obviously they do not exhaust all the possibilities for responses to the blots. Where entirely new responses are given by an individual, the tables are scrutinized to see if any interpretations similar in form appear. If there is no basis for comparison, the new forms must be scored subjectively on the basis of fitness to the area in question.

Even with those forms that do appear in the frequency tables, each must be considered on its own in terms of the information obtained in the inquiry and in terms of the total record and the skill and experience of the examiner. In the last analysis an $F+$ score is assigned when in the judgment of the scorer the form fits the area into which it is projected. An $F-$ response is one where the shape of the form fails to fit the outline of the area into which it has been projected. Fitness is the criterion applied here.

Vague forms (v) are those based on a general impression of the blot. As a rule such forms are indefinite in that they may take various shapes. They could be projected into many areas of the blot indiscriminately. These include maps, islands, x-rays, charts, and the like.

Original responses are those which are given least frequently. Those responses given most infrequently by our experimental groups were listed as original (O) in the frequency tables. Originality was applied to (a) usual forms in an unusual setting; (b) usual settings but with unique form or forms; and (c) totally unusual responses, originality being determined by the frequency one in one hundred and checked by three to five judges.

Responses infrequently given and not appearing in the frequency tables must, of course, be subjectively evaluated. If they do not appear in the tables and if they are not at all like any forms in the tables, originality is assumed. Obviously this score is highly subjective. The more experience one has with normal populations, the better one is able to recognize that which is different and unique.

Thus, with this weighting scheme, the adequacy of reality testing is taken into consideration, as well as the complexity, vagueness, originality, and popularity of the response. Responses which are infrequently given (original) where organization has taken place get highest weighting when accuracy of fit is established for the form or forms involved $(F+)$. They get lowest weighting when the form or forms involved are poorly perceived, irrealistic or distorted, and/or the relationships themselves are inappropriate and distorted. Similarly, vague and popular responses where organization takes place get low weighting.

At first, lower figures (.25, .10, .05) were used for weighting organization in responses with poorly perceived forms and relationships. After many trials, it was discovered that too little is added to the significance of the total score to warrant the use of a more detailed weighting system. Therefore, the weighting of .5 was applied to vague and popular forms seen in relationship as well as to the poorly perceived forms and combinations.

The combination score is also used in *combinatory responses* where two or more responses which take separate scoring formulas are associated. The same scheme of weighting is followed.

1. Where the relationship itself involves forms which are accurate and the combination is realistic, appropriate, and original, a weighting of 1.5 is assigned.

2. Where the forms are accurate and the relationship realistic and appropriate, a weighting of 1.0 is applied.

3. Where the combination involves inaccurate forms, the score of .5 is assigned.

4. Where the relationships themselves are inappropriate and irrealistic, where, e.g., the size or the spatial relationships are out of keeping with reality, the lowest weighting of .5 is assigned, whether the forms involved are accurate or not.

Separate scoring formulas are used and a special notation made of the poor combination. The $g - O - combination!$ is considered an indicator of impairment of some kind, even pathology.

Organizational score abbreviations.   These are, of course, abbreviations for the organizational patterns described above.

The notation $g\,O+$ stands for responses involving organization where forms are plus and original; $g+$, responses involving organization where forms are plus but neither original, vague, nor popular; $g\,P$, responses involving organization where forms are popular; and $g\,v+$, responses involving organization, where forms are vague, but because of the criterion of frequency, some few receive a plus score.

The notation $g+\,O+\,comb$ refers to responses which take separate scoring formulas where the forms and the combinations are fitting, appropriate, and original; the $g+\,comb$ refers to the same type of responses where the forms and combinations are fitting but not original.

It may be noted that all organizational responses where forms and combinations are fitting are summarized on the psychogram, *sum $g+\,wt$.*

The notation $g-\,O-$ refers to responses involving organizations where forms are minus and original (infrequent and/or unique); $g-$, responses where they are minus but neither original nor vague; and $g\,v-$, responses where organization is indicated but forms are vague and not fitting the outline of the area.

The notation $g - O - comb!$ refers to responses which take separate scoring formulas where the relationships seen are inappropriate and irrealistic, whether the forms themselves are fitting or not, and where the combinations are highly infrequent and unique, the $g - comb$ refers to the same type of combination involving forms which are minus and/or relationships which are inappropriate but not too infrequent or unique.

Again it may be noted that organizational responses which are scored minus are summarized in a *sum g− wt* score.

Finally the *total sum g wt* is computed for all organizational scores.

Examples of scoring. The following illustrate the scoring of the organization factor according to the simple scheme developed.

Card II (conelike projection, top middle)— "Oriental figures back to back"	$\dfrac{D}{1.5}$ $M+$	H	$O+$
Card X (grey figures at top with center projection)—"Hooded figures holding up a post"	$\dfrac{D}{1.5}$ $M+$	H *Post*	$O+$
Card I (side figure)—"Witch with cloak (wing projection at side) flying out"	$\dfrac{D}{1.0}$ $F+$ $Fm+$	H *App*	
Card X (pink figures with inner blue)—"Cliffs joined together by some kind of bridge"	$\dfrac{D}{1.0}$ $F(C)+$	*Mt* *Str*	
Card VII (upper two-thirds of side figure)— "Map of one country next to another"	$\dfrac{Dv}{.5}$ $F+$	*Map*	
Card VIII (red and orange area)—"Anatomical chart of some kind in color, this orange representing one organ and the pink another organ"	$\dfrac{Dv}{.5}$ $C/F+$	*Anat-Obj*	
Card VII (top third)— "Women's faces, as if they are making faces at each other"	$\dfrac{D}{.5}$ $M+$	*Hd*	P
Card II (black area at side)—"Dogs looking at each other"	$\dfrac{D}{.5}$ $FM+$	A	P
Card II (top red area)—"Something colored like caterpillars fighting"	$\dfrac{D}{.5}$ $FM-$ $CF-$	A	$O-$
Card VIII (grey-blue top area)—"Wolves all together sort of climbing up"	$\dfrac{D}{.5}$ $FM-$	A	

As Beck has indicated, the parts of the blots seen in relationship may be adjacent to each other, distant, or one inside the other. The areas into which forms are projected may be the whole, normal details, rare details, or details combined with spaces.

It should also be emphasized that organization as herein defined applies only to different forms seen in combination, not to parts of one form. For example, a response "Person because this is the head, body and feet," is not weighted for organization. Although it is true that analysis of areas and combination of parts have taken place, this is not the kind of organization which is scored by the g. The g score is applied only where forms are seen in combination and where the final response gives a new meaning because of the relation seen between the different parts.

There is one exception which we make to this rule, however. On occasion, parts of one form may be projected into areas which are seen in combination, and the meaning given depends clearly upon seeing something which is new by virtue of the relationship. The following table illustrates this:

Card II (red areas at top seen together)— "Andirons"	$\dfrac{D}{.5}$	$F-$	Hh	$O-$
Card II (tiny lines, upper part of middle space form)—"Representation of electric current"	$\dfrac{Dr!}{1.5}$	$F+$	$Current$	$O+$
Card X (inner green figures bottom seen as unit)— "Sort of like a lyre, but the strings are missing"	$\dfrac{D}{.5}$	$F-$	$Obj\text{-}Music$	$O-$

In these rare instances, the subject seems to see first one area and then another, projects one part of the form and then another into these areas, and then sees them in combination. Hence the organizational score is applied in these few cases.

Of course, where no form is projected, no organization weight is given. On occasion, many kinds of organization take place in one response. For example, good forms may be combined with popular forms in original settings. The procedure generally followed is to assign the highest weighting, as illustrated by the following cases:

Card II—"People doing a Russian dance in costume with red hats just beginning to squat sort of"	$\dfrac{W}{1.5}$	$\begin{matrix}M+\\FC+\end{matrix}$	$\begin{matrix}H\\App\end{matrix}$	(P)	$O+$
Card X—"Scene in Bermuda, viewed from a glass bottom boat, with octopi and other forms of animal life and colored vegetation"	$\dfrac{W}{1.5}$	$\begin{matrix}FM+\\CF+\end{matrix}$	A	$Sc(P)$	$O+$

Some examples of *combinatory respones* are as follows:

Card IX—"This is a fantastic figure (top orange figure) of some kind emerging from or perched on a heavy billowy cloud" (green middle area)	$\begin{matrix}D\\+\\\overline{D}\\g \text{ comb } 1.5\end{matrix}$	$\begin{matrix}M+\\\\ChF+\end{matrix}$	$\begin{matrix}(H)\\\\Cl\end{matrix}$	$O+$

Card II—"A toy dog, wooly dog (side black figure), and here is a red hat (top red figure)—gifts piled up under a Christmas tree maybe"	D $+$ D	$Fc+$ $FC+$	(A) App	(P)	$0+$
	g comb 1.5				
Card II—"Two men here at the sides . . . they are holding something (conelike projection, middle top), candles"	W $+$ D	$M+$ $Fc+$	H Hh	P	
	g comb 1.0				
Card II—"A dog's head (side black figure) and this is a red balloon on top of it, I guess (top red figure)"	D $+$ D	$F+$ $CF-$	Ad Toy	P	$0-$
	g comb .5				
Card VIII—"Two animals (side red figure), and this is an animal skin torn into two parts (middle blue areas). I guess the animals are holding a skin"	D $+$ D	$FM+$ $F-$	A Ad	P Obj	$0-$
	g comb .5				
Card VIII—"An animal (side red figure) climbing up from a colored butterfly (red-orange middle bottom) to a green tree (top grey-green area)"	D $+$ D $+$ D	$FM+$ $CF+$ $FC+$	A A Bo	P P	$0-$
	$g-$ comb .5				
Card IX—"Two people (side orange figures) fencing on top of two big bears (large green areas)"	D $+$ D	$M+$ $F+$	H A		
	$g-$ comb .5				

As illustrated, the organization score is written under the location category. It has been found helpful to compute the different organizational scores separately especially in cases of maladjustment and pathology. Thus on the psychogram (14), space is allowed for the more differentiated organizational patterns:

g $0+$	$g+$	$g\,P$	$g\,v+$	sum $g+$ wt
$g+$ $0+$ comb	$g+$ comb			
$g-$ $0-$	$g-$		$g\,v-$	sum $g-$ wt
$g-$ $0-$ comb!	$g-$ comb			
				sum g wt

Correlation with Beck's Z. The records of several groups of adolescents in the Brush series were scored for organization, utilizing Beck's Z and our g. In all of them, high correspondence was observed as can be seen from the correlations presented below for two groups of children, 12 and 15 years of age respectively.

		Sum g wt		Sum $g+$ wt	
Beck's Z wt	75 twelve-year-old children, 41 boys, 34 girls	.953±	.011	.881±	.026
	57 fifteen-year-old adolescents 29 boys, 28 girls	.958±	.011	.936±	.016
Beck's $Z+$ wt	75 twelve-year-old children, 41 boys, 34 girls	.890±	.024	.937±	.014

It appears that for "normal" groups at least, there is a close relationship between sum Z wt and sum g wt. It does not appear necessary therefore to use the involved table of Z weights developed by Beck.

VALIDITY OF THE ORGANIZATION FACTOR IN THE RORSCHACH

The Z Score

The organization score is utilized today rather widely in the analysis of records in clinical practice. Unfortunately, comparatively little systematic work has been done to establish its scientific validity. In the course of the years, isolated and fragmentary studies have appeared. For the most part reliance has been placed on theoretical assumptions and on empirical findings with normal and pathological subjects.

A few studies have appeared dealing directly with Beck's Z score. Z was subjected to systematic research by Goldfarb in 1945 (10), and more recently by Wilson and Blake (41), Batt (1), Sisson and Taulbee (34), and Kropp (22). It has, of course, been utilized in other research. It has been considered, for example, with other aspects of the Rorschach in studies of children by Thetford et al. (37), college students by Varvel (39), normal adults by Beck et al. (7), superior men of the U.S. Maritime Service by McCandless (24), mental defectives by Jolles (19), Sarason (30), and Sloan (35), neurotic and psychotic depressive patients by Varvel (39), neurotic patients by Wishner (42), manic patients by Schmidt and Fonda (32), and schizophrenic cases by Beck (6), Schmidt and Fonda (32), Taulbee (36), and Thiesen (38).

There has been much critical comment on Beck's rationale for the scoring of Z. As has been emphasized by Sarason (31) and Kropp (22), Beck's assumption that frequency of organizational acts implies degree of difficulty may not hold. It has not yet been demonstrated that the most infrequent kind of organizational activity is the most difficult. Furthermore, the Z values were developed from the records of a small and selected sample, only 39 superior adults. It is maintained that such a sample is inadequate to serve as a basis for determining order of difficulty of any types of responses. Kropp also demonstrates by reviewing norms published for Z values that the Z activity is not normally distributed in the general population. Beck has, of course, indicated several times that the distributions are markedly skewed for several of the Rorschach categories, including Z.

Kropp developed another set of sigma values for each of the five organizational acts identified by Beck, based on the 53 records found in Beck's volumes II and III. It is interesting to note that despite Kropp's criticisms, in his cross validation of the Z weights originally developed by Beck, his set relates highly to Beck's set of weights.

Several studies question the value of the weighting system as devised by Beck in relation to the various types of organizational activity. On the basis of a study of the records of five different normal and abnormal groups, 104 subjects in all, Wilson and Blake (41) show high correlation between Beck's total weighted Z score and the frequency of occurrence of organizational acts. The total number of times organization takes place, i.e., when Z appears, may be substituted for the total weighted Z score. A table is presented for predicting total weighted Z score when the number of Z responses is known.

Sisson and Taulbee (34) present further evidence of the high relationship between the sum of the responses containing Z and the weighted Z scores, on the basis of an analysis of the records of five groups of subjects, 235 in all, consisting of schizophrenic, neurotic, and organic male patients and normal male and female children. Employing the table of Wilson and Blake for the total weighted Z prediction when the total number of Z responses is known, they correctly identify from 71% to 100% of the cases within one and two standard errors.

A few studies are concerned with the relationship between Beck's Z score and intelligence. Beck presented no validating data in his original study. Goldfarb interpreted Beck's Z as a measure of "volitional and intellectual aspects of the abstract attitude" (10, p. 525). More specifically, he thought Z reflected an individual's "ability to organize his experience and to generalize from it, and his will or drive to think along the lines of abstraction and generalization" (10, p. 525). He therefore hypothesized a relationship between the Z score and various scores on other tests measuring the level of concept formation or categorical behavior.   He selected as his criteria scores on the block design and the similarities tests in the Wechsler-Bellevue Intelligence Scale, the Weigl Color Form Test, and the Vigotsky test of abstraction.   Studying the records of 30 normal adolescents, mean age twelve years three months, he could find no reliable relationship between Z and scores on these tests.   Since Beck's Z score does not make qualitative differentiations in terms of accuracy of forms or adequacy of organizational activity, Goldfarb studied, in his subjects, only that Z activity which was $F+$, and also a score based on the form-level rating scale of Klopfer and Davidson (21).   Beck's sum $Z+$ score did not relate to the scores of the other tests either.   He could show, however, that the form-level rating scores were reliably related to the scores of the other tests and, hence, could be hypothesized to reflect the organizational or conceptual ability measured in those tests.

The writer was similarly unsuccessful in obtaining significant relationships between Z and either M.A. or I.Q. based on the Higher Otis Test or the Stanford-Binet.   On the basis of scores of 75 twelve-year-old children, 41 boys and 34 girls in the Brush series, Pearson correlations were obtained as follows:

$$Z:M.A.\ .156 \pm .113; \qquad Z:I.Q.\ .174 \pm .112$$

Considering only the $F+$ forms in the responses which rated organization, $Z+$ correlates with M.A. $.182 \pm .112$ and with I.Q. $.198 \pm .111$. Again, for 57 fifteen-year-old children, 29 boys and 28 girls, using Binet scores, the correlations were Z with M.A. $.205 \pm .127$ and with I.Q. $.213 \pm .126$.

Similarly, Sarason (30) could find no relationship between M.A. and Z values when studying the records of two groups of mental defectives.   However, using the measure $Z-\%$, consisting of the number of minus responses scored Z over the total number of Z responses, she obtained correlations of $-.55$ and $-.63$ between the $Z-$ score and M.A. for the two groups.   The $Z-$ score can thus be said to be associated with lower intelligence.

Kropp (22) reports that Jolles (19) found insignificant correlations between total Z scores and Binet and Wechsler-Bellevue I.Q.'s in a group of 66 mental defectives.

On the other hand, a few studies report a positive relationship between weighted Z scores and intelligence. Wishner (42), for example, obtained a correlation of .536 between Z and full weighted scale of the Wechsler-Bellevue, in his study of the intellectual factors in the Rorschach records of 42 neurotic subjects 16 to 42 years of age, I.Q. 79 to 130. For a neurotic group, then, he could say that Z measures intellectual capacity as reflected by this scale. Similarly, Sisson (34) reports that he and Yager, working with the records of 50 psychiatric patients randomly selected, obtained a correlation of .428 between the weighted Z score and the full-scale Wechsler I.Q., and .52 between unweighted Z response and the full-scale Wechsler I.Q.

Two other studies corroborate this positive relationship between Z score and intelligence. Batt (1) obtained statistically significant correlations of .49 and .46 between weighted Z score and the verbal and reasoning parts of the Primary Mental Abilities Test in a study of 32 high school students. Accordingly the Z score might be assumed to reflect the capacity to understand ideas expressed in words, to solve logical problems, and to foresee and to plan.

Taulbee (36) was concerned with the Rorschach as a method of evaluating the intellectual levels of functioning of a group of 60 hospitalized schizophrenic patients. In this study, Z along with R, W, M, and F+ showed a positive relationship with the full-scale Wechsler-Bellevue I.Q. The W and Z correlations, although low, were significantly reliable. Studying Z in relation to the subtests, he obtained especially high correlations with digit span, similarities, and vocabulary. He concluded that Z in the records of schizophrenic patients could be said to relate to the ability to engage in verbal abstraction and the ability for concept formation.

Beck et al. (7) developed norms for Rorschach factors in their study of the normal personality as projected in the Rorschach test on the basis of 157 subjects, age range 17 to 69, all employees of the Spiegel Mail Order House in Chicago. They give norms for Z, along with other factors, for the group as a whole and for the group subdivided into subgroups in terms of the following vocational categories: I—executives and junior executives; II—skilled occupations; III—semiskilled occupations; and IV—unskilled occupations. These have been reproduced in Table 2.1. It may be seen that the higher the vocational group, the higher the sum Z values. Beck et al. say: "The intellectual energy represented by Z has a selective potency in the competitive field which present day industry is" (7, pp. 252–253).

Norms are also presented for normal children, 6 to 17 years of age in three age groups, 6 to 9 years, 10 to 13 years, and 14 to 17 years of age, by Thetford et al. (37). Medians for Z are presented in Table 2.1. The investigators show that the Z activity increases from 4.88 in the youngest group to 5.61 in the middle group, and to 24.50 in the older group. The differences are significantly reliable between weighted Z scores of the 6- to 9-year group and those of the 14- to 17-year group, and between those of the 10- to 13-year group and the 14- to 17-year group. The investigators conclude that, if there is no interference with the level of functioning, there is an increase in the ability to organize relationships (37, p. 61). The ability of the child to organize relationships meaningfully increases with his chronological development and manifests itself to a pronounced degree during the adolescent years. The investigators suggest that their finding may be "interpreted in relation to our knowledge of the normal growth curve emphasizing the freedom of mental energy which accompanies the maximum release of intellectual capacity during adolescence" (37, p. 76).

Organization is also analyzed in connection with prediction of academic success in the study of McCandless (24) on the basis of Rorschach records of two matched groups of officer candidates in the U.S. Maritime Service differing in academic achievement. Rorschach patterns failed to differentiate reliably between the "high-grade group" and the "low-grade group." The Z score did not discriminate the groups either. Contrary to expectation, the mean Z score in the high-point group was 43.3 as compared to 48.5 in the low-point group. The difference was not statistically significant, however.

A few studies of mentally defective children show the organization score helpful in differentiating groups. Sloan (35) matched a defective group of 26 children, I.Q. ranging from 44 to 79, with a similar number of nondefective children, I.Q. 80 to 100, this latter group having been considered defective prior to institutionalization. The purpose of the study was to determine whether certain personality disturbances may be mistaken for mental deficiency. The Rorschach records were studied for ten "signs" of mental deficiency, one of which was Beck's Z, the sign being the "normative range" 5 to 31. The deviation of each subject on each sign was computed. Total Z score was one of five factors on which the defective subjects deviated most frequently, the others being A%, F+%, F%, and R. Conclusion is made that analysis of these patterns then would help diagnose mental deficiency.

Jolles (19) was interested in a similar problem, namely, the importance of personality adjustment as a factor in the etiology of mental deficiency. The 66 children, ages 10 to 15, I.Q.'s 65 to 79, utilized in the case studies were divided into three groups according to Rorschach patterns, indicating: (1) normal mental ability; (2) at least one indication of normal ability in an otherwise abnormal picture; and (3) no indication of normal mental ability. Jolles made certain inferences in relation to the influence of emotional disturbances on intellectual development and functioning. For the present purposes, it is sufficient to point out that, for Jolles, high Z in conjunction with qualitatively good W, M, adequate range of content, and adequate F+ would contraindicate mental deficiency.

The Z score also appears in the literature as part of batteries of Rorschach factors characterizing different clinical groups. Thiesen (38), for example, identified five Rorschach patterns which discriminated normal adults from schizophrenic patients. Of these, one, pattern B, is of interest in the present review. Low F+% with low Z score is associated with the schizophrenic group, reflecting perceptual inaccuracy with low mental drive. In Beck's study of the six schizophrenias (6), of the six variables in which the schizophrenic children exceeded the norms, the high W and even higher Z were conspicuous, suggesting greater application of energy and more drive. Comparing the normals with the neurotics and schizophrenics, both clinical groups exceeded the normals in four variables, W, Z, M, and crude C. Intellectual drive appears to be released more in neurotic and schizophrenic children than in the normal group.

Again, in describing the Rorschach test behavior in the six schizophrenias identified by Beck (6), the Z score plays a part. For example, in the grouping S-1, "projection" is reflected by the triad, high Z, low F+%, and high S%. Another item of behavior, "accidental and tangential thought processes," is revealed by a combination of position responses, perception of artifacts in the cards, and peculiar and odd relations inferred from the Z scores. Z also is involved in "cramped and rigid attitudes," as inferred from low R, high A+%, Ad, high lambda index,[2] constricted experience balance, rejection trends, excessive qualifications, as well as low Z; "isolation defenses" are shown by emphasis on Dd, high R, obsessive-compulsive tactics, and Z lower than expectancy.

The Z score figures also in a study by Schmidt and Fonda (32). Rorschach scores of 42 manic patients are compared with those of 42 schizophrenic patients, the groups matched on the basis of age, sex,

---

[2] The lambda index, according to Beck, is the ratio of all scorings involving any determinant other than F, to the total number of F+, F− and F scoring [Editor].

number of responses. Manic patients give a Z score of 36.2 (S.D. 23.79), as compared to 27.2 (S.D. 17.96) given by the schizophrenic group, a difference which is statistically reliable. Also, the manics all exceed Beck's normals in Z score. The manics then are highest in discharge of intellectual energy. This higher output of intellectual energy is also reflected in their stronger tendency to generalize (W). Although the investigators did not study the Z score qualitatively, their figures do show that the $F+\%$ and the number of P are much lower in manics as compared with Beck's normal subjects. Thus, while the Z score tends to be high, no doubt it involves more poor forms $(F-)$ and fewer P.

A few intercorrelational studies are reported between Z score and other Rorschach factors. Varvel (39) reports the following correlations on the basis of a study of the records of 144 normal college students: Z correlates with $F+\%$, $-.29 \pm .05$; with $A\% + P\% + F+\%$, $-.46 \pm .04$; and with $M+$, $.79 \pm .02$. He concludes that "constricted stereotyped individuals show rigidity of personality structure, lack of that perceptual-cognitive 'fluidity' which in combination with attentiveness and intellectual precision $(F+\%)$ is associated with productive, differentiated intellectual and easy adaptability" (39, p. 12).

Kropp (22) computed intercorrelations on the basis of the 53 records given by Beck (4, 5). Z correlates with W, .843; with M, .581; and with R, .565. He also obtained multiple correlations of Z with W and M, .93; and Z with W and M and F, .95. On the basis of these correlations he concludes that a Z score might be estimated from W and M scores and, hence, finds it unnecessary to evaluate weighted Z scores.

The g Scores

An investigation of the organizational factor, g, was included in the preliminary survey research which was conducted on the Rorschach categories at the Brush Foundation. This research involved exploratory studies of normal children and adult patients from psychiatric hospitals. The following hypotheses concerning g were formulated.

1. The organization factor or g reflects capacity to analyze situations, to see relationships, to combine and organize parts into meaningful relations, to abstract meanings out of the combinations, and to generalize.

2. Since the power to analyze and synthesize into logical and meaningful wholes is one of the essential features of intelligence, sum

g wt is an indication of intelligence. Sum *g wt* should be high for individuals of superior intelligence and low for those of inferior intelligence, or in those where there is some impairment in intellectual functioning.

3. Since the individual must persist if he is to analyze a situation into its component parts, see relationships, and assemble and recombine into whole units, he must be motivated. Hence *g* reveals intellectual drive and effort.

4. Qualitative differentiations of the organization score reflect the complexity, the adequacy, and the appropriateness of the subject's thinking processes.

(*a*) *g*+ reveals thinking which is realistic; ability to see relationships between elements in a situation realistically, hence the capacity to see situations in proper proportion and perspective.

(*b*) *g O*+ reflects superior organizational ability; thinking is realistic, rich, varied, and original.

(*c*) *g P* reflects organizational ability which is devoted only to the more commonplace combinations.

(*d*) *g*− points to unrealistic thinking. Reality is seen in an inaccurate or distorted manner and/or relationships are seen as unreal, distorted, or bizarre. The higher the sum *g*− *wt*, the more irrealistic or autistic the thinking of the individual and the greater the intellectual impairment.

(*e*) The *g*− *O combination!* is a pathological indicator. It points to combinations which are constructed on the basis of unrealistic and false relations. It reflects inferior judgment and faulty reasoning, and suggests the possibility of delusional developments.

In the light of the very high correlation between Z and *g*, it is likely that results reported for Beck's Z, whether positive, negative, or equivocal, carry meaning for *g* as well. A few of the results of the fragmentary studies conducted at the Brush Foundation are reported below. Unfortunately, termination of this research program prevented more systematic exploration of the problems.

The total number of Rorschach responses is significantly related to weighted *g* score and organizing acts. On the basis of an analysis of the organizing activity of 50 fourteen-year-old boys and girls, correlations were obtained of .396 between *R* and organizing acts and .263 between *R* and sum *g wt*. In the present group, however, the correlation is not as high as that indicated by Kropp (22) between *R* and Z. There is a low positive correlation, then, between the giving of

TABLE 2.2. Norms for Organizational Scores Based on g

| | | | Organizational Acts | | | | | | | | | Sum g Weighted | | | |
| | | R | | g O+ | | Sum g− | | Total Sum Org. Acts | | Sum g+ wt | | Total Sum g wt | | | |
N	Groups	M	Q	Md	Q	Md	Q	Md	Q	Md	Q	Md	Q	M	S.D.
41	1. { 12-year-old children boys	34.25												12.01	6.35
34	girls	38.71												12.44	5.56
75	Total group	36.43												12.22	5.98
29	2. { 15-year-old children boys	33.87												10.80	6.02
28	girls	41.37												11.87	6.14
57	Total group	37.54												11.33	6.11
25	3. { 14-year-old children boys			9.0	2.8			10.0	3.7	9.0	2.8	8.0	2.8	9.82	
25	girls			8.6	2.8			10.0	3.7	8.6	2.8	8.0	2.9	10.62	
50	Total group	30.1	13.9	8.9	2.8			10.0	3.6	8.9	2.8	8.0	2.9	10.22	
25	4. { Very superior, ages 11–16 yrs. boys							11.3	3.5			11.7	2.8	12.52	
25	girls							10.1	2.9			9.4	4.0	12.54	
50	Total group	31.1	4.3	9.5	2.9	1.4	.9	10.8	3.5	9.7	3.4	10.5	3.2	12.53	

Extreme groups on Otis I.Q., age 12 yrs.

Group	n												
5. High boys	28										15.8	5.2	
High girls	28										15.5	3.6	
Total high	56										15.1	3.3	
Low boys	28										8.5	3.2	
Low girls	28										9.8	3.1	
Total low	56										9.2	3.0	
6. College women (young adults)	40	14.3	3.1	12.5	5.4	14.0	6.3	12.5	6.6		13.0	5.5	16.67
7. Subnormal, ages 10–13 yrs. (boys and girls)	25			1.2	1.5	1.9	1.7	1.1	.9		1.3	1.0	1.86
8. Depressed patients (adults)	25	24.0	6.4	4.9	2.3	7.7	4.0	3.4	1.7		5.6	2.9	5.36
9. Delusional schizophrenics (adults)	35	22.5	6.2	4.3	1.4	3.6 1.3 / 7.6	2.8	3.4	1.9		6.1	2.3	6.07
10. Brain-injured male patients (adults)	50	17.7	5.1								5.1	1.7	
11. Old-age group, age range 60–74 yrs.	28	23.5									4.8		
75–90 yrs.	22	17.7									4.8		
Total	50	20.8	6.2								4.8	2.6	

responses on the Rorschach and organization as herein defined. This need not mean however, as is so often interpreted, that increase or decrease in g is to be explained exclusively in terms of increase or decrease in the number of responses.

Relationship of g scores and intelligence. Intelligence as measured by the standard intelligence tests shows very low positive relation to weighted sum g or sum $g+$. Studying the records of 75 twelve-year-old children, 41 male and 34 female, Otis I.Q.'s ranging from 86 to 140, the following Pearson correlations were obtained for M.A. with g and $g+$ respectively: $.209 \pm .110$ and $.226 \pm .110$.

Again, correlations based on a study of the records of 57 fifteen-year-old children show similar low correlations, i.e., M.A. with g and $g+$ respectively: $.249 \pm .124$ and $.243 \pm .125$; I.Q. with g and $g+$ respectively: $.256 \pm .124$ and $.250 \pm .124$. For these groups at least, g does not measure the intellectual level which is reflected by either Otis scores or the Binet scores. This was also demonstrated with Z. It must be concluded that the organization score has little in common with tests like the Binet, Otis, or Wechsler-Bellevue Scale, or it reveals only a small part of what is revealed by them. Again, it may indicate something other than the kind of general intelligence reflected by them.

Normative data taken from the files of the Brush Foundation are presented in Table 2.2, which gives means and/or medians for the number of organizing acts, i.e., the number of times organization takes place, and the sum g weighted according to the scheme already described (pp. 30 ff.). With some groups, tabulation is made of the median number of organizing acts and the median weighted g score for organization involving plus forms and combinations ($g+$), original plus forms and combinations ($g\,O+$), and minus forms and combinations ($g-$). Table 2.3 shows proportions of the groups giving a certain number of responses rated "organization" (organizational acts) where originality, accuracy of forms, and appropriateness of combinations are considered. Qualitative differentiations of organizing acts include (a) $g\,O+$, where the forms involved and the combinations made are not only realistic but original; (b) $g+$, where forms and combinations are realistic; (c) $g-$, where forms and combinations are unrealistic and (d) $g-\,O-$ combinations!, where different responses are combined but the combinations are irrealistic and inappropriate.

The groups listed consist of normal children and clinical subjects.

TABLE 2.3   Proportions of the Groups Showing Appropriate and/or Inappropriate Organizational Acts (in Percentages)

		Scores					
		$g\,O+$	$g+$	$g-$		$g-\,O-$ comb!	
		Number of Occurrences					
		0–1	2 or more	8 or more	0–1	4 or more	1	2 or more
N	Groups	0–1	2 or more	8 or more	0–1	4 or more	1	2 or more
50	14-year-old group	52	48	56	58	18	—	—
50	Very superior group, ages 11–16 yrs.	18	82	74	54	8	10	2
40	College women (young adults)	33	68	90	43	33	13	—
25	Subnormal group ages 10–13 yrs.	96	4	—	72	8	16	4
25	Depressed patients (adults)	88	12	32	64	12	12	—
35	Delusional schizophrenics (adults)	80	20	9	14	51	34	31

The twelve- and fifteen-year-old children were taken from the Brush series. They were generally above average in intelligence and of higher social status and income group. The high and low Otis groups consisted of twelve-year-old boys and girls also taken from the Brush series, representing the upper and lower 20% of a larger twelve-year-old group. The low Otis group showed I.Q.'s of 86 to 105, and the high Otis group, I.Q.'s of over 120. The fourteen-year-old group were children tested in the public schools of Cleveland.

The superior group of children were selected at random from a larger group of superior children, ages 11 to 16 years, who participated in a contest sponsored by a Cleveland newspaper to select "the most superior child" in that age range in the public schools. The children were selected in the schools on the basis of school achievement scores, teachers' estimates, rating scales by supervisors and peers, and other test data. They were sent to the Brush Foundation for physical measurements and mental tests.

The subnormal group consisted of boys and girls, age range 10 to 13 years, who scored between 50 and 65 I.Q. on the Binet 1937 Scale. The college groups were students in an elementary psychology class. Patients in a state mental hospital and Veterans Administration hospital made up the clinical groups. They were not selected on the basis of any specific nosological grouping. The depressed patients included those individuals showing prominent depressive features. Similarly, the schizophrenic patients showed prominent delusional activity.

It may be of interest to include organizational scores which are available for brain-injured patients and old people utilized in other studies. The brain-injured were all cases of posttraumatic encephalopathy studied by Loehrke (23). The old-age group were all institutionalized old people, subjects in the study by Hertz et al. (16).

Of course, most of the groups presented are not comparable because they represent different populations and have not been matched for important variables. Medians and means are presented to describe the performance of the individual groups on organizational patterns.

The twelve-year-old group shows a mean of 12.22, S.D. 5.98, and the fifteen-year-old group a mean of 11.33, S.D. 6.11. There is no significant difference between the means. The range for both groups is approximately 5 to 18. The fourteen-year-old group is of a more representative population, since it consists of children taken at random in the public schools, whereas the twelve- and fifteen-year-old children in the Brush series consisted of a more selective group above average in intelligence and of higher social status. They show a median of 8.0 sum $g\,wt$, Q 2.9, the range being from about 6 to 11. Other groups studied above the age of 11 years show approximately the same median and range. The normative range tentatively used for adolescents of average intelligence is 6 to 11. It may be noted in Table 2.3, that 48% of the fourteen-year-old group give two or more $g\,O+$, and that 56% give eight or more organizing acts that involve realistic forms and combinations. Again, only a small part of the group give four or more organizing acts where forms and combinations are inadequate $(g-)$. Not one in this group gives the highly negative pattern, $g-\,O-$ comb!

The children of the superior group have a median of 10.5 sum $g\,wt$, Q 3.2, the range being 7 to 14. Children of the high Otis group show a higher median: 15.1, Q 3.3; here the range is 12 to 18. College women give 13.0, Q 5.5. As shown in Table 2.3, as many as 82% of the superior group and 68% of the college women give two or more organizing acts that involve originality. Again, 90% of the college women and 74% of the superior children give eight or more $g+$. Thus the groups of high intelligence give more organizing acts which involve realistic forms and combinations than acts involving inaccurate forms and combinations. A small proportion of the superior group give four or more organizing acts involving minus forms and combinations. However, a considerable proportion of the college group, 33%, give four or more $g-$ acts. Although the college women show organizational activity well adapted to reality, they also show unrealistic organization. As will be discussed below, emotional and personal factors influence reality testing and, hence, reflect on the quality of the organizational activity in all groups, whatever the level of intelligence.

The subnormal group shows a low median, 1.31, Q 1.00. There is hardly any distribution in scores, because 56% of the group falls below 1.5 sum $g\,wt$. Of course, it is generally observed that mental defectives have very low capacity to combine elements into more comprehensive whole units. They are not capable of much conceptual thinking, especially the kind that is in tune with reality. As seen from Table 2.3, very few of the group give even two or more organizing acts where forms are plus. It may also be observed that 16% of the group give different and strange combinations ($g-$ $O-$ comb!). Although the above groups are not comparable, there is a marked difference between the median of the subnormal group and those of the groups of higher intelligence.

This may also be seen in a study comparing the medians of the high Otis group with the low Otis group of boys and girls. The following results show statistically reliable differences between the medians of all the high and low groups, at the 5% level of confidence or less.

	Diff.	C. R.
High Otis boys with low Otis boys	6.8	3.33
High Otis boys with low Otis girls	5.5	2.68
High Otis girls with low Otis girls	5.7	3.11
High Otis girls with low Otis boys	7.0	3.87
Total high group with total low group	5.9	4.37

Children at the higher levels of intelligence, as determined by the Otis test, show higher sum $g\,wt$ than those at the lower levels.

Pertinent to this discussion is a study of the human movement in the records of a group of 137 children, 69 boys and 70 girls, 14 and 15 years of age, by Hertz and Kennedy (17). The I.Q. range was from 96 to 159 based on the revised Stanford-Binet. The group was divided into average and superior levels based on I.Q. Among the patterns studied, M was studied in combination with g, i.e., $W M g$, $D M g$, $Dr M g$, $S M g$, and sum $M g$. In this study, reliably more of the superior group than the average groups gave M which were $M g$ and more gave $D M g$, and $D M O+ g$. Thus more individuals of superior intelligence give human movement responses which rate "organization" than individuals of average intelligence. Further, responses rating "organization" where human forms are well perceived, experienced in movement, and projected into normal detail areas, are prone to reflect superior mental functioning.

The g scores in clinical groups. The group of depressed patients shows a low median of 5.6 sum $g wt$, Q 2.9. From clinical experience we know that individuals who are tense, anxious, and constrained give low g. They appear unable to analyze situations and see relationships. They are unable to respond to other than a limited perceptual aspect of a situation. They are "stimulus-bound." Varvel (39) shows this close relationship between limited perceptual organization and constricted personality. With the present group of depressed patients also, organizational activity is reduced.

From Table 2.3 it may be seen that of the present group of depressed patients, 32% give eight or more $g+$. Thus many who show organizational ability see forms clearly $(F+)$. Indeed, it may be noted that a large proportion of the group (64%) gives no or one $g-$. Those who have had experience with the depressed know, however, that this $F+$ reflects chiefly a rigid adherence to reality due to extreme cautiousness and guardedness.

A few of the present depressed group (12%) give one $g- O-$ comb! They see relations between areas of the blots which are unrealistic and peculiar. This would, of course, point to breakdown in reality testing, misinterpretation, and/or distortion of reality, which we know may occur in depressed conditions.

The schizophrenic group characterized by delusions has a low median sum $g wt$ of 6.1, Q 2.3. The median number of all organizational acts is 7.6, Q 2.8; of organizational acts which are minus it is 3.6, Q 1.3. In this group, 20% give two or more $g O+$, and a large proportion, 31%, give two or more $g- O-$ comb! About half of this group give four or more $g-$. We know that patients who show elaborate delusional trends tend to distort reality. They are not objective in their judgments. Their reasoning is faulty in certain respects. All of this may be reflected in the $g-$ score. The $g-$ $O-$ comb! appear to be associated with delusional developments.[3]

Experience with patients showing prominent obsessive-compulsive trends impresses us with the variability of the organizational score in their records. A study is now in progress analyzing Rorschach behavior in records showing obsessive-compulsive defensive operations. In some of the records being used, sum $g\,wt$ is surprisingly high. We can account for this at least in part in terms of the meticulous approach, the drive to perform, the striving to see as many things in as many relationships as possible, striving which is often compensatory in nature, which inflates the g sometimes well out of proportion to the actual capacity of the patients. On the other hand, sum $g\,wt$ is often low, even zero, in records showing obsessive-compulsive features. These individuals select detail after detail, giving them in unadorned and unelaborated fashion, without attempting any combinations and without seeing any relationships.

Similarly, with the records of excitable, impulsive, and manic patients, sum $g\,wt$ may be either high or low. Where high, qualitative

---

[3] In a recent, unpublished study, the author and Albert F. Paolino compared the organizational patterns of 35 neurotics and 35 paranoid schizophrenics, and found that the paranoid schizophrenic group gave reliable evidence of:

1. More organizational acts involving poor form $(g-)$ and inappropriate and unrealistic relationships $(g-$ comb$)$.

2. More instances of infrequent, unique, or bizarre organized concepts $(g\,O-,$ $g-$ $O-$ comb$)$.

3. Greater variability in the quality of the organized acts reflecting variable and unpredictable intellectual functioning.

4. A mental procedure which showed greater tendency to organize detail and space areas, with impaired form level.

5. A greater tendency to infuse organizational concepts with feelings of tenseness and conflict (m), with chaotic emotions $(C'\,CF)$, and with diffuse, primitive, or inappropriate emotional reactions.

6. More impaired thinking and less intellectual control $(\%\,\text{org}+)$.

7. More themes and more fabulized content in the organizational acts reflecting emotional aggressiveness, sado-masochistic tendencies, sexual preoccupation, and homosexual trends.

8. A higher total original score reflecting highly personalized, peculiar, or bizarre thinking.

9. More of the "negative" stylistic features as confabulation, contamination, autistic logic, fluidity, inappropriate specificity, and reference relationships.

10. More peculiarities in choice of vocabulary and language, with more pseudo-intellectual language and more sadistic verbalizations.

analysis reveals predominance of $g-$. Where low, the Rorschach performance is either sparse or erratic, unconnected, and disorganized. Unfortunately, qualitative analysis of various kinds of organizational activity for well-defined groups of patients showing obsessive-compulsive and manic features has not yet been systematically reported.

The brain-injured group attain a low median of 5.06, Q 1.66 for sum g wt. In the study by Loehrke (23), organizational activity was not studied by itself, but in conjunction with configurations which were quantitatively and qualitatively described in Rorschach terms. In certain of the configurations which were found to differentiate the brain-injured group from comparable groups of neurotic or schizophrenic patients, the g patterns figured prominently.

The old-age group also has a low median of 4.81, Q 2.58. The group as a whole showed considerable intellectual deterioration and constriction by other criteria. Analysis of the individual records revealed a variety of prominent neurotic and psychotic features. The reduction in sum g wt may be caused by intellectual deterioration, retardation, and constriction, or by the influence of neurotic and psychotic processes, or by a combination of two or more of these conditions.

SUMMARY

Comparatively little systematic work has been done with the organization factor in the Rorschach. A few studies point to the validity of certain aspects of the organization score. Results obtained by different workers, however, are at times at variance with each other. Even those that are in agreement must be repeated and cross-validated.

At the present time, we justify the use of this pattern in terms of available research, theoretical rationale, and clinical observation. Summarizing in terms of the hypotheses enumerated, we can say the following:

Hypothesis 1

The organization score appears to reflect ability to analyze material into component parts, to see relationships between and among these parts, to combine them, and to integrate them into wholes. It reflects the ability to conceptualize and to abstract.

Hypothesis 2

The organization pattern tells us something about the intellectual capacity of the individual, especially about certain verbal components of intelligence in relation to conceptual activity. Individuals of superior intelligence tend to give high organizational scores. Those who are mentally defective, intellectually defective, or intellectually retarded or deteriorated tend to give low organizational scores.

Hypothesis 3

The organizational score reflects intellectual effort, initiative, energy, and drive. It is increased by liberated energy and emotional expansiveness. Manic patients tend to give higher organizational scores than normals or schizophrenic patients. Depressed patients, on the other hand, tend to give much lower scores.

Hypothesis 4

Qualitative analysis of the organizational patterns tells something of the degree of reality testing, the complexity of the responses, and the appropriateness and constructiveness of the relationships seen. Organizational activity which involves accurate forms and combinations reflects realistic, logical, and constructive thinking. Individuals of average to superior intelligence tend to show more of this kind of organizational activity. Inferior organizational ability reflects inadequate reality testing, intellectual distortions, and confusion. Patients who are mentally and emotionally disturbed tend to give more of this type of organization. Finally $g-O-$ combinations! appear to be associated with faulty and irrational thinking and suggest delusional developments.

Hypothesis 5

In general, the organizational factor on the Rorschach helps gage the intellectual level of the individual, the efficiency with which the individual functions, the influence of emotional factors and mental disturbance on the intellectual functioning. High organizational score is associated with relatively high mental functioning, liberated energy, emotional expansiveness, and drive. Low organizational score is associated with mental deficiency, retardation, deterioration, anxieties, constriction, depressed conditions, and other emotional interferences. Neurotic and psychotic processes may inflate or deflate the organizational score.

Since the organizational score shows some relationships to the number of responses given, it should be considered and evaluated in conjunction with productivity. If a total organizational score is utilized, the sum of the organizational acts is probably as effective as a weighted organizational score. There appears to be considerable value, however, in utilizing the weighted scheme and studying the qualitative differentiations of the organizational score in order to study the nature and the adequacy of reality testing, the complexity, the originality, the constructiveness, and the appropriateness of the organizational activity.

The systematic study of the organizational pattern encounters difficulties. The multidimensional nature of this score, as all Rorschach scores, still presents methodological problems. As has been repeated so often, Rorschach scores take meaning only from the constellation in which they are embedded. The Rorschach score is determined and influenced by innumerable variables, not only by other Rorschach variables but also by extra test variables (mood, mental set, interpersonal relationships, examiner personality, and the like), variables which have been so appropriately emphasized in recent literature. Research with the organizational score must involve research with a large number of variables concomitant within the general personality configuration. To make the task harder, it must be studied in its qualitative and quantitative aspects as well as in terms of its interaction among other variables, a procedure which has not shown itself to be amenable to systematic research.

Ideally it would appear more appropriate, and certainly more profitable, to start with the unit personality itself rather than with Rorschach scores or even composite scores like the organizational pattern, and study how Rorschach patterns shape up and interact within the personality. Taking the ideographic approach, each Rorschach record would be studied not only in terms of its scores but also in relation to and as a function of the interaction of the individual with the total situation. As is done clinically with each case, interpretation would be global, consisting of a description of the personality dynamics and the functioning of the individual in a specific situation, based on all material available—other test data, interview material, social, medical, and psychiatric data, and the like.

In studying organizational ability, then, everything about the record and the individual would be taken into consideration. The mental ability, emotional make-up, emotional disturbances, efficiency of functioning, inhibiting or liberating pressures from the outside, defensive operations, everything known from the test itself, from the individual, and from sources outside the test would be weighed. Although appropriate normative material with healthy groups must be utilized in this appraisal to serve as a frame of reference, the organizational patterns like other Rorschach patterns take meaning for the individual only in relation to his unique psychological status and functioning at the moment. Research then would be directed toward establishing the validity of the varying forms of organizational activity in different kinds of individuals in specific settings and under special conditions. Such procedure would, of course, cut through the traditional diagnostic groupings and take into consideration the uniqueness and the complexity of the individual personality.

BIBLIOGRAPHY

1. Batt, H. V. *An investigation of the significance of the Rorschach Z score.* Unpublished Ph.D. dissertation, University of Nebraska, 1953.
2. Beck, S. J. Configurational tendencies in Rorschach responses. *Amer. J. Psychol.*, 1933, **45**, 433–443.
3. Beck, S. J. *Rorschach's test. Vol. I. Basic processes.* New York: Grune and Stratton, 1950.
4. Beck, S. J. *Rorschach's test. Vol. II. A variety of personality pictures.* New York: Grune and Stratton, 1949.
5. Beck, S. J. *Rorschach's test. Vol. III. Advances in interpretation.* New York: Grune and Stratton, 1952.
6. Beck, S. J. The six schizophrenias. Res. monogr., *Amer. Orthopsychiat. Assn.*, 1954, **10**, No. 6.
7. Beck, S. J., Rabin, A. I., Thiesen, W. G., Molish, H., and Thetford, W. N. The normal personality as projected in the Rorschach test. *J. Psychol.*, 1950, **30**, 241–298.
8. Ford, M. The application of the Rorschach test to young children. *Univ. Minn., The Institute of Child Welf. Monogr. Series,* No. 23, Minneapolis: University of Minnesota Press, 1946.
9. Friedman, H. Perceptual regression in schizophrenia. *J. proj. Tech.*, 1953, **17**, 171–185.
10. Goldfarb, W. Organizational activity in the Rorschach examination. *Amer. J. Orthopsychiat.*, 1945, **15**, 525–528.

11. Guirdham, A.   On the value of the Rorschach test.   *J. ment. Sci.*, 1935, **81**, 848–869.
12. Hemmendinger, L.   Perceptual organization and development as reflected in the structure of Rorschach test responses.   *J. proj. Tech.*, 1953, **17**, 162–170.
13. Hertz, M. R.   The scoring of the Rorschach ink-blot method as developed by the Brush Foundation.   *Rorschach Res. Exch.*, 1942, **6**, 16–22.
14. Hertz, M. R.   *The summary sheet: The Rorschach psychogram.*   Cleveland: The Press of Western Reserve University, 1942.
15. Hertz, M. R.   *Frequency tables for scoring responses to the Rorschach inkblot test* (3rd ed.).   Cleveland: The Press of Western Reserve University, 1951.
16. Hertz, M. R., Grossman, C., and Warshawsky, F.   The personality characteristics of a group of institutionalized old people.   Paper read at the Midwestern Psychological Association in Chicago, April 28, 1951.
17. Hertz, M. R., and Kennedy, S.   The *M* factor in estimating intelligence.   *Rorschach Res. Exch.*, 1940, **4**, 105–106 (abstract).
18. Janoff, I. Z.   The relation between Rorschach form quality measures and children's behavior.   Unpublished Ph.D. thesis, Yale University Library, 1951.
19. Jolles, I.   The diagnostic implications of Rorschach's test in case studies of mental defectives.   *Genet. Psychol. Monogr.*, 1947, **36**, 89–198.
20. Klopfer, B., Ainsworth, M. D., Klopfer, W. G., and Holt, R. R.   *Developments in the Rorschach technique.*   Yonkers: World Book Co., 1954.
21. Klopfer, B., and Davidson, H.   Form-level rating.   *Rorschach Res. Exch.*, 1944, **4**, 164–177.
22. Kropp, R. P.   The Rorschach "Z" score.   *J. proj. Tech.*, 1955, **19**, 443–452.
23. Loehrke, L. M.   An evaluation of the Rorschach method for the study of brain injury.   Unpublished Ph.D. thesis, Western Reserve University Library, 1952.
24. McCandless, B. R.   The Rorschach as a predictor of academic success.   *J. appl. Psychol.*, 1949, **33**, 43–50.
25. Peña, C. D.   A genetic evaluation of perceptual structuralization in cerebral pathology: An investigation by means of the Rorschach test.   *J. proj. Tech.*, 1953, **17**, 186–199.
26. Phillips, L., and Smith, J. G.   *Rorschach interpretation: Advanced technique.*   New York: Grune and Stratton, 1953.
27. Rapaport, D., Gill, M., and Schafer, R.   *Diagnostic psychological testing, II.*   Chicago: Year Book Publishers, 1946.
28. Rorschach, H.   *Psychodiagnostics.*   A diagnostic test based on perception.   Bern: Hans Huber, 1942.
29. Rosenblatt, B., Solomon, P.   Structural and genetic aspects of the Rorschach responses in mental deficiency.   *J. proj. Tech.*, 1954, **18**, 496–506.
30. Sarason, E. K.   The discriminatory value of the Rorschach test between two etiologically different mentally defective groups.   Unpublished Ph.D. thesis, Clark University Library, 1950.
31. Sarason, S. B.   *The clinical interaction.*   New York: Harper Bros., 1954.
32. Schmidt, H. O., and Fonda, C. P.   Rorschach scores in the manic state.   *J. Psychol.*, 1954, **38**, 427–437.
33. Siegel, E. L.   Perception in paranoid schizophrenia and the Rorschach.   *J. proj. Tech.*, 1953, **17**, 151–161.
34. Sisson, B. D., and Taulbee, E. S.   Organizational activity on the Rorschach test.   *J. consult. Psychol.*, 1955, **19**, 29–31.

35. Sloan, W.   Mental deficiency as a symptom of personality disturbance. *Amer. J. ment. Def.*, 1947, **52**, 31–36.
36. Taulbee, E. S.   The use of the Rorschach test in evaluating the intellectual levels of functioning in schizophrenics. *J. proj. Tech.*, 1955, **19**, 163–169.
37. Thetford, W. M., Molish, H. B., and Beck, S. J.   Developmental aspects of personality structure in normal children. *J. proj. Tech.*, 1951, **15**, 58–78.
38. Thiesen, J. W.   A pattern analysis of structural characteristics of the Rorschach test in schizophrenia. *J. consult. Psychol.*, 1952, **16**, 365–370.
39. Varvel, W. A.   The Rorschach test in psychotic and neurotic depressions. *Bull. Menn. Clinic.*, 1941, **5**, 5–12.
40. Vernon, P. E.   The Rorschach ink-blot test. III.   *Brit. J. med. Psychol.*, 1933, **13**, 271–295.
41. Wilson, G. P., and Blake, R. R.   A methodological problem in Beck's organizational concept. *J. consult. Psychol.*, 1950, **14**, 20–24.
42. Wishner, J.   Rorschach intellectual indicators in neurotics.   *Amer. J. Orthopsychiat.*, 1948, **18**, 265–279.

3 | by Laurence Hemmendinger

DEVELOPMENTAL THEORY

AND THE

RORSCHACH METHOD

In this chapter an attempt is made to assess a particular use of Rorschach's test as a tool for psychological research. The basic approach is through the analysis of the kind and patterning of the test responses.

If research data are to be meaningful, the observations they represent must be guided by questions that are formulated in terms of concepts derived from a systematic theoretical position. This does not necessarily imply the testing of deductions from theory since there are other ways of working within a conceptual framework, e.g., by the ordering of observations selected from diverse sources. The choice and suitability of any particular observational technique (in this case, Rorschach's test) depend in large part on what one wants to observe.

The material which follows is intended to illustrate the research potential of Rorschach's test when used in conjunction with a particular theory. The test as a procedure and the subjects as sources of test responses are the familiar, usual ones; but the analysis of the Rorschach location scores has been carried out consistent with some implications of a particular theoretical framework, namely, Heinz Werner's developmental theory.

DEVELOPMENTAL THEORY

Heinz Werner's developmental approach to behavior states that developmental changes take place in terms of a systematic, orderly sequence, and that a "direction" is implied. The regulatory principle that describes how these changes take place is stated as follows: "When development occurs, it proceeds from a state of relative globality and lack of differentiation to a state of increasing differentiation, articulation and hierarchic integration" (38–41).

This orthogenetic principle is not so much a statement allowing predictions about specific developmental events or behavior changes, as it is a manner of viewing, ordering, and interpreting behavior in all its manifold aspects. For example, it is assumed that the orthogenetic principle applies uniformly to all behavior, to the extent that behavior can be viewed as taking place over a period of time. In contrast to this uniformity is the multiplicity of specific developmental changes that may be observed in behavior.

There are three other specific aspects to this developmental conceptualization. These more detailed statements of the orthogenetic principle are that: (a) Changes in development take place according to the principle of abrupt, discontinuous change and developmental shifts—the emergence of new functions, etc.; (b) attained developmental level is characterized by a high degree of variability of functioning—that there is mobility rather than fixity of developmental level of operation; and (c) the achievements of various individuals may have come about by processes genetically quite different—that an analysis of the types of operations underlying a performance rather than the measurement of the accuracy of performance reveals a truer picture, and that the kinds and characteristics of the processes underlying behavior may change.

Werner defines organic development as "increasing differentiation and centralization—or hierarchic integration." The qualitative distinction between "undifferentiated" and "differentiated," "unorganized" and "hierarchically organized and integrated" can be further clarified by using other descriptive terms. Thus, the undifferentiated structure or process is said to be "syncretic," "diffuse," "labile," "indefinite," and "rigid"; when differentiated and organized, the terms "discrete," "articulated," "stable," "definite," and "flexible," are applicable. These terms are paired "opposites," descriptive extremes that have qualitative value for understanding genetic differences (41).

RORSCHACH APPLICATIONS

This developmental approach is hardly new or revolutionary (3, 17, 29, 36). A great many psychological theorists speak of development in terms of a reciprocal sequence of extension, differentiation, and integration of psychological structures and processes (e.g., Freud, Lewin). Recently, a series of attempts have been made to link some of these ideas with regard to development and genetic theory with clinical theory, i.e., to study the characteristic perceptual functioning of different clinical groups, or normal human beings of different ages, and the way perception develops in normal and clinical groups. This research started with the work of Howard Friedman, then at Clark University, who applied the principles of Werner's developmental approach to the structural aspects of Rorschach location scores (10, 11).

Friedman applied these qualitative "paired opposites" to Rorschach standard scoring locations. The resulting modified scores are an attempt to get at certain "formal" aspects of the variety of perceptual functioning reflected in a Rorschach response.

Precise definitions of the term "formal" or "structural" are difficult to give, but the meaning here is a simple one: One's concern is with the forming or fashioning of the thing seen. The simple $F+$ or $F-$ [1] designation for Rorschach content in a certain location is an attempt to describe adequacy of achievement. The developmental location scores, however, are concerned with the structure, or the arrangement of the parts of the percept, essentially without regard for the content of the structure.

It is true that one cannot deal with structure wholly without regard for content—indeed, this developmental theory would indicate that one could not do so in a pure sense. Some Rorschach percepts are determined not so much by the structure of the blot as by color or shading, or by the mere something-extended-on-a-ground quality of the blot. "A dog" or "a human," on the other hand, clearly require some orderly arrangement of parts in a fairly well prescribed order. In the latter case, the score deals with the "form" of content, and thus with structure. The second difficulty of dealing with structure in its pure form is that, particularly with mental patients, some percepts are clearly bizarre or erroneous. In this case, one believes that

---

[1] For explanation of scoring symbols, see Appendix, pp. 441 ff. [Editor].

the subject is responding not so much to the qualities of the external stimulus as to some inner experience of his own.

Another important qualification about dealing with pure structure is that at least some of the psychological determinants of structure are imaginal–motor-emotional in nature. Thus, to the extent that non-geometrical, sensory, imaginal, and emotional aspects of form play a role in perception, the attempt to deal only with structure becomes a recognizably artificial one, albeit desirable or necessary.[2]

As a consequence, some of the structural scores defined by Friedman are based upon nonform criteria, some are based upon $F+$ and $F-$ tables, and some are based upon the literal putting together of the forms of the blots; all are attempts to reveal the variety of perceptual functioning previously grouped together under a single unitary location score.

DEVELOPMENTAL LOCATION SCORES

In the following, the criteria for all scores utilized in the Clark University studies are defined, and examples of each score, taken from the test protocols, are given. The usual Detail (D) and rare Detail (Dd) blot areas are those delineated by Beck. The plus and minus form quality is determined primarily from Beck's tables, and in those few cases in which these do not suffice, the tables published by Hertz can be used.

Wa: An amorphous response in which the shape of the blot plays no determinable role. Such responses are based solely on chromatic or achromatic aspects of the blot, and, in customary scoring procedure, no form element would be included in the score.
    EX: Card I–"Black paint."
        Card II–"Sort of looks like some football team colors–black and red."

Wv: A vague response in which there is diffuse general impression of the blot. Although some form element is present, it is of such an unspecific nature that almost any perceptual form is adequate to encompass the content.

---

[2] Wertheimer (42) has described how all perception is organized by a combination of autochthonous (structural) principles, as well as by principles of organization involving idiosyncratic characteristics of the perceiver (past experience, motivation, etc.) and related this specifically to Rorschach percepts.

EX: Card II—"Rock formation."

Card I—"Could be an island—with water in between and water surrounding it on the outside of the island."

$W-$: A response in which the content produced requires a definite specific form, which, however, is not provided by the blot. (Goodness of match between blot and content is based upon the plus and minus form tables mentioned before.)

EX: Card IV—"A starfish."

Card I—"A frog."

DW: Rorschach's confabulatory response in which "a single detail, more or less clearly perceived, is used as the basis for the interpretation of the whole picture, giving very little consideration to the other parts of the figure."

EX: Card IV—"A monkey, a chinchilla," solely on the basis of seeing the top central area of the face of a monkey.

Card IV—"A boat," solely on the basis of seeing the lower projecting central area as "the front."

Wm: A mediocre response in which the gross outline and articulation of an unbroken [3] blot are taken into account so that the specific form implied in the content matches the blot.

EX: Card V—"A bat."

Card I—"A mask."

$W+$: A response in which all the discrete portions of a broken blot are combined into a unifying whole, and in which the specific form implied in the content matches the blot.

EX: Card II—"Two fellows at a bar toasting each other."

Card VIII—"A sail boat."

$W++$: A response in which a unitary blot is perceptually articulated and then reintegrated into a well-differentiated unifying whole, the specific form of which matches the blot.

[3] A "broken" card is considered as one in which the white background completely surrounds a usual detail (D), or the white background isolates the majority of a usual detail from the remainder of the blot, or where a major portion of white background intervenes between the two lateral halves of the total blot. Thus, cards I, IV, V, VI, and IX are considered unbroken, and cards II, III, VII, VIII, and X broken. It should be noted then, that although Wa, Wv, $W-$, and DW can occur on all cards, Wm and $W++$ can be scored only on unbroken cards, and $W+$ only on broken cards. Although normally card VII cannot yield a Wm score, it has been found necessary to allow a certain few exceptions. This card brings forth, in a few cases, relatively clear-cut "schematic" W responses in which the perceptual functioning is seemingly governed solely by a general contour feature of the blot, as its "U" shape. Such W responses, as "harbor," "bridge,"

EX: Card V—"A man dressed up in a grasshopper suit on skates—the finale of a show, and there's two girls resting in his arms."

Card I—"Can imagine it's a fountain with two dogs on each end. . . ."

The criteria for the *W* responses apply to the *D* responses, except, of course, that the blot area referred to is a usual detail. Consequently, with the exception of the *D+* score which requires a slightly modified definition, only examples will be provided for the *D* scores.

Da:

EX: Card II—Top red area, "Fire."

Card X—"Blue, yellow, brown, and green areas, "That's lighting rooms—lights."

Dv:

EX: Card IX—Large green area, "Looks like a map of some sort."

Card X—Blue area, "That's water . . . a splash of water."

D—:

EX: Card IX—Large top orange area, "Looks like sea lions."

Card VIII—Side pink areas, "That's a bee."

DdD:

EX: Card X—Large pink area, "Cocoons or worms," solely on the basis of the rounded top edge outline.

Card II—One lateral large black area, "Looks like an elephant to me," solely on the basis of an outer edge outline detail as the "head."

Dm:

EX: Card III—Red center area, "Suggests a bow tie."

Card X—Outer yellow area, "This is a little bird."

D+: A response in which two or more discrete blot areas (two or more *D*) are combined into one percept, the specific form of which matches the blot.

EX: Card VIII—The side red figures and top center area, "Two rats climbing up on the tree simultaneously, one on each side."

Card III—All black areas, "Two men beating drums as in a tribal dance. . . ."

D++:

EX: Card IX—Large green area, "These here look like comedy caricatures—person riding on some sort of animal."

Card IX—Orange area designated as a man with hat blowing a bugle.

"bowl," are scored *Wm*, for it is felt that the gross outline of the contour is clearly involved, rather than any true integration of discrete portions.

FaC: A fabulized combination in which two or more acceptably inter-preted areas are combined, on the basis of spatial relationship, into one absurd percept.

    EX: Card VIII—One lateral red area interpreted as a "tiger," the other as a "grapefruit," remainder of blot as a "church," and response becomes, "This is a funny church and the grapefruit is climb-ing up the church."

    Card II—Red interpreted as "fire," black as "animal's face," with center white space as "mouth," and response becomes, "It's fire and it's catching on to an animal (onto his chin) 'cause here's his mouth."

CoR: A contaminated response, in which two interpretations to the same area are fused into one.

    EX: Card V—Entire blot area seen as a "beetle," then seen as a "bear," and response immediately becomes, "A beetle near a bear."

    Card IV—Entire blot seen as "front of a bug," then as "front of an ox," and response immediately becomes, "Oh, a front of a bug-ox."

This scoring system of Rorschach response location has been created to reflect genetic changes as, for instance, the amount of separation of the blot areas into parts (differentiation), and the organization of these areas together into a "combined" whole (hierarchic integration). Both the developmental theory and ontogenetic evidence allow these scores to be distinguished dichotomously into "genetically low" or "imma-ture," and "genetically high" or "mature" scores. Or, in terms of the theoretical definition of the scores, they may be considered as re-flecting levels of operation of the subject.

When these scores are applied to the Rorschach responses of 160 children between the ages of three through ten years, one finds that the basic principle of development appears to be confirmed (13).[4] With increasing age there is a decrease of the undifferentiated, diffuse whole and detail responses, an increase of the highly articulated, well-integrated whole and detail responses, and an interesting shift from the early whole responses toward small details between the ages of six to eight years, then declining in favor of the integrated whole responses later on.[5]

    [4] The scoring system was initially developed by Friedman. The research as reported here is in terms of theoretical relationships rather than in its actual historical order.

    [5] The comparisons of median per cent, made by the chi-square technique, allow statements about statistically significant differences between age or diagnostic groups; these differences occur in the theoretically indicated directions and places.

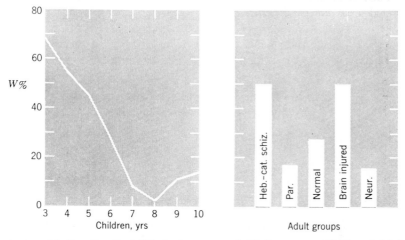

Fig. 3.1. Median Per Cent Whole Responses of All Responses: Child and Adult Groups.

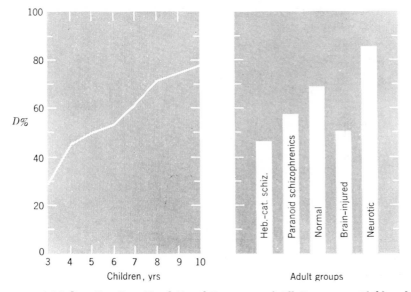

Fig. 3.2. Median Per Cent Usual Detail Responses of All Responses: Child and Adult Groups.

A detailed look at Hemmendinger's ontogenetic research shows that the data not only reflect the expected sequence of developmental processes but also indicates that development is never quite complete: the adults' behavior retains some of the fused-function global properties that are especially characteristic in young children. Conversely, there are already present in the youngest children traces of what will be their characteristic level or type of operation when they become

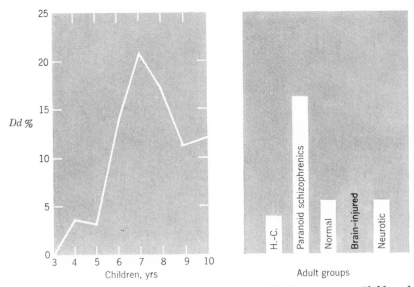

Fig. 3.3. Median Per Cent Rare Detail Responses of All Responses: Child and Adult Groups.

older. It is not a matter of either/or, but of more or less. Thus, the ontogenetic research provides a developmental scale that can be applied to a wide variety of research problems in which a change of function and/or performance is relevant.[6]

[6] In Klopfer's *Developments in the Rorschach technique,* Vol. II, there is an article by Dworetzki describing some of the research into the genetic aspects of Rorschach determinants that have been carried on in Europe. These studies focused on perception (in the same way that Rorschach did) as ways of reflecting the subject's adaptation to reality. Development was conceived of in the same way as described here: "differentiation" and increasing "complexity" as well as growing "flexibility."

Dworetzki first studied perceptual development in the reactions of different children and adult groups to ambiguous figures, e.g., a line drawing of various fruits (*D*) that together have the gestalt of a person on a bicycle (*W*). In her

Of particular interest in Hemmendinger's data is the fact that there remain in the perceptual behavior of older children and adults the residuals of the primitive kinds of perceptual functioning so characteristic of the younger children. As had been previously hypothesized by Friedman, the reverse of "growth" or "development" could also be studied by this technique.

The works of Friedman (10, 11), Siegel (34) Peña (24), and Frank

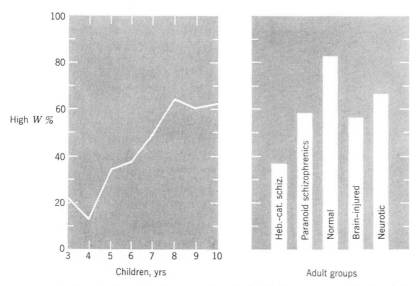

Fig. 3.4. Median Per Cent Developmentally—High Whole Responses of All Whole Responses: Child and Adult Groups.

(8) deal with perceptual regression. Regression is operationally conceived of as the relative accentuation of genetically low levels of functioning in various clinical groups. The developmental approach would predict that the most seriously impaired clinical groups should

application of the three laws of mental development that are reflected in reactions to the ambiguous figures ["1. General and confused perception of the whole (syncretic perception). 2. Distinct and analytic perception of the parts. 3. Synthetic recomposition of the whole with awareness of the part" (25, p. 112)], Dworetzki has not so adequately and quantitatively defined the kinds of perception of location areas as has Friedman, but she has related various response determinants, such as movement, shading, and color, to perceptual organization. Dworetzki, furthermore, discusses the influence of color and shading during development, and the development of movement responses themselves. A critical study of this article is fundamental to all future work with the Rorschach and to the developmental approach as an organizing theory.

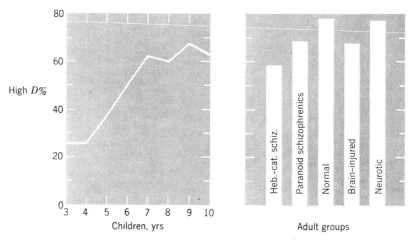

Fig. 3.5. Median Per Cent Developmentally—High Usual Detail Responses of All Usual Detail Responses: Child and Adult Groups.

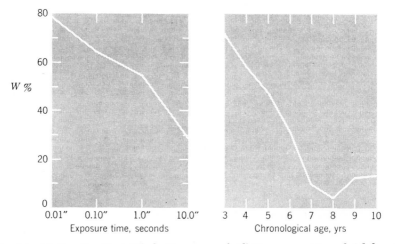

Fig. 3.6. Median Per Cent Whole Responses of All Responses: Normal Adults at Tachistoscopic Exposure, Children at Full Exposure.

show a preponderance of the genetically lowest responses, and that there should be a decrease of these responses and an increase in the genetically high responses with the lesser impaired groups. The relative degree of impairment was predicted from psychoanalytic theory, and would order the clinical groups (in increasing maturity) in the following positions: Hebephrenic-catatonic schizophrenics, paranoid schizophrenics, psychoneurotics, and normal adults.

The other most familiar impaired group of patients are adults who are brain-injured and who have suffered some cerebral damage. Peña (24) studied such a group of adults and, on theoretical grounds,

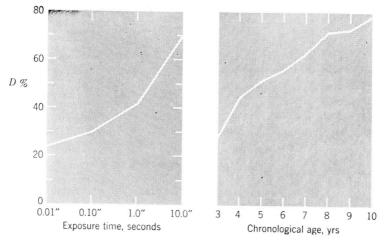

Fig. 3.7. Median Per Cent Usual Detail Responses of All Responses: Normal Adults at Tachistoscopic Exposure, Children at Full Exposure.

hypothesized that they would rate among the other patients on a range between the hebephrenic-catatonic schizophrenics and normal adults.

The over-all evidence is in good agreement with these expectations: The hebephrenic-catatonic schizophrenics generally resemble (in their genetic scores) children three to five years of age; paranoids are similar to children six to ten years of age; the psychoneurotics are intermediate between ten year old children and normal adults; and the cerebrally damaged adults are generally like older children, but with some of the perceptual characteristics of the youngest children, and yet possessing some of the stabilizing and economical features of normal adults. These data are shown graphically in Figs. 3.1 through 3.5.

In the researches described so far, ontogenetic concepts have been

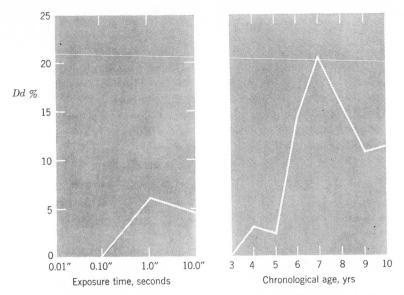

Fig. 3.8. Median Per Cent Rare Detail Responses of All Responses: Normal Adults at Tachistoscopic Exposure, Children at Full Exposure.

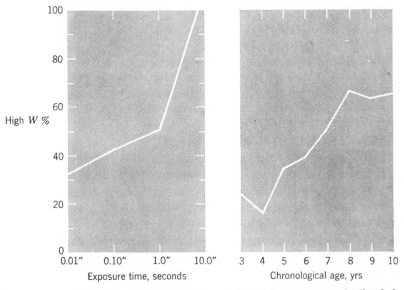

Fig. 3.9. Median Per Cent Developmentally—High Whole Responses of All Whole Responses: Normal Adults at Tachistoscopic Exposure, Children at Full Exposure.

used either to compare different age groups (the usual comparison) or to study the end products of perception in adult groups. In other words, while the processes of growth and regression have been studied, the intergroup comparisons were made on the basis of the end products of perception and perception itself as a developing process was not studied.

It is also possible to think of perception as a process taking place in time, and to apply the orthogenetic principle to perception as a developing process rather than as an end product. These are stud-

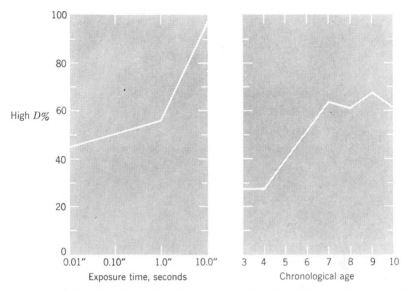

Fig. 3.10. Median Per Cent Developmentally–High Usual Detail Responses of All Usual Detail Responses: Normal Adults at Tachistoscopic Exposure, Children at Full Exposure.

ies of the "microgenesis" of perception. The development of perception is not only predictable from developmental theory but is also demonstrable in tachistoscopic presentation of the Rorschach cards. This was shown in the work of Framo (7), who studied microgenesis by tachistoscopic exposure of the Rorschach cards to eighty normals. Twenty subjects in each of four groups were presented with the cards exposed for .01 second, for .10 second, for 1 second, and for 10 seconds.

A comparison of the data of Framo's microgenetic study with the data from the ontogenetic study by Hemmendinger shows a striking

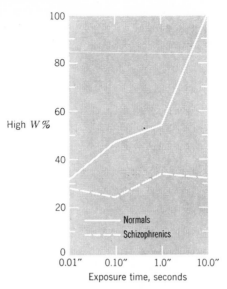

Fig. 3.11. Median Per Cent Developmentally–High Whole Responses of All Whole Responses: Normal and Schizophrenic Adults at Four Exposure Times.

similarity in the shape of the curves as exposure time increases for normal adults and as chronological age increases for the children. These data are shown graphically in Figs. 3.6 through 3.10. The reader may compare for himself the microgenetic changes and levels with the genetic levels of the two schizophrenic groups, the brain-injured, the neurotic groups, and the genetic characteristics of normal adults, all at standard-time presentation of the Rorschach cards.

The original research reports in detail the comparisons that can be made between these various groups for all of the many genetic location scores, and the reader is referred to them for these data and for the suggestions as to specific clinical use of these comparisons. However, the over-all conclusion is that the responses of the clinical groups represent various immature levels of perceptual functioning, and that these levels of functioning are as indicated by the theory (pages 59 ff.).

The developmental theory further implies that the most immature groups (either children or schizophrenics) would fail to show increased differentiation and hierarchic integration in their perception with time. Part of just such a study has been carried out by Freed (9), with the same design as Framo, using a group of sixty hebe-phrenic-catatonic schizophrenics as his subjects. At the shortest exposure time, the performance of schizophrenics is not obviously different from that of normals, but as exposure time increases, the schizophrenics lag further behind the normals in the development toward perceptually mature responses.   Figures 3.11 and 3.12 show graphically that the schizophrenic groups did not utilize the increase in exposure time for the improvement of perceptual performance.

It would seem that if such a comparison could be carried out for groups of children at various ages, as well as for a greater variety of clinical groups, more light could be shed on how perception takes place in time.

The Rorschach research reported thus far has to do with an attempt to provide supportive evidence for the orthogenetic principle as it applies to growth (ontogenetic or microgenetic studies), and with the application of this principle in describing the levels of perceptual functioning in various adult groups.   It is possible to think of these levels separately from "growth"; these genetic levels may be more broadly conceived as reflecting the kind of psychological processes characteristic of different kinds of people.   One can, for example, study some of the psychological processes of people who are high social achievers as compared to those who are low social achiev-

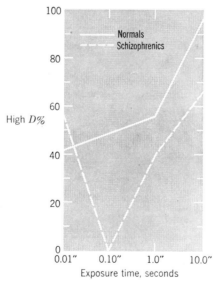

Fig. 3.12. Median Per Cent Developmentally—High Usual Detail Responses of All Usual Detail Responses: Normal and Schizophrenic Adults at Four Exposure Times.

ers, or various kinds of creative people, or people who are prone toward impulsive or self-destructive behavior, or people who test at different levels of intelligence.

The following brief research reports will illustrate two such uses of these Rorschach scores: Studies in which the Rorschach scores are used to understand certain characteristics of people, and those in which the scores have been used to separate groups (into those of different genetic levels) whose psychological functioning is then studied by other means.

The "level of regression" studies by Friedman, Siegel, Peña, and Frank have shown that psychiatric intactness corresponds to developmental level; one may also conceive of the form of symptom expression as being related to developmental level as indicated by the genetic Rorschach scores. Thus, studies by Misch (23) have shown that individuals whose behavior is characterized by immediacy of overt reaction (assault) are developmentally different than individuals whose symptomatology reflects more delayed or mediated behavior. Similar differences have been found by Kruger (18) for patients who either only threaten suicide or fear perversions from those who make serious suicidal attempts or who demonstrate overt sexual perversions.

In another setting, Fowler (6) has been able to demonstrate these kinds of developmental differences between subjects of high and low social adequacy and attainment. Becker (1), in using this approach to studying the process-reactive distinction in schizophrenia, has found a meaningful relationship between the process-reaction dimension and the disturbances of thought processes as reflected at the genetic-level Rorschach scoring system. In addition, Becker found that Whitman's Elgin Prognostic Scale (based on the same factors on which the process-reaction distinction is made) is also related to developmental level as indicated by this Rorschach scoring system. Fine and Zimet (5), using the same population as used by Brackbill and Fine (2) in a study of schizophrenia and central nervous system pathology, found differences in developmental level between process and reactive schizophrenics in essential agreement with the work of Becker.

Rosenblatt and Solomon (33) applied the developmental approach and the genetic Rorschach scoring to the problem of mental deficiency. They were interested in studying some structural aspects of perception, and the differences between the structure of perception in mental defectives and other subjects. They found that it was possible to discriminate among levels of mental deficiency in this way, and that normal children showed more differentiation and integration than defectives of the same mental age. Again, supporting some of the findings of Friedman, schizophrenic and brain-damaged subjects showed vestiges of a former level of functioning higher than that of the mental defectives. There is, furthermore, support for the idea of Friedman that vague whole perception stands for a regressive failure of attempts at integrative functioning on a functional basis, and would enable the clinician to distinguish between "fixation" and "regression."

Except for the studies by Becker (1) and Rosenblatt and Solomon (33), work with this Rorschach scoring system has tended to stick closely to the idea of "genetic and structural aspects of *perception*." It is, of course, possible to think of Rorschach responses, including the location categories, as reflecting other psychological processes, such as thinking. There are two studies not yet reported in the literature (one by Roger Bibace, the other by Charles Hersch) on the apprehension of numerical relationships in adults at different genetic levels and on creativity in artists. There also have been a number of studies from Clark University and Worcester State Hospital on the relationships between genetic level as defined by these Rorschach scores and such other factors as adaptation to stress, social attainment, and various psychological control mechanisms (16, 21, 25, 26, 27, 31, 37, 43).

There is, in addition, an attempt by Grace (12) to relate the developmental continuum of perceptual functioning with social adjustment and the content of the verbalizations. It was found that developmental aspects of content, defined as level of vocabulary usage in terms of frequency of use at various age levels, were related to social adaptation as well as to a variety of genetically conceived scores for the Rorschach.

This brief review of present research with the developmentally defined Rorschach location scores serves to illustrate ways in which the Rorschach method can be used to provide answers to problems in basic psychological science and to specifically clinical-psychological problems.

There are, of course, dozens of immediately obvious comparisons between groups or kinds of people in terms of genetic levels that would be of practical interest to the clinician or psychological scientist who is interested in intergroup comparison data. There are also other uses for this linkage of "theory" and "clinical-observation technique." One is a study of thinking. For example, one would expect that different kinds of "projection" (paranoid projection, infantile projection, and projection in transference phenomena, as well as the projective-test concept of unique and private organizing principles within an individual) would take place by different externalization processes. These externalization processes, like any kinds of organizing processes—e.g., those that create and develop the motivations that further organize thought processes—can be conceived of in developmental terms.

If psychologists were in possession of concepts relating motivating processes and externalizing processes by the developmentally conceived Rorschach factors of "determinants" as well as of "locations," it would be possible to study some of the processes and products of thinking in various age and clinical groups. Some early aspects of this work have been done by Dworetzki (22); Rapaport has long advocated a distinction between the "fixed tools of thought" (clearly involved in tests like similarities and differences) and "processes of thought," the latter called for especially where already existing concepts are not so relevant (28). It should be possible to study the conditions of the appearance, and the particular qualities, of processes of thinking by an organized combination of Rorschach inquiry and the subject's further free associations to the apperception of the Rorschach percepts themselves.

It would be anticipated that this inquiry and free association material would reflect some aspect of how thought processes occur and develop. Although there are other, in many ways better, observation techniques than the Rorschach for studying thinking, the congruence of intellectual, motivational, imaginal, etc., factors already recognized in the determination of Rorschach responses indicates that such a research program would be profitable.

No one yet knows enough of what an examination of developmental sequences in the "other-than-form-determined" Rorschach scores would reveal about the creation of the ego's various control functions, although certain implications emerge from the information provided by the genetic location scores and from emphases on $F+$ and $F-$ responses. Many of the present researches in this area are unfortunately based on simple reports of how well signs stand up (35, 36); it is suggested that research of the type outlined here can be more than a "sign" approach.

BIBLIOGRAPHY

1. Becker, Wesley C. A genetic approach to the interpretation and evaluation of the process-reactive distinction in schizophrenia. *J. abnorm. soc. Psych.,* 1956, 53, 229–236.
2. Brackbill, G., and Fine, H. J. Schizophrenia and central nervous system pathology. *J. abnorm. soc. Psych.,* 1956, 52, 310–313.
3. Crandell, V. J. Observations of the use of projective techniques in child development research. *J. proj. Tech.,* 1956, 20, 251–255.
4. Dallenbach, K. M. The place of theory in science. *Psych. Rev.,* 1953, 60, 33–39.
5. Fine, H. J., and Zimet, C. N. Process-reactive schizophrenia and genetic levels of perception. *J. abnorm. soc. Psych.,* 1959, 59, 83–86.
6. Fowler, N. Psychopathology and social adequacy: a Rorschach developmental study. Unpublished doctor's dissertation, The Pennsylvania State University, 1957.
7. Framo, J. L. Structural aspects of perceptual development in normal adults: a tachistoscopic study with the Rorschach technique. Unpublished doctor's dissertation, University of Texas, 1952.
8. Frank, I. K. Perceptual structuralization in certain psychoneurotic disorders: a genetic evaluation by means of the Rorschach test. Unpublished doctor's dissertation, Boston University, 1951.
9. Freed, E. Perceptual differentiation in schizophrenia: a tachistoscopic study of structural Rorschach elements. Unpublished doctor's dissertation, Syracuse University, 1952.
10. Friedman, H. Perceptual regression in schizophrenia: an hypothesis suggested by the use of the Rorschach test. *J. gen. Psychol.,* 1952, 81, 63–98.
11. Friedman, H. Perceptual regression in schizophrenia: an hypothesis suggested by the use of the Rorschach test. *J. proj. Tech.,* 1953, 17, 171–185.
12. Grace, N. B. A developmental comparison of word usage with structural aspects of perception and social adjustment. Unpublished doctor's dissertation, Duke University, 1956.
13. Hemmendinger, L. Perceptual organization and development as reflected in the structure of Rorschach test responses. *J. proj. Tech.,* 1953, 17, 162–170.
14. Hersch, Ch. Perceptual structure in creative artists: an analysis by means of the Rorschach test. Doctor's dissertation in progress, Clark University, 1956.
15. Holzberg, J. D. Symposium: implications for projective methods in recent developments in personality theory. *J. proj. Tech.,* 1954, 18, 418–447.
16. Hurwitz, I. A developmental study of the relationship between motor activity and perceptual processes as measured by the Rorschach test. Unpublished doctor's dissertation, Clark University, 1954.
17. Kass, W. Projective techniques as research tools in studies of normal personality development. *J. proj. Tech.,* 1956, 20, 269–272.
18. Kruger, A. Direct and substitute modes of tension-reduction in terms of developmental level; an experimental analysis of the Rorschach test. Unpublished doctor's dissertation, Clark University, 1954.

19. Kutash, S. B.   The impact of projective techniques on basic psychological science.   *J. proj. Tech.*, 1954, **18**, 453–469.
20. Lane, J. E.   Social effectiveness and developmental level.   *J. Pers.*, 1953, **23**, 274–284.
21. Lofchie, S. H.   The performance of adults under distraction stress: a developmental approach.   *J. Psychol.*, 1955, **39**, 109–116.
22. Meili-Dworetzki, G.   The development of perception in the Rorschach.   In: Klopfer, B.   *Developments in the Rorschach technique.*   Vol. II.   New York: World Book Co., 1956, 104–176.
23. Misch, R. C.   The relationship of motoric inhibition to developmental level and ideational functioning: an analysis by means of the Rorschach test.   Unpublished doctor's dissertation, Clark University, 1954.
24. Peña, C. D.   A genetic evaluation of perceptual structuralization in cerebral pathology: an investigation by means of the Rorschach test.   *J. proj. Tech.*, 1953, **17**, 186–199.
25. Phillips, L.   *Developmental theory and social adaptation.*   Mimeographed manuscript, Worcester State Hospital, 1954.
26. Phillips, L., and Framo, J. L.   Developmental theory applied to normal and psychopathological perception.   *J. Pers.*, 1954, **22**, 464–474.
27. Phillips, L., and Smith, J. C.   *Rorschach interpretation: advanced technique*   New York: Grune and Stratton, 1954.
28. Rapaport, D.   Projective techniques and the theory of thinking.   *J. proj. Tech.*, 1952, **16**, 269–275.
29. Reichard, S.   Discussion: Projective techniques as research tools in studies of normal personality development.   *J. proj. Tech.*, 1956, **20**, 265–268.
30. Ricciuti, H. N.   Use of the Rorschach test in longitudinal studies of personality development.   *J. proj. Tech.*, 1956, **20**, 256–260.
31. Rochwarg, H.   Changes in the structural aspects of perception in the aged: an analysis by means of the Rorschach test.   Unpublished doctor's dissertation, Michigan State University, 1954.
32. Rorschach, H.   *Psychodiagnostics* (Eng. translation).   Bern: Huber, 1942.
33. Rosenblatt, B., and Solomon, P.   Structural and genetic aspects of Rorschach responses in mental deficiency.   *J. proj. Tech.*, 1954, **18**, 496–506.
34. Siegel, E. L.   Genetic parallels of perceptual structuralization in paranoid schizophrenia: an analysis by means of the Rorschach technique.   *J. proj. Tech.*, 1953, **17**, 151–161.
35. Spiegelman, M.   Rorschach form-level, intellectual functioning and potential.   *J. proj. Tech.*, 1956, **20**, 335–343.
36. Stein, H.   Developmental changes in content of movement responses.   *J. proj. Tech.*, 1956, **20**, 216–223.
37. Waldman, M.   Personality factors and performances under stress.   Unpublished doctor's dissertation, University of Chicago, 1956.
38. Werner, H.   *Child psychology and general psychology.*   Mimeographed manuscript, Clark University, 1953.
39. Werner, H.   *Developmental approach to general and clinical psychology.*   Mimeographed manuscript, Clark University, 1954.
40. Werner, H.   The concept of development from a comparative and organismic point of view.   *The concept of development.*   Conference at the University

of Minnesota, December 1955. (To be published by the University of Minnesota Press.)

41. Werner, H. *Comparative psychology of mental development* (rev. ed.). Chicago: Follet, 1948.

42. Wertheimer, M. Perception and the Rorschach. *J. proj. Tech.,* 1957, **21,** 209–216.

43. Wilson, M. T. Regression in perceptual organization: a study of adolescent performance on the Rorschach test. Unpublished doctor's dissertation, Clark University, 1954.

> *Can we, then, by the citation of some of those instances wherein this thing of whiteness—though for the time either wholly or in great part stripped of all direct associations calculated to impart to it aught fearful, but, nevertheless is found to exert over us the same sorcery, however modified;— can we thus hope to light upon some chance clue to conduct us to the hidden cause we seek?*
>
> HERMAN MELVILLE

4

by Charles P. Fonda

THE
WHITE-SPACE
RESPONSE

Two affluent streams of psychological investigation converged in Rorschach's discovery of the white-space response. One of these was the academic study of perceptual processes involved in the experience of figure and ground (52); the other was psychiatric concern with the problems of negativism and hostility (10). It was due to Rorschach's brilliant ingenuity that these two seemingly remote branches of the behavior sciences could be made to coalesce. In this chapter, we shall review some of the circumstances surrounding Rorschach's creative act, and discuss some of the *a posteriori* amendments to it that have emerged from a third-of-a-century's experience with the ink blots.

DEFINITION AND NOTATION

Rorschach (49, p. 39) described space responses (*Zwischenform-antworten*) as "those answers in which the white spaces are interpreted rather than the black or colored parts of the figure which surround them." Although he made no reference to the concept of reversal of figure and ground, it is clear that this is the perceptual process he had in mind as mainly responsible for the space response. It was left for later students (6, 45) to show that persons who give space responses also reverse figure and ground (Rubin figures) and perspective (Necker cube) more readily than do those who fail to use the white spaces.

Most clinicians follow Rorschach's translators in using the symbols W, D, and Dd [1] to indicate the area chosen to support a person's percepts on the ink blots, but a minimum of slavishness has characterized Rorschach's successors in their choice of notation to symbolize the *space* response. Perhaps this is because it has always seemed like some kind of anomalous hybrid. On the one hand, it is a response to some definite area on the card, and its *location* aspect warrants consideration from the point of view of *intellectual* approach; it has its own D or Dd characteristics, but these are not always specifically noted in the evaluation of *approach*. On the other hand, the space response also implies the operation of important dynamic processes within the subject, and at least one innovator (13) has been sufficiently impressed with its determinant aspects to feel that it deserves the same kind of scrutiny as that accorded to the *movement* or the *color* responses. Accordingly, he scores such a response as "a lake" (to an inner space detail on card I), $Dd FS+ Ls$. This innovation failed to arouse much enthusiasm among other clinicians and has by now been pretty well forgotten. A common practice today is to symbolize responses to large spaces as S and to small spaces as s; both are listed in the location, rather than in the determinant, column.

What Rorschach recognized as space responses are now often called primary or main S responses in order to distinguish them from what are now known as secondary or additional S responses. The latter designation is applied when the white spaces play a more incidental role and no true figure-ground reversal has occurred, the black or colored parts of the ink blot serving as the principal stimulus. Most workers will add an S (or s, depending upon the size of the area) to the main location score whenever the percept is elaborated by the inclusion of some of the white space, but these so-called additional S scores are incorporated into the final summary only by Beck (8) and his followers. Accumulating evidence (6, 24, 45) is vindicat-

---

[1] For explanation of scoring symbols, see Appendix, pp. 441 ff. [Editor].

ing Rorschach's lack of interest in the secondary S response, since it appears to be unrelated to primary S and is of dubious reliability.

THE MEANING OF SECONDARY S

The personality correlates of secondary or additional S are still poorly understood. Bandura (6) for example, was unable to demonstrate a significant partial correlation (holding R constant) between primary and secondary S; from this he concluded that "the practice of using primary and secondary space responses as measures of the same thing seems unwarranted" (6, p. 117). Perhaps the best we can do with them, in the light of our present knowledge, is to apply a variety of more intuitive interpretations. For example, it has been suggested (30, 46, 53) that the piling up of secondary S in a record indicates undue concern with the lack of solidity in the inked figures. The implication is that the subject is unduly sensitive to the lack of stability in his own interpersonal relationships, that he is tensely preoccupied with his own sense of insecurity. Interpretations of this kind would seem most reasonable when the content of the secondary S response is of the "hole," "gap," or "cut-out" variety. On the other hand, when the secondary S responses have the appearance of attempts to account for everything on the ink blot, as in the case of the "lakes," "rivers," or "roads" seen on maps or landscapes, the implication seems clear that needs for thoroughness, or pedantic attention to detail, are in evidence. It sometimes happens that the white spaces are described as "eyes." Responses with this content always alert the examiner to the probability that projective tendencies or paranoid trends are present in the personality under examination. Occasionally one encounters a response like "a black-and-white butterfly" or "black-and-white smoke," where there has been a failure to differentiate the white space from the darker aspects of the blot. Such responses are extremely rare in adults; their presence in a record may be associated with profound dullness and apathy, as Phillips (46) has suggested.

Whether responses like "an entrance to a cave" (center space on card II) or "a bay" (card VII) are primary or secondary S depends upon the relative emphasis given by the subject, usually during the inquiry, to the meaning of the surrounding darker areas. Schachtel (53, p. 87) has observed that responses like these may denote "either 'need for shelter' or 'fear of enclosure.'" Loosli-Usteri (40) writes of "void shock"—a phenomenon similar to the familiar color shock—which she defines as "the stupor that subjects show upon viewing the empty spaces of plates VIII and IX" (40, p. 27). She reports that this reaction is observed in about 50% of normal men and women; her interpretation of its meaning closely parallels Schachtel's formulation as described above.

THE USE OF WHITE AS COLOR

In the case of both primary and secondary S, the use of white as color occurs in a minority of records. In these instances, of course, the appropriate symbol (e.g., C' or Y, depending upon the scoring system used) is added to the determinant score. The white may be used in a way that is analogous to the pure C response, e.g., "snow," "ice." Or it may be more adaptively integrated with the form, as "a white swan," "a marble bust." The foregoing are examples of primary S and deserve, in addition to the rich implications of the content, to be interpreted in the same way as any other reversal of figure and ground on the Rorschach. Whether the *whiteness, per se,* has any kind of symbolic value has been the subject of some very interesting speculations. Schafer (55, p. 255) believes that it may often stand for "innocence, loveliness and hope." Piotrowski (14) has suggested that, if the gray and black aspects of the ink blots seem especially prominent to the anxious and depressed, then perhaps the white is more often noticed by persons with a capacity for intermittent ecstatic moods. This problem has intrigued others besides professional psychologists. In a chapter entitled "The whiteness of the whale" in *Moby Dick,* for example, Herman Melville (42, Chap. 41) somewhat obscurely calls attention to the association between whiteness and the ideas of nothingness or death. Conceivably, therefore, sensitivity to the whiteness of the spaces on the ink blots may sometimes be an indication of susceptibility to the experience of eerie and uncanny terrors. In this connection, it should be noted that at least one writer (12) has described what he calls a "white shock" reaction. It must be admitted, however, that the true meaning of the use of white as color remains to be convincingly demonstrated. The reader is referred to the discussion of white as an achromatic determinant on pages 214 f. in this book.

THE MEANING OF PRIMARY S

The personality correlates of primary S are much better under-stood today than are those of secondary S. As will be shown later in this chapter, a sizable array of phenotypical concomitants of primary S has been confirmed in recent years. The coordination of these find-ings with systematic personality theory has been slower to arrive, however, probably because of certain shortcomings in the frame of reference within which the original formulation of the meaning of S was conceived. In this section, Rorschach's hypotheses about the meaning of primary S will be presented and subjected to critical evaluation. We shall find that the predominantly negative connota-tions attributed to S by Rorschach have not been supported by the available evidence; in subsequent sections it will be shown that em-pirical observation indicates instead that S is usually the manifesta-tion of an essentially *positive* asset in the personality. In an effort to align the most probable core meaning of S with some systematic theory of personality, an attempt will be made to coordinate S with a specific set of psychoanalytic formulations.

Rorschach's basic assumption was that "space responses always indi-cate some sort of oppositional trend" (49, p. 199). Yet he seems not to have been too sure about the *always*, for he also said that "if there occurs more than one S in a protocol abnormality should be sus-pected" (49, p. 39). The benign inference to be drawn from the presence of a single S in the protocol was not spelled out, nor did Rorschach seem to regard the *absence* of S as interpretable.

Hypothesis I: The Tendency to Opposition

The "opposition trend" meaning ascribed by Rorschach to S seems to have a considerable degree of plausibility. The person who pro-duces S does indeed seem to be performing in a way contrary to the instructions. Instead of interpreting the black or colored parts of the ink blot, as Rorschach quite naturally expected him to do, the sub-ject interprets the white space. "Precisely that is left undone or the contrary is done which one would otherwise expect under the existing conditions." The quotation is from Bleuler's (11, p. 10) definition of *negativism*. Inasmuch as Bleuler was one of Rorschach's most influ-ential teachers, it is not unreasonable to suppose that Rorschach formulated his concept of the meaning of S within the general framework of Bleuler's theory of schizophrenic negativism. At any rate, we do know that Rorschach (49, p. 39) believed that S responses "are most common in stubborn, eccentric normals and in negativistic, scattered schizophrenics."

The phenotypical character of the concepts "opposition trend" and "negativism" has retarded the alignment of S with genotypical concepts in contemporary theories of personality. Bleuler (11) himself called attention to this defect when he acknowledged that negativism "does not show itself uniformly but at times is present and at times is absent in accordance with the psychical constellation . . . we are not as yet able to distinguish between the various psychic processes which call forth negativism" (11, p. 9). More recently, Levy (38) has published an exhaustive analysis of oppositional syndromes and oppositional behavior. He notes that the purpose of such syndromes is to favor the individual's separateness and independence, and he concludes that "what has been called negativism, resistance and oppositional behavior . . . has its origin in a basic protective function. . . . We have lost sight of their original positive values . . . of the adaptive features of the mechanism" (38, pp. 222–223). Allport (2, p. 432) sums up the situation neatly with his observation that generally negativistic and *contredisant* individuals are encountered too frequently to justify the construction of "negativism" as a measurable dimension of personality.

It often happens that after a clinician has interpreted the presence of S in a record as an indication of underlying stubborn, hostile, negativistic, or rebellious tendencies, as Rorschach did, he discovers that he has failed to exploit the wealth of information conveyed by the S responses. Such an interpretation often turns out to be either redundant or nonspecific to the individual under examination. It is usually redundant if the color nuances and the content of other responses in the record have been adequately interpreted (18, 34); and it fails to differentiate the person from others to the degree that most of us are carriers of *underlying* hostile potentials.

Hypothesis II: The Experience Balance

Bleuler's influence can also be seen in Rorschach's (49, p. 200) attempt to relate the meaning of S to the experience balance. This attempt involved a series of deductions from which the following predictions were derived: In an *extratensive* record, S should stand for aggressive stubbornness, negative suggestibility, mistrust of others, defiance, and tendencies to indulge in polemics and contradictions. With an *introversive* balance, S should denote self-criticism, circumstantiality, feelings of inadequacy, and constant self-distrust. Finally, when the balance is *ambiequal*, S should reflect emotional ambivalence, doubt, vacillation, hesitancy, skepticism, and indecision.

In Rorschach's own interpretation of protocols, however, he seems not to have followed this scheme too rigidly. For example, he drew the following inferences from the presence of three S in a 34-response record with an introversive experience balance of 4:1.5: "There will be a predominance of ideas of insufficiency . . . a distrust of himself." But in addition, he also mentioned "skepticism, doubt, and ambivalence" (49, p. 200). And finally, in discussing the color responses, he concluded that "the patient must necessarily be capable of showing spite and revolt tendencies . . . and aggressive adjustments" (49, p. 203).

Again, in his interpretation of a 71-response record with four S in a more nearly ambiequal experience balance of 10:7.5, he wrote: "There is skepticism in regard to the introversive features, a deep sense of insufficiency," as well as "compulsive doubts . . . pedantic thoroughness." Yet he also went on to say that "the S responses represent opposition to everything, even the extratensive features, so that there is mistrust regarding others" (49, p. 150).

In a recently published discussion of still another 70-response record, this time with two S in an extratensive experience balance of 5:12.5, Rorschach (50, pp. 487–488) wrote: "If there were many S responses, they would suggest . . . an ascetic tendency, doubt about herself, feelings of inadequacy." He also said that "the opposition which comes out in her S turns against the outer world in the form of defiance, stubbornness, and negative suggestibility," although "these trends are rather weak" because there are only two S in the record. Rorschach suspected, in this case, that the labile affect indicated by the *CF* responses had prevailed over the subject's oppositional trends.

Unfortunately, the hypothesis that the interpretive significance of S depends upon the experience type in which it occurs has never been adequately reconciled with the findings of either clinical or laboratory-type research (3, 5, 15, 21, 34, 43, 45). Accordingly, we are obliged to agree with Bandura's (5, p. 20) recommendation that "the practice of interpreting the behavioral significance of the S score in terms of the experience type deserves to be discontinued until cogent evidence for its justification becomes available."

A Psychoanalytic Formulation

In an effort to understand the basic personality correlates of S, it might be helpful to make use of Freud's (25, p. 128) concept of *Bewältigungstrieb*—a "general instinct of mastery." The meaning of *Bewältigungstrieb* in Freudian ego psychology has been discussed in a series of theoretical papers by Hendrick (31, 32, 33), who also credits Angyal (4) with having formulated this same concept "in an especially constructive way" (33, p. 563). Hendrick deals with the instinct to master as one of the so-called ego instincts, others being hunger and self-preservation.

According to his formulations, one aim of the mastery impulse is "to control or alter a piece of the environment, an ego-alien situation, by the skillful use of perceptual, intellectual, and motor techniques" (32, p. 314). He feels that the mastery-impulse hypothesis provides "an adequate theory of the need to integrate which impels development and use of the executant functions of the ego" (32, p. 327). In short, *self*-mastery is an indispensable prerequisite to the development of mature and adaptive independence *vis-à-vis* the environment. It is not to be confused with frequently observed attempts to dominate and control *others*, and it should be carefully distinguished from the concept of "aggression." The latter term, according to Hendrick, refers to destructive and possibly disintegrative id impulses, especially to forces motivated by the desire to destroy the rival for a sexual object or the antagonist of a narcissistic need; the aims of the *Bewältigungstrieb* are, by contrast, both useful and constructive.

Pointing out that ego pleasures exist which can be clearly distinguished from id gratifications, Hendrick insists that reduction of tensions associated with the drive to attain mastery is undoubtedly one source of ego pleasure. Angyal (4, p. 218) describes this drive as "a trend towards increased autonomy," and Murray (44, pp. 156–159) has also included "*n* Autonomy" in his well-known catalogue of human needs. His discussion of this need makes clear its close kinship both to Freud's *Bewältigungstrieb* and to Rorschach's concept of *oppositional trend*. Adler (1) treated the need for autonomy as a "will to power" which acts as an organizing force in patterning the style of life, and Sullivan (59, p. 6) says, "We seem to be born with something of this power motive in us." Erikson (20) distinguishes autonomy and initiative as positive outcomes—contrasted with shame, doubt, and guilt as negative outcomes—of the "basic nuclear conflicts" which occur during early phases of ego development.

The distinction between the impulse to master, on the one hand, and hostility or aggression, on the other, is clarified in Fenichel's (22) assertion that mastery can be achieved in the realm of *any* instinct. Thus hostile and aggressive impulses must themselves be mastered by the very ego whose autonomy they threaten.

In his discussion of the psychoanalytic concept of *Bewältigungstrieb,* Fenichel takes a somewhat different position. He feels that although the capacity for mastery depends upon constitutional factors, it is not a separate, specific *instinct* but depends upon "all of the individual's previous experiences" (22, p. 117). Active mastery, according to Fenichel, is achieved by the gradual acquisition of the ability to bind primitive reaction impulses with countercathexes. In this way, for example, the child's play evolves from mere attempts at discharge to mastery of the external world by means of repeated practice. What happens is that before engaging in a feared activity, he passes through an anxious tension of expectation, the overcoming of which is enjoyed. The active repetition, on a limited scale, of what has been experienced passively is one of the principal mechanisms for fighting anxiety. Within the mastery impulse itself, therefore, there is a latent tendency to compulsive repetition. "The type of pleasure achieved," says Fenichel, "proves that the person is by no means really convinced of his mastery" (22, p. 480).

S as Reversal of Figure and Ground

Granting the existence of a fundamental need for autonomy, or an impulse to master, how is this related to the S response? Perhaps a short discussion of figure-ground reversals will help to clarify the assumed relationship between S and the need for autonomy. The laws of *prägnanz* (36) provide some clues for determining whether a reversal of figure and ground has occurred, but the ultimate criterion is strictly empirical. In one experimental study of this problem, Belden and Baughman (9) systematically varied the degree of black-white contrast in the configuration of Rorschach card II, and found that, no matter how great the alteration, the center white area was perceived as part of the *ground* in from 57% to 93% of the cases studied. According to Beck's (8) norms, this area ranks fifth among all of the areas on card II in frequency of perception as *figure*. When this area is perceived as figure, therefore, it is correct to say that perceptual *reversal* has occurred because (a) the area is barren of ink and is alike in color and texture to those portions of the card which are almost invariably experienced as ground, and (b) only a minority of all subjects perceive it as figure. On every occasion when these conditions are present in a Rorschach response, a primary S has occurred.[2]

One might with some precision measure the power of an area in the stimulus field to "compel" perception of *figure:* the proportion of observers who so view it could be taken as one index of that power. In Angyal's terms, power exerted by a particular constellation of the external environment is the resultant of *heteronomous* forces. When the power of a given area to induce perception as figure is small, another portion of the constellation must possess correspondingly greater power to generate such perception, since it is known that *some* portion of every more-or-less heterogeneous field will be experienced as figure (36). The extent to which the heteronomous influence must be neutralized and counteracted by forces operating *within* the observer (as must occur if a figure-ground reversal is to take place) is a measure of the strength of these inner forces. By some (35, p. 309), this strength is known as "daringness." Using Angyal's terminology again, we can define the power exerted by inner forces as the result of a trend towards increased *autonomy*. Appearance of a figure-ground reversal, and hence of the primary S response, then becomes an indication that the person has sought reduction of tensions associated with the need for autonomy. The frequency of such occurrences, therefore, quantifies the extent to which a person is concerned with the repetitive need to demonstrate his own autonomy.

There is something analogous to a latent tendency for compulsive repetition (which Fenichel says characterizes the mastery impulse) in the fact that each individual has his own rate of S emission which is stable and consistent over time (24). It looks as though even a healthy person must reassure himself regularly that his capacity to exercise autonomy is intact, that it has not been impaired by heteronomous forces. Yet the rate of S emission seems not to be highly correlated with the actual pressure of *external* events (16); it follows, therefore, that forces conceived as having power to determine S-emission rate, though they be experienced as arising in reaction to

[2] Although it has been customary to follow Rorschach's example and score as S any response to the frequently noticed inside area of card IX (e.g., "a cello"), it may be doubted if this is fully entitled to be considered as S. Not really white at all, even though its actual coloring is very faint, it is different from those portions of the blot which are almost invariably seen as part of the ground. Klopfer et al. (35) recommend that responses to this area should be scored *D* rather than *D, S or S.*

heteronomous events, actually emanate from within, from the *unconscious* regions of the personality, and so might properly be regarded as "ego-alien." Inasmuch as conflict over self-determination or self-government may be found at the core of nearly every personality disorder (26), it is easy to see how Rorschach could have written so long ago that "study of the space responses defines the neurotic aspects of the record" (49, p. 200).

An Illustrative Case

The role of S as an indicator of repeated attempts by a normal person to demonstrate his capacity for mastery is nicely illustrated in one of Schafer's (55, pp. 355–376) published cases. This author reproduced the full 76-response protocol of a normal physician whose clinical picture was described as one of "surface passivity in an obsessive-compulsive character." This subject produced nine S responses —about twice the average number in records of this length. In Schafer's interpretive summary, he writes that the subject's "impulses and anxiety rarely get out of hand. If they threaten to break through, they are usually quickly and cleverly minimized, negated, or otherwise stripped of threatening implications" (55, p. 375). Inspection of the content and circumstances surrounding production of this subject's S responses reveals that *their* principal function also had been to minimize and negate the threatening implications of underlying ego-alien impulses which constantly hovered near the borderline of awareness.

This subject's initial S followed immediately after the center red detail on card II had instigated his first impulse-dominated response ("blood"). In the act of reversing figure and ground to produce this S, the subject had reassured himself by demonstrating his capacity to achieve active mastery of the underlying hostility that had colored the previous response. He did this again in a second S, which followed shortly after the partial breakthrough of aggressive impulses into the imagery of a "not well-integrated" response to card III. Schafer comments here on the element of conscientious self-observation in the S response, by means of which the subject had re-established autonomous control.

The next three S responses occurred in quick succession and terminated the subject's performance on card V. As he gave his final response in this especially revealing sequence, he said, "I think that's enough!" Schafer notes here that the subject was apparently trying in this way to "beat the examiner to the draw" (i.e., to assert his own autonomy) because it had been the *examiner* who interrupted the subject's performance on one of the earlier cards.

The next two S responses again occurred together, this time at card VIII. They had aggressive content, but now the subject showed some awareness that he had maintained intellectual mastery; he uttered a triumphant "which would take care of *that!*" after the second S of the pair. Here Schafer observes that in this way the subject had kept himself "one step ahead of his threatening sadistic impulses— *but it is an important step*" [italics added].

This same process was repeated on card IX, when a single S seemed to give the subject sufficient reassurance that his capacity for autonomy was still intact. The content of this S was frankly aggressive, but the manner was now one of unruffled self-confidence; for the moment, at least, mastery over the ego-alien impulse had been complete. On card X, however, the defenses were once again in peril: an oral-aggressive fantasy emerged into awareness and quickly threatened to get out of hand. The subject immediately reasserted his autonomy, using an S response in the process; yet he felt obliged to concede that this achievement (of S) had not been easy. Following the final S, he signed off in complete control: "Really," he said, "I've exhausted it."

The subject's total of nine S responses (12% of R) in this record stands out like a price tag. The sheer number of S, of course, tells us little about the nature of his ego-alien impulses; this we must learn from the *content* of his responses. But the high S% puts on public display the heavy cost of defending his autonomy against predatory raids by these impulses. Though the cost is excessive, the subject's assets were apparently sufficient to allow him to make the payments. Except for what Schafer call his "out-of-tune emotionality," this man seemed able to function normally in his interpersonal relationships and was adequately productive in his professional life.

The Optimum Rate of S Emission

It is convenient to think of the S response in terms of rate of emission, or S%. Individual differences in S% are remarkably stable and persistent (24), and the average rate among healthy and intelligent young adults may be taken as a reflection of optimal conditions in the sphere of autonomy and independence. When the rate is at the optimum, the presumption is that, at least with respect to achievement of active mastery, the ego is functioning adaptively. According to a rough rule-of-thumb, the optimum rate is about 4%—or one in every 25—of all responses in the protocol. Actually, the average rate rises from 2% in 15-response records up to 6% in protocols having 60 or more responses (24). The average 25-response record will contain one S response; a 40-response protocol will, on the average, contain two; a 55-response protocol, three; a 70-response protocol, four; and so on. Any substantial deviation from this rate deserves special attention whenever it is observed. Departure from the optimum rate in either direction gives reason to believe that the ego is operating *defensively* in its efforts to ward off anxiety associated with the need for autonomy and achievement of active mastery.

Individual differences in the rate of emission of S could be a function of at least three variables: (a) the strength of the need for autonomy; (b) the capacity to gratify this need by perceptual reversal of figure and ground—in Fenichel's terms, a "constitutional" factor; and (c) the degree to which satisfaction of this need seems threatened. There is some increment in capacity for perceptual reversal as an individual emerges from infancy into maturity, and it is thought that brain injury impairs this function (29, 56, 61). But in the absence of techniques for distinguishing *capacity* from *need* in chronologically mature and neurologically intact individuals, clinicians generally ignore the role of possible variations in *capacity* when interpreting S because needs are assumed to have such powerful effects upon perception.

The Empirical Correlates of S

From a number of laboratory-type investigations we can draw some tentative inferences about phenotypical correlates of the primary S response. For the most part, these phenotypical variables are actual observations of behavior, rather than merely what Ainsworth (35, p. 374) and others have called *test correlates*. Thus, S scores have been related to ratings of interpersonal behavior (5, 16, 21, 34, 48), to observed reactions in experimental situations, including paper-and-pencil tasks (6, 24, 27, 34, 43, 45), and to interpretations derived from projective or sociometric techniques (21, 58, 63). A few of these investigations (21, 24, 62) have also included some of the more conventional scores on intelligence tests or self-descriptive questionnaires. But only one (51) is ostensibly a *test-correlate* study, and even this one is concerned with psychiatric diagnosis as the main criterion.

The most clear-cut findings show that the higher a person's rate of S emission, the more likely is he to be bright (21, 62), productive (24, 63), flexible (45, 56), ingenious (21, 34), and self-sufficient (21). A high rate of S emission has been found among negativistic adolescents (5) and negatively suggestible students (48), but the available evidence fails to confirm the hypotheses that S contributes to persistence (27), on the one hand, or to intellectual opposition (43, 45), disagreement and antagonism (21), and hostile, resistive tactics (34), on the other. Producers of many S do seem to be more hesitant and indecisive than other people (24, 58), but they are no more likely to concede that they have feelings of inadequacy or self-distrust (5, 24). It is apparent from results like these that Piotrowski (14, p. 48) was giving expression to a growing consensus when he wrote that primary S responses "do not seem to be so unfavorable as Rorschach thought."

S as One Indication of Ego Strength

The two principal components of ego strength—reality testing and active mastery—seem to be relatively independent of each other, at least in psychiatric patients. Thus, among the hypomanics and schizophrenics studied by Schmidt and Fonda (57), the correlation between S% and F+%, though slightly negative, was not significant. Wittenborn (63) found a highly significant positive relationship between S% and O% among hospitalized patients, but he did not evaluate form level, and in view of the apparent lack of correlation between S% and F+%, his explanation of the relationship between S% and O% may be a trifle premature. According to him, this relationship could be due to the fact that the patients' disturbance manifests itself simultaneously in both bizarre (O) and negativistic (S) responses. One would then expect patients to be differentiated from normals on the basis of both factors. Unfortunately for this hypothesis, it cannot be shown that psychotics are differentiated on the basis of average rate of S emission (57).

In a study of psychiatric patients at an out-patient clinic, Fiske and Baughman (23) did find a tendency for the median scores for primary and secondary S (combined) to be higher than among normals (8), after differences due to R had been removed. The meaningfulness of this result is somewhat clouded, however, by the inclusion of secondary S in their data. They also made the interesting discovery that a curve depicting the growth in production of *space* responses as a function of R shows a marked dip at the interval for

R from 30 to 34. This curious phenomenon appears in both patient and normal groups. Inasmuch as the average R of healthy normals lies within the 30–34 interval, it may be that the optimum rate of S emission for this interval reflects the most adaptive level of preoccupation with the problem of autonomy in our culture, and departure of either S or R from this level could represent, at least in part, *defensive* aspects of ego functioning.

Wittenborn (63) and also Williams and Lawrence (62) identify a factor underlying Rorschach scores which they designate as "lack of perceptual control." Items highly saturated with this factor include CF, C, C', K, c, and W, but its loading on S is either negligible or negative, and S is the only score which fails to show a positive relationship to *lack* of control. These findings lend support to the concept of S as an indication of the ego's efforts to control, assert autonomy over, or master reactions to the external situation. Their failure to demonstrate a relationship between S and the color-dominant responses is noteworthy and may come as something of a surprise to clinicians, who, like Rorschach (50), believe that a positive correlation exists between S and CF after removing the effects of R. Actually, of course, S stands for the exact opposite of the impulsivity revealed in CF. This finding was foreshadowed in an observation by Cyril Burt, and later confirmed by Bandura (6, p. 116) who demonstrated that "three times as many primary S responses occurred in the last two minutes of exposure [of any single ink blot] as in the first two minutes." Thus, it is prolonged observation and not impulsivity that seems to facilitate the production of S responses.

The foregoing results give meaning to the conclusion recently formulated by Klopfer et al. (35, p. 310) that "ability to use white space is considered one indication of ego strength, the implication being that the personality has resources to resist inundation by environmental forces or motivational confusion."

PRINCIPLES OF INTERPRETATION

In practice, it has been found useful to interpret relative overproduction of S as a measure of the extent to which a person feels that gratification of the need for autonomy and active mastery is being threatened, and to interpret underproduction of S as a measure of the extent to which a person feels that the exercise of autonomy might be threatening to him. Unfortunately, in a fairly large proportion of cases, no basis exists for deriving inferences from the S response. When, for example, R is less than 25, no inference is permissible unless at least one S appears. The fact that no S appears in a record having less than 25 responses does not tell us whether the person's characteristic rate of S emission is one in 26 or one in a million. In any event, inferences based upon S must be confirmed by, or at least be consistent with, other evidence in the protocol. Fortunately, the clinician is not limited to S for information about needs for activity and independence, nor about preferred modes of coping with tensions associated with them. Alternative cues supporting inferences about the status of ego controls are described in detail elsewhere in this book (pp. 109 ff., etc.).

When the clinician is interpreting a Rorschach protocol, he should remember that the significance of S% is nearly always *characterological* and rarely *symptomatic*. With the exception of brain injury and depression, the rate of S emission is unaffected by major changes in the life situation and is singularly resistant to the effects of most types of treatment. For example, although Rorschach (49, pp. 146–155) published a pair of protocols obtained from a young professional man whose emission of primary S increased from 5.6% to 6.6% after five months of psychoanalysis, he did not regard this change as sufficiently impressive to warrant interpretation. Moreover, clinicians know that any relationship between overt behavior and the dynamic processes underlying appearance of S is usually equivocal and indirect. This was strikingly demonstrated by the discovery (15, p. 46) that "normal individuals who are very *compliant* and eager to be accepted produce many S" [italics added].

If we view the occurrence of S in the light of (a) general Rorschach assumptions regarding personality values of M, C, F, etc., and (b) clinically accepted notions about dynamisms that operate in conjunction with the various defense mechanisms, then the following interpretative scheme may be tentatively proposed: A first step is always to determine from *other* aspects of the subject's performance, usually from the movement and color responses as described in Chapters 6, 7, and 9, whether the basic orientation is passive or aggressive, and whether impulses from this orientation are being warded off, acted out, or sublimated. Ordinarily these determinations should not be attempted from S alone. Once they have been made, however, the rate of S emission enables the clinician to make reasonably accurate predictions about the intensity of overt reactions in the subject's behavior.

Thus if the rate of S emission is *low* and the inner orientation is *passive,* the passive needs are either being acted out or sublimated; if the inner orientation is *aggressive,* the aggression is being warded off by means of outright repressions and inhibitions, and the behavior is likely to be cramped, rigid, indolent, or naive.

If the S rate is at the *optimum* and the inner stance is *aggressive,* the aggressions are either being acted out or sublimated.   If the inner stance is *passive,* the passive needs are being warded off by means of reaction formation, and the behavior is likely to be domineering, demanding, obnoxious, or irresponsible.

If the S rate is *high,* the underlying orientation is an *aggressive* one, but the aggressive impulses may or may not be acted out.   If they are being acted out, the subject's behavior will be self-willed, destructive, or delinquent.   If they are being warded off, the mechanisms employed may include reaction formation, isolation, or projection.   Which of these mechanisms the subject prefers is usually not indicated by S itself but may be inferred from the structure of the protocol.   If the subject is using reaction formation against ego-alien aggressions, his behavior will seem most of the time to be sweetly reasonable, compliant, and scrupulously trustworthy.   If he is relying upon isolation as a defense, the overt behavior is likely to be obstinate, pedantic, vacillating, and compulsive.   And if projection turns out to be his preferred defense, he is likely to be suspicious, truculent, grandiose, or deluded.

In every case where prediction is made to overt behavior, it is not the S% that tells *what* a subject *is* (e.g., rigid, demanding, destructive, compliant, obstinate, truculent, etc.).   This must be determined, as was indicated above, from inspection of the entire protocol.   The specific contribution of S% is to tell *how much, how strong,* or *how impressive* the reactions are likely to be.   Like a speedometer, the rate·of S emission tells how fast, but not where, a person is going; how far, but not from whence he has come.

UNDERPRODUCTION OF S

The absence of S and the meaning of a lower-than-expected S% have not been studied as extensively as the positive deviations in S emission.   One reason for this neglect is that R may be curtailed by factors other than lack of the tensions required for production of S. For example, one excellent device for demonstrating capacity to exercise autonomy is *not* to yield to an examiner's request for responses. Many suspicious paranoids who may have enormous capacity for the production of S will often, perhaps deliberately, give very short and guarded records in which no S would be expected in any event. Or, to take another example, consider patients who are depressed. We know that these patients are often totally lacking in *Bewältigungstrieb*, sometimes even to the point of self-destruction. Yet it is difficult, if not impossible, to elicit enough Rorschach responses from a depressed person to demonstrate that his S is actually below expectation.

When S% is low in longer protocols, we are entitled to assume that the larger response total is itself an indication of passive-dependent orientation, and that the subject feels he must somehow placate others with a docile display of compliance. In such individuals, analysis often uncovers archaic prohibitions against self-realization and development of the capacity to exercise mature autonomy.

OVERPRODUCTION OF S

The Paranoid Character

In practical clinical work, as we have seen, the meaning of S% above expectancy varies with the type of defensive structure in which it appears. Thus in persons having a paranoid character structure and relying heavily upon projection as a defense, the rate of S emission is often high because, as is well known, these individuals are excessively concerned with problems of autonomy. In Rapaport's (47) data from patients at the Menninger Clinic, for example, it was a group with the diagnosis of paranoid condition who showed the highest average rate of S production. That the ego-alien impulses of paranoids are projected and perceived as heteronomous does not, of course, make their implied threat to autonomy any less menacing. These patients are constantly on guard to protect their sense of separateness and integrity from delusional encroachment; often they become almost insatiable in demanding repeated assurance that their capacity to exercise autonomy is still intact. When a person with a high rate of S production becomes psychotic, he is more likely to be able to cling to paranoid delusions because the ingenuity and unconventionality that go with S also enable him to be especially adroit in finding ways to reconcile the contents of his delusional system with contradictions that must confront him in the real world. In particular, when reality testing $(F+\%)$ is weak, creative fantasy (M) and intellectual vigor (Z) high, and S abundant, the patient can be expected, as Beck (8) has so aptly observed, to be vexingly unbending in the stickiness with which he refuses to give up twisted ideas.

S in Obsessive-Compulsives

Persons with obsessive-compulsive character structures are so determined to "leave no stone unturned" that their response totals often become highly inflated with Dd, and this sometimes serves to mask an intrinsically high rate of S emission.   These are said to be people who have never accepted a truce in the struggle which made its first appearance in infancy, during the earliest phases of ego development. In them, it is the compulsion, the "strange command" (22, p. 269), that is experienced as a coercive and ego-alien force which constantly threatens their autonomy.   Little wonder, then, if they feel driven to demand continuous reassurance that the capacity for active mastery, for autonomy, is unimpaired.

When a neurotic character structure is found in a person who is capable of giving a high rate of S responses, we have learned to expect that the intellectualizing and ingenuity which accompany S have facilitated his discovery of the endless exceptions, qualifications, and occasions for undoing that are so beloved by the obsessive personality.   In studies which have identified hesitancy and indecision as concomitants of S (24, 58), the subjects have been either college students at universities where obsessive characters are probably quite numerous, or they have been veterans in a mental-hygiene clinic.   It may be that it is the obsessives in both groups who give more evidences of indecision, as one would expect, and also produce S at a higher rate, as one would also expect.   Perhaps only in this somewhat indirect way can S be understood as a sign of *ambivalence*.

The Aggressively Antisocial Character Disorder

A common characteristic encountered in antisocial psychopathic personalities is their erratic incapacity for delaying gratification of even the most primitive impulses.   It follows, therefore, that CF and C responses are often more useful in detecting aggressive, antisocial individuals than is the S%.   When parental prohibitions have been incompletely internalized in the superego, they may be experienced as intolerably oppressive and ego-alien forces in the personality (13).

This may be why some psychopaths try to rationalize their impulsivity and egocentricity as vigorous assertions of their inalienable right to exercise untrammeled autonomy. The more intelligent and ingenious the psychopath, the more likely will the defense of rationalization be available to him, and the more likely will he reveal his so-called moral imbecility—his defective capacity to sustain loyalties—in behavior that is impressive for its extreme disregard of social standards. Thus, although S% does not distinguish psychopaths as a group from other groups, it was possible for Boss (13), who examined a sample of antisocial psychopathic personalities, to conclude that, *within this group*, "the more white space responses a subject produces, the greater the evidence for deviation with respect to social standards" (13, p. 545).

Unfortunately, the fact that this generalization applies only to the class of person sampled by Boss (i.e., antisocial psychopaths), and not to *all* subjects, has sometimes been overlooked by subsequent investigators. Rosen (51), for example, thought that Boss had claimed that psychopaths could be distinguished from other patients on the basis of the S-response score. When he tried this on a group of hospitalized patients, however, he reached a conclusion which, he said, directly contradicted Boss' findings: Rosen's psychopaths obtained a *lower* S-score mean than did his nonpsychopaths! Since Rosen did not include the response totals in his published data, however, nothing is known about differences in S% between his groups. Moreover, he eliminated all subjects having excessive "?" scores on the MMPI, and in this way excluded those most likely to give the highest S-emission rates (24). There was only one significant relationship between S and the various MMPI scales. This occurred, as expected, with the psychopathic deviate (*Pd*) scale, but only among *non*psychopaths. Among psychopaths, the relationship between S and *Pd* was not significant; and as a crowning paradox, the *Pd* score itself failed to differentiate the psychopaths from other patients! We have no way of knowing how many subjects in Rosen's psychopathic group were of the aggressively antisocial—as opposed to the dependent-inadequate—type. Even though they too might have been diagnosed as psychopathic personalities, the latter individuals could scarcely have been expected to give many Rorschach responses of any kind, and hence would certainly not be likely to produce S.

Other investigators (19, 28, 39, 54, 60, 64) have attempted, without conspicuous success, to differentiate psychopaths from other deviates, or delinquents from nonoffenders, on the basis of the S response. The uniformly disappointing results suggest that intelligence, ingenuity, flexibility, unconventionality, and self-sufficiency—the known empirical correlates of S—must be distributed similarly within these groups. Evidently, membership in such groups is unrelated to degree of concern, or lack of concern, with the need to exercise autonomy and achieve active mastery.

S in Schizophrenia

Emphasis upon S in a record certainly gives no guarantee that the struggle for autonomy or mastery has been successful. Actually, of course, S% is only a measure of effort, not of achievement. In some schizophrenic patients, for example, the struggle for mastery has been totally abandoned, and S is absent; in others, however, the struggle may be conducted with great desperation, while the remaining components of ego strength—i.e., reality testing (F+%), or, in the affective sphere, emotional integration (as shown by the color balance)—are gravely impaired. In the latter cases, S% will be high and the content of the S responses may offer a *via regia* into the patient's psychotic preoccupations. In addition, the originality or bizarreness of the S responses will have intellectual implications, and their Dd or Z aspects will have additional meaning. Some of the most impressive and dramatic S responses on record have been found in the protocols of schizophrenics. Occasionally, one of these patients will actually describe nonexistent details within the white area, and although guided to some extent by contours provided by the darker figures, will create a picture in much the same way that a person produces an imaginative scene on card 16—the blank card—in the Thematic Apperception Test. A schizophrenic patient may or may not impress others as stubborn, rebellious, or negativistic. This will depend not merely upon S% but mainly upon the patient's perception of incompatibility between what he is trying to do and what others expect of him. The impulsivity with which he resists coercion can rarely be inferred from S%.

Hypomania and S

Hypomania is a symptomatic constellation that occurs periodically in persons having cyclothymic personality dynamics. In such persons, the rate of S emission tells something about the character structure in which a psychiatrically conceived regressive shift to the primitive defense of *denial* has occurred. Hypomanic patients, more often than normals, show excessive deviation from the optimum rate of S emission. But in group data, their positive and negative deviations are symmetrically distributed around the optimum rate and cancel each other out in such a way that no differences have been found between hypomanics and normals in the *average* rates of S emission (57). Consequently, even though we know that the one predominant mode of adaption common to all hypomanics is a constant attempt to *dominate* the human environment (41), we must be prepared to find that some hypomanics neglect S while others overemphasize it, and few produce S at the *optimum* rate.

Fortunately, hypomanics are nearly always so productive on the Rorschach that we seldom have any difficulty in identifying those who represent excessive deviations in rate of S production. We do not need the S response to tell us that hostile and rebellious undercurrents are seething in the hypomanic patient; what we do ask of S is that it help us to decide whether, in an attempt to ward off his hostile impulses, the individual has been in the habit of relying on hysterical repression or compulsive reaction formation. If S% is low or absent, we are entitled to believe that the hypomania has roots in a hysterical character structure; if S is present and overemphasized, we may recognize the compulsive aspects in the premorbid character structure. In either case, the magnitude of the deviation from an optimum rate of S emission indicates the degree to which the individual has failed to resolve conflicts over autonomy by the adaptive development of techniques for active mastery.

SUMMARY

In this chapter, a core meaning of the primary S response has been developed by coordinating the perceptual process of figure-ground reversal to a psychoanalytic concept of the drive to achieve active mastery. Some contemporary theory builders, notably Murray (44) and Angyal (4), conceptualize the drive to achieve active mastery as a trend towards increased autonomy. Alignment of the meaning of S with these concepts enriches the usefulness of a Rorschach clinician's interpretations by enabling him to incorporate implications and generalizations from a systematic theory of personality into his diagnostic appraisals.

Rorschach's original formulation of S as an indicator of "some sort of oppositional trend" attributed unequivocally *negative* values to this response in patterning out the structure of an individual personality, but subsequent experience with the ink blots has shown that S is usually a manifestation of more *positive* values. Indeed, capacity for active mastery is now regarded as one of the two principal components of ego strength, the other being efficiency of reality testing.

While S% gives some indication of the amount of *effort* that a person is devoting to the defense of autonomy, it is by no means a measure of *achievement*. There seems to be an optimal rate of expenditure of this effort, and excessive departure from the optimum, in the direction of an S% that is either too high or too low, gives warning that all is not well in the individual's struggle against ego-alien impulses.

The secondary S response, which uses white space but does not entail a complete reversal of figure and ground, was briefly discussed. The consensus is that it must have unfavorable implications for the personality that produces it but, in the light of its unreliable and arcane character, routine interpretation of secondary S is not recommended.

The primary S response, on the other hand, appears to have been one of Rorschach's most provocative discoveries and, although its true meaning still remains to be fully uncovered, it already gives promise of becoming an indispensable adjunct in the art of psychodynamic personality appraisal.

BIBLIOGRAPHY

1. Adler, A. *The practice and theory of individual psychology.* London: Kegan Paul, 1927.
2. Allport, G. W. *Personality: a psychological interpretation.* New York: Holt, 1937.
3. Ames, L. B., Learned, J. Metraux, R. W., and Walker, R. N. *Child Rorschach responses. Developmental trends from two to ten years.* New York: Hoeber, 1952.
4. Angyal, A. *Foundations for a science of personality.* New York: Commonwealth Fund, 1941.
5. Bandura, A. The Rorschach white space response and "oppositional" behavior. *J. consult. Psychol.,* 1954, 18, 17–21.
6. Bandura, A. The Rorschach white space response and perceptual reversal. *J. exp. Psychol.,* 1954, 48, 113–118.
7. Bätcher, U. Die Zwischenantworten, das Versagen, die Schocks und die Inhalte gestörter Einordnung im Rorschachtest bei verschiedenen Schülergruppen. *Prax Kinderpsychol. Kinderpsychiat.,* 1953, 2, 70–72.
8. Beck, S. J. *Rorschach's test. Vol. I. Basic processes* (2nd ed.). New York: Grune and Stratton, 1950. *Vol. II. A variety of personality pictures.* New York: Grune and Stratton, 1945. *Vol. III. Advances in interpretation.* New York: Grune and Stratton, 1952.

9. Belden, A. W., and Baughman, E. E.   The effects of figure-ground contrast upon perception as evaluated by a modified Rorschach technique.   *J. consult. Psychol.*, 1954, **18**, 29–34.

10. Bleuler, E.   *Dementia praecox oder Gruppe der Schizophrenien.*   Leipzig: Deuticke, 1911.

11. Bleuler, E.   The theory of schizophrenic negativism.   *Nervous and mental Disease Monograph* No. 11, Nervous and Mental Disease Publications Company, New York, 1912.

12. Bohm, E.   *Lehrbuch der Rorschach-Psychodiagnostik.*   Bern: Huber, 1951.

13. Boss, M.   Psychologisch-charakterologische Untersuchungen bei antisozialen Psychopathen mit Hilfe des Rorschachschen Formdeuteversuches.   *Z. ges. Neurol. Psychiat.*, 1931, **133**, 544–575.

14. Brussel, J. A., Hitch, K. S., and Piotrowski, Z. A.   *A Rorschach training manual.*   Utica: State Hospitals Press, 1950.

15. Buhler, C., Buhler, K., and Lefever, D. W.   *Development of the basic Rorschach score with manual of directions* (rev.).   Los Angeles: Rorschach Standardization Studies, No. 1, 1949 (mimeo.).

16. Counts, R. M., and Mensh, I. H.   Personality characteristics in hypnotically-induced hostility.   *J. clin. Psychol.*, 1950, **6**, 325–330.

17. Dalla Volta, A.   Contributi allo studio della percezione con particolare riferimento alla psicologia differenziale.   I. Forma e significato nel processo di inversione del rapporto di figura e sfondo.   *Arch. Psicol. Neur. Psich.*, 1949, **10**, 1–112.

18. Elizur, A.   Content analysis of the Rorschach with regard to anxiety and hostility.   *Rorschach Res. Exch. and J. proj. Tech.*, 1949, **13**, 247–284.

19. Endacott, J. L.   The results of 100 male juvenile delinquents on the Rorschach ink-blot test.   *J. crim. Psychopath.*, 1941, **3**, 41–50.

20. Erikson, E. H.   *Childhood and society.*   New York: Norton, 1950.

21. Eschenbach, A. E., and Borgatta, E. F.   Testing behavior hypotheses with the Rorschach: an exploration in validation.   *J. consult. Psychol.*, 1955, **19**, 267–273.

22. Fenichel, O.   *The psychoanalytic theory of neurosis.*   New York: Norton, 1945.

23. Fiske, D. W., and Baughman, E. E.   Relationships between Rorschach scoring categories and the total number of responses.   *J. abnorm. soc. Psychol.*, 1953, **48**, 25–32.

24. Fonda, C. P.   The nature and meaning of the Rorschach white space response.   *J. abnorm. soc. Psychol.*, 1951, **46**, 367–377.

25. Freud, S.   The predisposition to obsessional neurosis.   In: *Collected papers, Vol. 2.*   London: Hogarth, 1924.

26. Fromm, E.   *Escape from freedom.*   New York: Farrar and Rinehart, 1941.

27. Gallup, J.   The white space response in the Rorschach test as an index of persistence.   Unpublished honors study, Connecticut College, 1953.

28. Geil, G. A.   The similarity in Rorschach patterns of adult criminal psychopaths and pre-adolescent boys.   *Rorschach Res. Exch.*, 1945, **9**, 201–206.

29. Goldstein, K.   *The organism.*   New York: American Book Co., 1939.

30. Halpern, F.   *A clinical approach to children's Rorschachs.*   New York: Grune and Stratton, 1953.

31. Hendrick, I.   Instinct and the ego during infancy.   *Psychoanal. Quart.*, 1942, **11**, 33–58.

32. Hendrick, I. Work and the pleasure principle. *Psychoanal. Quart.*, 1943, **12**, 311–329.
33. Hendrick, I. The discussion of the "instinct to master." *Psychoanal. Quart.*, 1943, **12**, 561–565.
34. Ingram, W. Prediction of aggression from the Rorschach. *J. consult. Psychol.*, 1954, **18**, 23–28.
35. Klopfer, B., Ainsworth, M. D., Klopfer, W. G., and Holt, R. R. *Developments in the Rorschach technique. Vol. 1. Technique and theory.* Yonkers: World Book Co., 1954.
36. Koffka, K. *Principles of gestalt psychology.* New York: Harcourt, Brace, 1935.
37. Lapi, L. Contributo allo studio del processo di inversione del rapporto figura-sfondo. *Riv. Psicol.*, 1947, **44**, 506–516.
38. Levy, D. M. Oppositional syndromes and oppositional behavior. In: *Psychopathology of childhood.* (P. H. Hoch and J. Zubin, eds.) New York: Grune and Stratton, 1955.
39. Lindner, R. M. The Rorschach test and the diagnosis of psychopathic personality. *J. crim. Psychopath.*, 1943, **5**, 69–93.
40. Loosli-Usteri, M. A propos du choc au vide. *Beih. schweiz. Z. Psychol. Anwend.*, 1954, **25**, 21–43.
41. Lorenz, M. Language behavior in manic patients. *AMA Arch. Neurol. Psychiat.*, 1953, **69**, 14-26.
42. Melville, H. The whiteness of the whale. In: *Moby Dick or the white whale*, Chapter 42. New York: Dodd, Mead & Co., 1942.
43. Murray, D. C. An investigation of the Rorschach white space response in an extratensive experience balance as a measure of outwardly directed opposition. Unpublished Ph.D. dissertation, Northwestern University, 1954.
44. Murray, H. A. *Explorations in personality.* New York and London: Oxford University Press, 1938.
45. Nelson, W. D. An evaluation of the white space response on the Rorschach as figure-ground reversal and intellectual opposition. Unpublished Ph.D. dissertation, Michigan State College, 1954.
46. Phillips, L., and Smith, J. G. *Rorschach interpretation: advanced technique.* New York: Grune and Stratton, 1952.
47. Rapaport, D., Gill, M., and Schafer, R. *Diagnostic psychological testing: the theory, statistical evaluation, and diagnostic application of a battery of tests. Vol. 2.* Chicago: Year Book Publishers, 1946.
48. Ray, J. B. B. The meaning of Rorschach white space responses. Unpublished Ph.D. dissertation, University of Oklahoma, 1954.
49. Rorschach, H. *Psychodiagnostics, a diagnostic test based on perception.* (Trans. by P. Lemkau and B. Kronenburg.) Bern: Huber, 1942.
50. Rorschach, H. Three Rorschach interpretations. *J. proj. Tech.*, 1954, **18**, 482–495.
51. Rosen, E. MMPI and Rorschach correlates of the Rorschach white space response. *J. clin. Psychol.*, 1952, **8**, 283–288.
52. Rubin, E. *Synsoplevede Figurer.* Copenhagen: Gyldendal, 1915.
53. Schachtel, E. G. The dynamic perception and the symbolism of form: with special reference to the Rorschach test. *Psychiatry*, 1941, **4**, 79–96.
54. Schachtel, E. G. Notes on Rorschach tests of 500 juvenile delinquents and

a control group of 500 non-delinquent adolescents. *J. proj. Tech.*, 1951, **15**, 144–172.

55. Schafer, R. *Psychoanalytic interpretation in Rorschach testing.* New York: Grune and Stratton, 1954.

56. Scharmann, T. Die Zwischenraumdeutungen im Rorschachtest. Versuch einer gestaltpsychologischen Erklärung. *Beih. schweiz. Z. Psychol. Anwend.*, 1950, **19**, 64–72.

57. Schmidt, H. O., and Fonda, C. P. Rorschach scores in the manic state. *J. Psychol.*, 1954, **38**, 427–437.

58. Shatin, L. Relationships between the Rorschach test and the TAT. *J. proj Tech.*, 1955, **19**, 317–332.

59. Sullivan, H. S. *Conceptions of modern psychiatry.* Washington: W. A. White Foundation, 1947.

60. Watters, R. H. A preliminary analysis of the Rorschach records of 50 prison inmates. *J. proj. Tech.*, 1953, **17**, 437–446.

61. Werner, H. Thought disturbance with reference to figure-background impairment in brain-injured children. *Confin. neurol.*, 1949, **9**, 255–263.

62. Williams, H. L., and Lawrence, J. F. Further investigation of Rorschach determinants subjected to factor analyses. *J. consult. Psychol.*, 1953, **17**, 261–264.

63. Wittenborn, J. R. Level of mental health as a factor in the implications of Rorschach scores. *J. consult. Psychol.*, 1950, **14**, 469–472.

64. Zulliger, H. *Jugendliche Diebe im Rorschach Formdeutversuch. Eine seelenkundliche und erzieherische Studie.* Bern: Haupt, 1938.

CATEGORIES OF ANALYSIS: DETERMINANTS

*The extremes of vice and virtue are alike
detestable; absolute virtue is as sure to kill
a man as absolute vice is, . . .*

SAMUEL BUTLER

5 | by Sheldon J. Korchin

FORM PERCEPTION
AND EGO FUNCTIONING

I

Perceiving, whether highly structured objects or ink blots, always represents a joint interaction of the organism and the stimulus. In Murphy's phrasing, "The percept . . . develops as an organized response to a matrix of stimulation in which the structure of the environment and the structure giving tendencies of the perceiver converge in the determination of a unitary response" (36). Perception can range from the one extreme of complete autism to the other in which stimulus determination prevails, and any given perceptual act reflects in varying degree determinants from various points along this continuum. In the main, the greater the structuredness of the stimulus, the more likely will field-organizational factors decide the final perception; the less the external structure, the greater will be the contribution of the individual perceiver. However, the personality is active in every perceptual act—not only in the "distortion" of perception through the penetration of demanding needs but as well in the achievement of reality-oriented, objective perception. The interpretation of form level in the Rorschach depends on the assumption that in neither case does perception consist simply of the passive reception of "what is there." In Stern's (54) classic dictum, there is "Keine Gestalt ohne Gestalter." The perceiver organizes selectively, and the percept bears the imprint of individual modes of organization (perceptual styles).

In this chapter the adequacy of Rorschach form perception, interpreted as an index of the integrity of ego functioning, will be discussed. In a strict sense, the final Rorschach response involves more than a narrowly defined perceptual act; rather it is the resultant of a coordinated series of cognitive activities in a total process of forming, testing, critically evaluating, and communicating perceptual hypotheses. The term "form perception" is used in the present context as a shorthand designation for this total process, and form level, or operationally $F+\%$,[1] is used to describe the accuracy with which the form qualities are utilized. Stated another way, the Rorschach task presents the subject with the problem, "What might it be?" The type and adequacy of the solutions reached depend on the subject's ego organization, showing the requisite cognitive abilities, which, however, must be understood in terms of internal drive and affective pressures and the demands of the external situation as he interprets them. Some of the differences in form perception among clinical and personality groups will be examined, and an attempt will be made to distinguish the various mechanisms responsible for good or poor form response. Problems involved in scoring will be considered, since they bear on the interpretation of form-perceptual behavior. It is hoped that better understanding of the theoretical relationship between form perception and ego functioning, and of the concept of ego strength will emerge.

The infant initially perceives and responds diffusely to the immediate stimuli of its inner and outer worlds. There is no time perspective and a minimum ability to delay response or gratification. Objects are perceived in terms of their "physiognomic" (58) characteristics and their immediate need-reducing values. In this period, behavior is largely under control of the "pleasure principle" and thinking reflects the "primary process." Slowly there is an emergence of ego functions through which the individual becomes less reactive to the immediately present external stimulus and to the demands of current drives. In Piaget's terms, the child moves from participation to eventual objectivity. The world is seen, so to speak, in its own terms rather than in terms of the child's needs. The development of the reality principle, as Freud (15, 16) originally argued and Rapaport (42, 43) more recently has stressed, depends on the growing capacity to delay grati-

[1] For explanation of scoring symbols, see Appendix, pp. 441 ff. [Editor].

fication and, consequently, motoric discharge, and to substitute instead thought processes through which actions can be tested vicariously.[2]

Mature ego functioning involves a capacity for undistorted perception. Though often described as "ambiguous stimuli" or, in Rorschach's original phrase, "indeterminate forms," a primary characteristic of the ink blots is that they do have contours and are in varying degree organized. The responses given by a subject may be more or less congruent with the stimuli forms. This dimension of Rorschach performance—the degree to which the subject is attentive to, or departs from, the "reality" represented in the blots—has often been taken as a measure of the subject's ability to deal with, and his respect for, reality in general. In this sense, it becomes a measure of ego strength.

Although accurate form perception is a necessary function of a strong ego, it is clearly not its only characteristic. The individual's ability to plan and to organize behavior over extended periods of time, to maintain integrated behavior under stress, to have insight into his impulses and in so doing control and direct them, and other such aspects of ego organization, as Murray and Kluckhohn (37) point out, are all aspects of what might properly be called ego strength. However, central to these is the ability to discriminate and to deal with reality. The growth of reality testing parallels the development of other ego functions and is a necessary condition of psychological maturity.

II

According to Rorschach (46), a high percentage of $F+$ responses depends on: (1) the ability to concentrate; (2) the availability of clear memory images (engrams); (3) the ability to bring such memory images into consciousness; and (4) the ability to select from among these the most fitting for the stimulus. It assumes control of the perceptual and associational processes, and critical interpretation. For Rorschach these abilities were the *sine qua non* of intelligence.

The production of $F+$ responses is dependent on the ability to or-

---

[2] Thus, reality testing and phantasy, Rorschach's $F+$ and M are parallel aspects of ego development. The concept of delayed gratification, as Singer discusses in Chapter 9 and elsewhere (51), contributes to the theoretical understanding of the reciprocal relationship between phantasy and motor activity.

ganize, integrate and control perceptual and associational processes and to bring these into appropriate relationship with one another. There must be minimum distortion by unconscious and emotional factors. The achievement of adequate form perception results, as Rapaport (44) has emphasized, from the individual's capacity to delay the discharge of impulse, thus allowing for the critical formation of the reality-appropriate response. Beck (7) states, "F plus, then, is the critical work of the intellect." It depends on the effective functioning of the highest levels of cerebral organization.

The ego activity involved in form perception is seen in the contrast of form and color perception. Rorschach originally interpreted color as indicative of affectivity largely on the basis of the empirical findings that impulsive and labile individuals have more, and stable and dysphoric individuals fewer, color responses. Rickers-Ovsiankina (45), interpreting these findings in a broader context, shows that many perceptual studies point to a similar color-form duality and find that preference for one or the other mode of response is individually consistent. Color dominance is not only characteristic of the emotionally labile adult but also is more characteristic of earlier stages of psychological development, yielding to form with increased maturity (see also pp. 10 f. and 154 ff. of this book).

Further evidence for the role of integrative factors in Rorschach form perception is found in Stein's studies of performance under tachistoscopic conditions (53). Among the most decided differences in records produced at .01, .10, 3.0 seconds, and full exposure was a steady increase in the proportion of $F+$ to $F-$ with increased viewing time. By contrast, the trends for color, shading, and movement responses were much less clear cut; there is a tendency for color-predominant response (CF and C) to decrease more rapidly at longer exposures than those having better form-color integration (FC). The organizational activity required for accurate form perception needs time for its operation. There is evidence, too, that the better adjusted subject maintains a higher $F+\%$ under the stress of tachistoscopic presentation and, perhaps, that the responses obtained at the faster speeds may be an even better gauge of the subject's over-all adequacy of functioning than those obtained under usual conditions of administration.

III

Scoring Form Level: The Criterion of Accuracy [3]

The problem of scoring starts from a truly difficult question: "What is accuracy?" Inherent in the definition of good form—that the percept offered fit the "realities" of the blot—is the problem of knowing what that reality is and how to judge that the given response fits. Basically two types of criteria have been used, each dependent on a somewhat different answer to the question.

Frequency of occurrence. One way of deciding what is accurate is in terms of the responses actually given by a sizable sample of normal individuals. On probabilistic grounds alone, it would seem reasonable that pathological thinking would more usually lead to diversity of response, whereas reality-directed thinking would lead to greater commonness of response. A large group of healthy individuals, from the same culture, sharing basic experiences, should more often give similar than diverse responses. On this basis, frequency of response defines reality. Thus Beck's statement:

Our starting assumption is that since there is no accuracy, or reality at all within these originally chance ink blots,—therefore the forms which these normal people perceive in them are the absolute accuracy or reality that obtains in the blots (9, p. 263).

In establishing standards for plus and minus, Beck takes as a basic criterion that $F+$ should differentiate healthy from unhealthy psychological functioning.

Under differentiation I have in mind selection of persons of good intellectual control who see their world accurately, separating these from those who see less of the world in this manner, and from those who twist much of it. The groups in our society who see their world in clear outlines, are presumably they who make up the rank and file, and those who run our society—that is, the average and superior. The next premise is that the forms they see in the Rorschach test are the reality that obtains in these figures. They are F plus. Contrarily, the forms that a feeble-minded or a schizophrenic group see, and that are not seen by the healthy, are not real. They are F minus (4, p. 155).

[3] The purpose of this section is to examine some of the methodological issues involved in scoring, rather than to consider in any detail the several proposed scoring systems. For a critical review of a number of scoring methods, see Kimball (25).

In a later statement Beck tempers this distinction by pointing out that a normal sample does not have "*carte blanche* to interpret the presented blot figures arbitrarily and to call anything which they see an *F* plus" (9, p. 263). Thus, the criterion for including a new response found in the Spiegel sample of 157 normals into the existing list of *F*+ was that it be seen by at least three individuals.

Using this criterion and extensive samples of subjects, Beck has carefully evolved norms for plus and minus responses. Similarly, Hertz (21) has derived norms from the responses given by an adolescent population. In his original work, Rorschach (46) used the form-determined responses of 100 normal subjects as a basis for judging plus and minus, though apparently coupling a judgmental with this statistical criterion.

The judgment of the examiner. A second criterion for the accuracy of response depends on the empathic judgment of the examiner. In its simplest form this consists of the decision: "Does it seem to fit? Can I see the response which the subject gives as making sense in terms of the blot?" Implied in this criterion is the assumption that what is accurate is what another—albeit skilled and experienced—individual can appreciate as an adequate solution to the problem. Whereas an occurrence criterion assumes that what is actually *given* by healthy individuals defines accuracy, this criterion assumes that what can be *appreciated* by healthy individuals is accurate. Although these approaches imply two logically different solutions to what ultimately is a metaphysical question, we do not really know to what degree estimates based on them do differ in practice. Some experiments (26, 57), in which judges evaluated the "goodness of fit" of numbers of responses taken from published lists of plus and minus based on occurrence, are relevant and will be discussed later.

Klopfer and Kelley (32) and Rapaport (44) have depended principally on the judgment of the examiner. In the effort to provide both standards of judgment and a quantitative form-level score, Klopfer (30, 31) has more recently proposed a rating system for assessing form level in which the examiner makes quantitative ratings of each response depending on his estimation of the accuracy with which the percept fits the blot outlines, the type and degree of specification of the response, and the degree of organization (i.e., the inclusion of disparate portions into the response). Not only in the mechanics of scoring but also in the psychological mechanisms involved, Klopfer's present handling of form level overlaps Beck's organizational score, Z.

Whatever the criterion used, there is likely to be a problem in the evaluation of the essentially new response. Take, for example, the very creative response which, although unusual and original, is not (in some absolute sense) minus. Although it differs from the commonly agreed solutions, it need not violate the "realities" of the blot. Yet, on a literal interpretation of an occurrence criterion it cannot be $F+$ if it has never or rarely been reported before, nor, however, is it $F-$.[4] Although it is more likely that the sensitive examiner will appreciate the response, still his ego has limits for accepting the strange. Copernicus was "accurate" though his contemporaries neither independently held his views of the universe nor certainly did they recognize the correctness of his position in evaluating it.

Although not dependent on published lists of plus' and minus', it seems unlikely that any examiner evaluates each response *de novo*. As in any judgmental act, there is always a frame of reference, perhaps in part derived from the examiner's own observations of occurrence (i.e., "clinical experience"), or perhaps consisting of implicit definitions of the limits of accuracy. The establishment of norms based on frequency of occurrence has the advantage of providing explicit standards, but the examiner's judgment is by no means obviated. This is always true in evaluating the wholly new response, and often true in deciding whether the given and the listed response are in fact the same. Although a wholly qualitative system may put more strain on the examiner's judgment, and allow greater play to his projections, the obvious dangers in trusting his empathic behavior exist in some degree whatever the method used, the more so if the examiner is inexperienced or emotionally disturbed. Thus, in one study, Kimball (26) found that 100 W responses were given significantly higher ratings for accuracy by inexperienced than by experienced judges. There was considerable disagreement among judges; many responses were rated at virtually every point on her six-point scale. Moreover, the examiner's judgments are made within the same interpersonal context as the subject's responses. The estimates of accuracy are subject to halo effects and may reflect the action of countertransferent tendencies. Withal, the critical judgment of the examiner is indispensable in any scoring system, and these dangers merely point up the necessity for training and discipline.

[4] All Rorschach workers have been sensitive to this problem. Beck, for example, suggests that when dealing with the original response, the judgment of the examiner is called into play to decide whether the new response is more like known $F+$ or whether it has the form quality of known $F-$ (4).

Some recent studies suggest a method for reducing the subjectivity of examiner judgments which, at the same time, may provide a new criterion for form-level norms, dependent neither on frequency of occurrence nor on individual examiner judgment. Many responses are shown to a number of judges, each of whom evaluates the accuracy with which they match the blot. Whether a response is called plus or minus depends on the extent of agreement among a number of judges in their accuracy ratings rather than on the basis of its frequency in the records of normal subjects. Thus, in a study by Walker (57), 100 normal adults naive in the Rorschach method judged 299 W responses (191 plus and 108 minus) from Beck's norms simply in terms of whether the response did or did not seem to fit the blot. Although the plus' and minus' arrived at through group judgment were significantly related to Beck's plus' and minus', it was found that the $F+\%$ derived from this method differentiated significantly the records of normal adult from paranoid schizophrenic patients, whereas Beck's $F+\%$ did not. In another study, Kimball (26) had 103 judges, varied in their experience with the test, rate 100 responses drawn from Beck and Hertz on a six-point scale of accuracy. If a response was rated 4 or better by 50% of the subjects, it was considered plus; If 2 or below by 50% of the subjects, minus. She found that the populars were generally rated highly, although they were not always considered to be the most accurate. In a number of cases, the plus and minus standards arrived at by this method did not agree with the Beck or Hertz standards. This type of approach has the obvious advantage of supplying quantitative norms of examiner judgments, thus minimizing the uncertainties inherent in single-examiner evaluation, while preserving the theoretical rationale of a judgmental criterion.

Categories for Good and Poor Form

Authorities differ, too, in the number of categories to be used for describing good and poor form. While sharpening the criteria of plus and minus, Beck (9) has followed Rorschach's original practice and includes virtually all form-determined responses in the categories $F+$ and $F-$. Klopfer and Kelley (32) used three categories: $F+$, which are excellent, well-organized forms; $F-$, which are notably poor or distorted forms; and F which includes all other forms. In Klopfer's present form-level rating method, each response gets a numerical value in addition (30, 31). Rapaport (44) distinguishes four levels of quality: $F+$, $F\pm$, $F\mp$, and $F-$. In addition, he distinguishes four qualitative categories: "special $F+$" for the sharply defined and very convincing form response; "special $F-$" for the definite but arbitrary form response; F_v for the vague form response, and F_o for the mediocre but acceptable response. These categories have the value of directing attention to different qualities in the production of good or bad form.

The Form-Level Ratio

Lastly, practices differ in the methods by which the over-all level is represented. Basically, the $F+\%$ is the ratio between clear and distorted form perception. But methods differ in whether the calculation is limited to "pure" form response or include also other responses in which there may be a distinct or primary form element but which include also other determinants. However, both Rapaport and Hertz ($R+\%$) use ratios based on all responses which use form either as the sole or principal determinant. Although one study (14) has shown Beck's $F+\%$ and Hertz' $R+\%$ to be correlated highly—in the mid-eighties for both a neurotic and normal sample—there has not been sufficient research to explore the possible differences, both theoretically and empirically, between these various methods of assessing form level.

IV

Differences among Personality and Clinical Groups in $F+\%$

Beck gives the mean $F+\%$ for normal subjects as 83.91 and the critical minimum for psychological health as 60. With these values for reference some of the differences among personality groups may be briefly characterized.[5] It has generally been found that the $F+\%$ rises from early childhood (31, 41, 55, 56), though a lowering is found in the adolescent years which may well reflect the temporary ego weakening of this emotionally stressful period (8, 55). During the adult years the level is stable, falling again in advanced age (10, 12, 54, 56). $F+\%$ is high in adults with superior intelligence, and decreases at lower

[5] More extensive discussion and some of the evidence for these general characterizations may be found in Beck (4, 5, 6, 7, 8), Klopfer, Ainsworth, Klopfer and Holt (30), Rapaport, Schafer and Gill (44), Rorschach (46) and other texts, as well as in numerous papers describing specific clinical groups.

levels, being lowest in the feeble-minded. The brain-injured patient may have an adequate form level, perhaps in a constricted and generally coarctated record, but it will tend to be lower under emotionally stressful conditions or in more confused patients. In schizophrenia the level is generally low, decreasing with the extent of confusion, excitement and intellectual deterioration. The greater the involvement and disorganization of the thinking processes, as in Beck's recently described S-1 schizophrenic reaction pattern (8), the lower the form level. Studies have shown that with clinical improvement there is a general rise in $F+\%$ (27, 39). In agitated and manic states the $F+\%$ is quite low. Similarly, the very anxious individual, generally less able to integrate perceptual and associational processes, also tends to a somewhat lower level. Interestingly, however, the depressed patient can have an exceedingly high form level, as does the rigid and pedantic normal. This finding will be commented on later, for it makes the important point that form level is not a simple and direct function of mental health and psychological maturity, but rather is curvilinearly related.

$F+\%$ and Behavior under Stress

Overt behavior is always the resultant of a number of interrelated personality processes operating in terms of the various demands and constraints of particular situations. Consequently, as Ainsworth (30) points out in her review of Rorschach validation research, one is inclined to look askance at "single-variable" studies attempting to predict behavior in complex situations. Yet, where it is possible to derive pointed hypotheses relating test variables to measurable behavior, and one can reasonably manipulate the experimental situation, such research can contribute greatly to the understanding of the test variables.

The hypothesis that subjects with good form perception should function better in experimentally induced stress situations has been tested in a number of experiments. Baker and Harris (3) measured the intelligibility and variations of intensity of speech during nonstress and stress conditions. Although all subjects showed a significant decline in both intelligibility and variability under stress, both form level and color-form integration ($FC:CF$) were positively correlated with the increased variability of intensity. Williams (59) found that the maintenance of digit-symbol test performance under stress was correlated with both $F+\%$ ($r = .71$) and color-form integration ($r = .35$). The multiple r using both Rorschach variables was .82.

However, these findings could not be replicated in subsequent experiments (11, 13). Although not reporting $F+\%$, Hertzman et al. (22, 23) found that the ability to tolerate anoxic conditions in high-altitude pressure chambers is related to a number of Rorschach indices of psychological health. The records of subjects with low anoxia tolerance were more often marked by low M, color and shading shock, refusal or inability to respond, no FC, and negative color balance ($CF + C > FC$). Using a multiple-choice group, Smith and George (52) studied the proportion of form-determined responses ($F\%$) as an index of control, using the decrement in performance of digit-symbol and information tests given before and after severe criticism as a measure of stress response. There was a significant nonlinear relationship between $F\%$ and the stress measure. Control in this situation increased with $F\%$ to the 50% level; above this point control broke down. Taken together, these experimental studies suggest that subjects with more accurate form perception are better able to perform under stress. They supplement clinical and personality studies, and in general give support to the interpretation of form perception as an index of ego control.

V

Let us consider in closer detail the various psychological mechanisms which may account for $F-$ responses. As already noted, an optimum $F+\%$ as an index of ego strength depends on the segregation and delay of impulsive and affective processes which might otherwise encroach into perception. Specifically, it assumes the intactness of the integrative functions of the ego (to focus attention, discriminate, consciously scan and select from memory), the availability of experience (memory or associational context), and the subject's desire to give accurate responses (in general, his set and motivation in the task). Deficiency in any of these factors singly or in combination may result in $F-$, but the quality differs with the particular factors involved. This is recognized in such distinctions as Beck's (6) personal and impersonal $F-$.

The Effect of Need

A personal $F-$ may occur when the pressure of internal needs is great and the reality organization of the subject is overwhelmed. The response, given with minimal respect for the contours of the stimulus, represents in one or another fashion the subject's need expression. The existence of strong drive as such is not sufficient to produce $F-$; there must be simultaneous weakness in the subject's ability to control the emergence of the drive and its effect on conscious perception. Thus, in studies of semistarvation there is no decrease in form level (28).

The Effect of Defense

Not only the drive but also the defense against its expression may lead to perceptual distortion. Though it is precisely the defensively constricted individual who achieves very high $F+$ levels, in other instances defensive action may lead to the hasty production of harmless but poor responses. If the blot stimulates threatening phantasy, the reported response may represent a denial of such a percept or involve the avoidance of the suggestive area. Clearly, the nature of the defense may influence the adequacy of the percept as well as its content, as Schafer (50) has most recently and fully described.

The Lack of Integrative Ability

However, the subject may simply be unable to meet the demands of the task and to integrate a response from the available stimulus material. This implies not a pressure of uncontrollable impulse, but rather a deficit in the control itself. The subject lacks *Gestaltungskraft*, and hence may give $F-$ responses which are, however, "impersonal." The brain-injured patient required to make something of the meaningless stimuli may do no more than give the obvious responses. Staying within the limits of his ability, there is minimal distortion but little richness or variety. However, venturing beyond these limits or because of the anxiety generated by his inability to cope with the test, his performance deteriorates and $F-$ responses appear. An interesting illustration of such a process was seen in a patient examined at Michael Reese Hospital. This man, a physician with a long-standing barbiturate addiction, gave a well-elaborated airplane as a whole response to card I. Most of the succeeding cards he again described as airplanes; in each case, however, giving considerable technical information about the particular model, style, and construction. Although impressing the examiner with his knowledge, most of these responses were little related to the forms of the blot. This patient used a particular fund of knowledge to cover his inability to integrate responses in terms of the stimulus qualities unique to each blot. Perseveration of response leading to a lowered form level has been described often in the brain-damaged and senile. However, perseverative response can also appear under the pressure of inner need, although in such cases the $F-$ produced will be more clearly personal. Thus, the neurotic patient with obsessive sexual thoughts may give genitalia in response to every conceivable, and many inconceivable, portions of the blots. Klopfer (32) has distinguished the two forms of perseveration by the terms "mechanical" and "fixed idea." Other types of pathological thinking leading to lowered form level are seen in confabulation, contamination, positional responses, or the like. Though all are $F-$, the distinctions among them are of diagnostic value.

Paucity of Associational Material

Still another source of poor form perception lies in a paucity of associational material out of which to construct responses. This may well be the more important determinant of the feeble-minded individual's low $F+$ than either a lack of integrative capacity, or, certainly, the overwhelming pressure of need. Since the final response depends on the subject's perception of the blot area and then drawing from his experience a likely percept to fit its perceived contours, it is clear that any reduction in the fund of material from which a response can be drawn, whether owing to cultural isolation or to limited intelligence, will reduce the possibilities of $F+$ responses.

Task Set, Interpretation, and Motivation

Lastly, the form level reflects the motivation of the subject in the task. An individual may be capable of, but unconcerned with, good form. It has often been assumed that the motivation of the subject in this as in any test procedure is "to do as well as you can." Thus, by presenting him with a piece of "reality," one can see how well he is able to deal with the demands of that reality.[6] But the subject may be unconcerned with our reality and rather prefer to do it his own way.

[6] Harris (18) has interpreted behavior in any testing situation in similar terms. He points out that whether the test presumes to assess personality, intelligence, or any other aspect of psychological functioning, the subject's ability to adjust to the requirements of the procedure yields evidence of his ego strength.

One extreme is typified by the schizophrenic, another by the compulsive who, in Rorschach's phrase, "takes the test very seriously."

Test performance depends, both generally and specifically with regard to $F+\%$, on the subject's interpretation of the test situation—the purpose of being tested, the rationale of the procedure, the behavior required of him—and on his relation with the examiner. It has too often been assumed that the test performance is strictly the resultant of the interaction of the test stimuli and the subject's personality, while neglecting to note that this behavior occurs within a social setting and is conditioned by the pre-existing orientations of the subject. Schachtel (49) and, more recently, Sarason (47) and Schafer (50) have described in considerable detail the dynamics of the patient-test and patient-examiner relationships. That such factors may have considerable influence on the final protocol is also attested to by a variety of empirical studies in which the attitude of the subject, relation to the examiner, and other such test-situational factors have been experimentally manipulated (17, 24, 35).

Rorschach early recognized that $F+\%$, along with sequence and approach, is one of the factors which can most easily be varied voluntarily and, by extension, through the action of more subtle attitudinal and situational factors. Set for accuracy, a subject with adequate intellectual resources can reach a perfect hundred. And as Schachtel notes (49), many subjects enter the examination with the expectation that their intellectual abilities are under test, that there are "right" responses, that "the essential requirement of the task is doing systematic accurate work rather than letting their imagination play" (49, p. 438). Their relation to the examiner may be defined in authoritarian or competitive terms. In other cases, a lowering of form level may reflect a regression of the subject in terms of his set toward the task and examiner, just as the excessively high $F+\%$ shows the others' need to appear exact and meticulous to the examiner. A common experience is the basically well-integrated subject tested prior to, or early in, psychoanalysis who, projecting the role of analysand into the Rorschach situation, applies the "first rule" willynilly. (A young doctor, with excellent ego strength, gave many responses of the sort: "My mother's menstrual blood.") How free the "free association" part of the examination is, often reflects the subject's role definition, and his willingness to relax his criticalness as well as his ability to apply it.

Certainly, it is important to distinguish such behavior from a more enduring inability to give accurate responses. For this, it becomes important to understand the meaning to the particular subject, possibly through direct inquiry or through the observation of other cues in the situation. The subject who interprets the situation competitively—"I'll show him!"—may be driven by a quantity ambition and, consequently, may produce large numbers of responses, some of them poor. Similarly, another, awed by the omniscient doctor and feeling that his fate hangs on the outcome, may limit himself to safe and accurate responses. Recognizing the importance of task-motivational factors also indicates the value of varying them in the interest of discovering the range of potential response. By manipulating the demands of the task—as in "testing the limits"—the production of plus responses (or, conversely, the relaxation of critical attention) can be encouraged. If none are forthcoming, then one can speak more readily of incapacity.

These considerations point up the rather obvious fact that the final production cannot be taken as a literal representation of the subject's capacity for reality contact, but that this may well be determined by test-situational, motivational, and attitudinal factors, some of which, in turn, reflect enduring and habitual personality trends, others more transitory ones.

VI

The healthy ego is not only able to maintain critical control but also is able to relax it as well. As recent workers in psychoanalytic ego psychology have pointed out (19, 20, 34, 42, 43), creative behavior often depends on regression, which is, however, under control and "in the service of the ego." In play, in art, and in spontaneous social intercourse, the psychologically healthy individual does not have to maintain a vigilant reality testing, but voluntarily releases control in the interest of spontaneous affective expression or phantasy. Indeed, it has been argued that artistic production may depend largely upon this ability for controlled regression. Stated another way, Kubie has recently suggested that creative thinking may depend upon the free utilization of preconscious processes and may involve the relative constraint of both the logic and reality orientation of conscious thought as well as the distortion of the unconscious.

The fact that form level is not linearly related to psychological health was recognized by Rorschach, who pointed out that optimum and maximum are not synonymous.

. . . we find the best forms in the pedants and depressed subjects, especially in psychotic depressions. These subjects take the test very seriously. They search laboriously for good forms, bringing to bear all their attention and faculties of self-criticism so that they achieve an F plus percentage of almost 100, though the answers are extraordinarily stereotyped, showing a poor range of variation (46, p. 57).

More recent writers have invariably pointed to the fact that the highest level of $F+$ is found in the individual with constrictive defenses who is neurotically unable to relax control. "The critical-controlling processes may have become rigid and intolerably accurate, making for meagerness of productivity and for rigidity in thinking and behavior" (44, p. 194). Such behavior is usually paralleled by a generally high proportion of form-determined responses indicating the decreased spontaneity and the inhibition of phantasy and affective processes. In Schachtel's (49) interpretation, both the pedantic and depressed patient share a lack of relatedness to the world in general, which, within the Rorschach situation, does not permit any spontaneous interest in the ink blots. Each views the task as something imposed from outside by a strange and threatening authority with which one is relatively powerless to deal. The pedant has to a degree repressed the feeling of strangeness and helplessness, and the compulsive defenses are in the forefront. By contrast, the depressive is overwhelmed by his inadequacy and guilt, and by the attendant affect. But both "have to check constantly whether they are really on the right track, the depressive considering this unlikely, the pedantic making sure he has followed the right protocol" (49, p. 439).

VII

Thus, the psychologically healthy individual, viewed in terms of form perception, emerges as one whose perception is neither diffuse nor distorted nor rigid, but accurate. The central integrative functions upon which such behavior depends emerge in psychological maturation and are damaged in psychopathology. They are part of the ego organization which includes also internalized value systems. Before concluding, I should like to consider the relationship between accurate form perception and such values, and, more specifically, to distinguish between reality-oriented behavior and conformity in the well-functioning personality.

In the concept of the "ego" two highly related but conceptually separate types of psychological phenomena can be distinguished. First, there are the organized values, attitudes, conscious needs, goals, and ideals which define the psychological self. These, as Allport (1) discusses, are the center of the personality organization from which the individual gains identity and continuity. This is "ego" in terms of its content, and can be distinguished from ego in a more structural sense. For the present discussion, clarity might be served by using a term such as "self." Second, the term "ego" defines the capacity to organize and synthesize experience, perceive, remember, plan, and, in general, exercise control over behavior. The term "ego strength" has come into use to describe variations in the adequacy of such functioning (38). Thus far, the ego functioning seen in $F+$ has been discussed principally in terms of this latter meaning.

Ego and self are clearly parallel and related concepts. In psychological development, the individual must be capable of distinguishing self and not-self before a self-system can emerge. The ability to relate past memories, present events, and future consequences in causal sequences paces the emergence of the self as a temporally continuous structure. The delay of gratification which makes possible the development of ego functions allows the self, as subject to be gratified, to have internalized goals which can be represented in phantasy. Similarly, in the developed organism, self and ego processes remain tightly related. The individual who has incorporated unrealistic goals may of necessity have to resort to irrational mechanisms to live without anxiety. Thus, the existence of strong ego functioning assumes an organized self-system. In social behavior, critical judgment implies a set of values in terms of which such judgment is made. Although many of these are derived from the cultural environment, they are integrated within the psychologically individual self.

Accurate form perception implies an awareness of, and in general a respect for, the social values which define the rules of organized social life. The ego-strong individual has learned the conditions allowing expression and those requiring inhibition of impulses, and he has the control necessary for directing their expression or inhibition. Similarly, he can flexibly accept various roles in a complex and changing social situation. He is neither, on the one hand, compulsively constrained to a single pattern of behavior, nor, on the other, does he lose the identity of the self in chameleonlike adaptation.

But knowledge of social definitions does not imply conformity to them. Perceiving accurately does not mean valuing things as everyone else does. The existence of an integrated self involves holding values which to greater or lesser degree must be in conflict with social demands. Prior to the formation of the ego, there is conflict between the blind expression of instinct and the requirements of social reality, but the reality testing which arises in the mediation of these conflicting demands also provides a basis for a new conflict between the values of the self and social demand. Indeed, psychological maturity requires the ability to accept social disapproval and isolation in the pursuit of long-term goals, and not to have one's self-esteem dependent upon the approval which goes with conformity.

Thus, deviance does not imply ego weakness. True, the individual with profound unresolved emotional conflicts will have poor reality contact and be characterized by aberrant behavior. The existence of certain deviant values may be presumptive evidence or a deficit in psychological growth, while holding others may put such strain on the ego's resources as to require distortion for their maintenance. But the fact of deviance is neither proof for or against ego strength. It is precisely the weak ego who is unable to assert independent values and who "escapes from freedom" through conformity. And, conformity, as so often happens, depends on continued self-deceit, compromise, and the renunciation of one's own perceptions for its justification and continuance (2).

In sum, the healthy individual is capable of detachment and objectivity in perceiving and organizing both internal and external events. He knows social standards, and may in the main abide them, but he is not compulsively constrained by them. He has interiorized value systems that are the unique expressions of his development and give direction to his behavior. He is not compelled to judge his actions by existing social standards, nor does he feel it necessary to flaunt them. There is sufficient flexibility to adjust to changing demands, but this behavior is not so fluid as to conform to the immediate requirements of the social world or to the pressures of inner needs.

BIBLIOGRAPHY

1. Allport, G. W. *Becoming.* New Haven: Yale University Press, 1955.
2. Asch, S. E. *Social psychology.* New York: Prentice-Hall, 1952.
3. Baker, L. M., and Harris, J. S. The validation of the Rorschach test results against laboratory behavior. *J. clin. Psychol.,* 1949, 5, 161–164.
4. Beck, S. J. *Rorschach's test.* Vol. I. *Basic Processes.* (2nd ed. revised.) New York: Grune and Stratton, 1949.

5. Beck, S. J. *Rorschach's test. Vol. II. A variety of personality pictures.* New York: Grune and Stratton, 1945.
6. Beck, S. J. *Rorschach's test. Vol. III. Advances in interpretation.* New York: Grune and Stratton, 1952.
7. Beck, S. J. Rorschach F plus and the ego in treatment. *Amer. J. Orthopsychiat.*, 1948, **18**, 395–401.
8. Beck, S. J. *The six schizophrenias. Res. Monogr. Amer. Orthopsychiat. Assn.*, 1954, **10**, No. 6.
9. Beck, S. J., Rabin, A. I., Thiesen, W. G., Molish, H., and Thetford, W. N. The normal personality as projected in the Rorschach test. *J. Psychol.*, 1950, **30**, 241–298.
10. Caldwell, Bettye M. The use of the Rorschach in personality research with the aged. *J. Geront.*, 1954, **9**, 316–323.
11. Carlson, V. R., and Lazarus, R. S. A repetition of Meyer Williams study of intellectual control under stress and associated Rorschach factors. *J. consult. Psychol.*, 1953, **17**, 247–253.
12. Davidson, Helen H., and Kruglov, Lorraine. Personality characteristics of the institutionalized aged. *J. consult. Psychol.*, 1952, **16**, 5–12.
13. Eriksen, C. W., Lazarus, R. S., and Strange, J. R. Stress and its personality correlates. *J. Pers.*, 1952, **20**, 277–286.
14. Feldman, M. J., Gursslin, Carolyn, Kaplan, M. L., and Sharlock, Nidia. A preliminary study to develop a more discriminating F+ ratio. *J. clin. Psychol.*, 1954, **10**, 47–51.
15. Freud, S. *The interpretation of dreams.* (Translated by James Strachey.) New York: Basic Books, 1955.
16. Freud, S. Formulations concerning two principles in mental functioning. In: *Collected Papers. Vol. IV.* London: Hogarth Press, 1953, 13–21.
17. Gibby, R. G. The stability of certain Rorschach variables under conditions of experimentally induced sets: 1. The intellectual variables. *J. proj. Tech.*, 1951, **15**, 3–25.
18. Harris, R. E. Psychodiagnostic testing in psychiatry and psychosomatic medicine. In: *Recent advances in diagnostic psychological testing.* Springfield: Charles C Thomas, 1950.
19. Hartmann, H. Comments on the psychoanalytic theory of the ego. In: *The psychoanalytic study of the child. Vol. V.* New York: International Universities Press, 1950, 74–96.
20. Hartmann, H. Ego psychology and the problem of adaptation. In: D. Rapaport (ed.), *Organization and pathology of thought.* New York: Columbia Univer. Press, 1951, 362–396.
21. Hertz, Marguerite R. *Frequency tables for scoring responses to the Rorschach inkblot test.* Cleveland: Western Reserve University Press, 1951.
22. Hertzman, M., Orlansky, J., and Seitz, C. P. Personality organization and anoxia tolerance. *Psychosom. Med.*, 1944, **6**, 317–331.
23. Hertzman, M., Smith, G. M., and Clark, K. B. The relation between changes in the angioscotoma and certain Rorschach signs under prolonged mild anoxia. *J. gen. Psychol.*, 1949, **41**, 263–271.
24. Hutt, M. L., Gibby, R. G., Milton, E. O., and Pottharst, K. The effect of varied experimental "sets" upon Rorschach performance. *J. proj. Tech.*, 1950, **14**, 181–187.

25. Kimball, Alice J.   History of form-level appraisal in the Rorschach. *J. proj. Tech.*, 1950, **14**, 134–152.
26. Kimball, Alice J.   Evaluation of form-level in the Rorschach. *J. proj. Tech.*, 1950, **14**, 219–244.
27. Kisker, G. W.   A projective approach to personality patterns during insulin shock and metrazol convulsive therapy. *J. abnorm. soc. Psychol.*, 1942, **37**, 120–124.
28. Kjenaas, Nancy K., and Brozek, J.   Personality in semi-starvation. *Psychosom. Med.*, 1952, **14**, 115–128.
29. Klopfer, B.   Personality patterns in old age. *Rorschach Res. Exch.*, 1946, **10**, 145–166.
30. Klopfer, B., Ainsworth, Mary D., Klopfer, W. G., and Holt, R. R.   *Developments in the Rorschach technique. Vol. I. Technique and theory.* Yonkers: World Book Co., 1954.
31. Klopfer, B., and Davidson, Helen H.   Form level rating: a preliminary proposal for appraising mode and level of thinking as expressed in Rorschach records. *Rorschach Res. Exch.*, 1944, **8**, 164–177.
32. Klopfer, B., and Kelley, D. H.   *The Rorschach technique.* Yonkers: World Book Co., 1942.
33. Klopfer, B., and Margulies, J.   Rorschach reactions in early childhood *Rorschach Res. Exch.*, 1941, **5**, 1–23.
34. Kris, E.   On preconscious mental processes. *Psychoanal. Quart.*, 1950, **19**, 540–560.
35. Lord, Edith.   Experimentally induced variations in Rorschach performance. *Psychol. Monogr.*, 1950, **64**, No. 316.
36. Murphy, G.   *Personality: a biosocial approach to origins and structures.* New York: Harper, 1947.
37. Murray, H. A., and Kluckhohn, C.   Outline of a conception of personality. In: Kluckhohn, C., Murray, H. A., and Schneider, D. (eds.). *Personality in nature, society and culture.* New York: Alfred A. Knopf, 1953, 3–49.
38. Nunberg, H.   Ego strength and ego weakness. *Amer. Imago*, 1943, **3**, 25–40.
39. Piotrowski, Z. A.   Rorschach manifestations of improvement in insulin treated schizophrenics. *Psychosom. Med.*, 1939, **1**, 508–526.
40. Prados, M., and Fried, E.   Personality structure in the older age groups. *J. clin. Psychol.*, 1947, **3**, 113–120.
41. Rabin, A. I., and Beck, S. J.   Genetic aspects of some Rorschach factors. *Amer. J. Orthopsychiat.*, 1950, **20**, 595–599.
42. Rapaport, D.   On the psychoanalytic theory of thinking. *Int. J. Psychoanal.*, 1950, **31**, 161–170.
43. Rapaport, D.   *Organization and pathology of thought.* New York: Columbia University Press, 1951.
44. Rapaport, D., Schafer, R., and Gill, M.   *Diagnostic psychological testing. Vol. II.* Chicago: Year Book Publishers, 1946.
45. Rickers-Ovsiankina, Maria A.   Some theoretical considerations regarding the Rorschach method. *Rorschach Res. Exch.*, 1943, **7**, 41–53.
46. Rorschach, H.   *Psychodiagnostics.* New York: Grune and Stratton, 1942.
47. Sarason, S. B.   *The clinical interaction.* New York: Harper, 1954.
48. Schachtel, E. G.   The dynamic perception and the symbolism of form. *Psychiatry*, 1941, **4**, 79–96.

49. Schachtel, E. G. Subjective definitions of the Rorschach test situation and their effect on test performance. *Psychiatry*, 1945, **8**, 419–448.

50. Schafer, R. *Psychoanalytic Interpretation in Rorschach testing*. New York: Grune and Stratton, 1954.

51. Singer, J. L. Delayed gratification and ego development: Implications for clinical and experimental research. *J. consult. Psychol.*, 1955, **19**, 259–266.

52. Smith, S., and George, C. E. Rorschach factors related to experimental stress. *J. consult. Psychol.*, 1951, **15**, 190–195.

53. Stein, M. I. Personality factors involved in the temporal development of Rorschach responses. *J. proj. Tech.*, 1949, **13**, 355–414.

54. Stern, W. *General psychology*. New York: Macmillan, 1937

55. Thetford, W., Molish, H. B., and Beck, S. J. Developmental aspects of personality structure in normal children. *J. proj. Tech.*, 1951, **15**, 58–78.

56. Vorhaus, Pauline, and Kay, L. Rorschach reactions in early childhood: Part II. Intellectual aspects of personality development. *Rorschach Res. Exch.*, 1943, **7**, 71–78.

57. Walker, R. G. An approach to standardization of Rorschach form-level. *J proj. Tech.*, 1953, **17**, 426–436.

58. Werner, H. *Comparative psychology of mental development*. Chicago: Follett, 1948.

59. Williams, M. An experimental study of intellectual control under stress and associated Rorschach factors. *J. consult. Psychol.*, 1947, **11**, 21–29.

6

by Zygmunt A. Piotrowski

THE

MOVEMENT

SCORE

Rorschach's system of personality analysis can be called percept-analysis because it consists mainly of an analysis of percepts or visual images elicited by ambiguous visual stimuli, a set of ink blots. The most original part of this system is the human movement response, or M.[1] Rorschach's discussion of the M and its relation to the color responses occupies a full third of his *Psychodiagnostics,* excluding the sample records (20). The psychological traits corresponding to the M and the C are different but not mutually exclusive in Rorschach's system. Rorschach described an individual who produced more M than sum C as an introvert and an individual with more sum C than M as an extravert, the degree of introversion or extraversion depending on the excess of M over sum C and sum C over M. These terms were taken from C. G. Jung, but they do not have quite the same meaning in Rorschach's perceptanalysis as they have in the Jungian personology. At first Jung viewed these two functions as mutually exclusive; later he reduced their incompatibility by making of them a pair of complementary attitudes or functions. They cannot occur on the same psychological level. If an individual's consciousness is dominated by his introverted attitude, his unconscious is dominated by his extraverted attitude, and vice versa (7). Rorschach believed at first that these two functions were independent of each other: "The psychological processes producing introversion and extraversion are not opposite but different. They are as different as thinking and feeling, as motion and color. . . . In general,

---

[1] For explanation of scoring symbols, see Appendix, pp. 441 ff. [Editor].

however, the introverted person is understood to be one who is turned in upon himself, who lives more within himself than in the outer world, and who has difficulty in his approach to the world outside himself" (20, pp. 82–83). The M type (or introvert) possesses the following traits: "(1) predominance of personalized productivity; (2) intensive rapport; (3) stable affect and motility, awkwardness, insufficient adaptability to reality and insufficient extensive rapport" (20, p. 81). The implications are that the M type is more original and creative than the C type (or extravert). The M type establishes an intensive rapport with rather few people, whereas the C type tends to establish superficial relationships but with many people. The M type achieves stability of affect by a reduction or suppression of spontaneous acting out. Rorschach never explained this fully but this appears to be the conclusion from his strong emphasis on the negative correlation between the number of M and the degree of overt motor behavior. "Kinesthetic engrams act as inhibitors of physical activity; motor activity inhibits kinesthetic engrams" (20, p. 80). By contrast, speaking of the C, the indicators of affectivity, Rorschach stated, "There is a very close relationship between motility and affectivity, almost a parallelism" (20, p. 80).

Rorschach knew that the absolute numbers of M and sum C varied in a test protocol under the influence of mood swings—depression and elation, fatigue and exuberance—but he believed that the M:sum C ratio remained essentially unchanged, shifting but slowly and gradually during a life time (20, pp. 94–95). Increased experience made him alter this view. In letters, excerpts from which were published by Bash, Rorschach raised questions "about the view still upheld in my book that a relatively strong constance pertains to the *Erlebnistypus*" (M:sum C ratio); he concluded: "I must draw nearer to Jung, who distinguished an attitude of the conscious and an attitude of the unconscious, and says: 'When the attitude of the conscious is extraverted, then the attitude of the unconscious is complementarily introverted'" (1, p. 238). Bash performed an experiment to investigate this statement. He had 28 subjects look at card IX 200 times in succession (5-second periods of exposure alternated with 15-second periods of darkness), and asked them to tell each time what they saw, permitting repetitions. The M:sum C ratio of the 8 subjects whose regular pre-experimental records contained an equal number of M and of weighted sum C did not change. The ratios of 18 of the 20 remaining subjects (10 M types and 8 C types) changed during the experiment: The M and sum C became more and more nearly equal, both through the numerical decline of the component (M or C) that was originally the stronger one, as well as through rise of the originally weaker component. "Jung's principle of complementarity is thus given a formal confirmation through the Rorschach" (1, p. 239). The same tendency to gradual ambiequality can be observed in successfully treated psychoneurotics. The average M:sum C ratio of 13 patients who received intensive and prolonged psychoanalytically oriented psychotherapy was 3.8:5.5 at the beginning of treatment; it was 9.8:9.4 at the end of treatment. Ten neurotic but nontreated control patients showed no significant change during a similar time interval (17). The successfully treated patients improved also in many other respects, e.g., showing qualitative changes in the M and sum C; these changes were more significant than the numerical equalization of the M and sum C.

EXPERIENCE TYPE AND OVERT BEHAVIOR

Rorschach's fundamental view of the M presupposes mutual exclusion of kinesthetic experience, underlying the M response, and overt physical activity. This idea recurs in the *Psychodiagnostics* and is expressed in a variety of ways. It is a basic concept:

The factors which are essentially "inner" or self-determined, and are expressed primarily in experience of motion in the test, are in some way opposed to physical activity, the actual execution of motion. I would like to add an example so that this conclusion is not left simply hanging in air. Dreams are "inner" or self-determined productions and kinesthesias play an important role in them. On awakening, necessary movements, physical motion begins at once. This movement sets the dreams aside. There is, however, a way to recall dreams: lie perfectly motionless on awakening in order not to cover up the kinesthesias of a dream by present physical movement (20, p. 72).

Rorschach cited Mourly Vold's experiments in support of his view concerning the essential role played by kinesthetic sensation in dreams when the body is motionless. Mourly Vold found that obstructing free movement (e.g., by placing light weights on the limbs of sleepers) caused dreams with intense activity (20). Rorschach stressed the great difference between the imagination revealed during the taking of his test and the overt behavior of the testee:

The experience type (i.e., the ratio of M to sum C) indicates only how the person experiences [notices] but not how he lives [acts overtly], or toward what he is striving. A person with strong introversive traits and less strong extratensive traits may be decidedly extratensive in his behavior. . . . These discrepancies between experience type and living can be explained only by the fact that the "active energy," the effective energy at the moment, the will, the libido, or whatever it may be named, is so oriented as to allow only a part of the faculties for experiencing to be in operation. It is instinct which transforms constitutional features into active tendencies. It is always daring to draw conclusions about the way an individual experiences life from the results of an experiment (20, p. 87).

Relationship of M to the Unconscious and Fantasy

It would seem to follow from this emphatic differentiation between manifest motor behavior and the images which the test elicits that Rorschach's explanation of extensor and flexor M applies not to overt behavior but to covert fantasy. "Subjects who see extension movements are active individuals with strong drives toward importance and activity though they often show neurotic inhibitions. Those who see flexion movements have passive and resigned natures" (2, p. 206). Beck wrote:

The M response, as Rorschach understands it, really reproduces movements or activities that the subject is carrying on within his mental life. Since these mental activities are those in which we should like to engage in the outer world but cannot, or dare not, they are our wishfulfilling activities. Thus they are our fantasy life—which means that the associations encased in them actually project the subject's intimately personal living (2, p. 92).

In his blind analysis of Oberholzer's patient, Rorschach concluded that flexor M revealed "an unconscious passive attitude," and that the predominance of M over sum C disclosed "a tendency to regression" (20, p. 207). This opinion marked a great change in Rorschach's evaluation of his test because earlier he had emphasized that "the test cannot be used to probe into the content of the subconscious" (20, p. 123). He defined the difference between extensor and flexor M in terms of conscious attitudes toward inner fantasy life. An individual with extensor M "struggles against his introversive tendencies," while a subject with flexor M "surrenders himself to his imagination" (20, p. 123). The self-assertiveness implied in the extensor M is directed not at other people but at one's own imagination revealing an inner struggle; the compliance associated with the flexor M indicates peace with one's self in the sense of accepting one's imagination and the wishes contained in it, according to Rorschach.

If Rorschach's definition of the meaning of the M is valid, then the content of the M, be it self-assertive or compliant, should not be noticeable in overt behavior. This meaning has been challenged by Piotrowski in 1937 on the basis of clinical experience, and the meaning of the M was redefined to reflect action tendencies which directly influence the individual's basic attitudes when dealing with others in personally vital matters (12). Thus the M tendencies became overt attitudes and were not considered indicators of repressed action tendencies. This new view did not imply that the M tendencies were always easily and fully manifested in overt conduct. In the first place, the personality trends revealed by Rorschach's perceptanalysis are an inventory of possible behavior patterns, all of which are never simultaneously expressed in a motor activity. In the second place, instead of viewing the M as representing repressed tendencies and the sum C as representing overt action tendencies (as did Rorschach), Piotrowski assumed that both the M and the sum C directly influence overt behavior, and that interference with this influence could be detected by other perceptanalytic components. Among these the most important are: the light shading responses; the ratio of the sum of light shading to the sum of color responses; the number, degree of differentiation, and form-quality level of whole responses; and the percentage of sharply perceived forms (13).

More recently, there has been advanced a third view of the meaning of the M which is strongly influenced by psychoanalytic ideas about the nature of transference and countertransference between examiner and examinee (21, 22). According to this view, the significance of the M depends on the rapport between examiner and examinee, and on the examinee's interpretation of the meaning of the examination. The acceptance of this standpoint would be justified if both the number and the textual content of the M varied with the fluctuations of transference and countertransference at every examination. Moreover, we would need a proof that the same changes in transference and countertransference regularly produce predictable changes in the content and the number of the M. The difficulties involved in analyzing satisfactorily the nature of transference and countertransference, and their effect upon the test data, are so great as to make this view of the M far more complicated and less definite than it appears at first sight. Besides, the content of the M, if not their number, is one of the stablest Rorschach components, as shown in multiple re-examinations of the same patients (17).

CRITERIA FOR SCORING M

Rorschach insisted that the active movements or the immobile postures which constitute the M response should be felt: a tension, a readiness to act, and effort to maintain a posture should be consciously felt by the subject; otherwise the response is not an M even if the verbal content of the response plainly implies movement. This requirement makes scoring extremely difficult and unreliable. Roemer reported that he and Rorschach had spent a great deal of time discussing this matter and would, after a thorough reanalysis of a scored record, greatly change the number of M, in one case reducing it from seven to two (19). Rorschach concluded from self-introspections that some of the responses which contained no textual hint of movement or muscular tension were accompanied by strong kinesthetic sensations, whereas some responses with full descriptions of movement were produced without any kinesthetic experience. He pointed out the difficulties in the scoring of M, and warned that examiners who produce many M themselves tend to score too many M, whereas those with few M frequently fail to score M when such a score is warranted. Rorschach's preconceived idea that the content of the M, like that of dreams, expresses repressed tendencies, made him reject as M responses those that were accompanied by verbal and overt bodily gestures illustrating movement. It seems to me that Rorschach's preconceived notion that fantasy as revealed in the perceptanalytic human movement response must differ from actual overt living is responsible for the complexities which Rorschach introduced into the scoring of M. With the acceptance of the other view, that the tendencies revealed in the M are not repressed but, on the contrary, influence directly observable relationships with others, a search for the muscular tension inwardly felt but not associated with any external motor behavior becomes unnecessary. Not being obliged to establish any incompatibility between the content of the M and actions (or gestures) accompanying the response, we can rely largely on the content to determine the score. Most psychologists actually follow this procedure. One should be on guard against spurious M, in which the movement is intellectually inferred and not genuinely experienced, but they seem rather rare. If subjects assume movement merely to explain form, the response is a spurious M. Some individuals infer that the dark figures in card III could not bend the way they do unless they were in the midst of some movement. This is an example of a spurious M. Whenever the subject shows that he reacts kinesthetically, his response is a genuine M. It is unnecessary to ascertain the presence or absence of kinesthetic sensations when the content plainly suggests a movement or muscular tension. Nevertheless, the evidence of a kinesthetic experience spontaneously offered by the examinee strengthens the validity of th M score. Many a response reveals its M character after a delay, e.g., during the inquiry following the examination proper. At times, the M develops slowly and gradually. Anything spontaneously added to the original response can be considered as an integral part of the response. However, this too can become a controversial issue. Rorschach asserted that the speed and immediacy of a response were necessary conditions of its genuineness. This notion seems to be based on the belief that, when given time to elaborate upon their ideas, subjects tend to rationalize them and to change them under the influence of their neurotic defense mechanisms. It is very doubtful that the same argument applies with equal validity to perceptanalytic examinations. If subjects are unaware of what they are disclosing about themselves during a Rorschach examination, they do not know how to modify their responses in order to present themselves in a more favorable light. Examination anxiety affects the content of responses rarely, although it easily reduces their number. Thus, it is of little significance for the validity or the genuineness of the responses whether they are given all at once or whether they are completed in two or several phases, provided they are genuine and spontaneous and are not deliberately changed because of knowledge of the conclusions that may be drawn (13). This matter is important and deserves a thorough investigation. Psychologists differ on this point, but do so evidently more for theoretically determined than for empirically supported reasons.

M AND INHIBITED MOTION

Experiments have shown that subjects tend to produce more M after a period of deliberate motor inhibition than under normal conditions (10). Although the increase, measured in terms of group averages, is statistically significant, the absolute degree of the increase is quite small. Nonetheless Rorschach and others have reasoned that, if restraint imposed on overt bodily movements increases the number of M, the M must represent inhibited action tendencies. This reasoning poses several questions. May it be assumed that conditions which facilitate the communication of an action tendency (through the perceptanalytic response) are the same as conditions under which the action tendency manifests itself? Does hesitation about communicating a drive mean that the drive is manifested outwardly with hesitation, and, conversely, does a free and spontaneous communicating of a drive mean that the communicated drive is behaviorally manifested in a free and spontaneous way? Does a denial of the commission of an impulsive act mean that the individual had not acted impulsively? Is it not rather unlikely that rules of psychological interpretation valid in one situation (revealing drive during a preceptanalytic examination) are equally valid in another situation (manifesting the drive in behavior on a fantasy or motor level)? If it is, the slight increase in the production of M following a period of physical restraint does not imply that the M reveal repressed tendencies, but simply means that some subjects give more complete records when deliberate self-restraint increases their conscious attention to their own mental processes. Thus, the experiments with the effect of physical restraint on the number of M do not undermine the validity of the statement that the M disclose action tendencies which are not repressed but are acted out whenever there is an opportunity, i.e., when there are no external obstacles, physical or social, and when the subject is not in a state of debilitating anxiety.

M AND SELF-ASSERTION

The first experimental evidence that the M press for direct outward manifestation was offered by Mirin (11). Behaving as if he were a fellow subject in an alleged memory test, Mirin deliberately contradicted schizophrenics (one at a time) in order to find out whether patients with extensor M will insist on acceptance of their version, and whether patients with flexor M will give in to the experimenter even if they are right. The type of M in the pre-experimental records was significantly and positively associated with the patients' reactions to Mirin's attempts at influencing them: patients with flexor M gave in, the ones with extensor M insisted that they were right. Hammer and Jacks (5) determined the relative frequency of extensor and flexor M in records of imprisoned rapists, and of imprisoned pedophiles whose offenses consisted of a passive and seductive appeal to children to expose themselves. Significant statistical differences were found to support the hypothesis of extensor M being associated with assertive behavior orientations and flexor M with submissive or passive ones. Brecher (4) compared the M responses of maternally over-protected and maternally rejected male schizophrenics of equal intel-ligence. The rejecting mothers were abusive, both mentally and phys-ically; they humiliated their sons through constant criticism, and gave no signs of approval, creating a feeling of great insecurity. The over-protective mothers limited their sons initiative and curbed their self-expression, but took excellent physical care of them, breast-fed them for a year or more, and overfondled them. Brecher found that the overprotected patients produced more than twice as many M as the rejected ones, the respective averages being 5.4 and 2.1, although the averages for W were 5.4 and 9.3, and for the total number of responses 43.5 and 23.9 respectively. This result supports Piotrowski's theory that the development of M is facilitated by two factors: (1) an un-satisfactory childhood relationship with the parents, especially with the mother, awareness of this situation, and a wish to improve upon it; (2) sufficient satisfaction of basic needs (physical security, shelter, food), mainly on the part of a stable and protective mother (13). Time and calm surroundings, i.e., a certain amount of security, are needed to develop the habit of thoughtful contemplation.

When he discussed the M concept, Rorschach had in mind the gen-eral idea that people who spend much time thinking (who are ab-sorbed in their inner life) are unlikely to engage in much motor ac-tivity. Since he believed that the number of M indicated both fan-tasy (inner life) and motor restraint, he concluded that the number of M was positively correlated with the habitual amount of thinking. However, the logical relation of the number of M to thinking or to overt motor behavior is a different problem from the logical relation of the textual content of specific M responses to overt motor behavior. The solution of one of these problems does not determine the solu-tion of the other. Specific M content can reveal deep-seated motives for action regardless of the relative strength of the tendencies to lose oneself in thought or to express oneself in action. The idea presented here, linking M content with the overt handling of vital interhuman relationships, should add to the usefulness of the M without conflict-ing with Rorschach's principle that an increase in the number of M is associated with an increase in thinking and a decrease in overt motor activity.[2]

[2] This paragraph was written in response to a comment by the editor.

The *M* is such an important psychological reaction that it retains great significance even in group testing, although group tests are much less reliable and valid than individual tests. About fifteen years ago the author administered group Rorschachs to U.S. Army prisoners. Slides showing the Rorschach plates were projected onto a large screen. The men—no more than 40 of whom were examined at a time—were asked to write down their responses. When the written examination paper was not clear enough for scoring, the man was called in for an individual inquiry on his potential movement and color responses. Each slide was exposed for three minutes during which the responses were written down. An exception was made for the last, tenth slide, which was exposed for four minutes. The second part of the examination consisted of a group-written inquiry, the directions to which ended with an appeal to "write down anything that you think is necessary to make us understand why you wrote down each particular answer." These group Rorschachs as well as other data were used to predict future parole conduct upon restoration to duty. Eighty per cent of the prisoners had been court-martialed for AWOL (absence without official leave), at the Fort Jackson Rehabilitation Center. Most of these men were subsequently paroled and we had an official report on the men's conduct during the first six-month period after restoration to active duty. If a man was reported to have gone AWOL again, or to have been court-martialed for whatever reason, he was placed in the poor-conduct group. All other men were placed in the good-conduct group. These reports were used to check the accuracy of the preparole predictions of future parole conduct. One of the many factors, Rorschach and non-Rorschach, which contributed to the prediction concerning possible future parole conduct was the quality of the *M*. Any *M* in which only one figure appeared, or which was characterized by inhibition, doubt, or inconsistency when two or more figures appeared in it, was considered prognostically unfavorable. *M* free of any restraint, in which the two or more figures cooperated freely, were considered prognostically favorable. Examples of favorable *M* are: "Two men working on some engine"; "two bears standing at a bar"; "men or women sort of bowing" (toward each other); "two old hens [meaning women] gossiping"; "squatting with knees together"; "waiters serving"; "sitting at a table and saying a toast"; "dancing"; "two men tearing a crab apart." The essential point is not whether the intent of the movement or action was friendly or hostile, but only whether the two *M* figures cooperated or fought each other. If they disagreed or fought each other, the *M* was classified as unfavorable, e.g., "two men fighting over a purse," Other unfavorable M were those in which there appeared but one figure, e.g., "woman dancing on stage," or part of one figure, e.g., "heavy feet tramping"; M in which there is an obstacle, e.g., "ugly persons trying to kiss through a partition," "two men want to budge this heavy bag"; M in which doubt was expressed, e.g., "two Martians pulling something apart, I don't know if they can do it," "people dancing or pulling a tire off a wheel," "washing clothes or trying to pick up a basket"; "sitting on the ground or maybe bowing"; M with divergent and inconsistent action tendencies, e.g., "tug of war," "kneeling down but raising hands up," "men trying to get the same thing which only one of them can have." Sixty-eight per cent of the men with follow-up reports (115 out of 168) produced at least one M. Prognosis was believed to be unfavorable if the Rorschach record contained at least one unfavorable M. Good parole conduct was predicted only for men with exclusively favorable M. Among the 115 M cases, 69 gave no unfavorable M; of these, 57 (e.g., 83%) conducted themselves well during parole. Each of the remaining 46 produced at least one unfavorable M and, of these prisoners, 32 (70%) manifested poor parole conduct. In the total group of 115, the predictions, based merely on the quality of the M, were proved correct in 89 cases (77%).

The difference between restraint and absence of restraint in the action tendencies of genuine M is of universal importance. Its importance is independent of differences in intellectual level, in degree of social responsibility, and intensity of living. Business executives differ greatly from Army prisoners. Yet the main difference between executives who continued being successful, despite increasing responsibilities and promotions, and those who had failed after they had reached the highest rungs on the managerial ladder could be expressed in degrees of freedom of action shown in their M. The author analyzed 50 individual Rorschach records of successful and unsuccessful top business executives on the initiative of the psychology department of E. N. Hay and Associates at Philadelphia. The following types of M were found with significantly greater frequency in the successful group: Self-assertive and confident postures ("an athlete, standing erect, before a boxing match," "men about to conquer the world"); constructive cooperation for a common purpose ("two men lifting a weight," "two men trying to catch an animal"); display of mutual respect ("men politely greeting each other"); friendly or non-hostile facing of each other ("two men facing each other and discussing something"); and dancing. The unfavorable group produced significantly more M of the following sort: Blocked or circular movement ("pulling in opposite directions," "twirling around"); lying down, hanging down, or descending, i.e., passively giving in to the force of gravity; bending toward and adjusting to a fixed inanimate object ("talking into a microphone"); hostile and tense facing of each other ("two women glowering at each other," "two teenagers telling each other insults"); and movement alternatives, i.e., giving at least two different types of movement with the implication that both apply and there is no reason to prefer one over the other ("two people dancing or sitting down," "two men fighting or playing pattycake"). These types of M were weighted and assigned plus or minus scores. Each of them was scored when it appeared in the record. The final M score was the algebraic sum of the plus and minus weights. M not comprised by the scale were disregarded. The distribution of the final M scores separated the successful from the unsuccessful executives very well; only one case overlapped. The scale remains to be validated on a new group of executives.

A difference in absolute numbers of M given by two people also is apt to indicate an unfavorable interpersonal relationship. For example, if this difference between marital partners exceeds more than three points, the marriage is not likely to last; husband and wife are likely to continue living together despite conflicts if the difference is small (16). Complete absence of M (or very small numbers of them) has repeatedly been found to be an unfavorable prognostic sign in schizophrenia. As long as the schizophrenic can produce some good quality M, he is capable of resisting deterioration; when he ceases to produce them, he is likely to slip gradually down to lower levels of social and occupational functioning (15).

Booth (3) classified the M according to two different criteria. He based one on the effect of the action tendency and the other on the function assigned to the central vertical axis of the blots. Primary kinesthesias are goal-directed actions, the effect of which is a direct and practical change in the individual's environment; examples are "running," "walking," "cooking," "carrying," "fighting." Secondary kinesthesias do not effect changes, but maintain a position in the environment; being determined by social conventions, they do not introduce innovations. Examples are dances, ceremonies, "holding on to something," "just standing," "praying," "bowing," "greeting." His primary M, said Booth, reflect independent creative ability. The individual who is not stimulated to creative effort by conventions produces primary M for he rather expects the environment to conform to his personal expectations and he resists changes in his environment which do not suit him. The secondary M reflect an ability for constructive work within the prevailing social and cultural norms. The life goals of the individual who produces secondary M are determined by his social milieu for he intends to conform to what society expects of him. Booth's second classification of the M was influenced by Roemer's (19) division of whole responses. Roemer found that his axial or "primitive whole responses" (e.g., "bat" in card I) constitute the majority of wholes in the records of children and of the low occupational classes. The lateral or "bilateral whole responses" (e.g., "two clowns" in card II) make up the majority of wholes in records of adult members of the middle class. By analogy, Booth divided the M into axial and lateral. In his study of 60 locomotor patients (half of whom suffered from arthritis and half from Parkinsonism) and 60 vascular cases with arterial hypertension, Booth (3) found that M which were both primary and axial were produced by 10% of the locomotor group and by not one vascular case. However, secondary M which were also axial were given by 40% of the vascular patients and by no locomotor patients.

M AND CREATIVITY

The M type's "predominance of personalized productivity" is associated with a preference for thinking over feeling, a capacity for productive imagination and greater creative ability than is demonstrated by the color type. Roe's (18) studies showed that many leading representatives of the physical and physiological sciences produced few M, whereas psychologists and anthropologists gave many. There are several possible explanations of this finding and they are not mutually exclusive. One explanation lies in the definition of "creativeness." If being creative means producing something new that was unknown before, one could argue that it is possible to be a leading scientist or even an artist with little true creativeness. Modern mathematics is so complex and difficult that the mere mastery of several of its fields, though nothing new has been contributed, is a remarkable achievement. An artist can be an outstanding craftsman and produce noteworthy work even though he is essentially an imitator. Many scientists are renowned only because they have mastered techniques created by others and make sound use of these techniques.

There is no doubt that, other conditions being equal, the individual with many M has a much more lively intellect and a greater diversity of active interests than a person with few or no M. Conversely, the capacity to produce M is drastically reduced by organic brain disorders, particularly those which lead to irreversible deterioration. It would be wrong to infer from these findings that the more M the better. Rorschach noted that the maximum is not the optimum. This axiom applies to the M as well as to other components. The qualitative aspects of the M may be of greater importance than the quantitative ones. After all, it is not desirable to have large numbers of passive or compliant M. There is then the uncompleted task of setting up criteria for the optimum number of the M. A simple statistical survey, designed to check Rorschach's claim that the "number of M shows the most definite direct proportion to the variability [in content] of the responses . . . [and that] the direct proportion between the number of good original answers and the M responses is even more clear" (20, pp. 64–65) has not been carried out on any large number of subjects.

Another reason for the difficulty in demonstrating a high positive relationship between the number of M and intellectual creativeness may be related to the psychological function performed by Rorschach's perceptanalysis. This technique is not primarily a test of intelligence or of creative mental potentialities. When a very intelligent, sensitive, and creative individual is in a deep depression, his Rorschach record may not reveal either his superior intelligence or his creativeness. A depression may be severe enough to prevent the individual from manifesting his assets even in his Rorschach responses. This and similar examples warrant caution in the assessment of the potential of perceptanalysis. As a test of personality, perceptanalysis may reflect only those psychological traits or action tendencies which the individual utilizes in his relationships with others. The concept of human interrelationships and the role which the individual plays in them are central in the psychological definition of personality (13). If in a depression the patient loses all interest in others, his Rorschach becomes impoverished for the duration of the depression. This suggests the possible explanation that the creativeness indicated by the M reveals itself primarily in interpersonal relationships. Psychologists, psychiatrists, social workers, novelists, artists, and other individuals intensely interested in psychosocial relations produce, on the average, many more M than those whose interest in this area is weak or not genuine. Among the latter are engineers, financiers, physicists, anatomists, and many other scientists (18). The relatively low number of

M in highly intelligent and creative physicists might thus be explained by the nature of their greatest interest. They are interested primarily in inanimate matter and abstract formulas, their preoccupations and creative efforts being associated with nonhuman phenomena. This important problem, too, deserves more attention than it has received.

The further traits ascribed to the M type, intensive rapport and stable affect, together with awkward physical movements, cannot be investigated without simultaneous study of other test components which pertain to rapport and emotions, such as the number and quality of color responses, the M:sum C, and the $F+\%$. Intensive rapport can be studied more easily and decisively than can the combination of awkward physical movements and emotional stability. More significant than this combination is the apparent association of the number of M with pride or, more specifically, with a code of conduct which tends to forbid the use of easy ways out of difficulties and imposes complex or disadvantageous methods of handling social relations. This is an almost completely unexplored characteristic of the M type.

CHANGES IN M DURING THERAPY

Repeated examinations of ten nonpsychotic adult patients benefiting from intensive and prolonged psychotherapy showed that the quantity of the M changed more rapidly than their quality. The number of M was about doubled in the first six to twelve months of treatment, but the quality of the M underwent a slow and gradual development (17). These changes in the M, which paralleled the patients' clinical improvement, were marked mainly by two features. One was the increasing expansiveness and decrease in restraint in the movements of M figures. For example, at the beginning of treatment, the card-III figures would be lifting an object with difficulty due to the heavy weight of the object, the unsteady posture of the figures, or the absence of one leg, etc. At the end of treatment the lifting would take place with no reference to any difficulty. The other feature was the gradual change in the physical characteristics of the M figures, in the direction of similarity to the patient; i.e., when at the beginning of treatment the patients' M productions differed strikingly in physical traits from himself, there was a tendency for the M figures to resemble the patient more toward the end of treatment. Thus a movement might be performed by women in the first and by men in the last

Rorschach record of a male patient. In the case of the ten patients, only trends were established. Not every patient's M changed in the same way or to the same degree, but the changes tended to be in the same general direction of diminished aggressiveness, greater expansiveness, and increased use of M figures which closely resembled the subject physically. Some M, especially the undesirable ones—the passive, blocked, or aggressive variety—disappeared altogether. It is perhaps significant that the color responses changed in quality more easily than did the M, and the change during treatment in the absolute number of color responses differed more from patient to patient than did the number of M. The highly selected small group of ten patients is not, of course, representative. However, these findings do point up the desirability of checking the conclusions as to the great resistance of the M quality to change and the association of changes in the direction of a freer and more expansive M with clinical improvement under various conditions. If the number of the M varies more frequently and more widely than the quality of the M, and if the quality change is gradual and related to important personality changes, then the quality of the M may be more significant than the number of M for a personality analysis. If this can be demonstrated to be the case, then we have to assume, e.g., that schizophrenics demonstrating sudden and marked changes in the M quality without undergoing any treatment, must be undergoing important personality change.

M IN PERSONALITY DEVELOPMENT

If the M are indicators of a deep-seated conception of the individual's life role which strongly influences his interhuman relationships, and which does not change easily (17), it is worth finding out whether there are any general rules regulating the distribution and development of the different types of M, at least in the majority of the population. Because childhood is a period of intense growth and maturation, it is probable that, barring inhibitions, nearly all of us would have only expansive or extensor M, since this type of M seems to go with self-confidence and with an inner need for demonstrating to oneself and to others what one can do. During the first years of life, up to about the sixth year, many children produce no M at all. By the age of six, conflicts with adults could have led to a loss of self-confidence, a weakening in self-assertion (measured by the extensor M), and an appearance of compliance (flexor M). Constitutional weaknesses, congenital or acquired, lack of physical vigor (for whatever reason), lack of stamina theoretically may also favor the development of compliant M.

M AND PERSONALITY INTEGRATION

Incompatible M, flexor and extensor, occur at times in the same individual. Instead of qualifying one another, they seem rather to influence overt behavior at different times. The traits which the Rorschach perceptanalysis reveals are not manifest at all times. An individual's inner feelings and external conduct are not a result of the global effect of all his traits mutually modifying, strengthening, or weakening one another. This is an important principle which is disregarded by many. A lone but definitely aggressive M in a record with many compliant, even passive (e.g., "sleeping") M does not mean that the individual's compliance is tempered by an element of aggressiveness; it means rather that at times, possibly very infrequently, and probably under special circumstances, the individual behaves overtly in an aggressive way. The prediction of the manner in which the aggressiveness is manifested depends on the analysis of other components, especially of the sum of light shadings, sum of color responses, the number of whole responses, and the form level. The degree of personality integration seems to determine the degree to which the personality traits, represented by the various perceptanalytic components and their combinations, qualify one another's influence upon the individual's thoughts, feelings, and actions. It seems that the process of mutual qualifying grows more intense with integration and becomes less intense with decreasing integration. It is probably for this reason that the validation of Rorschach conclusions (most of which are based on an analysis of single or at best two components) is easier and more successful in the case of poorly integrated psychotics than in that of well-integrated normals. This is a problem which is hardly ever raised, let alone worked on, although it is a basic one for the process of validating Rorschach generalizations, including those about the M. The right combination of the pertinent components probably could provide a measure of the degree of personality integration.

MEANING OF FLEXOR AND EXTENSOR M

The exact meaning of the two main types of M, extensor (self-assertion) and flexor (compliance), must be defined clearly before verification of conclusions based on the M can begin to be valid. It is not certain that we are in possession of the best possible definitions. Self-assertion has been defined as the need to demonstrate one's capacities when challenged and when vital personal matters are involved (13). This does not necessarily imply activity or initiative. An exhibitionist is self-assertive but may not be active and may not display any initiative in trying to dominate or direct other people. In fact, too much confidence in one's potential worth tends to discourage diligence and inventiveness. Compliance has been defined as a need to lean on a psychologically powerful person in whose benevolent protection the compliant individual may develop activity and initiative when challenged or threatened in one of his vital interests. Apparently the greatest need of a compliant person is to feel the protection (not necessarily guidance) of someone strong and willing enough to take the final responsibility for the compliant person who trusts him. Compliance, then, according to this definition, is not synonymous with passivity or submissiveness. Many a person with compliant M is quite active and inventive. On the other hand there are M which plainly suggest passivity and avoidance of challenge and initiative; e.g., a very intelligent and educated young man who underwent a marked personality change after his first severe schizophrenic episode interpreted the reversed card V as "two gentlemen peacefully sleeping in coffins," a response which epitomized his changed fundamental conception of his life role. Anyone who tries to develop a detailed scheme for the classification of the numerous varieties of M (of which the extensor and flexor are prominent but not the only subgroups) will soon discover how difficult a task it is to interpret the meaning of the M according to consistent, objective, and standardized rules of interpretation. A very detailed inquiry of each M, during which the subject is encouraged to elaborate on and free-associate to his M percepts, facilitates this task greatly.

The conclusions inferred from the difference between flexor and extensor M are not valid unless the blots into which the M have been projected elicit both types of M with equal ease and plausibility. In such a case, the personality of the subject determines the type of M, and, consequently, conclusions regarding the subject's personality can be made from the type of M he has produced. If a blot favors one type of M and makes it hard to see the other because of strong visual clues, the blot is not a valid instrument to measure self-assertion versus compliance. The Levy movement finger paintings (9) are sometimes used to experiment with M. It is customary to follow Levy's procedure and to ask subjects to visualize people in his finger paintings, and then inquire about the activity of the imaginary people. Once subjects "see" human beings there (which is not difficult), they see them far more frequently in flexor than in extensor movements. The suggestion of flexor movements is strong regardless of whether the human beings are perceived spontaneously or at the suggestion of the examiner. This factor alone introduces an essential difference between the psychological meaning of the Levy movement responses and the M elicited by the Rorschach plates. No equivalence can be assumed between the movement responses obtained by these two methods.

ANIMAL AND INANIMATE MOVEMENT

Rorschach had but one movement response category. Any response, regardless of content, is an M according to Rorschach's criterion provided it is accompanied by a kinesthetic experience. Rorschach said explicitly that some individuals are capable of responding with a kinesthetic experience even to inanimate and geometric forms, e.g., a spiral, a bridge, a volcano. He also said that many subjects respond similarly to animal forms. Despite this plain statement according to which all these responses should be scored M, Rorschach did not score animal movements and inanimate movements as M. In the *Psychodiagnostics* proper, not a single animal movement is scored M. The sole exceptions are animals whose physical movements are almost identical with those of humans, e.g., bears standing up and kissing, monkeys bowing. Monkeys hanging by their tails, however, would not be an M because this is a movement or posture which humans cannot perform. In the blind analysis (which is appended to the *Psychodiagnostics*), Rorschach again took animal and inanimate movements out of the M category, but this time he provided for those movements a separate category: F tending toward M. This is one of many proofs of Rorschach's sense of reality and respect for clinical facts.

He observed that animal and inanimate movements did not have the same meaning as human movements, and he preferred to be inconsistent in his definition of the M rather than to go counter to his experience. The problem is whether to treat the nonhuman movements as special movement responses and, to be consistent, modify the requirements for the scoring of human and nonhuman movements, or whether to treat the nonhuman movements as pure form responses. Klopfer (8) and the author (12, 13) have separate scoring symbols for the animal movements, FM, and the inanimate movements, m. However, their psychological interpretation of the assumed meaning of the FM and m is not identical. Klopfer views the FM as an indicator of instinctual forces which are near the conscious level and threaten to influence overt behavior; if the FM are more numerous than the M, Klopfer feels that we deal with immaturity in psychological development. I have suggested that the FM are positively though not necessarily highly correlated with physical vigor; subjects with many FM do not mind physical exertion. I also believe that the FM reveal action tendencies likely to become apparent in the subject's behavior when he is in a state of diminished consciousness, i.e., in a state of altered consciousness, of intoxication, severe debilitating anxiety, great physical fatigue, exhaustion through illness, etc. This interpretation of the M relies on several premises. First, it is assumed that the M, FM, and m represent potential behavior patterns, each of which can be reflected in the individual's overt behavior. Second, the action tendencies represented by each movement response can at times influence the individual's behavior with little or no interference from action tendencies represented by other movement responses, be they M, FM, or m. It is highly unlikely that two M which disclose incompatible behavior patterns, e.g., a strikingly assertive and strongly compliant one, would be manifested outwardly at the same time. Third, it is assumed that if any of the FM is more expansive than the most expansive M, i.e., if it expresses a movement in which the force of gravity and inertia are overcome with greater ease and speed than in the most confident and assertive M, the individual is likely to behave in a more active and expansive manner when his consciousness is diminished than when his span of consciousness is broad and deep and he is functioning efficiently. Thus, a man with FM that are more expansive than his M is likely to be more outgoing, active, and enterprising when intoxicated than when sober, and vice versa. This was a conclusion based on a study of sexual offenders, about half of whom were under the influence of alcohol when committing the aggressive offense (14). Should the principle regarding this psychological implication of the difference between the quality of M and that of FM be true of all subjects and of all states of diminished consciousness and not only of alcoholic intoxication, the usefulness of the Rorschach method would be extended greatly. The establishment of such a principle would greatly advance the search for a good experimental measure with which to attack problems of personality integration versus the extent of being at cross purposes with oneself.

The FM action tendencies probably represent the life roles which were dominant in early childhood, up to about the fourth or sixth year of life, but are not the dominant ones at present (12). During treatment the quality of the FM changes at times. One might infer from this that, even if the FM represent past basic conceptions of life role, they disclose only some of them. It was observed that when the M change, the FM too change accordingly (17), but more observations are needed before we can be definite about this. Presumably the roots of the M life roles also go back into the past. The differences between them and the FM life roles appear to be twofold: First, the FM life roles failed to be integrated into the core of personality and did not develop into forces which motivate the individual when he is in a state of highest personality integration, in such a way that his various mental functions, conscious and unconscious (motives of which he is unaware), act in relative harmony; in these states of greatest personal integration, it is the M that are believed to influence the individual's goals and conduct. The second difference is that the FM —provided they are qualitatively different from the M—reflect the life roles dominant in the individual's past, while the M reflect the life roles dominant in the present; conversely, the M are less important indicators of the past than are the FM.

It was suggested (12) that the inanimate movement response category, symbolized by the small letter m, be reserved exclusively for movements or positions (dynamic balance) of inanimate objects, either solid, liquid, or gaseous; e.g., "plane flying," "volcano erupting," "clouds driven across the skies," "rocks balanced on a semicircular base," "smoke rising," "ocean waves breaking on the shore," or a power holding these inanimate objects apart. If the m refer exclusively to inanimate objects in movement or in dynamic balance, they might be presumed to represent wished-for life roles which the individual feels to be beyond his ability to assume; such conviction about the unattainability of the m role implies being conscious of limitations and thus points to a feeling of bitterness and some depression (13). Some support for this meaning of m is provided by the observation that after successful psychotherapy the m tend to disappear altogether or to change into human movements. In other words, they are given up and are no longer desired, or they become realizable by changing into M (17).

Only a minority of subjects, practically all of them of at least average intelligence and with a well-developed habit of psychological self-observation produced m; and a still smaller minority produce more than one m. Eighteen of 50 schizophrenics of a mean high average intelligence produced at least one m; 7 produced more than one. When re-examined, after an average interval of 4 years, 17 gave at least one m, and 8 gave more than one. Half of 50 neurotics with a mean high average intelligence produced at least one m, and 7 of them produced more than one. In a sample of 40 normals, all with I.Q.'s of over 115 and nearly all college-educated, m were found in 27 records; 14 subjects had more than one m. Most of the m are extensor, containing percepts of movements overcoming the force of gravity. The most frequent single m is "explosion." This response can be interpreted as pointing to a desire for an unrestrained and powerfully assertive handling of interpersonal relationships; however, there is no danger that such unbridled actions will be carried out, because—by definition—every m expresses an unrealizable wish. Passive m ("water dripping," "plane falling") indicate an unrealizable wish to give up striving and competitiveness, and to surrender to strong environmental forces; it may be further assumed that a counterforce such as fear of possible consequences of passive surrender is responsible for making the wish appear unrealizable to the individual who harbors it. Passive and destructive m ("house falling apart") are quite rare and are produced by very masochistic and morbid individuals.

Klopfer's "minor movements" are not identical with my m. The Klopfer m concept is broader and includes (in addition to movements of inanimate objects) grotesque faces, masks, symbols, i.e., representation of sexual force, and even "ambiguous dynamic terms" (e.g., "man hanging," "attached to something") when it is not clear whether the response is a genuine movement response of any kind, human, animal, or inanimate (8, pp. 114–125). Although Klopfer did not change the scoring of his "minor movements," he revised their meaning, saying that they reveal "an awareness of conflict which might exist either between different impulses within the personality or between the impulses of the individual and some frustrating forces in the environment; this awareness serves as a 'warning system' against seeking immediate gratification for such impulses" (8, p. 579). This new definition is compatible with the idea that the *m* (provided they are limited to inanimate movements or their active suspension) disclose desirable but unrealizable attitudes towards others in personally vital matters (13). The frustrating opposition of others has a great deal to do with an individual's conviction that some of his wishes are unrealizable. In the Rorschach literature the *m* have received little attention as a separate perceptanalytic component. Their textual content is frequently interpreted with the aid of such symbols as used in psychoanalysis. The conclusions drawn therefrom are as uncertain as our knowledge of symbols.

It is hoped that this chapter demonstrates the progress that has been made in exploration of the challenging but complex area of human and nonhuman movement responses. Full logical clarification and validation of the concepts involved, however, must await further investigation by relevant empirical observations and experiments.

BIBLIOGRAPHY

1. Bash, K. W. Einstellungstypus and Erlebnistypus: C. G. Jung and Hermann Rorschach. *J. proj. Tech.*, 1955, 19, 236–242.
2. Beck, S. J. *Rorschach's test. I. Basic processes.* New York: Grune and Stratton, 1949.
3. Booth, G. C. Organ function and form perception: Use of the Rorschach method with cases of chronic arthritis, parkinsonism, and arterial hypertension. *Psychosom. Med.*, 1945, 8, 367–385.
4. Brecher, S. The Rorschach reaction patterns of maternally overprotected and maternally rejected schizophrenic patients. *J. nerv. ment. Dis.*, 1956, 123, 41–52.
5. Hammer, E. F., and Jacks, I. A study of Rorschach flexor and extensor human movement responses. *J. clin. Psychol.*, 1955, 11, 63–67.
6. Hay, E. N., and Associates. Monograph on top managers. Philadelphia, Pa. (To be published.)
7. Jung, C. G. *Psychological types.* New York: Harcourt, Brace, 1933. (1st ed., 1921.)
8. Klopfer, B., Ainsworth, D., Klopfer, W. G., and Holt, R. *Developments in the Rorschach technique: technique and theory. Vol. I.* Yonkers: World Book Co., 1954.
9. Levy, D. M. *Levy movement cards.* Madison: College Typing Co., 1948.
10. Meltzoff, J., Singer, J. L., and Korchin, S. J. Motor inhibition and Rorschach movement responses. *J. Pers.*, 1953, 21, 400–410.
11. Mirin, B. The Rorschach human movement response and role taking behavior. *J. nerv. ment. Dis.*, 1955, 122, 270–275.
12. Piotrowski, Z. A. The *M, FM* and *m* responses as indicators of changes in personality. *Rorschach Research Exch.*, 1937, 1, 148–157.

13. Piotrowski, Z. A. *Perceptanalysis: A fundamentally reworked, expanded, and systematized Rorschach method.* New York: Macmillan, 1957.

14. Piotrowski, Z. A., and Abrahamsen, D. Sexual crime, alcohol, and the Rorschach test. *Psychiat. Quart: Suppl.,* 1952, **26**, 248–260.

15. Piotrowski, Z. A., and Bricklin, B. A long-term prognostic criterion for schizophrenics based on Rorschach data. *Psychiat. Quart. Suppl.,* 1958, **32**, 315–329.

16. Piotrowski, Z. A., and Dudek, S. Z. Research on human movement response in the Rorschach examinations of marital partners. In: V. W. Eisenstein (ed.). *Neurotic interaction in marriage.* New York: Basic Books, 1956, 192–207.

17. Piotrowski, Z. A., and Schreiber, M. Rorschach perceptanalytic measurement of personality changes during and after intensive psychoanalytically oriented psychotherapy. In: G. Bychowski and J. L. Despert (eds.). *Specialized techniques in psychotherapy.* New York: Basic Books, 1952, 337–361.

18. Roe, A. A psychological study of eminent psychologists and anthropologists, and a comparison with biological and physical scientists. *Amer. Psychol. Assoc.,* 1953, **67**, No. 352.

19. Roemer, G. A. Vom Rorschachtest zum Symboltest. *Zbl. Psychotherapie,* 1938, **10**, No. 6.

20. Rorschach, H. The application of the form interpretation test. In: *Psychodiagnostics: a diagnostic test based on perception.* Bern: Hans Huber, 1942, 184–216. (1st ed., 1921.)

21. Sarason, S. B. *The clinical interaction: with special reference to the Rorschach.* New York: Harper, 1954.

22. Schafer, R. *Psychoanalytic interpretation in Rorschach testing: theory and application.* New York: Grune and Stratton, 1954.

23. Singer, J. L., Meltzoff, J., and Goldman, G. D. Rorschach movement responses following motor inhibition and hyperactivity. *J. consult. Psychol.,* 1956, **53**, 42–47.

Vowels: black A, white E, red I, green U,
blue O,
Someday I shall name the birth from which
you rise. . . .[*]

J. N. Arthur Rimbaud

7

by David Shapiro

A
PERCEPTUAL UNDERSTANDING
OF COLOR RESPONSE [†]

INTRODUCTION

The practical Rorschach problem of the interpretive meaning of color response has not been a subject of much debate among clinical Rorschach workers. It is safe to say that there are not many working with this test clinically who would disagree, in essentials, with Rorschach's own original formulation: [‡]

The *C* and *CF* answers express the more ego-centric affective responsiveness, while the more adaptive affective responsiveness is expressed in the number of *FC*'s (22, p. 33).

However, notwithstanding its general acceptance and its wide areas of clinical applicability, it must be noted that in certain specifics this formulation has not always proved to be an accurate one. For example, ordinary clinical experience suggests at least two types of cases —severe narcissistic or psychopathic character disorders and chronic schizophrenics—in whose Rorschachs pure color or color-dominated responses may appear conspicuously without evidence of corresponding affect-experience in the ordinary sense. Nor has the general acceptance of Rorschach's interpretive principle linking color with affect

[*] Translated by Muriel Rukeyser.
[†] This article has been completed with the aid of research grant M–2477(C1) from the U.S. Public Health Service.
[‡] For explanation of scoring symbols, see Appendix, pp. 441 ff. [Editor].

been matched by an equally wide acceptance of any of the proposed explanations of this linkage.

Some Rorschach workers, convinced of the linkage but not able to explain it, have in effect tried to skip over the problem of rationale simply by assuming some sort of given, intrinsic affective value to color. Others have assumed the existence of culturally established, highly charged and affective associations to colors. But as has often been pointed out, this explanation does not explain; at best it only postpones the explanation.

An understanding of the meaning of color response can come only through an understanding of the perceptual processes involved in it. Specifically, the issues are these: Does color perception, and therefore color response, involve special perceptual processes which are essentially different, for example, from those involved in form perception? If so, different in what respects? And, can the nature of those differences clarify the interpretive meaning of color response, especially in those cases where the affect-color linkage seems not to hold up?

The aim here will be to answer these questions, which have, I believe, an intrinsic interest quite aside from their practical implications for test interpretation. In line with this aim, we will put aside for the time being questions of the interpretive meaning of color response, and first concentrate only on the nature of color experience and the color response process as such.

It is important to begin with a reminder to the reader of the three basic contributions, in addition to Rorschach's own discussion, to the understanding of color response. These are: Schachtel's (23), Rickers-Ovsiankina's (19), and Rapaport's et al. (17). Each of these contributions takes as its starting point the assumed relationship between color response and affect, but each also contains certain views, or certain principles, of color perception or color response as such. It is not possible to summarize the three contributions here, but I would like simply to indicate these views or principles of color perception, since the following discussion will lean on them, particularly on Rapaport's, quite heavily.

Schachtel refers to the subjective experience of seeing color. He points out that this experience is of something perceived without effort of will, or of one's attention being captured, in contrast to the experience of form perception. He suggests the example of walking into a room in which there is a colored area on the wall—the color "seizes" one. The perception of color, therefore, requires little activity on the part of the perceiver and may be described as primarily a *passive* process.

Rickers-Ovsiankina speaks more explicitly of the nature of the perceptual processes themselves. A color perception, she states, is a relatively *direct* sense datum as compared with the complex, more energy-consuming processes, e.g., of gestalt organization, involved in form perception. Color perception may also be described, therefore, as a more *immediate* process than form perception. Rickers-Ovsiankina presents important evidence for this point, some of which will be referred to later (see pp. 10 ff. of this book).

Rapaport's emphasis is somewhat different. He considers, first of all, that color response is merely an indicator of affective response, not necessarily affectively toned in itself any more than the dial of a gasoline gage needs to contain fluid. Although he does not discuss explicitly the nature of color experience as such, he speaks to the problem of the integration of the "impact" of color with articulated form. The Freudian concept of capacity to delay tension discharge is central to Rapaport's discussion, and he indicates that, in general, the more successfully form-integrated color responses reflect a capacity for such delay sufficient to allow for the optimal integration of color impression and form. The color-dominated responses, in contrast, generally represent an insufficient integration of the perceptual impact of color with form; and the pure *C* responses reflect a "short-circuiting," an absence of the delay capacity which is a precondition for further perceptual and associative elaboration. One may assume therefore that, from this point of view, color experience as such *requires less complex psychological organization* (i.e., discharge-delaying organization) than the perceptual articulation of form.

I have previously [Shapiro (27)] attempted to define a mode of perception which may be associated with color experience in general, and I have proposed in that connection the concept of *perceptual passivity.*[1] This concept, I believe, is essentially consistent with the views of color perception contained in the three contributions described, with one qualification regarding Schachtel's position which is discussed below.

Perceptual passivity refers to the perceiver's relationship to the visual stimuli. It means a condition of relative absence, immobilization, or

---

[1] Suggested by a concept of activity-passivity developed by Rapaport (16) in connection with drive-restraining psychological organizations, i.e., "activity" describing a condition of active organization, control, and modulation of drives, and "passivity" describing a condition of helplessness in the face of those drives.

temporary relaxation of active perceptual organizing capacities, and, accordingly, a condition in which the perceptual experience is to a large extent dominated by, and subject to, the most immediately manifest and sensorially most vivid aspects of the visual surroundings, such as color. Such perception would tend to be, *though would not necessarily be,* associated with conditions of impaired or less highly developed psychological organization. And perception of this sort, in contrast to perception which organizes more actively such as in complex perceptual form articulation, would ordinarily be accompanied by a subjective feeling of passivity of the sort Schachtel describes, an experience of being held, distracted, or struck by the stimulus. But, this subjective feeling of passivity is not a reliable indicator of the objective condition of passivity in the sense described; the *feeling* of passivity, in such a connection, may be avoided, as will be demonstrated later. With this qualification, therefore, the assumption that color experience tends to be associated with a passive mode of perception is consistent with the three views described above.

One corollary, namely, a developmental one, may be added to this conception of color perception. We know, from Werner's work (31) in particular, that perception undergoes a development, in mode or style, from infancy to adulthood. Werner indicates that the very young child is "stimulus-bound," i.e., he is passively subjected to sensory stimulation. In contrast, he describes, normal adult perception is relatively more free from the influence of adventitious aspects of sensory stimulation, and is characterized by increased articulation and increased dominance of form as the basis of reaction to stimuli. This picture of perceptual development suggests that color experience tends to be a more prominent aspect of visual life in childhood than in maturity.

These formulations regarding color perception will be considered in the following sections as working hypotheses, to be examined in the light of certain experimental, clinical, and Rorschach literature. I believe these hypotheses to be essentially sound, but the place of color experience in perception is by no means settled by them. The data to be considered have, therefore, not been selected with a view merely to substantiate these initial formulations or to render them more convincing, but rather to clarify and extend them. In the final section, the interpretive or clinical significance of color response, and with it the question of the color-affect relationship, will be reconsidered and the formulations will be recast.

DATA ON COLOR PERCEPTION

The data that will be taken up in this section are not for the most part Rorschach data but pertain more to color perception in various other situations. The studies considered fall roughly into three groups: (1) Developmental data including experimental studies of children's sorting behavior that seem to throw light on certain aspects of children's perception, and some data from developmental Rorschach studies; (2) studies of special pathological states—schizophrenic and brain-damage conditions—in which certain changes in perception appear and seem associated with thought disorder; and (3) the material collected by Senden (26), describing the early visual experiences of previously blind people with surgically repaired vision.

Color Perception in Children

The relative prominence of color in the visual experience of very young children is obvious even to the casual observer. Their response to brightly colored objects, as compared with uncolored or less saturated ones, is unmistakable.[2] It is quite clear also, in general observation, that this response is not only a matter of sensory pleasure, but is more far-reaching. Objects tend, to a much greater extent among children than adults, to be *identified* primarily or exclusively in terms of color. For example: a 2½-year-old child sees a brilliantly colored maple tree in autumn, at a range quite close enough for her to identify even the shape of the leaves; she can readily identify them when they are green but, in this case, exclaims that it is an apple tree. A good deal of experimental work appears to confirm this heightened significance of color for children.

A number of studies have been carried out on object-sorting behavior in children which are of interest here for one reason in particular: the experimental task, which is usually to sort simple geometrically formed objects either on the basis of form or color, has an appreciable perceptual component.

Revesz (18) and Thompson (29) have reported such studies, and additional studies of this sort are described by Werner (31). The results indicate a clear tendency in the groups of young children to

---

[2] Children's preference for bright colors, in contrast to adults' preference for pastels, is documented in a study by Honkavaara (11).

sort initially on the basis of color rather than on the basis of form—
at least as "form" is defined by such materials as triangles, circles,
squares, etc. Several similar studies have been made on a relatively
large scale with subject populations covering a fairly wide and continuous age range, an advantage over those which compare younger
children with only one or two older age groups. Descoudres, in an
experiment described by Werner, and Lindberg (15), using his ring
test,[3] have been able to demonstrate a more or less *continuously* increased preference for form and decreased preference for color as a
sorting basis through the age ranges of 3 to 18, and 7 to 14 respectively.

Since these experimental tasks put no special logical advantage on
either the color or the form sorting, it seems justifiable to assume that
the results reflect, at least in part, a developmental change of a perceptual sort, i.e., a change in the relative perceptual importance of
form and color factors within the task. Insofar as the direction of this
change is clearly toward a decrease in the significance of color with
age and maturation, the results support our general assumptions.
However, it is not clear from the data alone exactly what this developmental shift in the significance of color consists of. The difficulty
of interpreting the results is, in fact, compounded by a special problem, namely, the likelihood that the task itself is subjectively something different for the younger children from what it is for the older
ones or for adults. It is likely, for example, that for the youngest
children tested the task is one of immediate identification of the most
manifest similarity among the objects presented. For the older subjects, the task is probably something closer to finding the logically most
essential aspect of the objects or representations, even though the nature of the test does not prejudice the logical choice one way or the
other.

Three ways of understanding the development suggest themselves:
(1) The difference in *attitude* toward the task and in *understanding*
of its nature, and the undoubted inclination of the younger children
to proceed in a more immediate and less detached fashion are primarily responsible for the shift from color emphasis to form emphasis; (2)

[3] Lindberg's results are especially clear-cut, possibly because his procedures
involve printed material and thus escape the problem, which is often insufficiently
considered, of whether a child's form-choice has more to do with the perceived
form configuration or with concrete object qualities of the cut-out forms. I imagine that this problem is one of the reasons why studies of this sort do not *always*
show the sort of development described, although the preponderance of such
studies do.

the shift represents a *perceptual development* in which color experience actually comes to occupy a modified and on the whole less significant position in visual life; and (3) there may be, along with maturation, an actual *diminution of color sensitivity*, as the psychophysicist would measure it. These three possibilities by no means exclude each other, and it is not out of the question that all three are correct. It is, in other words, possible that the more immediate response and less detached attitude of the younger children are associated with a mode of perception in which such sensory qualities as color have heightened significance and are actually subjectively more vivid. These issues will come up again later in connection with other data.

It is of interest to compare the results of the sorting studies of children with developmental Rorschach data. Systematic Rorschach studies as well as clinical reports on children's Rorschachs seem quite consistent and unvarying regarding the appearance of color response in children. Klopfer and Margulies (14), Ford (4), Ames (1), and Halpern (7) have all described that among the color responses in Rorschach records of very young children pure *C* responses tend to predominate; in somewhat older children *CF* responses occupy a more important role and the pure *C* responses drop out rapidly; and at a still later age, *FC* responses play an increasing part. It is not necessary to consider here the specific age ranges which seem to be correlated with these phases.

There is, however, one aspect of the Rorschach data on children which seems, at first, to contradict the general picture of a more or less continuous development from a predominance of pure *C* to increasingly form-dominated color response. Most Rorschach workers have noted the fact that, among the very youngest children tested— 2 to 2½ years of age, for example—color responses tend to be few or even to be absent altogether. This matter, noteworthy in itself, also involves certain more general issues that warrant discussion.

The explanation of the apparent discontinuity in the development of color response can be found in the nature of the demands which the Rorschach itself imposes. The Rorschach test does not require of a subject simply any perceptual reaction. It requires rather a response that meets certain standards of conceptualization if it is to be counted as a *response* at all. The Rorschach instructions, regardless of their minor variations, clearly indicate that mere verbal expression of a sensory impression of color is inadequate. What is called for is the integration of that impression with form aspects of the card, if possible, or at the least an integration of the color impression with an appropriate, more or less realistically representational content. As far as the Rorschach is concerned, most pure C responses are already at the bottom of the conceptual scale; mere color naming is generally considered off the response scale altogether (some Rorschach workers considering such responses to be in the pure C category, others not counting them among responses at all). However, it is clear that color responsiveness in children, if one foregoes the technical response standards of the Rorschach test, extends far below this conceptual level. For example, Werner (31) indicates that, on the basis of studies of bodily reactions, very young infants seem to be able to discriminate the primary colors.

The absence, therefore, of what may be technically accepted as color responses in the Rorschachs of very young children by no means indicates an actual absence of responsiveness to the color stimulus. The situation can be summed up as follows: As one goes *down* the chronological scale, Rorschach responses altogether become progressively more diffuse, global, and concrete and, correspondingly, the predominant mode of color response shifts from *FC* to *CF* to pure *C*; before this, color may well occupy a prominent part in the over-all impression but this is the point at which the Rorschach response scale, so to speak, stops. The significance of this issue in evaluating the Rorschach data on children with respect to color response is easily illustrated. Both Ames and Ford, for example, consider color-naming responses as beneath the conceptual level required for Rorschach responses, and they do not include color naming in their over-all tabulations or in their tabulations of pure color responses. Ford, however, reports that 48% of her three-year olds gave color-naming responses, and Ames also reports a high incidence of color naming in the early age range. These tabulation procedures, as far as ordinary Rorschach work is concerned, are not in question, but the apparent absence of color responsiveness in very young children looks very different in this light.[4]

[4] It may be mentioned that essentially the same issue appears in Stein's (28) tachistoscopic experiment with the Rorschach. With normal adults as subjects, he administered the Rorschach tachistoscopically, the exposures ranging down to .01 second. In general, the bright color determinants steadily *decreased* as exposure time was *increased*. Pure color responses dropped especially rapidly with increased exposure time. In apparent contradiction to this development, at the very shortest exposure time, Stein found a drop in color responses. He indicates, however, that the card was considered rejected and no responses were counted if the subject responded in such a way as the following: "It looked like it was col-

Dworetzky (2, 3) makes essentially this same point in connection with her extensive developmental study, and offers some empirical confirmation of it. With her Rorschach subjects (2) from approximately 4 years old through puberty she found, in line with the other work described, a gradual diminution of pure color and color-dominated responses in favor of form-dominated responses. Among her three- to four-year-old subjects, however, color tended to drop out altogether as a basis for scorable responses, very much as has been described. She was able to note, however, that various aspects of the test behavior and other aspects of the test performance of these children (e.g., number of subjects who gave their first response to a red area) indicated the attraction and stimulation value of the color for them, notwithstanding that they were not, at this age, able to use the color to produce scorable responses.[5]

With this amendment, the Rorschach data on children are quite consistent with the sorting results described but, in at least one sense, they offer more. The sorting data are, aside from behavioral observations, limited to a single dimension: the number who sort one way as compared with the number who sort another way. The quantitative Rorschach data, however, contain additional dimensions, namely, those defined by the Rorschach scores, and it is accordingly possible to see clearly an answer to one question which could not be answered on the basis of the sorting studies alone. Although the Rorschach data do not indicate that color responsiveness *per se* diminishes with development, they do indicate unmistakably that the relative significance of color as the central and overriding aspect of the percept diminishes. What can only appear in the sorting data as a progressive diminution in number of color choices, appears in the Rorschach data to be a modification of the position of color in the final percept, namely, from an immediate color experience which tends to dominate a final percept to one in which the color is progressively integrated, in essentially a secondary position, with form articulation. Dworetzky (2) relates this change in the nature of color response

---

ored but it didn't mean anything to me" (28, p. 363). It seems clear, in this illustration, that color was in fact an effective stimulus, but that there was insufficient time for sufficient mobilization of the organizing and associative processes necessary to arrive at a percept which would be technically acceptable as a Rorschach response.

[5] In her recent article, Dworetzky (3) does not seem to extend this same interpretation to the data of her youngest group (2.4–3.6 years), where color responses are few, for reasons that are not clear to me. She reiterates it, however, in connection with the 3.6- to 5-year group.

to a more general perceptual development from a "receptive and global" stage to a more "active and analytic" one.

Perceptual Tendencies Associated with Impairment of Thought Processes

Studies of schizophrenic and brain-damaged patients with color-form sorting tests (or the more complex Vigotsky test) offer valuable data on perceptual tendencies in these groups also, especially so since certain of these studies include relatively detailed clinical or behavioral description.

Weigl's study (30) on patients with cerebral lesions and Hanfmann and Kasanin's (9) on schizophrenic patients show a consistent result in regard to color versus form preference. These patients, in contrast to normal adults, have a decided tendency to make sortings *first* or *exclusively* on the basis of color.

In addition to the quantitative results, however, these investigators observed certain qualities of behavior or attitude which tended to be associated, respectively, with color and form sorting. Repeatedly, these authors describe the apparently passive, gripped, or stimulus-bound quality of the patient's perception of the material in connection particularly with its color qualities.

Weigl, for example, says, in describing his impression of the (typical) color choice of one of the brain-damaged patients: this response "*was forced upon* [him] by the sensorially manifest aspects of the situation" (30, p. 2) [my emphasis].

This is in contrast to the apparent attitude of detachment and reflective choice which is usual in the normal subjects and is typically associated with form choice.

Weigl explored further the differences in attitude associated with the form and color choice respectively by inquiring into the immediate responses of the normal subjects when they first looked at the given material and before they had time for reflection. It turned out that, "without exception . . . their first impression was that of 'color variety' in which the colors of similar qualities seemed to join together" (30, p. 10). Here again, the subjective experience of something happening, visually, beyond deliberate control in connection with the immediate color response is noteworthy ("seemed to join together").

In Hanfmann and Kasanin's study of thinking in schizophrenia (9), with the Vigotsky test, observations of this sort are described in greater detail. Specifically, these authors note a relationship, although a significantly limited one, between the visual qualities of the materials to which their subjects seemed to respond and the level of thinking, primitive or concrete, "intermediate," or abstract and truly conceptual, which they demonstrated in the test. They state:

Color, and to a lesser degree general size (height and area), seem to have a more immediate perceptual, at times even physiognomic appeal, and consequently prevail on the primitive level. Shape (prevails as a basis for sorting) on the intermediate level . . . on the level of true classifications there seems to be no definite preference for any one quality of the blocks . . . (9, pp. 39–40).

On the most primitive, concrete level the sorting is not made with a detached, "objective" attitude or with any concept or principle in mind; it is made rather on the basis of the most (visually) impressive groupings which immediately "thrust themselves" upon the subjects. On this level, characteristic of the schizophrenic patients, the sortings tend to be made in terms of color. At a higher level, the "intermediate" level, there is a somewhat greater tendency toward a detached attitude and a conceptual principle, and here the shape of the objects seems to outrank color in its perceptual significance and becomes the basis of sorting. At the highest conceptual level, characteristic of the more intelligent normal-control cases, the attitude is a detached and objective one, and the subject is no longer *directed by* the immediate sensory or perceptual impressions but can, as it were, *make use of* these impressions, shift freely from one to another, and consider them without bias for the purpose of solving the logical task.[6]

The pertinence of these studies of thought disorder is twofold:

[6] The substantial identity of these conclusions with those of Goldstein and Scheerer (6), and others in studies of abstract and concrete behavior, is evident. Goldstein and Scheerer do not report, and are essentially not interested in, the relative frequencies of color and form choices. Their interest is rather in description of the qualities of the abstract and concrete attitudes (e.g., dependence upon a unique aspect of an individual object; "matching" as opposed to "sorting"; capacity to learn with aids; shifting; etc.), either of which may eventuate in color or form choice where those are alternatives. It is undoubtedly true that there is no perfect relationship between the operating mode of perception or attitude and the final sorting choice (form or color). This fact was mentioned in connection with the sorting studies of children, and another aspect of the same fact is indicated in the Hanfmann-Kasanin results described above. Nevertheless, the general tendency for color choice to be associated with the more concrete attitudes seems clear. This is implicit in the Goldstein-Scheerer monograph also, particularly in their repeated emphasis on passive "surrender" to the most sensorially vivid aspects of the stimulus as one critical feature of the concrete attitude.

First of all, they confirm our expectation of an increase in the signifi-cance of color under circumstances of disorganization or primitiviza-tion of thought. Secondly, they give evidence of the behavioral and subjective attitude of passivity in relation to the visual stimulus which is associated with this increased color significance. The second fact gives special meaning to the first. It indicates that the significance of color in these conditions is not merely increased but also different in quality. These differences in the quality and significance of color experience appear then to reflect differences of a more general sort in the mode of perception, and, at the same time, in thought organization. Although the normal subjects,[7] as a whole, are undoubtedly perfectly capable of considering the color, or of weighing in a detached way its possible significance, it does not have for them the compelling, grip-ping quality [8] that it has for the pathological subjects.[9]

The question that was raised before, concerning whether the heightened perceptual significance of color or its compelling quality is associated also with heightened subjective vividness and a lowered color threshold, as a psychophysicist would measure it, is still not answered. Some light, though it is not conclusive, is thrown on this interesting question by the work of Senden (26) discussed in the following.

[7] Of course, when we speak here of "normal" adult perception, we refer to the general group tendency. Hanfmann (8), with the Vigotsky test, was able to dis-tinguish several groups along the same dimension among normal subjects. She found that her subjects could be divided according to their approach to the task as follows: (1) those whose approach was characterized by "active thinking"— "subjects of this type show a strong preference for shape as a basis for groupings," and (2) those she characterizes as intuitive, "in whose approach the perceptual . . . factors seem to predominate." These subjects, she reports, favor color and over-all size of blocks in groupings. Of course, perceptual factors operate in the response of both groups, but in different ways. The division must be between those whose perception and response tend to be more passively dominated by the gross sensory aspects of the stimulus, and the more "active" subjects whose perception is not dominated by these aspects and whose approach is in terms of what would ordinarily be logically more relevant features, primarily shape.

[8] See also, in this connection, the concept of the "insistence" value of color in the gestalt literature, e.g., Katz (13).

[9] Clinical observations of brain-damaged patients, e.g., Schilder (25), also pro-vide very interesting descriptions of the increased significance of color and the modifications in its appearance under these circumstances. It is an open, but interesting, question whether the greatly increased vividness and the compelling quality of colors in the case of a person under the influence of Mescaline or similar drugs, e.g., Huxley (12), can be related to the same general process.

Visual Pathology: Senden's Survey

The last data to be taken up concern perceptual experiences associated with a certain type of visual pathology. These are the remarkable data on the early visual experiences of the newly seeing (after operation) formerly blind, collected by Senden (26).

The most significant features of these data, from the standpoint of our interest, may be summarized as follows: In the earliest visual experiences of these previously blind people, there is a remarkable deficiency in form vision. Not only is there an initial incapacity to recognize forms (on the basis of anticipated transfer from previous, nonvisual familiarity), which would not be so surprising to us, but there is an extraordinary difficulty in this initial phase in *learning* to identify forms or in learning to "see" forms of any degree of complexity. For example, even after a period of some weeks of visual experience, a typical patient had extreme difficulty in distinguishing a triangular cardboard cutout from a circular one, and the distinction could finally be made only by laboriously tracing the edge, visually, taking note of corners, etc.

In contrast to this marked incapacity for perceptual form-articulation, color recognition was very rapid in this initial stage, almost immediate for most of the patients reported. It is, however, not only the fact of the ease and rapidity of color vision and color recognition, in contrast to form vision, that is of interest. Senden's material also makes it clear that one reason for this rapid acquisition of color recognition was the very fact that vivid color sensation occupied an unusually dominant position in the earliest visual experiences of these people.

The case descriptions included by Senden leave no doubt about the general quality of these early visual experiences and the subjective feelings that accompany them. The sensation is of helplessness and passivity in the face of a confusion of attention-demanding stimuli: "A plethora of impressions . . . from which he obtained relief only by closing his eyes" (26, p. 60), "too many things . . . he becomes confused . . . only the colors interest him" (25, p. 64), are typical descriptions.

Senden summarizes them as follows: "There is now the experience of a tremendous wealth of visual impressions which overwhelmed him who only recently gained sight" (26, p. 57).

This "plethora of impressions," it must be remembered, does not consist of articulated form impressions but rather of the most gross and diffuse sensations of light and color, movement, figure, and background. The sensations are often of unusual vividness and brilliance, frequently actually painful, and Senden speaks, in this connection, of a "sensory oversensitivity," at this stage of vision.

There can be little doubt that the exceedingly compelling and vivid qualities of these visual sensations are of a piece with their diffuseness, and are essentially antagonistic to perceptual form articulations of any degree of complexity. The accomplishment of form articulation and reliable object recognition, out of this state of vision, becomes a task of such magnitude that it frequently precipitates a personal crisis which is overcome only after laborious training procedures.[10]

This process of increasing capacity for form recognition and perceptual form articulation is not, according to Senden's data, a gradual and continuous one. The development appears to consist of distinguishable phases. The critical phase, which appears to coincide with the time of the personal "crisis," seems to be one in which the rudiments of form perception are being laboriously acquired. It is during this period that the patient slowly emerges from the experience of being passively subjected to sensory stimuli of great vividness, at the same time compelling and distracting, into a stage in which the *basic equipment* for more active perceptual articulation is available. Senden says:

> When the blind-born operated person has acquired a certain fund of form-conceptions and is able to increase this fund independently in approaching new visual objects with a searching mind and by using previously acquired concepts, then learning how to see is no longer a problem . . . they [doctors or educators] can leave the rest to the patient . . . (26, p. 93).

One other noteworthy feature of this perceptual development deserves to be mentioned. During this same critical period, in the course of the patients' efforts toward an adequate visual orientation, it is observed that *object identifications* often tend to be made, at first, on the basis of color. There appears, in other words, to be a

[10] It should be mentioned that the more recent results obtained by Riesen and his associates (20) with chimpanzees reared in darkness fully confirm the incapacity for perceptual form articulations without a prior development of experience. Riesen speaks of "form blindness" in the early vision of these chimpanzees. Brightly colored, shiny, or moving objects provided much more effective visual stimuli.

development which very likely consists of several overlapping phases, from identification of objects at first on the basis of their most conspicuous and gross visual aspects to later perceptual identification primarily in terms of more abstract form qualities. It is the earlier phase of identification by color that is of special interest here. It reveals a process by which color sensation, initially only passively experienced and antagonistic to clear form articulation, comes to serve an active function, to be *used* actively, and the beginnings of an integration of color and form are suggested. This issue will be taken up below.

Summary and Reformulations

In certain respects the data of all these studies confirm the initial assumptions; in other respects they seem to raise new questions.

Color does appear to have increased significance for children, in conditions of pathologically impaired mental organization, and in conditions of primitive and undeveloped visual capacity as well, as compared with normal adults. It has greater significance, in other words, in all those cases in which optimal perceptual organizing capacity has not yet been achieved or has been impaired. This fact, together with the subjective experience of its compelling quality, in contrast to the more detached and subjectively deliberate or, in the case of the newly seeing person, effortful feelings associated with form articulations, seems consistent with the assumption that color experience involves more passive and immediate processes, and becomes more prominent under conditions that make for a passive perceptual mode. But the data suggest more than this general principle.

Senden's material suggests that the two sorts of visual experience, the passive and immediate experience of what is sensorially most vivid, on the one hand, and the more active and detached articulation of form, on the other, may originally be antagonistic to each other. It is primarily his description of the critical phase, in which the effort is made to achieve form vision and to overcome the distraction of what is simply vivid in the visual field, which suggests such an antagonism. At the least, it is clear that the overcoming of a passive and hypersensitive relationship to visual stimuli and the acquisition of basic elements of form perception, and with them a more active and autonomous way of seeing, *are two aspects of the same process.* The details of this transition are not clear. But it does seem clear that a stage is reached in which the acquisition, in effect, of basic tools of form perception at the same time allows for easier resistance to the otherwise compelling and distracting sensory qualities of the visual field. These latter no longer dominate perception, and rapid and less effortful visual learning experience becomes possible. This marks the end of the critical phase of learning to "see" in the patients.[11] If color is, in the earliest visual experiences, an extremely compelling and dominating aspect of the visual field, what happens to it as perception becomes progressively dominated by active and complex form articulations? It is obvious that color neither disappears nor retains fully its original gripping and too vivid quality. *Its place in perception is modified and, in one way or another or to varying degrees, it becomes integrated with the now predominantly formal perception, and secondary to it.*

It has been noted by painters and others, e.g., Schilder (25) that looking at a landscape upside down causes the colors to become more vivid. This process accomplishes the partial disruption of familiar, recognizable forms. Probably much the same thing is accomplished with the use of a reduction screen. The existence of color constancy, as well as the loss of color constancy [Katz (13)] with the use of reduction screens or other devices such as a tachistoscope which obscure or eliminate form outlines, offer additional evidence of the significant changes that come about in color experience as color sensation is integrated with form and with meaningful or familiar objects. It cannot be assumed that this integration *necessarily* involves a diminution in the vividness of the color experience, but I believe that this is the predominate tendency.

To speak of an "integration" of color sensation with form suggests, however, something more than merely a modification of the subjective experience of color. Form vision is an adaptive function of first importance, and this fact raises the following question: Does color sensation, when integrated with predominantly formal perception, have a functional or adaptive position in vision, and if so, what is it? Ordinary visual experience suggests three such functions that color sensation may perform within form-dominated perception, although all three are undoubtedly functions of secondary adaptive importance in vision: (1) Color sensation enriches a visual experience by investing it with an ordinarily pleasing sensual quality which is not present otherwise; (2) simply by adding another dimension to visual experi-

[11] The process is very suggestive of what has been described by Harlow (9) as "learning to learn," and, in fact, Riesen (20) has considered this type of hypothesis in explaining his data with chimpanzees.

ence, color sensation makes finer articulations possible and lends greater individuality to a given form articulation; and (3) color sensation may be an *aid* to form articulations, and under optimal conditions can undoubtedly make form recognitions easier, faster, and more accurate; in this sense, color performs an economical function. In these ways, at least, color sensation comes, *in the later stages of perceptual development*, to enhance form articulation and to fulfill adaptive functions. It should be added that the ultimate value of color sensation in fulfilling these functions seems to derive from *just those qualities of sensorial immediacy and directness which originally appear to be antagonistic to form vision.*

At the same time as we may speak of color sensation as predominantly integrated with form in normal adult perception, it cannot be forgotten that all individuals are capable of and ordinarily exercise a *range* of perceptual modes. We see differently from time to time, and we are capable of a variety of shifts in mode of vision. These shifts in way of seeing seem to be partly determined by the nature of the stimulus as, for example, when bright lights or, for that matter, vivid colors compel attention or distract us. Partly, however, the nature and the range of such shifts is undoubtedly a matter of individual differences. A painter, for example, may have an unusually great capacity for certain sorts of perceptual shifts; Katz (13) has suggested that painters may have a capacity to perceive color in its "reduced" quality, i.e., as it would be seen ordinarily through a reduction screen. It can be assumed that the variety of ways of seeing, in a given individual, is itself organized in a way which is superordinate to each single perceptual mode. Beyond that, however, it seems justifiable to assume that the extent to which perception remains passively gripped by the sensorially more vivid aspects of the stimulus or "stimulus-bound" (as in the early phase of Senden's cases), to that extent the development of a wide range of ways of seeing or of the capacity for deliberate shift from one way to another must be limited.

Along with the fact of the range of color experience in perception, it must be remembered that, although we have talked schematically of the development of color experience from an originally more dominant position in a stage of perceptual passivity to a position secondary to and integrated with form in later, form-dominated perception, actually this transition must include a number of developmental phases and must be a gradual and extended process. Senden's cases suggest some of the intermediate phases, e.g., that phase in the newly seeing patients in which object identification is attempted primarily on the basis of color.   The developmental sorting studies cited make clear the gradual nature, in normal development, of the modification of color significance.   The sorting studies of pathological cases give evidence of the regressive changes that can occur, in this respect, in individuals whose visual capacities can certainly not be compared with Senden's cases of "form blindness."   One can only conclude that the variations and transitional states in the development of active, form-dominated perception are many, and that the ways in which color may be integrated with form perception are equally numerous. Some of these will be discussed in the following section in connection with specific varieties of Rorschach color responses.

Before turning to these, which will also provide opportunity for more specific development of our general thesis, we can sum up as follows:

Color perception as such is a more immediate and passive experience than form perception, requiring less in the way of perceptual tools or organizing capacity.   It is associated with a passive perceptual mode in that it becomes more dominant, more compelling in quality, and perhaps even antagonistic to form articulation in conditions in which active perceptual organizing capacity is impaired or is only rudimentary; at the same time, under optimal conditions, color becomes integrated with form perception, is itself modified in subjective experience, and acquires new functions of economy and enrichment.

RORSCHACH COLOR RESPONSES AND THEIR INTERPRETIVE SIGNIFICANCE

A color response involves, from our point of view, the operation of a perceptual mode of the sort or within the range described above; i.e., a perceptual mode which retains, at some level, a significant aspect of passivity.   In psychological conditions of impairment of controlling, integrative, and expressive functions, we expect an impairment of active perceptual organizing functions also; the more immediate perceptual route offered by the color stimulus may then be especially opportune.   Conditions of excessive affect pressure constitute one *special case* within this general class. There are many others.   At the same time, under conditions where perceptual organizing and integrative functions operate well, passive and immediate sensory experience will still play a significant role, but it will be of a different sort and the sensory experience will be of a different quality. In general, the degree and quality of color response, including the subjective quality of the color itself insofar as this can be determined, will reflect the characteristic forms and qualities of immediate and passively experienced tension discharge. It will either be well-integrated, expressive, and adaptive, in which case it will tend to lose its distinctiveness, both subjectively and objectively in the over-all integrated operation; or it will be primitive, unmodulated, and perhaps eruptive, in which case its distinctively passive character will be conspicuous both objectively and, ordinarily, subjectively.

The varieties of color response on the Rorschach are very numerous, only grossly covered by our scoring schemes, and it is doubtful that all of these varieties can be accurately placed on any single continuum. Nevertheless, a very rough sort of continuum does exist, namely, from the completely formless pure C response to the highly articulated and well-integrated $FC+$ response. The discussion here, and the brief excerpts from Rorschach protocols that accompany it, will be divided into three loose categories: pure C responses, CF responses, and FC responses. It should be kept in mind, however, that our aim is not a manual of interpretation but rather illustrations of our approach.

Pure C

It has been indicated in the discussion of the previous section that even the most primitive pure C response which is scorable as such does not reflect the most immediate and primitive perceptual response to color, but is already, or it could not be a scorable response, integrated to some extent with appropriate content. The only exception to this would be color-naming responses which are clearly on the borderline of scorability. Nevertheless, the pure C responses as a whole, and particularly those varieties that are met with in cases of chronic schizophrenia, do seem to approach the immediacy and directness of an altogether diffuse and unformed color experience. As mentioned before, these responses have been described by Rapaport (17) as "short circuiting" the ordinarily more highly developed channels of perception and association. That is to say, the processes of active perceptual organization which operate in normal adults are in these cases by-passed to a considerable degree. This describes the condition of perceptual passivity, and, in Rorschach testing, such responses are in fact sometimes accompanied by indications of a relative helplessness and of a subjective feeling of passivity in relation to the stimulus, which are very close to those described previously in connection with the sorting studies of pathological cases and with the early experiences of the newly operated blind.

Pure color responses, such as those found in the records of chronic schizophrenics, and color-naming responses, which are an even more "pure" type of color response, provide difficulties for an understanding of color responses which ties their meaning exclusively to affects. Cases in which these primitive varieties of color response tend to predominate are, of course, just those whose affects are often described as shallow, "blunted," and the like.

At the same time, it is true that one sometimes meets with these responses in cases where the pathology may include exceedingly impulsive, perhaps psychotic, actions or exceedingly wild, unmodulated, unpredictable, and by ordinary standards inappropriate affect expressions. Sometimes both of these conditions may exist together in the same person, blandness being sporadically interrupted by impulsive outbursts. Since we know that pure C response can be a dominant Rorschach feature associated with any of these—blunted affect, impulsive actions, or unmodulated outbursts—it is clear that its essential significance relates to a factor which underlies all of them. This factor is just that condition of "short circuiting" or immobilization of integrative, modulating, and impulse- and tension-discharge-delaying functions, a short-circuiting which, as we have described, reflects itself also in a relative primitivization of the perceptual process. Perception tends, in such conditions, to become more diffuse and global [see Friedman (5)] and, with immobilization of the active form-organizing capacities that give it its autonomy, perception becomes also more bound to the sensorially most impressive aspects of the stimulus.

In organic cases of color naming and in connection with the pure C responses of blunted and deteriorated chronic schizophrenics, one gets no feeling of *affect* discharge or affect pressure. On the contrary, the impression is often of a concrete report of a sensory experience without any but the most direct, immediate, and primitive content and quite without the affective connotations which more highly organized color responses frequently have. Nor is there, in general, any indication of sensual-esthetic satisfaction in the color perception. Such satisfactions appear, and richer and more highly refined content and affect associations as well, only when some greater sense of autonomy and deliberateness is present in the perceptual act, i.e., only when active perceptual organization as a whole is more advanced.

The issue may be illustrated with several color responses, one a pure C and one scored F/C arb., from the Rorschach of a 42-year-old male chronic schizophrenic. This patient had barely managed an ambulatory adjustment for many years and, when seen at a psychiatric sanitarium, he was undergoing some further decompensation which made hospitalization necessary. His Rorschach contained 47 responses, somewhat more than one would have expected from the extent of his general dilapidation, but probably reflecting those retained adaptive capacities that had permitted him to function at a marginal level outside of hospitals for so long. Contamination, gross confabulations, perseverative responses, confused and peculiar verbalizations, and gross fluidity of thinking were all conspicuous in his test. His $F+\%$ was low. Among the determinants, he had one M, the popular on card III, four FC of which two involved an arbitrary use of color, one CF, and five pure C responses.

The following response, it will be noted, is quite innocuous and ordinary in content, but it is unusual in the extent to which it reveals the processes involved:

To card VIII—"These two red things here [the animal figures] look like rats . . . [pause] . . . only they're red . . . red rats . . . I never heard of that . . . only the shape looks like rats."

In this response, the form, certainly one of the most clear-cut and obvious in the Rorschach, was accurately perceived. But it is clear at the same time that this perception is not at the level at which we are accustomed to thinking of form perception. The concreteness of the response is obvious. An adequate form perception implies the capacity to abstract perceptually the outline or shape without regard for or distraction by the other sensory stimuli which may happen to surround or be enveloped by that shape. Here, this capacity was clearly not present. Once impressed by the gross, concrete sensory stimulus, the patient was not able to restrain his response to the color, to say nothing of making use of it, for example, in an adequate FC response.

A subjective feeling of helplessness and passivity which one might expect would accompany this process is, in fact, conveyed not only in his verbalization in connection with the original response but also in the inquiry.

When the examiner later returned to this response and asked, "Red rats?," he answered, "Very peculiar . . . but I mean I saw them that way . . . you don't see red rats . . . but they're shaped like rats." The patient was still bound to the color and unable simply to overlook it, even though he was well aware of the inadequacy of his production. A feeling of helplessness of this quality and extent seems substantially the same thing as what has been called "impotence" in the Rorschach behavior of organically brain-damaged patients. The similarity of the whole response, also, to some of the behavior that has been described, in connection with both the concrete sorting behavior of the pathological group and the perceptual reactions of Senden's cases, is noteworthy.

This response quoted was followed immediately by another one, and it seems possible to see in this sequence the further breakdown of an already extremely inadequate detachment, and the patient's even greater passivity in the face of the color stimulus. This second response was a pure C. He continued, ". . . and the redness [now all of the red area on card VIII] reminds me of tincture of merthiolate . . . like I have on my hand here."

His reference of the ink-blot color to the red tincture of merthiolate on his hand, which he held up in front of him at that moment, reveals again the loss of an attitude of active, detached perceptual organizing of the ink blot. Instead, he is held by the color even to the extent that the immediately striking color relationships override the ordinary separation, altogether unquestioned in the attitude of most subjects, between the card and the remainder of the visual field around it.

It will be noted that there is no suggestion here of affect discharge in connection with the color response; as mentioned, blandness and impoverishment of affect were clinically conspicuous in the patient. The color, after all, is itself only a *sensory* stimulus and response to it can only be productive of, or reflect, affective response when the psychological organization being stimulated is capable of such a response. But, as has been described, a passive perceptual mode and the high responsiveness to color that tends to be associated with it is far from being limited to such conditions. In the case of this patient, the impairment of perceptual organizing and integrating capacities was so great as to make the color stimulus attention demanding and passively experienced to the extent of not only precluding adequate integration with perceived form elements but also of overriding logical considerations and even detachment from the Rorschach card itself. Such a degree of impairment of perceptual organization and perceptual control must reflect a general impairment of psychological organization and control functions including an impairment of what are, after all, the relatively highly organized and differentiated discharge channels that would be necessary for true affect experience. Color response of this sort, therefore, cannot be said to reflect affectivity, but rather a condition of such disorganization or impairment of control functions as to preclude affective response in any ordinary sense of that term.

It happened that six months later this patient had recompensated to a considerable degree, and it is interesting to compare his handling of the same stimulus on card VIII at that time. His response was: "This looks like a rat—the same on the other side . . . [long pause] . . . I was going to say it looks like ink—I said it before . . . I can't see anything else." He handed the card back abruptly.

In the inquiry he was asked, "Ink?" He answered: "Because I think I said all the red looked like ink the last time . . . it doesn't look like ink this time . . . it feels funny . . . it feels like a lot of things disappeared the way I looked at things before."

In an unusually explicity way, and just because the process here is such an effortful and tenuous one, these verbalizations describe certain aspects of the patient's now reconstituted functioning. It is clear that his reference to the difference between this and the previous experience does not primarily have to do with the content of the response; it is altogether ordinary and unremarkable. His remarks seem rather to derive from a vague subjective feeling of increased control, perhaps including increased repressive capacity, but, more important in this instance, including a control that manifests itself in the capacity to detach himself from the over-all concrete sensory impression and to restrain immediate response to the color stimulus in particular. He is able now, although obviously barely able, to achieve a true form response. In the normal subject, of course, this process functions so smoothly and so quickly as not to be noticeable.

It may be mentioned that the color determinants in this second Rorschach consisted of two *FC*, two *CF*, and only one pure *C*, and that, along with this indication of better organization, at the time of the second testing, this man was a good deal more emotionally responsive in general clinical observation.

What about those cases of severe regression, e.g., chronic schizophrenics, where no color response appears at all? How is it that color, if it is the more immediately manifest stimulus, can be completely absent in these cases where impairment of perceptual organizing capacity along with impairment of thought and affect organization is otherwise obvious?   The problem may at first appear all the more peculiar in view of the fact that it is always among the same clinical groups—chronic schizophrenics, severe schizoid character disorders, and perhaps some of the more severe narcissistic character disorders —that one finds cases in which color responses are altogether absent and other quite similar cases in which pure C responses are a dominant feature.   It is not unusual, in fact, to find in retesting these patients that a Rorschach with one or two pure C responses will be replaced by one with no color at all, or vice versa.

It is just this close relationship between pure C responses, on the one hand, and complete absence of color response, on the other, that contains the central point.   It will be remembered that a similar issue arose in connection with the apparent disappearance of color responsiveness in very young children, and, also, at very short exposure times in tachistoscopic presentation of the cards.   In each of these cases the essential point is the same.   It is this: the pure C response tendency and the complete absence of color response do not stand, as it were, at opposite ends of a scale of perceptual organization, but rather side by side.

This fact may be made more clear if one considers that the two perceptual tendencies have an essential feature in common, namely, *that something* is conspicuously absent in both of them.   What is absent is exactly the capacity to achieve an adequate degree of integration of the sensory experience of color with appropriate content and with form articulation, the capacity to use the color actively in any degree, and it is this capacity which essentially distinguishes an adequate color response from *both* the pure C response and the total absence of color response.[12]   I do not mean to imply by this that the conditions which give rise to pure C responses, on the one hand, and to a total absence of color response, on the other, are identical, but only to clarify their relationship to each other and the relationship of both to more advanced and more adequately organized color responses.

There appear to be at least two sorts of conditions which may be responsible for a total absence of color response.   First of all, in cases of chronic schizophrenia, or possibly some cases of organic brain dam-

---

[12] There are many analogies to this situation, both in psychological phenomena and elsewhere: flood and drought, inhibition and vulgarity, stinginess and waste —all these look superficially like polar opposites, but on closer look they are often associated and always for the same reason, namely, an absence of development, or an impairment, of modulating and controlling organizations or discharge structures.

age, there may be an incapacity to articulate and to give expression to the color experience as a distinct perceptual dimension at all, at least at a level of a scorable response. Color naming would, again, be just on the borderline of scorability, and is likely to appear in such cases. In other types of cases, particularly schizoid or paranoid but not necessarily psychotic characters, one often suspects on the basis of clinical observation an underlying defensiveness or guardedness in the absence of color response. The guarded detachment which is so characteristic of these people seems to preclude the degree of abandonment which might be implied in responding to the color stimulus at all. Here, too, however, one may easily overestimate the gap between a total absence of color response and a helpless, immediate response to color, as in a pure C, if one forgets that a complete avoidance of color reflects, first of all, an *incapacity* for adequate form- and content-integrated use of it. Such a defensive avoidance of the color stimulus, therefore, is likely to be separated by only a very thin line from a passive, helpless response to it. In fact, one sometimes gets some clinical confirmation of this when, in the course of a Rorschach test, one has been impressed by such a total avoidance up until the last card or two when a pure C response finally occurs. It would not be correct, in any event, to assume that a defensive, total avoidance of color reflects simply an avoidance of expression of affects, because the incapacity for an adequately organized response to the stimulus, which is indicated by the necessity for such an avoidance, is precisely what suggests that more or less adequately organized discharge channels, such as are assumed for ordinary affective experience, are not in existence. The likelihood is, therefore, that such an avoidance will again correspond to a degree of blandness, possibly sporadic impulsive actions, and possibly even sporadic outbursts of diffuse affect, but not simply to inhibition or lack of expression of otherwise well-developed and continuous affect experience.

The CF Response

The CF response is a much more common sort of color-dominated response than the pure C, and its quality and interpretive significance in many ways are much more varied. We will have to limit ourselves here to discussing a few types of CF responses.

It is among records in which color response is predominantly of the CF type, much more than among those dominated either by pure C or FC, that one finds the cases where color truly seems to reflect a lability and unusual vividness of affects. Even among cases with a dominant *CF* tendency, however, it is necessary to distinguish at least two important groups: one, characterized in fact by vivid and usually unstable emotional reactions, and a second group characterized much more by impulsive action, frequently with only little or shallow affect accompanying the action, and sometimes even with a psychopathic coolness or blandness. Roughly speaking, these two groups are, diagnostically, the hysterical category, in the first case, and the category of narcissistic or impulsive character disorders, in the second.

The *CF* responses, of course, stand between the more immediate and passive pure *C* responses and the more highly articulated *FC* responses. It will be remembered from the previous discussion that the development from the most passive and concrete sort of perception, in which color tends to be a dominant feature, to a more active perception, in which color is primarily integrated with and secondary to form, must include many overlapping intermediate phases. Senden's material only hints at such phases, and this is not surprising in view of the fact that visual development in his cases was compressed into an extraordinarily short period. Still, he describes, for example, a phase in which the newly seeing person attempts object identifications primarily on the basis of color, yet with some attention also to at least the more gross or visually more evident form characteristics. There is no intention here to suggest any exact parallel between such a phase of perceptual development and a specific sort of Rorschach response; such a parallel would be misleading. But it is important to note that such intermediate phases do exist, that there are various levels and degrees of integration of passive and active perceptual modes, and that these, in turn, must reflect various levels of more general psychological organization.

Of the two types of subjects to be considered first for whom the *CF* response is frequently a dominant Rorschach feature—impulsive, action-oriented, highly narcissistic people, on the one hand, and hysterical, extremely and unstably emotional people, on the other—no one can doubt that in both cases there is an impairment of capacity for delay of tension discharge or an impairment of impulse- or affect-organizing, modulating, and expressive functions. Yet it is clear that this impairment is not on the same level as that evident in the case of chronic schizophrenia described before. In these nonpsychotic cases, no matter how great the pressure to discharge may be, or how abrupt or extravagant the discharge itself may be, the form or channel which that discharge takes is still in its essentials reasonably adapted to reality, i.e., it is a nonpsychotic form of discharge. Even though, therefore, abrupt, impulsive action or affect discharge reflects an impairment of control functions, this manner of discharge still generally presupposes a level of psychological organization which is distinctly more advanced and more intact than that of the schizophrenic case discussed before.

These people of the two types mentioned will typically find the immediate and visually obvious perceptual route offered by the color a congenial or provocative one. The subjective sense of immediacy and of being passively "struck" by a vivid color stimulus is, in fact, often very clear in the behavior and verbalization of these subjects. The fact remains, however, that as quick and passive as the response appears to be, as attention demanding as the color may be in these cases, the perceptual response does not reach the level of passivity, either in objective response product or in subjective sense of helplessness of the schizophrenic pure *C* response. The immediate and passive aspect of the perception is to some extent integrated with form-organizing and articulating capacities. A certain level of intact organization, *within which* an impairment of discharge control appears, is reflected therefore in the perceptual mode represented by a dominant *CF* tendency.

Of course, the *CF* tendency, itself, may be more or less prominent in a wide range of subjects. *CF* responses may reflect not only the sorts of impairment of controls that eventuate in pathologically abrupt and diffuse discharges through action or affects but also may reflect, at other times, the capacity for the wide range of affect discharges, immediate enough but quite nonpathological, which we call spontaneity. Or they may reflect a capacity for various degrees and types of more sensuous abandonment to the stimulus.

There are presumably differences in the perceptual quality of these sorts of *CF* responses, and there are marked differences in the subjective experience that accompanies them. Sometimes the quality of the subjective experience will be suggested by the behavior and tone of voice of the subject and sometimes by the "tone" of the content of the response itself. For example, the response "paint dripping" to the upper red areas of card III or the response "lipstick smear" to the upper red areas of card II suggest a different subjective experience from that suggested by the response "bursting fireworks" to the whole of card X. However, both of these responses will fall within the *CF* scoring category.

The first illustration is from the Rorschach of a young man diagnosed a narcissistic character disorder. An outstanding feature of his history and his life was impulsive action, frequently with a psychopathic flavor; business decisions, the buying of a car, even marriage or divorce were carried out speedily, with a minimum of reflection, and, as far as one could tell, with quite limited amounts of affect. In many ways, in fact, his affects could be described as shallow or bland, although not to the degree of a schizoid or schizophrenic person. His Rorschach was a long one, 77 responses, although many of the responses were pretentious and empty. His color responses included three CF, one C/F, and two pure C together with eight FC and F/C. In many ways the CF responses may be considered most characteristic of the man; both the FC responses, on the one hand, and the pure C responses, on the other, tended toward a CF quality. Many of his responses, including the color responses, were delivered in an exhibitionistic way, with special pleasure when he felt they might be considered remarkable or unusual, and his manner was one of dictating what he felt confident would be an interesting record.

To card II, for example, after an initial W response of "clowns," he went on, ". . . then, blood . . . blood stains," a pause followed by another response that did not become clear until the inquiry, ". . . toilet . . . this isn't particularly pretty," this last with particular emphasis as though to call attention to how disturbing the idea was.

A few responses later, he returned to the colored areas with the following: "It seems to be like red underwear there"; a few responses further on, he said: "Upside down it looks like an explosion . . . like a volcano exploding"; finally, his last remark on handling the card, again with special emphasis, "I don't like that red."

The "toilet" response turned out to be associated loosely with the previous "blood" response and included all of the black, center white, and lower red areas of the card; when asked about this in the inquiry, he said: "Ah, I was afraid you'd get to that. It seems to be a blast of blood. That's been a big problem of mine . . . it seemed to be associated with blood coming out of my rectum. . . ."

Thus, there were three color-dominated responses to the card, exclusive of the surrounding comments and elaborations: "blood," the vaguely formed "red underwear," and the equally vaguely formed "volcano."

I have tried to convey with these excerpts the exceedingly impulsive and diffuse quality of this patient's whole Rorschach. The immediacy and relative absence of restraint with which gross, only weakly articulated, and vivid sensory impressions appear as conscious percepts and, in that sense, as finished products are obvious. It is noteworthy, however, that notwithstanding this immediate and impulsive quality, there was no indication of affect fluctuations in connection with the color responses or, for that matter, during the entire test. In contrast to the typical reaction of hysterical neurotics, this patient seemed quite at ease with the immediate, impulsive style of his color responses.

In certain ways, in the primitive quality of the pure *C* responses and the diffuseness of many others as well, this record seems close to a schizophrenic one. Yet it is still different in several respects, speaking with regard to the issue of color alone. As primitive as the color responses often are, they remain predominantly on a level on which there is some degree of integration with form, and they include, in fact, a number of form-dominated color responses. Just as the patient's general behavior was characterized by extremely impulsive discharge through action—which was, however, never essentially disorganized action—had some direction, and was not unmindful of at least proximal realistic demands, so his perceptual mode was passive, impulsive, and dominated by immediate response to the most sensorially vivid stimulus, yet never without a certain degree of active perceptual organization, and never passive to a degree in which the sensorially vivid overrode or immobilized the capacity for form organization altogether.

There is another feature related to this. In this man's behavior, there was no indication whatever that he experienced a *subjective feeling* of passivity or helplessness. There was no evidence that he felt "struck" by the color stimulus, in spite of the fact that to the observer he *appeared* immediately attracted and gripped by it. On the contrary, there was every evidence of a subjective feeling of deliberateness and autonomy even as he gave the most (perceptually) impulsive responses. This situation closely paralleled certain aspects of the clinical observations. The patient's quick, impulsive behavior could not help but strike anyone as reflecting an *incapacity* to delay, to hold back, and to consider long-range consequences or possible alternatives; yet the patient himself in no way *felt* at the mercy of his impulses, but rather felt that every action was deliberate and willful, or at least allowed by him. Is the observer right, or is the patient? The answer seems to be that in certain respects both are right. The impairment of restraining and organizing functions, perceptual and otherwise, is certainly present and manifests itself in the ways described, but, again, this impairment is not so extensive that certain basic integrative functions are altogether overwhelmed or immobilized. The existence of some such level of intact organization must be, at least, one prerequisite for this man's capacity to maintain a subjective feeling of autonomy. This type of discrepancy between the subjective feeling of autonomy and the objective evidence of passivity will present itself again in a more gross form in connection with the productions of hypomanic patients, to be discussed later.

Probably the most frequently encountered records in which CF responses have an important place are those of hysterics. These records demonstrate more than any others a relationship between vivid, color-dominated responses and equally vivid and labile affects. As we said before, the labile and volatile affects of hysterical people reflect also an impairment or inadequacy of controlling and integrative functions; the immediate, provocative quality of the color stimulus for them, the perceptual "short-circuit" that occurs, is often especially apparent. It is so apparent because it is frequently accompanied by small-scale, but actual, affect discharges. However, just as an impairment of control which manifests itself primarily on a level of abrupt *affect* discharge, without discharge in action and without conspicuous impairment of thinking processes, implies an essentially more intact organization than would be indicated otherwise, so, typically, the impulsive color-dominated response of the hysteria, notwithstanding its immediacy, does not violate form aspects of the stimulus (as in the first, schizophrenic case), nor does it reach a level of diffuseness in which form aspects are ignored.

The following excerpts are from the protocol of a 39-year-old hysterical woman. Her adjustment had been characterized for many years by typically hysterical features: a general repressiveness and lack of reflectiveness, a good deal of romantic fantasy, and, above all, a conspicuously labile emotional life. It was, in fact, an increasing difficulty in emotional control, manifested in outbursts of tears or anger, that had caused her to seek psychiatric help.

Her Rorschach, except perhaps for one feature, was much as one might expect. There was only one M response, but an abundance of color responses including three FC, one F/C, two CF and three C/F. The total number of responses was 49; this unusual feature in an hysterical record is probably attributable to a rather ambitious, tenacious, compulsive aspect of her makeup.

Her first color response, which was her first response to card II was as follows: "Oh, my heavens! [flushes . . . a brief burst of nervous laughter] . . . Oh! . . . well, I could say it would look just like some pictures in a gynecological magazine or book of some kind."

In the inquiry, it became clear that this response was a rather vague W, determined largely by the immediate color impression which suggested menstruation, though it was integrated to some extent with form by way of the sexual-anatomical content. Other color responses which appeared later in the Rorschach had much the same perceptual quality as this one, though without the sexual content.

Her first response to card IX is an example: "That looks like a burst of something . . . just looks like a great big burst of color more than anything else"; and the first response to card X was: "Goodness! It looks like something . . . under a microscope . . . in color."

Both of these responses are W, and both were accompanied by the same sort of tension and affect discharge which was apparent in connection with the earlier response. In these responses also, however, she managed to achieve some degree of integration of color with form, though a quite weak one.

The exclamations, flushing, and nervous hesitations that accompanied these responses leave little doubt of a subjective experience of being struck by something or being taken by surprise. When one sees such reactions, in a Rorschach of this sort, it is tempting to assume that the color somehow contains an intrinsic affective value. The tone of the response content, e.g., "bursting," may also be construed to suggest this. Yet even in this case such an assumption is not necessary. It is necessary only to assume that the *perceptual* response to the color stimulus will, in its level and degree of immediacy, bear the stamp of whatever level of impairment or relaxation of control functions may exist. The qualities of that level will be reflected in the special visual qualities and formal aspects of the perception, ordinarily in its content as well, and in the special quality of the subjective experience that is associated with the perceptual process.

These special qualities of a response are often not revealed in scores. For example, both the color responses of this hysterical patient and those of the previous case are predominantly of a *CF* sort. But it would be as incorrect to miss the difference in level of color-form integration, the difference in degree of perceptual diffuseness and immediate sensory domination, the difference in content-tone, and the difference in subjective experience between this patient's responses and the previous patient's as to miss the difference between romantic fantasy and impulsive marriages.

One of the most interesting examples of the significance of color response appears in the records of hypomanic cases. At the same time, color response in these cases involves certain special problems.

The expansive, poorly controlled affect of hypomanic people is sometimes described as "forced" emotionality; similarly, the large number of color-dominated responses which usually accumulate in the Rorschach records of these people are sometimes described as "forced" or "artificial" color responses. What is the meaning of this description, and what process is described by it?

The fact that the color responses of hypomanic patients often seem forced seems to derive from two aspects of those responses: (1) They often consist largely of C/F responses, i.e., color-dominated responses in which the color and form are inadequately or only very effortfully and tenuously integrated; and (2) the fact that many of these responses are given in the manner of, or accompanied by, the driven expansiveness and high mood which are characteristic of hypomania; frequently the content of the responses themselves suggests that high mood (24). In connection with the first of these facts, the inadequate integration of color and form, there is a certain ambiguity. In a response in which color and form are inadequately integrated, the question remains open as to whether the color is "artificially" added to what was originally a form perception or, on the contrary, the form is inadequately integrated with what began as a vivid color experience. As to the second factor mentioned, the expansive way in which such responses tend to be produced and in which the color in particular tends to be described, it must certainly be said that this accurately reflects one level of the hypomanic person's subjective experience; he does obviously *feel* that he is producing deliberately, actively, and creatively, and he may very well feel so about his color use. But as we have already seen in the case of the narcissistic character disorder, the subjective feeling of activity and creativeness, and of autonomy in perception, by no means necessarily precludes that the state is objectively a relatively helpless one.

There is an alternative to understanding these color responses as "artificial": The abundant color reaction of these people reflects essentially a state of relative passivity in the face of this stimulus, a too immediate response to it, and an incapacity to integrate it adequately with form; but, in contrast to other conditions in which this passivity or helplessness is experienced *subjectively* as such, in hypomanics it is covered by denial. It is somewhat like a person who finds himself riding a wild horse and, though actually quite out of control, proclaims himself a great rider because he is able to go so fast.

In the color response, then, what is "artificial" and forced is not essentially the vividness of the color but the inadequate integration of it with form and content, and the denial of helplessness implied often in the content tone. One qualification has to be made: In the analogy, the fiction of good horsemanship can only be maintained if the rider is able to avoid falling off altogether, and so it is with the color response; to the extent that the capacity for active form integration fails altogether and CF or C/F responses give way to pure C responses, one may expect that what was only high mood will give way to chaotic action and to a subjective sense of disorganization.

Both paranoid and hypomanic features, clearly of borderline psychotic degree, were outstanding in the clinical picture of the patient whose Rorschach will be described. Along with the usual expansive mood, there were many quite megalomanic ideas, particularly in connection with her interest in world affairs. There were 76 responses in the Rorschach, of which three were M responses and 22 were color responses. Among the color responses were two pure C, two C/F, seven CF, six F/C, and five FC.

The first color response was the first response to card II, given almost immediately upon looking at the card: "A top of a woman's dressing table with spilt nail polish and mascara all over the place." The domination of this response by the gross sensory impression is conspicuous. The emphasis on spilling or spilling over is also noteworthy because it appears repeatedly in connection with other color responses in the remainder of the test.

For example, to the same card: "This part looks somewhat like a map of Russia—that would be very interesting—down here where the red is sort of spilling over into Red China and here into the eastern satellite states."

Or, to card VIII: "An aerial view of the Mississippi . . . flood stage . . . spreading over its banks." This whole response was determined primarily by the blue-green color in the center of the card, but included the other colors as indicating "a more turbulent area."

Other color-dominated responses, to illustrate further the vivid and gross quality, included the three red areas of card III seen as "red lights" and, again, the whole of card VIII seen as "the flame of a Bunsen burner."

The exceedingly poor control, including both impulse and affect control, is reflected not only in the immediacy of the perceptual response to the color impression and by its essential diffusiveness but also in content, as in the theme of "spilling over" or "overflowing" banks. She was, however, sufficiently intact to maintain not only a consistently high mood but also a superficial manner of detached intellectual interest throughout most of the test. This degree of actual intactness, i.e., the kernel of truth that was probably indispensable to her otherwise empty sense of autonomy, was reflected in the degree of form articulation she generally did manage to achieve in her color responses as well as in the quantity of her productions. Just such a capacity for enough active, integrative effort to go through at least the motions of productiveness and, as it were, to challenge the underlying sense of incapacity seems essential to a sustained hypomanic mood. It is difficult to observe such things, but it may be that with those responses which are least articulated formwise and, at the same time, with those in which the color experience is most immediate, vivid, and compelling (e.g., "red lights"), the sense of detachment and control did break down temporarily.[13]

It seems more difficult to account for those expansively toned color responses sometimes given by hypomanic patients to areas of color on the ink blots which are, in themselves, quite pale.

An example of this type of response is the following to the upper center area of card IX, from a mildly hypomanic patient: ". . . and here all the colors of the card [which she had previously responded to separately] blend in a rainbow. . . ."

It is this type of response which, as far as I can see, constitutes the strongest argument for an assumption of "artificial" or forced response to color. However, even here, this thesis seems doubtful.

The patient whose response is quoted above had, almost immediately upon seeing the card, named and described each of the colors in the different parts of the blot. This process revealed her initial reaction to the colors; it represented, as such color description ordinarily does, an altogether inadequate attempt to use them actively. Following that, there was a gross, and again inadequate, attempt at integration of all the color with form; she described the whole blot as a "varicolored doublet." Notwithstanding their inadequacy, the integrative efforts in connection with the color were, therefore, clear enough. Again, up to the last response—the "rainbow"—the effortful and forced quality seemed to reside, as in the previously described case, in the inadequate form integration rather than in the color reaction itself. This was the background of the "rainbow" response at which the patient arrived finally. It may very well be that this last color response

---

[13] Such an apparent vividness of color experience is also encountered on occasion in the Rorschachs of borderline or schizophrenic paranoid patients in more acutely disturbed states. One such response from a patient, and his only color response, was to card III: "Like the headlights of a car [center red] coming toward you on the beach at night." The vividness of this response harks back to the early phase of Senden's patients.

contained not simply a reaction to the pale area indicated, but was actually a further integrative effort to deal with *all* of the other, previously named, colors in the blot (". . . and here all the colors . . . blend"). In effect, then, this final color response, in which the color experience itself seemed forced and artificial, is seen as another effort to deal actively with the initially passive color experience. I believe that careful analysis will usually show this type of process in connection with such responses.

Responses of this sort seem to underscore that the defensive efforts in hypomanic conditions include not only denials of a sense of helplessness to deal with compelling sensory stimuli but also an aspect of active exercise of the remaining intact integrative functions, as though to challenge those underlying feelings. It is probably this active exercise that lends some substance to the content of the denials. It is in this sense only that an artificial-use-of-color hypothesis seems to have validity.

FC Response

On the whole, the processes that go into making an *FC* response seem more difficult to understand and more complex than those involved in the color-dominated responses. Perhaps this is so because the higher integrative capacities that go into the making of this type of response are less well understood. It also seems true that the interpretive meaning of *FC* responses varies more widely than that of more primitive color responses. In general, after all, people differ more widely from each other in the more complex mental functions than they do in the developmentally more primitive ones. It will be necessary to discuss the *FC* response in somewhat more general terms than has been the case with the other categories, since specific illustrations cannot, in this case, sufficiently convey the main aspects of the argument. First, I will sum up the understanding so far.

On account of the absence of capacities for active perceptual organization, more primitive perception involves a more passive relationship between the perceiver and the stimulus, in which color, because of its sensory quality and its ease of apprehension, becomes an especially compelling, vivid, and distracting aspect of the visual field. On account of these same qualities, color originally is probably antagonistic to form perception; the perceiver is distracted from form elements by what is sensorially more vivid. In certain sorts of adults, such an antagonism between color and form perception still operates to some degree, and, as we can see through the Rorschach, the more immediate response to the vivid sensory stimulus seems to abort or override the development of highly organized form articulations; or, the achievement of highly articulated form perception is possible only at the relative sacrifice of responsiveness to the more immediate and sensorially more vivid stimulus. However, optimally, as form perception develops, an integration between it and the originally antagonistic or distracting color sensation is achieved. The problem is, what does this integration actually consist of?

As described before, one significant intermediate stage in the integration of color and form in perception is achieved in the movement from being only gripped or distracted, passively, by the sensory experience to active *use* of that sensory experience for object identification. But the adaptive value of object identification predominately or exclusively on the basis of color is extremely limited, and vision ultimately, if it is to have significant adaptive value at all, must be predominately form vision. The development must be progressively away from what merely happens to be sensorially most impressive in the visual field and toward what is logically most essential.[14] Color must be displaced from a position of dominance, and it is displaced along with the development of capacities for active perceptual organization and the increasing freedom, concomitant with this development, from altogether passive response to what is sensorially vivid. However, color may still retain functions of value; by its very quality of sensory immediacy and ease of apprehension, color experience normally plays a significant role even in perception that is very largely dominated by form.

Let us continue at this point in Rorschach language. If we regard a good *FC* response, i.e., a response whose character is predominately defined by the form or configuration of an area of the blot but in which the color of that area also plays a significant and appropriate part, is it correct to say that such a perception has been achieved in a rapid but essentially additive fashion, by a process through which the component of color supplements the form perception through additional organizational effort? This question, most likely, must be answered in the negative, for two reasons. First of all, there is the fact that in the process of integration with form the perceptual experience of color undergoes some change. In a broad way, this is indicated by the body

---

[14] With the development of perceptual constancies, the perceiver achieves an adaptively valuable degree of independence even from transient and accidental variations in form or configuration.

of the material discussed here, but specifically, it can be confirmed by such simple devices as a reduction screen. Therefore, the process is certainly an integrative and not an additive one. In addition, if we ask whether an object or representation is more easily or more rapidly identified when it is with or without appropriate color, we see at once that under such circumstances, far from being a burden to the perceptual process or requiring more effort than already required by the organization of the form perception, appropriate color is an aid, can make accurate apprehension of the object or representation a speedier and easier affair, and functions more like a *useful* short-cut. It is, of course, partly for just such reasons of perceptual economy that color is useful in communication generally. That very immediacy which is inherent in color sensation, and which is originally antagonistic to highly organized form perceptions, can serve perceptual articulation in an economical way, assuming still that it does not override or short-circuit form elements altogether.

We know that there is more to the story. Apparently at the same stroke in which apprehension of color can provide a perceptual economy, it can enliven a form and lend an additional richness or sensory pleasure. Exactly what the sensory pleasure consists of, how it is related to the over-all perceptual organization, and in what possible ways it may be connected with the economical function of color, if at all, are questions which we cannot answer. But that is no reason to ignore the fact.

It is assumed, then, that within predominantly form-oriented perception, color retains from its original compelling quality both an economical and an enriching function. An optimal integration of this sort between form and color seems to be reflected in the *FC* type of response. The enrichment of virtually any form response when it is integrated successfully with color is self-evident. To call the large human figures on card II, for example, "Halloween witches," making use in that image of the red and black costume is to see something more distinct, more vivid, and more individual than to describe these same figures without the dimension of color. The same thing can be said for the ordinary "green caterpillars" or "green tomato worms" on card X, as opposed to describing these same figures as simply "snakes" on the basis of their form alone. The economical function of color in the Rorschach situation itself may be questioned, because, after all, in that situation there is no objective need for economy of recognition. Even so, the availability of a more economical mode of perception will have advantages; the subject who can allow color as well as form to suggest imagery is able not only to produce richer responses but also to produce them more easily. The capacity, for example, to allow the red and black colors on card II to suggest, together with the form, an appropriate content should, if the process works smoothly, be a less effortful one than a delineation which must rely on form exclusively to suggest an appropriate content.

The condition that is reflected in successful perceptual integration of form and color and, at least ideally, in the *FC* type of response, is one in which the immediate sensory experience of color is neither so compelling and distracting as to preclude adequate form articulation (and content elaboration) nor has it to be avoided altogether, but can be *used*. This condition implies a more autonomous perceptual attention (in contrast to a condition in which attention is bound to the vivid sensory qualities of the visual field) and a wider range of perceptual sensitivity than would otherwise be the case. It implies, therefore, rather a capacity for a more flexible and therefore more adaptive sort of perception.

Insofar as they can be determined, the subjective feelings typically associated with the color impression on the Rorschach when it is well integrated with form are not feelings of *helpless* passivity or of disruption of sense of (perceptual) autonomy; for example, such phenomena as have been described by the term "color shock" do not appear in connection with these responses. It is, in fact, only consistent with the integrated character of this perceptual process and the economical or enriching use of the immediate color impression that the visual quality of the color *as such* should be less attention demanding and that the subjective experience in connection with the color *as such* should tend to be less distinct, except insofar as it endows the whole perception with a special vividness or ease of apprehension.

FC responses have been considered, in line with Rorschach's original assumptions and the color-affect linkage, to reflect a more adaptive, reality-tuned emotional responsiveness. However, I believe that, here too, the characteristics of the perceptual mode represented by this score suggest a somewhat broader significance. This perceptual mode suggests a psychological organization in which passive and immediate experience or discharge may appear on a level not antagonistic to, or disruptive of, control functions or adaptive necessities, and which is not associated with a subjective experience of helplessness or loss of autonomy but on a level and of a quality integrated with and valuable to adaptive direction and interest in the ways indicated.

FC responses, therefore, may reflect not only an adaptive responsiveness in the narrow, socially oriented sense but also a range of sensitivity, a mobility of attention, and a susceptibility to pertinent impression all of which are equally significant in connection with such functions as judgment, planning, and, in general, style of thought. They may reflect, also, capacities for more durable, subjectively self-consistent, and also more individually stamped sorts of feelings, involvements, and interests.

Of course, it has again been expedient to speak in ideal, almost typological terms. It will be clear enough to anyone who is familiar with the Rorschach that a great deal that has been said here about the FC response can apply equally well to many responses that may be scored CF, and it is equally true that many responses which, technically, require an FC score do not convey at all the sense and meaning that has been described. Several of these latter sorts of responses, FC responses which, as it were, fall short of their goal will be considered further.

Most such inadequate FC responses are of a specific type; the integration of form and color is simply unsuccessful, not in the sense that it flatly violates reality but that it produces no essential unity in which one feels, of both the color and the form, that each contributes something to the other and perceptually modifies the other. These responses are usually scored F/C. For example, the upper red areas on card II may be seen, the card turned sideways, as representations of animals colored red for decorative purposes as in a stage backdrop; or the popular animals on card VIII may be seen as polar bears with a pink color because they are in a sunset. In such responses the form and the color seem to approach an additive combination; the form is not significantly influenced, or further delineated, or specified by the presence of the color, and the appearance of the color is probably subjectively no different than it would be if detached from this particular form, or seen through a reduction screen—it is uninfluenced by the form which marks its boundaries.

Sometimes it is said that these responses also contain a "forced" use of color. But here again, what is forced is not the response to color *per se*, but the integrative effort. Certainly there seems in such responses to be an integrative effort, but the resulting integration fails, at least partially, in that the color does not fulfill to any appreciable extent its essential functions, i.e., it does not particularly enrich or enliven the form, nor does it seem to have aided or to have been suggestive in the articulation of that form. What is the failure of the integrative process here? It can be made clear by a comparison with more successful form-color integration.

The condition for a successful *FC* response is a susceptibility to the immediate color impression in which that impression offers itself as a possibility to a mobile attention, but not gripping that attention and not, as it were, intruding itself until it becomes an aspect of the final, integrated percept. In the process of the *F/C* response, as much as one can reconstruct it, this does not quite happen. Visual attention seems in this case not to be so mobile and autonomous; although, many times, the subjective attitude toward the color seems to be one of detachment, actually the color seems to offer itself quite insistently. (Both the subjective detachment and the underlying insistence and attention-demanding quality of the color for these subjects are often conveyed in the explanations of their response, in inquiry, which may run as follows: "Well, the color *was there*, so I *had* to explain it some way.") In contrast to the process of a pure *C* or color-dominated response, this insistence of color seems not to be of a sort which aborts (or "short-circuits") form articulation but, nevertheless, occurs to the extent that the color, in contrast here to the successful *FC* process, does establish its final quality independently of the final, complete percept, and perhaps thereby limits, or at least does not extend, the range of acceptable content possibilities.

One sometimes gets the impression with *F/C* responses that a primitive and exceedingly immediate color response has barely been avoided. This expresses, in another way, the fact that the color aspect of these responses often seems so unmodulated perceptually and so little more than a direct and concrete report of a sensory impression (and, in fact, simple color descriptions do frequently appear in these same records, though given in a detached way and not intended as official responses). Yet, insofar as a logical coordination is achieved between the color and form, and a quality of detachment is maintained, a "short-circuit" is avoided. It will, in fact, be found in many cases where *F/C* responses figure prominently that there is a general avoidance of and an apparent incapacity for a freer or more frankly immediate response to the color, a playful use of it, or a sensory enjoyment of it, and *CF* responses will tend to be absent in these cases. Thus, the *F/C* response seems, on the one hand, in some way to be associated with a relatively unmodulated, sensorially direct, and insistent perception of color, yet, on the other hand, at least in one context in which it frequently appears, it seems associated with an avoidance of free response to color. What is the meaning of this apparently paradoxical circumstance?

It seems possible in certain cases that capacities for active perceptual form articulation have been achieved, not together with a more or less gradual modification of the perceptual position and function of more immediate sensory experience but only by way of an excessive detachment of attention from such sensory experience in favor of form elements. It is not clear how such a detachment of attention might be achieved and maintained, though possibly the persistent and unvarying fixing of attention on form elements of the visual field (such as we see in many obsessive-compulsive Rorschachs) is itself a critical factor in maintaining it. This sort of detachment is quite different from the more flexible and mobile attention described before. It does achieve facility in form articulation, but at a cost of more immediate sensory experience; it does achieve a degree of active, autonomous visual attention, but the range of that attention is limited; and it often has a quality of strain and of being only a short step from losing its autonomy to compelling sensory stimuli (as, in fact, in some rigid, compulsive Rorschachs, the detached accumulation of pure form responses is abruptly interrupted by a pure C response). The F/C response seems to involve such a detachment, but a detachment of a partial or less complete and wavering sort. It appears to involve a compromise in which a color experience, which is initially insistent and attention compelling and which, as we have said, establishes its final quality in the perception independently, is yet regarded with a degree of detachment until the form articulation is also independently established, and only then is it fully and officially admitted. It is some process such as this, I believe, that gives the F/C response its peculiar quality of an effortful combination of elements which are not really integrated perceptually.

F/C responses of this sort are found frequently in overcontrolled, compulsive people. They seem to reflect a kind of responsiveness, adaptivity, or spontaneity that may be described as "forced" in the same sense that the response itself may be called "forced"; i.e., one senses in this kind of responsiveness some quality of discrepancy or incomplete integration between a not quite sufficiently modulated impulse or tension discharge and the intent or direction with which it is coordinated and which it is supposed to serve.

This type of F/C response is by no means the only one; the process which has been described may have a number of variants, and so, accordingly, may the specific perceptual quality of the response and its specific interpretive meaning. It must be added, also, that there are various shades of responses that fall somewhere between the type of *F/C* response described and a successful *FC*. A less rigid, and perhaps more smoothly functioning, detachment, which is still essentially of this sort may allow for better integration of the color with form, and may even eventuate in a response scorable as *FC*. Such conditions are among those taken up below.

There are, of course, many different perceptual qualities even among *FC* responses in which form and color are, according to our criteria, perfectly well integrated. Two sorts of cases will be considered now in which such *FC* response seems to have a significance somewhat different from, and which in some ways falls short of, the general *FC* quality described. These are, first, cases in which one or two *FC* responses comprise the *only* color responses, and, secondly, cases of an apparent overabundance of *FC* responses.

There are several types of Rorschachs in which a few *FC* responses will comprise the only color response. First of all, there are the Rorschachs of extremely inhibited people, which are likely to be quite constricted in general. Secondly, there are the records of compulsive people, which are dominated by a large number of meticulous, pure-form responses. The general problem of these cases may be put as follows: Can *FC* responses, in such contexts, be said to reflect the wider range of perceptual sensitivity or the susceptibility to immediate sensory experience and the readiness to use it, which were previously described as characteristic of the *FC* tendency? Or, to put the issue another way, is it possible that a perceptual organization in which a frank, immediate responsiveness (of a color-dominated-response type) is so decisively avoided may still allow for such flexible use of color as the *FC* score has been said to imply? The answer appears to be "yes," but with certain qualifications.

It seems that in these cases of rigid and inhibited psychological organization a *limited* sort of attention may be allowed to the colors in the Rorschach. It is true that the functioning of a psychological control organization such as this seems to dictate a relatively consistent detachment from, or avoidance of, color in favor of exercise of more active, more controlled form-organizing perceptual capacities. Within this general orientation, however, the rigidity or constriction may be more or may be less severe, and the restriction of attention to form elements may be more or less marked. In connection with the *F/C* response we have seen one way in which such rigidity may *waver*, and one way in which detachment may be *partially* relaxed. When the general control organization is functioning more smoothly, some greater mobility of perceptual attention may be achieved, but perhaps only to an extent and under conditions which do not challenge the essential dominance of the more actively controlled form-organizing perceptual mode.

What are such conditions? For example, attention may be allowed to the more muted colors (e.g., the "brown-grey mice" in card X), whereas it is not allowed to the more vivid ones; or, attention may be allowed to colors in connection with form percepts which are very obvious and easily articulated, whereas it is not allowed otherwise. In the cases under discussion, where one or two *FC* responses comprise the total color response, richer responses involving the more vivid colors or larger colored areas (e.g., "Halloween witches in black and red costumes" on card II) are not likely to be present. In other words, the sort of mobility of perceptual attention which is associated with the *FC* response is not an all-or-none affair; it may operate within various limits and with various sorts and degrees of restriction. The perceptual quality of the resulting response will vary accordingly, and so will its interpretive significance. Thus, even one or two *FC* responses within such otherwise rigid or constricted records will generally reflect some of the flexible, responsive, or sensitive traits generally associated with the *FC* tendency, but in muted ways or within limited areas which are not inconsistent with the quality of the general control organization.

The second type of case considered in order to illustrate the various perceptual qualities which are possible within the *FC* category is that type in which there is an unusual abundance, in a sense even an excess, of *FC* responses. These *FC* responses, in contrast to the rigid or inhibited Rorschachs discussed above, may appear together with many *CF* and even pure *C* responses. It might be asked, with some justification, how *FC* responses could be too abundant, in view of their generally adaptive significance. The answer is, of course, in the fact that such a context suggests that the individual *FC* response must have a somewhat different quality and significance from what is usual.

One such record, for example, obtained from a male overt homosexual, included seven *FC*, two *F/C*, and four *CF* out of a total of 27 responses. Only five of these 27 responses were pure-form responses; wherever color was present and available, some sort of color-form response was preferred to a pure-form response.

Actually, his emphasis on color went further, in a certain way, than even this tabulation can demonstrate. In his verbalization generally, and particularly in the inquiry, wherever a response was by objective criteria a product of both color and form aspects, he invariably under-scored the color aspect.

For example, his remark, "It had to be something—the color just suggested it," was a typical answer to inquiry, even in connection with obviously well-articulated perceptions. Or, his description of card IX, "An arrangement of tropical plants—arranged more just for the combination of colors than for the beauty of the flowers them-selves," or even on card I, "The first thing I thought of was kind of the outline of a bat—maybe the color more than anything else."

We have indicated that the *FC* response reflects, ideally, a type of sensitivity to the color stimulus and a capacity to use it which result in an enrichment of the final perception and an economy in the per-ceptual process. This sort of readiness to make use of the more im-mediate color experience, together with form elements, has been de-scribed as indicating a more flexible kind of perception and a more freely ranging visual attention. But it is clear in the case described that we cannot speak simply of a *readiness* to use color in this way; instead, for this patient, there appears to be a marked *reliance* on some use of the immediate color experience, together with form ele-ments, to achieve a reasonably well-delineated response. Pure *F* responses, in other words, tend to be supplanted by *FC* responses. What does this mean, and, specifically, what is the interpretive mean-ing of *FC* in these circumstances?

It will be helpful, at this point, to consider certain features of the clinical picture that this patient presented. He was a capable enough person who arranged and organized his life in a way that for the most part would indicate to an observer some stability and direction. The patient himself, however, did not particularly feel such a direction or, at least, did not feel that it originated from him and was controlled by him. Whatever he did was felt by him either to be vaguely impulsive, or dictated by external necessity, or submissive to another person's wishes, and, in fact, his activities tended to be so arranged as to leave such issues unclear. He experienced little or no sense of active choice, decision, or autonomous action. A clear-cut and self-aware sort of planning, especially of a long-range sort, was largely absent, although, as mentioned, the objective course of his life was by no means chaotic.

Throughout the Rorschach, along with his tendency to underscore the color determination of his responses, this patient repeatedly em-phasized their intuitive, impressionistic nature (e.g., in such comments as, "It was the first thing I thought of . . . ," "It just looked that way at a quick glance . . . ," "The color just suggested it . . . "). The verbal emphasis on the impressionistic nature of actually well-articulated responses is consistent with the perceptual tendency described; i.e., it is consistent with what appears to be a *reliance on the suggestive value* of the more immediate and sensorially more impressive aspect of the stimulus for the initiation even of what may finally become a well-articulated percept. This sort of reliance seems generally to be involved when the *FC* mode dominates and tends to supplant pure-form articulations.

This tendency does not imply a severe impairment or "short-circuit" of form-articulation capacities. It does indicate, however, that complex form-articulation capacities either have not been maximally developed or tend to be avoided in favor of more impressionistic short-cuts to the achievement of articulated percepts. This perceptual mode, therefore, may be considered one that fulfills the adaptive requirement of perceptual articulation with the least amount of active and controlled perceptual organizing. The color experience here will not be an altogether compelling and attention-demanding one but, in its suggestive and percept-initiating value, will probably draw greater attention and assume greater visual importance than might ordinarily be the case in an *FC* response.

This type of dominant *FC* tendency will not necessarily be associated with impulsive behavior or affective lability. Nor will it, on the other hand, be associated with the sort of adaptive flexibility previously described in connection with the *FC* response. It will rather tend to be associated with that kind of life style which, though sufficiently well-organized and adaptive, is somewhat lacking in, or shrinks from, the sort of controls and the degree of detachment from transient external pressures that make for clear and autonomous direction, for the capacity to make long-range plans, for sustained though not necessarily rigid convictions, etc., and which, because of that insufficiency, relies heavily although quite selectively on the manifest external pressures of the moment and the passively experienced internal response to them. Such people prefer to feel "it happened to me" rather than "I did it." Where this dominant *FC* mode is surrounded by color-dominated response, the character will usually have a somewhat more impulsive quality; where color-dominated responses are fewer, it will generally be more submissive in tone.

It is clear, then, that within the *FC* category, as in the other major scoring categories, there exists a range of perceptual qualities with a corresponding range of interpretive meanings.   One additional point may be noted at this time.   It is apparent that at the *FC* end of the color-response scale as at the other, pure *C* end, the value of the color-affect hypothesis tends to diminish and the supposed linkage becomes foggy.   Although the various sorts of subjective experiences and forms of tension discharge other than affects which have been described in connection with various types of color response are not unrelated to affect experience in its ordinary meaning, it is in the *CF* range that the linkage between color and affect has its principal validity.

SUMMARY

We have selected a sample from the ordinary range of Rorschach color responses for the purpose of examining a variety of perceptual modes in which color plays some part and to illustrate an interpretation of color response in terms of the perceptual processes involved in it.

This perceptual understanding of color response rests primarily on three factors, which, of course, are separated and abstracted here only for purposes of exposition: (1) The more strictly sensory and perceptually immediate quality (i.e., requiring a minimum of perceptual organizing or deliberate direction of visual attention) that is intrinsic to color as a visual stimulus; (2) the special, more passive or immediate *aspect* which may be seen in one form or another or on one level or another in all Rorschach color responses; and (3) the nature of the individual perceptual organization and integrative capacities which will determine the quality and significance of this aspect of visual experience, from an altogether attention-compelling and distracting experience, antagonistic to form articulation, to a sensitive and smoothly operating use of color to facilitate and enrich an articulated percept. The quality of color response will therefore reflect aspects of the perceptual and general psychological organization, which pertain to the more passive and immediate varieties of subjective experience and tension discharge, and will indicate, also, something of their specific quality.   From this point of view, the affect-color linkage must be regarded as a special case of a more general phenomenon.

BIBLIOGRAPHY

1. Ames, Louise Bates, Learned, Janet, Metraux, Ruth W., and Walker, R. N. *Child Rorschach responses.* New York: Paul Hoeber, 1952.
2. Dworetzky, Gertrude. Le test de Rorschache et l'evolution de la perception, *Arch. Psychol.,* **27**, 1939.
3. Dworetzky, Gertrude. The development of perception in the Rorschach. In: *Developments in the Rorschach technique. Vol. II.* Yonkers: World Book Co., 1956, 104–176.
4. Ford, Mary. *The application of the Rorschach test to young children.* Minneapolis: University of Minnesota Press, 1946.
5. Friedman, H. Perceptual regression in schizophrenia: An hypothesis suggested by the use of the Rorschach test. *J. genet. Psychol.,* 1952, **81**, 63–99.
6. Goldstein, Kurt, and Scheerer, Martin. Abstract and concrete behavior: an experimental study with special tests. *Psychol. Monogr.,* 1944, **53**, 239.
7. Halpern, Florence. *A clinical approach to children's Rorschachs.* New York: Grune and Stratton, 1953.
8. Hanfmann, E. Study of personal patterns in an intellectual performance. *Character and Personality,* 1941, **9**, 315–325.
9. Hanfmann, E., and Kasanin, J. Conceptual thinking in schizophrenia. *Nerv. ment. Dis. Mongr.,* 1942, No. 67.
10. Harlow, H. F. The formation of learning sets. *Psychol. Rev.,* 1949, **56**, 51–65.
11. Honkavaara, Sylvia. The "dynamic-affective" phase in the development of concepts. *J. Psychol.,* 1958, **45**, 11–23.
12. Huxley, A. *Heaven and hell.* New York: Harper, 1956.
13. Katz, D. *The world of color.* London: Routledge and Kegan Paul, 1935.
14. Klopfer, B., and Margulies, H. A. Rorschach reactions in early childhood. *Rorschach Res. Exch.,* 1941, **5**, 1–23.
15. Lindberg, B. J. *Experimental studies of colour and non-colour attitude in school children and adults.* Copenhagen: Leven & Munksgaard · Ejnar Munksgaard, 1938.
16. Rapaport, D. Some metapsychological considerations concerning activity and passivity. Paper read at the Austen Riggs Center, 1953.
17. Rapaport, D., Gill, M., and Schafer, R. *Diagnostic psychological testing.* Chicago: Yearbook Publishers, 1945.
18. Revesz, G. An experimental study in abstraction in monkeys. *J. comp. Psychol.,* 1925, **5**, 293–343.
19. Rickers–Ovsiankina, Maria. Some theoretical considerations regarding the Rorschach method. *Rorschach Res. Exch.,* 1943, **7**, 41–53.
20. Riesen, Austin H. Plasticity of behavior; psychological aspects (multigraphed).
21. Riesen, A. H. Post-partum development of behavior. *Chicago med. Sch. Quart.,* 1951, **13**, No. 1, 17–24.
22. Rorschach, H. *Psychodiagnostics.* Bern: Hans Huber, 1942.
23. Schachtel, E. On color and affect. *Psychiatry,* 1943, **6**, 393–409.
24. Schafer, R. *Psychoanalytic interpretation in Rorschach testing.* New York: Grune and Stratton, 1954.

25. Schilder, P. *Medical psychology.* New York: International Universities Press, 1953.

26. Senden, M. *Raum and Gestaltauffassung bei operierten Blindgeborenen.* Leipzig: Barth, 1932. (Translation of notes on original by Laboratory of Psychology, Cornell University, 1950.)

27. Shapiro, D. Color-response and perceptual passivity. *J. proj. Tech.,* 1956, **20**, No. 1, 52–69.

28. Stein, M. Personality factors involved in the temporal development of Rorschach responses. *J. proj. Tech.,* 1949, **8**, 355–414.

29. Thompson, J. The ability of children of different grade levels to generalize on sorting tests. *J. Psychol.,* 1941, **11**, 119–126.

30. Weigl, E. On the psychology of so-called processes of abstraction (transl.). *J. abnorm. soc. Psychol.,* 1941, **36**, 3-33.

31. Werner, H. *Comparative psychology of mental development.* Chicago: Follett Publishing Company, 1948.

In the quiet of night when awaking
Loneliness treads near my place
How to go on living and laughing?
Darkness stares into my face.

Is there still a scent from candles
And a mother's softness near?
How the smoke envelops me in blackness
And only melancholy's here. *

ALBIN ZOLLINGER

8 | by Ewald Bohm

THE

BINDER CHIAROSCURO SYSTEM

AND ITS THEORETICAL BASIS [1]

It may be a matter of chance that Binder's fundamental essay (2), although it appeared as early as twenty years ago, even today remains little known in the United States. The work is seldom mentioned, and even then not always correctly. Nevertheless, European workers consider Binder's writings among the most important publications in the field.

It is no easy task to work one's way through this treatise and to master its complicated trains of thought. The effort is worth while, however, since the Binder system offers a number of advantages. Only after the analysis of a considerable number of test protocols did Binder arrive at his classification criteria. Following Rorschach, he treats the chiaroscuro reactions, analogous with form, color, and movement responses, in the light of the experiences determining them, whereas in scoring systems based on the distinction among surface, depth, and texture, the treatment appears to be more closely related to the content

---

* Translated by Morton Felix.

[1] This chapter is a translated and modified version of the author's publication *Das Binder'sche Helldunkelsystem*, Rorschachiana, **V**, 1959, pp. 3–21.

of the responses than to the underlying experiences. The widely used systems of Klopfer (10) and Beck (1) utilize three-dimensionality as a criterion for classification of chiaroscuro responses. Binder, too, realized that in many of these interpretations three-dimensionality plays a role, but did not consider this factor an essential or invariable aspect of the shading. Their summative nature rather than three-dimensionality is considered by Binder to be the distinguishing feature of chiaroscuro responses. It it consequently advisable to keep apart these two things—the mode of experiencing the shading and the criterion of three-dimensionality. I record the three-dimensional responses as "perspective," and take their occurrence into account as an independent phenomenon.

Binder's system has the further advantage that it is based on a carefully considered and very usable theory of feeling. Theory and practice are synthesized in a way which we do not meet even in Rorschach's own writings. It therefore seems appropriate to begin the presentation of his system with an exposition of this theoretical basis.

BINDER'S THEORY

Peripheral and Central Phenomena

In his theory, Binder essentially follows the Munich branch of the objectivistic, phenomenological school. He distinguishes between peripheral and central psychic phenomena.[2] In order to account for the great adaptability in coordinating functions between the incoming sensory and outgoing motor "sides" of the organism's periphery, Binder postulates a mediating agent which he calls the "sophropsyche," a term borrowed from Braun (4). The sophropsyche is a set of cognitive-conative systems, culminating in an "integrative organ" (2), the ego. Since the ego represents primarily the phylogenetically late developed "higher" mental activities, it is to be thought of as peripheral in nature. In contrast to these ego-syntonic processes, the ego-alien deep-seated urges and emotions constitute the core of the person or the id, and are to be considered central in terms of Binder's basic dichotomy. This differentiation does not coincide with that between

---

[2] This distinction into peripheral and central phenomena should not be interpreted as paralleling the differentiation of neurological processes into peripheral and central [Editor].

"conscious" and "unconscious." Peripheral as well as central processes may be conscious, half-conscious, or unconscious, according to the extent to which inner awareness is focused on them. Through constant interaction, the ego and the id combine into the superordinate unity of the individual.[3]

Characteristics of Feeling

According to Binder, all feelings are characterized by the following four criteria:

1. Feelings always show "a peculiar warmth"; they are pleasant or unpleasant; they have a quality of like or dislike; in other words, they are never indifferent.

2. Feelings show "a peculiar subjectivity." One may distinguish "a subjective and an objective component of feeling," but, in contrast to the objective one, the subjective component can never be absent.

3. Feelings *per se* are not "directed," but a direction may be superimposed upon them from the outside.

4. "Feelings are not acts, but merely states which the individual experiences passively" (2, p. 4).

The latter feature distinguishes them from strivings, which involve psychomotor activity. However, introspectively, feelings and strivings may be experienced as closely linked.

[3] The ego concept presented here as a "sophropsychic integrative organ" interpolated between the centripetal and centrifugal "sides" of the human organism and possessing regulative functions, essentially corresponds to Freud's conception of the ego. Freud's ego is "the organized part of the id" (6, p. 24), and has "controlling, mediating, and integrating functions" (6, pp. 15–16). In *The Question of Lay Analysis,* Freud writes: "We recognize in man a psychical organization which is interpolated between his sensory stimuli and perception of his bodily needs on the one hand, and his motor activity on the other; and which mediates between them with a certain purpose. We call this organization his 'I' (ego)" (7, p. 33).

Binder's conception of the id as the emotive and conative core of the personality, now conscious, now semiconscious, and now unconscious, differs however in one respect from Freud's id conception. The Freudian id is indeed also "the oldest of mental provinces" (5, p. 14), the original core of the personality, but it is always unconscious: "Everything which goes on in the id is unconscious and remains so" (7, p. 38).

Categories of Feeling

In accordance with the above division of psychic phenomena into peripheral and central, Binder arrives at the following classification of feelings:

I. Peripheral, reactive, discrete feelings.
    (a) Sensory   (b) Dispositional
II. Central feeling-tones (moods).
    1. Central, reactive, total-feelings (*Gesamtgefühle*).
    (a) Sensory   (b) Dispositional
    2. Endogenous vitality-feelings (*Lebensgefühle*).

The *peripheral discrete feelings* are aroused by sensations, perceptions, and ideas, and are closely connected with them. Usually they constitute rather specific reactions of consciousness and possess a relative independence within the momentary state of the person. Different discrete feelings may exist side by side at the same time. The *sensory* discrete feelings are connected with a palpable sensory element of a perception and their objective feeling component is pronounced. The *dispositional* discrete feelings are based on an "act intending a single object of perception, of ideation or of thought." They are directed and intentional (joy at, dislike of, love of, fear of). Here the subjective part is more evident (2, pp. 5–7).

The *central total-feelings* are also of a reactive nature, and are aroused by peripheral experience. Where an entire sensory area is experienced as total impression, a *sensory* total-feeling arises. A diffuse multiplicity is experienced, which through some common basic feature is merged into a whole. When a circumstance of broad implications combines a wide area of objects and events into a total situation, a *dispositional* total-feeling arises. Such sensory and dispositional total experiences may give rise to a "feeling resonance" in the deeper layers of the personality, which will then diffuse into a broad total-feeling. Total-feelings, as a rule, reverberate for a long time and their directional character is so faint that intentionality can no longer be ascribed to them. The subjective feeling component is preponderant. Two different total-feelings cannot exist at the same time in consciousness. The total-feelings are identical with Kuelpe's "generalized feelings" (*Gemeingefühle*) (12).

The *vitality-* or *life-feelings*, finally, are the "deepest central emotional background of everything experienced." They are not reactive, but endogenous. They are purely subjective and they are not directed. They are "tied to the totality of the . . . indistinct organic sensations and fused with these into a uniform experience" (2, p. 6). The endogenous vitality-feelings blend to a great extent with the reactive total-feelings. Thus these central feeling tones together form the *moods*, in which an endogenous and a reactive side are to be distinguished. At times, however, as a consequence of the general spreading tendency of feelings, very intensive and prolonged peripheral feelings may expand into the center of the personality, and then assume the character of a mood. These moods will then acquire an object-oriented, concrete direction. Thus there are no sharp lines of demarcation among the various categories of feeling.

Psychiatric Implications

According to these views of Binder's, *endogenous mood disturbance* constitutes "an organically determined fluctuation of the vitality-feelings," which also influences the mode of reaction of the total-feelings. This leads to a constantly heightened readiness for like reactive total-feelings. Occasionally, however, as, e.g., in light depressions, euphorically toned discrete feelings may appear. The *reactive mood disturbance* is the occurrence of a central total-feeling produced by a complex experience or by the expanding of very strong and lasting discrete feelings. Here, too, the readiness is increased for responding in a like feeling tone to almost every stimulation from outside. As a rule, the vitality-feelings remain unaffected in reactive depressions, although there are cases in which the total-feelings are of such depth that they may engulf even the vital feelings. The *autochthonous mood lability* consists of abnormally frequent changes of the vital feelings, the phases of which, however, last for at least a few hours. The *common reactive mood lability* appears to be a constitutionally based anomaly of central total-feelings, which respond readily even to mild stimulation, but fade rapidly. This kind of mood fluctuation may be very transitory. When total-feelings of only a single quality occur, Binder speaks of *one-sided reactive mood lability* (2, p. 8). In psychopaths this type of lability seems to be rooted in temperament, while in neurotics, it is more likely to be functional in nature.

Like Ribot (15) and Szymanski (18), Binder distinguishes four basic mood qualities, the euphoric and three dysphoric ones, namely, the sad, the anxious, and the irritable. In addition, these qualities may appear in mixed forms (2, p. 8).

Emotion and Perception

The problem under consideration in this chapter makes it desirable to say a few words about Binder's ideas regarding the relationship between perception and emotional experiences. He develops these ideas from the supposition that there are two principal attitudes under which it is possible to grasp a number of simultaneously occurring visual stimuli:

1. One may apprehend every sensory pattern as separate and interpret it objectwise. Such an attitude will be accompanied by a number of sensory and dispositional discrete feelings. Since the perceived "whole" is experienced as an aggregate of independent items, as something summative, mosaiclike, only incomplete fusion of these discrete feelings can occur. In the resulting so called "mixed feelings," the separate affective components can easily be discerned by directing one's attention toward them.

2. One may also take in the perceptual totality at a glance, without attending separately to its different sensory components. They are simply experienced as a diffuse multiplicity. Since the perceptual impression is a holistic one, awareness of its common undertone within the multiplicity is what primarily characterizes this experience and leads to sensory total-feelings or mood reactions. Any dispositional total-feelings arising at the same time will be fused with them.

These two extreme attitudes may combine. In such cases, single, especially striking, sensory items will be perceived separately and with object character, so that they are experienced as "foreground" on the "background" of diffuse total impressions into which the remaining perceptual material blends.

To a certain extent, both modes of experience may be brought about intentionally. The objective nature of the presented stimuli, however, greatly influences the mode of experience. If the visual stimuli consist mostly of sharply offset, disparate elements, the experience is usually correspondingly mosaiclike, and there is no "true total impression." On the other hand, visual stimulus material containing indistinctly separated details that blur into each other and are similar to each other is likely to produce a total impression, especially where these details are "tuned to" a common keynote. Such visual impressions thus bring about reactive moods (central total-feelings). We know these differences from art. The genre picture or still life of

Dutch realists appeals to our discrete feelings. It has been justly said about such a picture as the well-known "Iron Mill" by Adolph von Menzel (1875) with its multitude of well-defined details that here the eye could find no focal resting point. The landscapes of the Romanticists and the Impressionists, on the other hand, characteristically tend to arouse moods in the observer. In the same way we may distinguish between these two kinds of effect in music and in literature.

In nature, *chromatic colors* mostly appear to us in such a clearly differentiated way that this independence of distinct color blots from each other is experienced as a multitude of single objects. Accordingly, the emotional reaction is one of discrete feelings. The abovementioned "mosaiclike impression of a whole" has been created. In the same way, placing a variety of equally bright color patches side by side in a painting fails to produce any moods.

On the other hand, the *chiaroscuro scale* of white-grey-black is typically experienced in quite a different way. In nature it occurs mainly in the grey of dawn, in the twilight, in the moonlit landscape, fog, darkness, or the "floating light of distant atmosphere," where the chiaroscuro values blur indistinctly into each other, and thus "automatically" result in a total impression. The mood tends to be euphoric when brightness prevails, and dysphoric when darkness dominates. The creation of diffuse total impressions is particularly facilitated by chiaroscuro stimuli, because they are more homogeneous than the greatly varied chromatic hues, and thus one of the two conditions for the appearance of total impressions (indistinct delineation and similarity among the given elements) is always fulfilled in the case of chiaroscuro material. The perception of a colored landscape usually calls forth a combination of the two approaches. The play of lights and shadows produces the "background" of the experience, the total-feeling, the mood, whereas single, especially conspicuous, chromatic colors provide the "foreground" which arouses certain discrete feelings as leitmotif.

The essence of these reflections by Binder culminates in a statement that is basic for his Rorschach theory: "Chiaroscuro values primarily affect the total-feelings, produce mood-reactions; the hues of the chromatic colors mainly affect discrete feelings" (2, p. 11).

This proposition, however, does not apply without certain exceptions. The assumption that color perception, by virtue of its "object character," arouses discrete feelings, refers only to the *surface colors* [in the meaning of Katz (8)], which in the Rorschach test correspond mainly to the *FC responses*.[4] The *film colors*, on the other hand, do not show this strong affinity to discrete feelings, but seem to stand in a closer relationship to moods. In the Rorschach, this concerns especially the pure *C* and possibly also certain *CF* responses, as is well demonstrated by protocols of patients with agitated mood disturbance. Binder, who does not mention the work of Katz, was nevertheless fully aware of this psychologically important distinction between colors. He speaks (2, p. 12) of the justification for the expression "color mood," where a color is so predominant that it strikes the keynote which evokes a total color impression, and, hence, a mood reaction. This applies particularly to "large, relatively uniform color areas." This wording, with the examples he gives—"forest-green, ocean-blue, sunset-glow"—suggests that Binder had in mind more or less the same phenomena as those referred to by Katz as "film colors." Far more complicated conditions probably exist in such cases as the glaring color contrasts of an annual fair, which as a rule do not produce visually any mood (unless one squints to bring about artificially a total impression). Besides the over-all brightness, it is the general impact of noises and motion that is here mainly responsible for the mood effect.

In practice, a second exception from Binder's general proposition is of even greater importance. Occasionally chiaroscuro material may be experienced in a mental set toward detail, and in such cases will then lead to peripheral discrete feelings in the same way as do the chromatic colors. "This, however, is only possible," Binder says, "where in the totality of presented stimuli the shadings are sufficiently clearly demarcated, and are of sufficiently differing brightness, so that the individual shading actually is able to produce the effect of a separate form" (2, p. 12). We shall later see that this exception has suggested the main principle of classification in Binder's chiaroscuro system.

Emotion and Overt Behavior

Of relevance to Binder's theory of feeling are his ideas on the psychological problems involved in overt behavior. They center around the controlling functions of the "sophropsyche" discussed earlier in this chapter (p. 203). All organizational mental activity is seen as representing a synthesis between sophropsychic cognitive patterning,

---

[4] For explanation of scoring symbols, see Appendix, pp. 441 ff. [Editor].

on the one hand, and emotional-motivational forces, on the other. This synthesis results in a global formation "which is at once reason, feeling and striving" (2, p. 14). The role of the sophropsychic steering in this process is that of a regulating agent of infinite plasticity. It is directed against peripheral as well as central emotions and strivings, not in the sense of denial but of control (2, p. 14). Such steering does not prevent the arousal of emotions and motivations *per se*, it only checks selectively the overt expression of those that cannot be effectively integrated into rationally formed structures. "Normal steering is thus 'a striving for organization' in perception, thought and action" (2, p. 15).

Empathy

To complete the review of Binder's theoretical system, we shall touch upon his treatment of the controversial concept of *empathy*. Binder agrees with Scheler (16) and Klages (9) that the direct apprehension of another person's expression "does not result from empathy." Empathy is rather the projecting of one's own emotions and strivings, and of accompanying kinesthetic experience, into an external object. The sensory discrete feeling is most easily "objectivized" in this manner; "it is localized completely in the object" (2, p. 15). Volkelt (19) calls this "subjective, unaccentuated empathy," as, e.g., in "the cheerful yellow of the flower." On the other hand, there is no projection of dispositional discrete feelings; the enjoyment of the flower remains my own, and cannot be perceived as a property of the flower. With sensory and dispositional total-feelings, on the other hand, empathy is a frequent phenomenon. When the observer is in a sad mood, the landscape seems to be full of sadness; it acquires an "emotional character." But the mood is also felt as one's own ("subjectively accentuated empathy," according to Volkelt).

BINDER'S SCORING SYSTEM

Binder's Rorschach material consisted of the records of 51 normals, 101 psychopaths, 58 neurotics, and 61 psychotics, altogether 271 cases. The patients were diagnosed through detailed case studies at the psychiatric university clinic in Basel.

Analyzing the protocols, he soon realized that it would not be possible to assign any single interpretation to all chiaroscuro responses.

On the basis of careful, nonsuggestive inquiries into the experiences of his subjects, he arrived at a differentiation of the chiaroscuro responses into two large main categories, with quite different interpretative significance: (1) The faceted responses emphasizing a number of individual discrete shadings, which today are usually called *shading responses;* and (2) the *chiaroscuro responses proper,* which are based entirely on a diffuse total impression of chiaroscuro. In conformity with Rorschach's original scoring, Binder denotes the former group (*C*) responses, and scores them $F(C)+$, since their form by definition can only be good. This implies a narrowing of the category to which Rorschach originally gave the score. As Binder says, he now uses the symbol "in a much more precisely defined manner" (2, p. 27). The other group, Binder identifies as chiaroscuro or *Ch* responses proper.

Classification of Chiaroscuro Responses

Shading or (C) responses. Score: F(C). The frequency of these responses is inversely proportional to that of the other group, the *Ch* responses, and inversely proportional to the frequency of *M*. They have a high negative correlation with *W* and a high positive correlation with *D* and *Dd* (2, pp. 33, 38, 57). The $F(C)$ is a rather rare category of response, and since the score is so often wrongly used, we shall quote Binder's definition verbatim:

. . . Within the selected blot area, the subject, from among all the conspicuous shadings, *picks out each individual one,* primarily emphasizing the delimiting forms of the individual shadings, and only secondarily their chiaroscuro values (2, pp. 26–27).

Binder emphasizes the rarity of the $F(C)$ responses elsewhere with these words:

In each $F(C)$ response, *several* single shadings must be used, and each of them must be interpreted separately. These individual shadings must be objectively different in brightness and clearly delineated from each other (2, p. 31).

The shading response is thus a matter of summative multiplicity. In most cases, these responses are very minutely elaborated. As an example, Binder quotes the following response to the upper projection of card VI:

A fountain in the shape of a slender Triton of black marble [deep black]. It is clearly seen how the water emerges above his head and flows down across the marble. Behind it [the half-moon shaped detail] a Roman bowl made of light, strangely clouded marble. All over the bowl peculiar gargoyles are placed [the featherlike parts]. They are already half crumbled and in places overgrown with dark moss (2, p. 27). The score is D F(C)+ Arch. O+.

An example in which the space details are combined with F(C) and even seen in perspective is the following response to card II:

A parkway in glaring sunlight [white space], both sides lined with dark, overhanging trees [the black]. The street narrows down in the distance to a little path [light grey middle stripes of the point] lying in shade because both sides of it are lined with a fence, perhaps made of rocks. The lane leads up to a pagodalike pavilion [pointed detail] (2, p. 27). The score is WS F(C)+ Na.

The F(C) response, which occurs only rarely in the records of psychopaths and neurotics, always indicates a low threshold for sensory discrete feelings and for rather specific nuances of affective adaptability, while sophropsychic control is adequate and central feeling tones are rarely involved. Two groups of F(C) responses may be distinguished. A preponderance of darker shadings suggests "peripheral feelings of depressive-anxious bend" in insecurely functioning persons (2, pp. 36, 38). The FC occurring in these protocols are mostly a cool blue or green. In the other group, the light, single shadings are especially emphasized, intimate landscapes with idyllic nuances are affectionately described, finely chiseled, attractive or quaint heads are seen, or soft furs almost sensually enjoyed. This type of F(C) interpretation reveals the arousal of gently pleasurable emotional tones in compliant, plastically adapting individuals. These subjects also produce considerable numbers of FC responses, usually warm reds and yellows. It may be said that in a subject of extratensive experience type the F(C) are an indicator of sensitivity, whereas in the record of a subject of introversive experience type they rather suggest oversensitivity. In combination with the white-space interpretations [S F(C)+], the F(C) responses have the meaning of wish fulfillment, as Rorschach realized.

Elsewhere (3, p. 166) I have called the F(C) responses "the auxiliary troops of the color," since in deducing the total affectivity from a protocol the F(C) must always be considered in conjunction with the color responses. The F(C), like the chromatic FC, reflect the subject's emotional adaptability; however, the former indicate an especially finely nuanced capacity for empathy. There are three major kinds of color-shading configurations:

(a) $F(C)$ may occur in a protocol (at times with FCh or even ChF) without color responses. These are nearly always cases of "substitute contact," in which the subject tries to offset his lack of direct emotional adaptation and empathy by a more intellectualized, indirect, hesitant form of contact.

(b) In the case of a preponderance of $F(C)$ over FC, the sensitivity of the subject approaches oversensitivity, particularly in the case of an introversive experience type.

(c) Finally, $F(C)$ may occur together with a predominance of labile color responses, i.e., together with CF and C, and no or very few FC. This combination has proved to be typical of the specific form of oversensitivity found in schizoid persons who, behind a withdrawn facade, conceal an oversensitive core, so that their reactions are at times quite puzzling to the observer. As Kretschmer has expressed it so beautifully, they are "like bare Roman houses, villas, that have closed their shutters against the glaring sun, while in their subdued inner light feasts are being celebrated" (11, p. 159).

Chiaroscuro responses proper or Ch responses. Lacking a common designation for the two major groups, Binder uses the term "chiaroscuro responses" for both $F(C)$ and Ch responses, although he applies the chiaroscuro symbol Ch only to the group of genuine chiaroscuro responses. They are either W responses or refer to large details of the blot. The frequency of Ch responses is inversely proportional to frequencies of $F(C)$ and of color responses. Ch responses have a high positive correlation with W, a clearly negative correlation with D, and a high negative correlation with Dd. In these responses, "no single shadings are selected"; rather the interpretations are based on a diffuse total impression of the chiaroscuro values. "The delimiting forms of the individual shadings receive no attention" (2, p. 28). The outline form, however, may play a more or less significant role. On the basis of the latter criterion, Binder divides the Ch responses, in analogy with the color responses, into three subgroups, as follows:

(a) *The FCh+ or FCh− responses* (depending on the quality of the form perception) are responses in which the outline form is emphasized primarily and clearly, "while the diffuse chiaroscuro impression is given less weight than the delimiting form" (2, p. 29), e.g., "Scarecrow draped with dark material" (card IV) or "The silhouette of the ruins of a castle on rocks (upper half of card VI in > position). "Animal skin" (especially for cards IV and VI) should be scored FCh only where the chiaroscuro factor is emphasized (2, pp. 66, 67).

(b) *The ChF responses* are interpretations in which the chiaroscuro impression is so much in the foreground "that the form delineations of the area are only faintly and unclearly perceived, if not entirely disregarded" (2, p. 30), e.g., "Stormy clouds" (card VII), "X-ray pictures of an animal" (card IV), "Dark-wooded mountain slope, a sort of mountain ridge" (card V).

(c) In the *pure Ch responses,* finally, the form factor of the blots is entirely ignored in the interpretation, "so that the subject reports nothing but a diffuse chiaroscuro impression" (2, p. 30), e.g., "Stormy mood" (card IV), "Like a nightmare" (card IV), "The play of the waves" (card I, right side).

The *Ch* responses are more frequent in neurotics than in normals, and still more frequent in psychopaths. In contrast to the *F(C)*, which reflect peripheral discrete feelings, the *Ch* interpretations are always connected with central feeling tones, mostly of a dysphoric nature. In the case of the *FCh,* sophropsychic control of these moods may be assumed, since such responses usually accompany a high *F+%,* an orderly succession, and a normal apperception type. Control of moods is inadequate with the *ChF,* and entirely absent in the pure *Ch.* In the case of the *FCh−,* a striving for self-control is still present, but because of inadequately differentiated judgment, it is no longer effective.

Borderline Cases

To complete the discussion of Binder's classificational system, some borderline cases should be mentioned in order to differentiate them from the chiaroscuro responses. Binder emphasizes about all these borderline cases that they are *not* "genuine chiaroscuro responses" (2, p. 23).

1. Interpretations of the *white areas* occur in two variations. Such a response either is a *secondary* reference to the white color (e.g., "Lampshade of white china" to the space detail in card II), and is scored simply *F;* or is a *primary* reference to the white color (e.g., "Snowman" to the space detail in card IX), and, as a genuine color response, is scored *FC.* That these primary references to white are genuine color responses is indicated by their occasional appearance in conjunction with chromatic color responses (as figure-ground fusion, one might say). An example is the response to the central red in card VIII combined with the white space above: "Elegant red kimono with

especially nice white collar." These "genuine" white color responses seem to have a whole series of possible interpretations. As Binder himself mentions, they may be the expression of an euphoric mood. Rorschach found reference to the white as well as to the grey and black colors in epileptics, and sometimes also in disorganized schizophrenics. I myself have observed the use of black, grey, and white color as a not uncommon component of the ixothyme [5] syndrome. More recently Zulliger reported (20, p. 243) that he had found white-color responses mostly in records of oversensitive and easily hurt subjects who endeavor to hide their sensitivity. Furthermore, it should be remembered that, when the white color serves as a determinant, space responses are involved, and hence their interpretative significance must also be considered. In any case, they are never assigned a chiaroscuro score.

2. Similarly, responses to which only the outline of a darker or lighter inner detail has contributed, and in which the light-dark gradation has not played a role, do not belong in the chiaroscuro category. Such interpretations are frequently given to the black or the light figures inside the so-called boot on card IV, where the black is often seen as a human figure or a geographical map (e.g., Jutland), the light part as a dog or lion. These are either pure form or movement responses. The same detail may, of course, be perceived in quite different ways, as in the following example by Binder: one subject interprets the two dark stripes in the middle line of card IV in position ∨ as "Man, of whom only his long legs and his hips are plainly seen, while the upper part of his body [in the middle column] is indistinct." This is a pure form response ($Dd F+ H O+$). Another subject, however, interprets the same detail as "A sinister figure—only the legs and the abdomen are clear; on top it looks as if it were shrouded in a dark cloud. A mummified Egyptian—a giant from olden times" (2, p. 23). Here, besides the form, the chiaroscuro values have clearly played a part, and the score is ChF. This important distinction is often overlooked, and responses which are not determined by shading are scored as if they were, thus causing misinterpretations.

3. Again, the use of shading secondarily as an elaboration does not constitute a genuine chiaroscuro response. If, e.g., the subject says on card III: "Two men who take their hats off to each other," and then

[5] The ixothyme constitution, according to Stromgren, is a normal type, with character features analogous to those found in exaggerated and pathological form in epilepsy (17).

after a pause goes on: "One might also say, if one wishes, that they are English schoolboys because they are dressed in dark clothes" (2, p. 24), then this is a common popular response, and must be scored $W M+ H P$. At most, we may, with Zulliger, indicate the tendency as $FCh \rightarrow$. The full score, then, would be $W FCh \rightarrow M+ H P$.

4. Finally, a whole group of responses must be distinguished from the genuine chiaroscuro responses, because the subjects do not react emotionally but purely intellectually to the chiaroscuro impression. Binder calls these responses "intellectual chiaroscuro responses" (2, p. 25). They usually are given by subjects who want to put on airs "to create an impression of specialized knowledge and education." There are three kinds of such responses.

(a) The chiaroscuro namings are a special kind of description and should be dealt with as such, i.e., they are not given any score, but instead "chiaroscuro description" is noted. Here an effort to make an impression has induced the subject "in spite of lack of ideas nevertheless to say something." Binder illustrates this kind of response with the following example: "A person familiar with the technique of charcoal drawing is reminded of it by the shadings because everything is so blurred together" (2, p. 25).

(b) Another variety of intellectual chiaroscuro response is somewhat more concrete, and may be scored as real interpretation. It does not matter much whether they are scored $F-$ or ChF responses, as long as they are marked "intellectual chiaroscuro response" and are kept apart from the genuine chiaroscuro scores. Binder describes them as "'scientific' reminiscences," and gives this example: "When in a chemistry experiment two fluids are mixed together, then such clouds are created in one of the substances" (2, p. 25).

(c) A third, rather rare subgroup of the same phenomenon includes the responses which might be called *descriptions of the chiaroscuro symbolism*. They are closely related to schizoid symbolic interpretations. They are scored in the same way as are the "scientific" reminiscences. An example is the following reaction to card VII: "That [lower third] would be the dark grey life—and here [midline] it then goes through the narrow gate of death up to heaven [white space] which appears quite white" (2, p. 26).

DARK SHOCK

An outgrowth of Binder's chiaroscuro scoring system are his reflections on the dark shock, the aspect of his work that is most familiar to American readers. He observed this phenomenon first in "persistent neurotic depressions." It consists of failure to respond to the dark cards, especially to card IV or, more frequently, inhibition of interpretations on these cards, reflected in *Dd* or *Do* responses, poor form, trite stereotypes, disturbance of succession, or unusual perceptions (2, p. 279).

Since Binder drew attention to the existence of dark shock, it has been found on all achromatic Rorschach cards, and today we know that dark shock may appear as a component of such psychopathologic Rorschach syndromes as phobias, psychasthenias, etc. It is always an indicator of pervasive anxiety. As such it is less frequent than the color shock which is characteristic of peripheral and more isolated emotional imbalances.[6]

Dark shock may occur alone or together with color shock, in the latter case with or without interference phenomena on cards IV or VII (3, p. 103 ff.). Furthermore, the possibility of shock compensation and the simultaneous presence or absence of depression symptoms all have to be taken into consideration for an adequate evaluation of the dark shock on an individual Rorschach protocol.[7]

Mohr (13) has given us some interesting speculations regarding the psychogenesis of dark shock. Symbolically, black is frequently perceived as the "opposite of the impression of life inherent in light." It is lifeless, empty, dead. Since in a variety of cultures death is viewed as atonement for man's sins before God, the black color has become symbolic of the divine and of guilt. As pictured in the Prometheus legend, victory over nature has left man with a fear of the forces of nature, which, it may be postulated, is now transferred to the black, the dark of night.

Hence Mohr has deduced the following symbolic significance of the black color: Its *positive* meanings are the stable, the unalterable, the

---

[6] In some as yet unpublished research I have been able to demonstrate by measuring the skin temperature that the dark shock represents a diminutive anxiety attack, i.e., manifest anxiety, a finding which may be of importance for the differential diagnosis of neuroses.

[7] For more details on the symptomatic value of dark shock, see 3, pp. 100–105, 196, 199 ff., 218–220, etc.

solemn (*viz.*, its use in formal clothes), the symbol of authority, the majesty of death, the divine. The *negative* meanings are guilt, rebellion, anxiety, and judgment. Since the father is the first authority in the life of the small child, it appears understandable in the light of the above relationships, that those of Mohr's subjects who were in conflict with their father felt an "unpleasant, somber, anxious mood" on cards I, IV, and VI, whereas persons not bothered by such conflicts react to these cards "with moods of security and calmness." Negative reactions to the dark cards were also observed in girls who had experienced conflict with a man. Here, of course, man may mean the father figure, but the black may also directly symbolize "evil," the negative masculine, as it is found in the symbolism of some Western cultures.

However valuable these observations may be for the understanding of individual Rorschach protocols, the reader should be warned against mechanically considering the card IV *"the* father card," just as card VII cannot be called *"the* mother card." Not every disturbance on card IV in the form of dark shock must necessarily rest upon a father conflict or on a sexual conflict with a man. Such a conclusion may only be drawn where it is made probable by the total picture of the particular Rorschach protocol. Psychological insight and clinical experience are of particular importance here.

SOPHROPSYCHIC CONTROL

To demonstrate concretely how Binder applies his scoring system to a psychological analysis of Rorschach protocols, we shall present in some detail his deductions with respect to sophropsychic control (see p. 203 and pp. 209 f.).

Today it has become customary in superficial Rorschach practice simply to "read off" the degree of reality adaptation of an individual from the $F+\%$, as well as from the relation of the FC and FCh to the other color and chiaroscuro scores. This, however, does not provide an adequate picture of the subject's reality adaptation; rather a more complex pattern of test factors has to be taken into consideration.

Thus, Binder infers sophropsychic inhibitory tendencies from the particular manner in which his hypersensitive, asthenic subjects handle their chiaroscuro responses. For example, in sensitive psychopaths, a Ch response is frequently followed by an $F(C)$ response of labored objectivity. Binder gives the following example: First the subject responds to card VI in position > with, "A wreck in a sea of ice. Everything snowed under and covered with ice, quite abandoned. And below, the melancholy reflection. Arctic loneliness." The score is $D FCh+ Na O+$. Then the card is placed in $\wedge$ position, and the subject interprets the upper projection: "That is a newt in an embryonic stage seen under the microscope in transmitted light. The inside of the embryo, alimentary canal, ganglia, etc., are already firmly formed and hence appear dark. Then round it a semi-transparent mantle. In front, a little darker, the embryonic eyes. On both sides the extremities, flippers, etc., partially formed toward the periphery—the darker fibers of the tissue are clearly seen." The score is $D F(C)+ A O+$ (2, p. 235).

The first response reflects a relatively intensive mood reaction to the general diffuseness of the chiaroscuro. An emotion of such intensity may be expected to reverberate for some time, and so the second response is again prompted by the light-dark effect of the blot. What is significant, however, is that this time the interpretation does not fall into the Ch category, quite contrary: by means of pedantic elaborations on minute gradations in shading, the patient constructs an over-rational association. Any peripheral discrete feelings that had been touched off in this context, and that would have to be disphoric in tone because of perserveration of the earlier total-feeling, are blocked. The response is one of marked dry objectivity. It appears plausible to see in this strained scientific affectation an effort to compensate for the initial display of mood disturbance. Such $F(C)$ reactions of stressed matter of factness, devoid of any accompanying feeling, do not occur in the records of normal subjects. They are the result of compensatory mechanisms directed at the upsurge of an emotional attack. The quoted Rorschach responses thus might be viewed as a miniature reproduction of the inner struggle characteristic of the sensitive psychopath.

Sophropsychic inhibition may also affect directly the content of the shading responses, e.g., in the way the interpreted object is projected into great spatial distance. Thus an inner rejection of feeling expresses itself in spatial symbolism, as in the following reaction to card VI:

A cold winter landscape, but seen from far away. In the middle line a brook frozen over in spots, on each side a dark earth slope. Then above there is still some dirty snow lying; one can see the snow streaks running between the dark stones. Farther out some isolated grey snow patches are still seen on the slightly rolling ground. But it is all seen from very far

away, as if you were flying in an airplane far above it. The score is
$D.F(C) + NaO+$ (2, p. 236).

The implication here is that the subject wants to place himself "at a
distance" from his feelings.

Occasionally the rejection of initially experienced moods through
sophropsychic inhibition also affects the Ch responses. The inhibition
may be expressed through either spatial or temporal distance, as in
the well-known phrase, "bird's eye view," or as in the following for
card VI, main part, in ∨ position: "As if one were standing on a
mountain looking down at a distant prairie fire on the plains. Nothing
but fire and smoke." Score: $D\,Ch\,Na\,O-$ (2, p. 253). At times the
rejection of feeling is even given conscious representation, as in the
following response to card IV:

> Something depressing. Maybe a desolate landscape with a chaos of
> strange rocks. And there [dark stripes in the middle above] a very small
> slender figure seen from the back. It turns away from the landscape. Yes,
> I have experienced something like that myself. Score: $W\,ChF\,Na\,O-$ (2,
> p. 253).

Other interpretations stand out by their forced, dry objectivity, as in
the following response to card IV:

> The map of an island with a rugged coast. A certain island in the Malay
> Archipelago has such a shape, but I cannot think of its name. In the in-
> terior the shadings, that is how one indicates the contours on such a map.
> But I don't know—this is indeed somehow a quite unfamiliar island. Score:
> $W\,FCh+\,Map$ (2, p. 254).

Similarly, on card VI: "A newspaper-holder with torn newspapers"
$(W\,FCh+\,Obj\,O+)$ (2, p. 254). And finally, the blocking of feeling
can be inferred from the sudden appearance of a white space or an
artificial form interpretation after several Ch responses (2, p. 255).

The overcompensation of the mood effect may show itself when,
immediately after several mood-colored "genuine" Ch responses, a
Ch response of monumental architecture, devoid of mood, appears. A
subject first gives the following interpretation to the side figure of
card I in > position: "Like a cemetery. There [bat's wing] a cypress,
old and bent, and beside it overturned gravestones. Gives a sinister
impression," $D\,FCh+\,Na\,O+$. And then the somber mood is over-
compensated in the following response (card I in ∨ position): "The
outline of a triumphal arc or something like that. Crude rocks.",
$WS\,FCh+\,Arch\,O+$ (2, p. 256). The overcompensation can also be
recognized in the use of religious symbols, as in the following reaction
to card IV:

Torn clouds, quite dark—that is the first impression I got from that picture. But if one tries hard, one might see there above the clouds the Madonna floating with open arms, *W ChF Scene O—* (2, p. 256).

In all forms of sophropsychic inhibition, a capacity for control may thus be assumed, which is of special importance regarding indications and prognosis for psychotherapy.

CONCLUSIONS

By way of conclusion I should like to submit that through his ingenious interpretations of chiaroscuro reactions to the Rorschach blots, Binder has thrown new light upon the important and complex role played by moods in the total structure of the personality. With his patterns of emotional reactions on the one hand, and indicators of rational controls, on the other, he has so enriched Rorschach theory, that it is nowadays hard to imagine the Rorschach field without Binder's share in it. Hence it seems justifiable to term the European variations upon the original method of Rorschach, the Rorschach-Binder method.

BIBLIOGRAPHY

1. Beck, S. J. *Rorschach's test. Vol. I. Basic processes.* New York: Grune and Stratton, 1944.
2. Binder, H. Die Helldunkeldeutungen im psychodiagnostischen Experiment von Rorschach. *Schweiz. Arch. Neurol. Psychiat.,* 1933, **30**, 1–67 and 233–286.
3. Bohm, E. *Lehrbuch der Rorschach Psychodiagnostik* (1st ed.). Bern: Hans Huber, 1951.
4. Braun, E. Psychogene Reaktionen. In: Bumke, O. (ed.). *Handbuch der Geisteskrankheiten. Vol. 5.* Berlin: Julius Springer, 1928.
5. Freud, S. *An outline of psychoanalysis.* Strachey, J. (Tr.) New York: Norton, 1949.
6. Freud, S. *The problem of anxiety.* Bunker, H. A. (Tr.) New York: Norton, 1936.
7. Freud, S. *The question of lay analysis.* Proctor-Gregg, N. (Tr.) New York: Norton, 1927.
8. Katz, D. *Der Aufbau der Farbwelt.* Leipzig: J. A. Barth, 1930.
9. Klages, L. *Ausdrucksbewegung und Gestaltungskraft.* Leipzig: J. A. Barth, 1923.
10. Klopfer, B., Ainsworth, Mary D., Klopfer, W. G., and Holt, R. R. *Developments in the Rorschach technique. Vol. I.* Yonkers: World Book Co., 1954.

11. Kretschmer, E. *Körperbau und Charakter.* Berlin: Julius Springer, 1944.
12. Külpe, O. *Vorlesungen über Psychologie.* Leipzig: S. Hirzel, 1922.
13. Mohr, P. Die schwarze und dunkle Farbe der Rorschach-Tafeln. *Rorschachiana,* 1947, **2,** 24–36.
14. Mohr, P. Die schwarze und sehr dunkle Tönung der Rorschachschen Tafeln und ihre Bedeutung für den Versuch. *Schweiz. Arch. Neurol. Psychiat.,* 1944, **53,** 122–133.
15. Ribot, T. *Psychologie der Gefühle.* Altenburg: O. Bonde, 1903.
16. Scheler, M. *Wesen und Formen der Sympathie.* Bonn: F. Cohen, 1923.
17. Stroemgren, E. Om den ixothyme Psyke. *Hospitalstidende,* 1936, **79,** 637–648.
18. Szymanski, J. S. *Gefühl und Erkennen. Abhandlungen aus der Neurologie, Psychiatrie, und ihren Grenzgebieten, Heft 33.* Berlin: S. Karger, 1926.
19. Volkelt, J. *System der Aesthetik.* Munich: C. H. Beck, 1925–1927.
20. Zulliger, H. *Der Tafeln-Z-Test.* Bern: Hans Huber, 1954.

*Were it not for the motion and the colour-
play of the soul, man would suffocate and
rot away in his great passion, idleness.*

CARL G. JUNG

9 | by Jerome L. Singer

THE EXPERIENCE TYPE:
SOME BEHAVIORAL CORRELATES
AND THEORETICAL IMPLICATIONS

The concept of the experience type emerges from *Psychodiagnostics* as one of Herman Rorschach's most important contributions. Indeed, the rather warm and human quality of Rorschach's pages dealing with the ratio of human movement and color responses suggests that the author felt a close personal identification and an intuitive excitement about this material which are readily communicated to the reader. That people with differing life experience should see different things in ambiguous ink blots was almost a truism in Rorschach's day, but that a *specific* type of response determinant—human movement or color —should effectively measure a long-standing and important personality characteristic remains to this day a puzzling observation that calls for theoretical comprehension. Rorschach also concluded from his observations that, while relative emphases on human movement (introversive tendencies) or color (extratensive tendencies) represented human variations along two separate dimensions, some underlying relationship existed which merited juxtaposition of the two types of responses in order to estimate the experience type. For Rorschach the M:sum C relationship [1] apparently reflected a deeply ingrained life style most likely constitutional in origin, although modifiable to some extent by mood swings, aging, extreme situational disturbance, or psychotherapy. The ratio for a given individual derived from his

[1] For explanation of scoring symbols, see Appendix, pp. 441 ff. [Editor].

223

ink-blot protocol indicated a pattern that could be observed in day-to-day behavior, but which went beyond this readily observable level and suggested potentialities as well. As a concept the experience type had implications for unifying a vast number of personality characteristics ranging from the modes of expressing intellectual abilities to artistic talent, approach to interpersonal relationships, vocational potential, suitability of marriage partners, therapeutic accessibility, stress reaction, psychopathological symptomatology, and type of social or cultural interests.

Despite these potentialities, the concept of experience type in actual practice, as Beck (6) has noted, has proved difficult to use and is often relatively neglected in diagnostic reporting. This chapter represents an attempt to explore the data now available from an increasing body of experimental research, with the hope of exposing some of the known facts that bear on Rorschach's concept and some of the problems which arise concerning its theoretical worth. The focus of the chapter will be as much as possible upon the M :sum C relationship, and subtle nuances such as content of either human movement or color responses will not be considered here. Two general questions will be raised and will serve as the organizational framework for the chapter:

1. Are Rorschach's original observations concerning the experience type confirmed by other investigators using more formal and improved research methods?

2. Are data or formulations available which suggest the possibility of relating Rorschach's experience type to more general theories of perception and personality?

BEHAVIORAL CORRELATES OF THE EXPERIENCE TYPE

Since Rorschach emphasized the "empirical" nature of his results and explicitly stated that his conclusions were grounded in his observations rather than deduced from a theory, these observations must bear up under the detailed scrutiny of others if they are to be accepted. The heightened awareness of the existence of selective perception and recall which derives from the work of Freud and Rorschach makes it all the more imperative to check on the reported observations of these original and independent-minded investigators.

Although analysis of an individual Rorschach protocol calls for consideration of the interrelations of several response categories and their qualitative features, the argument that experimental variation of specific aspects of the Rorschach method violates the meaning of the technique overlooks the crucial question of how the interpretative scheme originated. In order for Rorschach to derive his conclusions about the meaning of the different determinants he must have had at one time to consider them in relative isolation and to correlate gross behavior with extreme scores on the various test dimensions. Since Rorschach did not hesitate to suggest overt behavioral characteristics associated with high M, high sum C, and M:sum C, it may be well to begin with his specific statements and consider some approaches to verify them.

Other chapters have dealt in detail with the specific significance of the human movement and the color responses. It may suffice here to state that for Rorschach, human movement (kinesthetic) responses to the ink blots gave an indication of gross tendencies for fantasy and imaginal activity which were linked to overt inhibition or delay of motor response. Color reactions represented affective tendencies which also bore a relationship to overt motility. By juxtaposing human movement responses and the weighted sum of color responses, one is afforded an indication of gross reaction tendencies that bear on relative capacities to resort to introversive or extratensive patterns in many areas of human functioning. The following table suggests some of the characteristics of persons who show predominantly either M or sum C in their experience types. As the experience type ratio becomes more nearly equal for both components, one may expect a richness of capacity for both inner- and outer-directed living:

Kinesthesis Predominant:	Color Predominant:
More individualized intelligence	Stereotyped intelligence
Greater creative ability	More reproductive ability
More "inner" life	More "outward" life
Stable affective reactions	Labile affective reactions
More intensive than extensive rapport	More extensive than intensive rapport
Measured, stable motility	Restless, labile motility
Awkwardness, clumsiness	Skill and adroitness.

(79, p. 78)

It is obvious from this table that Rorschach felt he had observed direct behavioral manifestations of the experience type patterns. It remains the task of the experimenter to formulate the terms in Rorschach's table operationally so as to permit specific verification. For some reason, despite Rorschach's obvious interest in such experiments, little was attempted. Only in the past five or six years has a body of data emerged which permits some evaluation of the validity of Rorschach's formulation of the experience type.

A critical issue which is outside the scope of this chapter, but which must be mentioned because it is frequently overlooked, is that of essential validity and reliability of Rorschach's scoring system itself (see Chapters 13 and 14). To the extent that human movement scores are not clearly distinguishable from animal or inanimate movement (FM and m), or color from shading or texture, we cannot anticipate clear-cut results from attempts at experimental validation. Certainly there is considerable question concerning the relative effect of color on the ink blots (1, 88). It appears possible that the outstanding feature in color responses is the relative diffuseness of the reaction (1, 21, 89, 116) and this may conceivably apply to shading or black-white as well as to color. It is possible that the experience type may be sacrificing information, since achromatic responses, either diffuse ones such as "Black clouds" or articulate ones such as "Face of a black poodle," are not considered in the $M:C$ computation.

Constitutional Factors and Physiological Correlates

What are some of the areas of human functioning in which we can expect manifestations of correlates of M and sum C? Obviously the constitutional make-up of the individual comes to mind, since Rorschach did feel the experience type was, within limits, an inborn response predisposition. This must mean that one may expect almost from birth gross differences in children along the dimensions of activity inhibition, delaying capacity, and, gradually, of the tendency to use fantasy. European psychologists have sought to link physique to introversive-extratensive personality characteristics: The work of Schmidt (85) and the research of the students of Kretschmer which have been reported on and followed up by Eysenck (17) suggest at least the possibility that gross introversive or extratensive characteristics are associated with body type, on the one hand, and perceptual preferences for form or color responses, on the other. Wenger (109, 110, 111) has found evidence of gross motor differences in children that might be taken as forerunners of subsequent introversive-extratensive tendencies. There is insufficient data on these points as they apply specifically to the Rorschach, for the obvious reason that, by the time it is possible to obtain suitable protocols from children, so much learning and variation in identification patterns have occurred as to prevent any clarification of the constitutional elements.

Developmental studies of Rorschach response patterns and of perception and concept formation indicate a general tendency for more primitive color responses to emerge prior to more controlled color and human movement, thus coinciding with children's progress from diffuse motor reactivity to increased control, as well as from egocentric speech with minimal delay or fantasy to socialized speech and greater internalization of fantasy. These studies do not, however, come to grips with the *origin* of individual differences in the experience type, and, hence, offer no support to any constitutional theory. Some indirect but suggestive evidence for the viewpoint that identification possibilities in the family setting may account for variation in experience type comes from the work of Goldfarb (28, 29), who reported that children raised from very early life under impersonal institutional conditions show primitive and markedly extratensive Rorschach characteristics in addition to difficulties in delaying capacity and conceptualization.

There have been relatively few attempts to relate the Rorschach experience type or M and sum C to various physiological measures. One intriguing study along this line has been recently reported by Rabinovitch et al. (69), who found EEG distinctions between extremes in the experience types and tentative evidence that high introversive subjects showed more "harmonizing activity" from various cortical areas. Since little is known of the correlates of the EEG measures, however, speculation as to the meaning of these findings is limited. Certainly we cannot conclude from this evidence that the experience type is constitutionally based, but merely that there appear to be concomitant cerebral activities which accord with Rorschach reaction tendencies. The same caution applies to a study by Brower (12) which provides some evidence of relationships of FC and general responsiveness to color cards (R VIII, IX, X/total R), to pulse pressure, and to diastolic blood pressure. A study more clearly translated into Rorschach concepts is that of anoxia tolerance reported by Hertzman et al. (34). These investigators found that the threshold for breakdown under anoxic conditions as measured by physiological and psychological instruments was lower for extratensives than introversives, suggesting greater response to environmental alterations by the high sum C group. It should be noted, however, that the group most susceptible was made up of the constricted subjects who gave few M or C responses. Generally it appears that persons who block or show impoverished use of various Rorschach determinants prove least stress-tolerant or flexible, and that production even of relatively uncontrolled color responses is indicative of more adaptive capacity in various situations (48, 99).

A suggestive model for research in this area is to be found in the work of Block (11), who reported that subjects who showed considerable psychogalvanic responsiveness in a lie-detector situation also revealed perceptual and behavioral characteristics similar to those which might be expected of Rorschach extratensives. Block did not base his classification into "over" and "undercontrollers" on Rorschach data, and it is suggested that a repetition of his study, using Palmer's (64) useful method for classifying experience types, might throw further light on the correlation of the experience balance with the lie-detector measure.

For the present it must be concluded that almost nothing of a systematic nature is known concerning the physiological or constitutional correlates of the $M:$ sum C ratio. Hunter's (37) findings of Negro-white differences in the experience type have been questioned by Palmer (63) as being possibly an artifact of her mode of inquiry. Palmer (63) himself found no racial differences in his experience-balance measure. Even if Hunter's results were accurate, they might well reflect subcultural group differences rather than differences in racial temperament. Two studies have failed to yield evidence of clear-cut sex differences in the experience type (18, 63), although both obtained some very tentative suggestions of greater adaptive affect on the part of the women. Dawo (13) has reported a shift from introversive to extratensive experience types in female medical students tested in the intermenstruum and again at the onset of menstruation, but this conclusion is rendered somewhat questionable by the fact that the second testing was with the Behn-Eschenburg ink blots which have been shown to yield more FC responses and less M than the original series (15, 90). Confirmation of Dawo's finding would not necessarily provide evidence of a physiological component in the $M:$ sum C ratio, since the emotional response of these women to the psychological meaning of the period might well be involved.

Perceptual Correlates

A knotty problem in understanding the experience-type concept derives from Rorschach's contention that M and sum C represent reaction tendencies and also modes of perceptual experience which presumably influence subsequent reaction tendencies. Thus the fantasy world of the M type leads to special kinds of selection in what is perceived, whereas the C type's emotional response or motor interchange with his environment similarly leads to a selection in perceptual experience. Palmer (63, 64) has pointed to some of the problems inherent in Rorschach's concept, and has suggested a solution in terms of functional dimensions similar to those which will be discussed below. In actuality, research data in the sphere of perceptual correlates of the experience type are largely limited to studies of behavioral correlates of the M and C components rather than to investigation of the mode of "experiencing."

Since one component of the M response is motion, it has seemed logical to compare Rorschach M tendencies with tendencies to perceive illusory motion, specifically the ϕ and other autokinetic phenomena. In view of the complex nature of the ϕ phenomenon and its extensive theoretical ramifications, several attempts have been made to relate M responses to low thresholds for stroboscopic or similar illusory motions. Werner (112) observed that endogenous mentally defective children showed lower threshold for ϕ and other forms of illusory motion than did the matched exogenous mental defectives. Since these two groups differed significantly in Rorschach movement responses (endogenous subjects showing more M and a more introversive protocol as well as generally more controlled or, at least, phlegmatic motor behavior), it is likely that M and ϕ bore some relationship, although no data specifically on this point were presented. Werner perhaps more than any other investigator has proceeded to draw extensive theoretical conclusions concerning perception and developmental theory from this inverse relationship of motion perception and overt motor activity. Klein and Schlesinger (38) also obtained some evidence that high-M subjects showed greater tendency to perceive ϕ than did low-M subjects, although their results are somewhat inconclusive when total Rorschach responses are considered.

Singer and Basowitz in an unpublished study also observed a relationship between a scoring of the M:sum C ratio and threshold for ϕ, the more introversive subjects showing lower thresholds for perception of illusory movement. More recently Schumer (84) has reported a trend for subjects with numerous M to show less variability in perception of ϕ, although ϕ threshold itself did not prove to discriminate between high- and low-M subjects. Two studies employing perception of autokinetic motion as correlates of M have also obtained suggestive, if not conclusive, results. Murawski (61) found that immobilized subjects with expectations of recovering motion showed a positive correlation between Rorschach M and a tendency to perceive the autokinetic phenomenon. Schumer (84) used the autokinetic situation as a measure of influence and suggestibility in the manner of the social psychological studies that have derived from Sherif's work. In this case, a negative correlation between M and extent of autokinetic perception emerged. The crucial difference between the apparently contradictory findings of Schumer and Murawski appears to lie in the fact that Schumer's procedure by its experimental instruction employed the autokinetic phenomenon in a social situation involving conformity or suggestibility. Hence Schumer's results are consistent with Rorschach's view that high-M subjects, being presumably more independent-minded and less responsive to external stimuli, should prove less suggestible. Leiman (46) employed two perceptual measures for comparing high- and low-M subjects. One involved perception of motion in kinesthetic figures which were presented tachistoscopically. The high-M group showed a trend toward reporting motion in the figures sooner than did the low-M subjects. Results obtained with the Street gestalt figures (silhouettes of figures which have been cut up and which subjects are required to integrate perceptually in order to ascertain their content) were even more conclusive. High-M subjects proved significantly more effective at integrating the cut-up silhouettes into meaningful wholes. Leiman has interpreted his basic data as supporting a view that "closure accuracy" is one of the basic components in formation of M responses. Matarazzo et al. (54) instructed their subjects (students and patients with anxiety neuroses) to report sensations other than merely flickering in response to an intermittent flickering light. They then scored these reported sensations by means of Rorschach determinants and found significant positive relationships for both movement and color between the flicker reactions and Rorschach responses. For the patients alone, the color relationship failed to hold, but the association of flicker movement and Rorschach movement persisted.

Perceptual data seem in general, therefore, to indicate that tendencies to structure Rorschach ink blots with movement correspond roughly with more general sensitivities to perceive illusory movement. The M type of person has not been shown, however, to be more responsive to general motion around him. The noteworthy point is that in the situations described the movement is not actually taking place in the stimulus constellations but is contributed by the subjects as a result of an integration of certain favorable environmental conditions. This is a crucial consideration, theoretically, since the implication of Rorschach's view of M and of the extensions of these views by Werner (112) is that certain persons by inhibiting direct reaction tendencies tend to develop sensitivities or predilections for *imposing* motion, either on ambiguous stimuli or on stimuli in what may be called "the mind's eye." Schumer's data point up the fact that when perception of motion is utilized as part of an environmental situation in which suggestibility plays a role, the relationship of M and motion perception is altered. So it would seem that, as there is less support from the stimulus itself for perception of motion, the introversive person becomes the more likely to *impose* motion on it; conversely, with more stimulus support, the more likely is the extroversive person to *perceive* motion in it. Indirect evidence for this supposition may be adduced from studies which suggest that introversive subjects (as judged by questionnaire measures rather than Rorschach protocols) show lower size constancy in perceptual experiments (selecting an object of the same size as a distant standard), where it is known that inability to isolate the stimulus from the environmental objects which surround it enhances size constancy (91, 108).

Further research into perceptual correlates of Rorschach's experience type is clearly necessary if we wish, on the one hand, to gain a greater understanding of what goes into the making of a particular response and, on the other, to advance beyond Rorschach empiricism to a theory that encompasses perception, imagination, and action.

Motor Activity and Environmental Responsiveness

One of the most fruitful outcomes of Rorschach's concept of extratensiveness has been the possibility of linking the motor habits and expressive behavior of the individual to habits of thought and perception. Through the medium of the color responses, and even more the experience type as a whole, the way has been opened for exploring such linkages and ultimately relating them in a theory of ego function or personality, generally. Indeed, although the linkages of the Rorschach ratio to other perceptual responses are relatively tenuous at the moment, data bearing on the relationship of the experience type to action tendencies and environmental responsiveness are more clear-cut. This may be, in part, because the perceptual situations utilized have themselves involved fairly subtle processes of dubious reliability, and, in part, because Rorschach's own conclusions about his response categories were no doubt derived to a great extent from observation of gross motor tendencies.

Most current theories of personality and ego development emphasize as a basic developmental dimension the gradual control, differentiation, and socialization of motility (23, 50, 51, 65, 70, 113). In Rorschach terms this implies a certain general pattern of response tendencies for various age groups. One should expect with increasing age in children an increase in M and a change in the nature and weighting of color responses from pure C and CF towards FC. This is roughly what has been found in normative studies (1, 20, 40, 103). The M response begins to appear most typically in the records of children of school age, at a time when there is a sharp increase in the demands on the child for inhibition of motor behavior and socialization of speech and gratification patterns. The increasing introversive trend of the experience type and the greater control of the color responses correspond with Piaget's descriptions of changes in the verbal behavior of children as well. Where once the child moved directly towards the source of gratification or spoke out his thoughts whether heeded or not, he must now check the impulse, raise his hand to request permission, or remain quiet during a lesson. In varying degrees, then, internalization of response is rewarded and, as reading is learned, the tools for internalization are vastly improved. Since effective and creative living involves a flexible shifting between control, internalization, delay, and direct action or spontaneous affect, one would ideally expect an optimal rather than maximal development of introversive tendencies. Levi and Kraemer (47) and Thetford (102) provide some data on variations in introversiveness and motor control, or precocity, which have pathological implications.

More direct studies of responsiveness, impulsivity, and control seem also to accord with Rorschach's views. The work of Siipola and Taylor (89) on responses to ink blots under free and pressure conditions affords evidence that fast responders give fewer M responses and that persons who give unstructured responses such as C and CF respond more rapidly. Similarly, as pressure for response is increased, there is greater tendency for C and CF responses to emerge. The authors conclude that the M tendency in contrast to the C tendency characterizes the person who excels in "the ability to delay." These findings were also confirmed by Bieri and Blacker (7). The latter investigators reported that extratensive subjects showed faster reaction times in producing all types of Rorschach determinants than did ambiequals and introversives, in that order.

Since the trait of impulsivity is obviously related to inability to delay, one would expect some relationship between measures of impulsive behavior and the M:sum C ratio. Holtzmann (36) failed to find such a relationship in a study of normal persons rated by their neighbors, while Gardner (26) did obtain positive results in a study of normal adults rated by clinical psychologists who knew them well. Thiessen et al. (104), studying equated groups of children differing in ratings of impulsivity, found ample support for the relationship of sum C and, particularly CF and C, to impulsivity and also to maladjustment, but the M:sum C ratio itself did not prove discriminating in the form in which it was employed. Misch (60), in a careful effort to obtain data on extreme impulsivity, selected two groups of individuals who differed in assaultiveness; one consisted of chronically assaultive criminals, the other of psychiatric patients who had a history of assaultive threats but who had never carried these verbal threats into action. The "motoric" group was characterized by more primitive Rorschach records, including more CF and C and less M than the "verbal" group. Finney (19), comparing assaultive psychiatric patients with others who had never been assaultive during their hospitalization, found significantly more CF and sum C in the records of the former group but no differences emerged in M. In general, grossly comparable results were obtained in a study by Singer et al. (98), in which color and shading responses and ward ratings of aggressiveness and diffuse energy had sizable loadings on a common factor, whereas M and a rating for ward cooperativeness were linked on still another factor.

Other evidence bearing on inhibition of motor response or environmental reactivity comes from a variety of studies. Mann (52) employed a clever criterion of environmental responsiveness or lack of imaginative inner resources. He obtained series of free associations from subjects, and totaled those associations to the immediate situation or the examination room, to obtain his measure. A negative correlation between M and environmental responsiveness, and a sizable positive correlation between sum C and this criterion emerged. This result seems clearly an indication of a relationship between introversiveness and the ability to free oneself from passive response to the environment. Ideational fluidity, a basic component of imagination, must also be involved, to be sure. Levine, Glass, and Meltzoff (48) sought to obtain evidence of inhibition of a habitual motor response by studying the Rorschach records of subjects who, in taking the Wechsler-Bellevue Digit Symbol subtest, erred by writing the letter

"N" instead of its mirror image, which is the correct symbol. A significantly greater percentage of these subjects than of controls gave fewer than two M responses on the Rorschach. Results obtained when color responses were considered, however, indicated that, for this sample, the more color, the less likelihood of a reversal. The authors found that coartated subjects were most likely to err and introversive patients with dilated experience types least likely to do so.

Herman (33) employed a clever measure of motor control in comparing equated groups of introversive and extratensive Rorschach groups. The subjects were asked to define out loud a list of words such as, "point," "knot," "twist," "squeeze," and "rub." Extratensives used significantly more gestures and body movements in the course of their oral definitions. Two studies employing a simple waiting-room observation procedure devised by Rickers-Ovsiankina (73) have found that schizophrenic adults grouped on the basis of Rorschach M and sum C differed correspondingly in the amount of spontaneous movement and speech during a 15-minute wait. Although M and particularly active M proved most discriminating, both Singer and Spohn (96), and Singer and Herman (93) found clear evidence of an influence of the experience type in the fact that rated amount of activity in the waiting period increased progressively through the four subgroups of high M:low sum C, high M:high sum C, low M:low sum C, low M:high sum C, or, in other words, as the group ratios changed from marked introversion to marked extratension.

Separate mention should be made here of a series of studies which have employed a motor inhibition task modified from Downey's Will-Temperament Scale. This technique calls for the subject to write a brief phrase as slowly as possible without stopping motion of the pencil. Performance on this task consistently proved to correlate with M (58, 93, 96, 98), but also yielded differences between subjects with introversive and extratensive experience types (33, 96). Meltzoff and Levine (49, 56) have demonstrated that Rorschach M responses, motor inhibition, and cognitive inhibition (ability to inhibit a habituated association and rapidly substitute a new one) are related, thus affording support to the entire theory of the linkage of motion perception, action, and thought.

Despite these encouraging findings, we cannot but notice some lacunae in the structure thus far built up in support of Rorschach's view of the experience type. These gaps appear particularly in the area of expression of affect. Although it is true that much of the data on motor and impulse control are indirectly relevant to affectivity, the fact remains that there are few studies which deal with the relationship between M:sum C and ease or inhibition in revealing feelings of anger, love, sympathy, or sadness.   Indeed, while free expression of feelings and spontaneity both in imaginativeness and in affect are facets of psychotherapy, concerning which individual Rorschach examiners have much to say in their reports, little effort has been made to carry out systematic studies along this line.   The studies on aggressive behavior cited above are relevant, but there has been no attempt to evaluate potentialities for warmth, for giving love, or for effective assertiveness rather than destructive aggression.   One technical difficulty among others here is the fact that the FC response, presumably indicative of adaptive rapport, is one of the least reliable of major Rorschach determinants both in retest and scoring (10, 15, 18).   But perhaps there has been too much preoccupation with "pathology" to the detriment of a fuller understanding of the richness of personality.   Perhaps, too, the populations available to researchers for extensive or intensive study have been clinic or hospital patients, thus leading to an overemphasis on behavior that is socially distressing.

Whatever the reasons, it seems essential that some attempts be made to carry through research on affective expression as a correlate of the experience type if the one of the most vital assumptions of Rorschach analysis is to be verified and if the Rorschach factors are to be brought into conceptual relationship with more general personality theories.   Some valuable first steps towards effecting this increase of our understanding have come in studies by Piotrowski and Schreiber, described in detail in Chapter 6, and in an ingenious experiment by Meltzoff and Litwin.   Piotrowski and Schreiber (68) found valuable evidence of increases in dilation of the experience type in the course of psychoanalytic psychotherapy as contrasted with supportive psychotherapy.   Changes in both M and sum C seemed to mirror personality changes in the individual patients.

Meltzoff and Litwin (57) studied conscious inhibition of affect by exposing normals to a Spike Jones "Laughing Record," which they had already demonstrated evoked an almost universal laughter response in a sample of their population.   They found that when subjects were instructed to listen to the record without laughing, the high-M group proved more successful than the low-M individuals.   They also observed an interesting progression and some individual differences in the modes of control employed.   Some subjects at first employed motor control to avoid laughing, e.g., tightening lips, and later resorted to cognitive or fantasy methods, e.g., thinking of sad events.   Some of the subjects emphasized motor methods, others fantasy, thus opening an avenue for exploration of such problems as symptom choice. Should further studies support these observations, a way may be opened for elaborating on Rorschach's original observations on mode of schizophrenic reaction, sense involved in hallucinations, obsessive or compulsive symptomatology, etc., as a function of experience type.

Even these two stimulating reports point up some of the problems raised in introducing this area, however. It should be noted that in both studies the M determinant proved most significant. The influence of the color factors therefore remains more shrouded in doubt. In addition, the very form of the Meltzoff and Litwin experiment calls for an emphasis on control of affect. In this experiment, success or compliance with experimental instructions hinged on control.

But what of the problem of *excessive* control of affect through ideation—the intellectual defenses? Little has been done in that connection. And what of the many times in life when a spontaneous, warm laugh or smile carries with it more than a thousand words or images in building constructive human contacts? Clinically, Rorschach examiners have often been aware that the rich use of FC and good CF responses betokens the sympathetic and loving person who can also assert himself clearly when crossed. Rioch (77), for example, in her studies of Rorschach records before and after psychoanalytic therapy, found evidence of increased FC responses and richer use of color in patients felt to have relaxed emotionally. One change in color responses reported by Piotrowski and Schreiber in the course of psychoanalytic treatment was a greater resort to warm colors, while Rickers-Ovsiankina (75) found that chronic schizophrenics who improved were chiefly distinguished from a static group by the former's avoidance of the red and pink portions of the blots. When the improving subjects do respond to these portions, however, their reactions are significantly less frequently of the form-dominant type than is the case in the static group. Some unpublished data collected by the writer on schizophrenic patients with dilated and constricted experience types also indicate that the patients with many movement and color responses were generally rated the most attractive and interesting personalities in the wards. Although the dilated personalities often showed persisting severe symptomatology, they were capable of establishing relationships and of evoking affection of a sort from other patients and the staff of the hospital.

The capacity for spontaneous intellectual or emotional release or playfulness, what Kris (41) terms "regression in the service of the ego," is almost certainly what was meant by Rorschach in his discussion of the adaptive features of the *FC* and the good *CF* responses. Exploration of this facet of the experience type through formal experiment remains to be done, however (35). It seems very likely to be related to talent and expression in what has been termed the "performing arts," and may have been expressed in Rorschach's reference to "reproductive ability and skill and adroitness" as characteristics of the color-predominant experience type.

Inner Life: Thinking, Fantasy, and Imagination

The correlates of the experience type in the area of the inner experience and in the capacities for fantasy, "individualized intelligence," and "creative ability," as Rorschach described them, have proved most fascinating to subsequent Rorschach workers. This is the domain of the *M* response *per se*, although Rorschach makes clear that both *M* and *C*—fantasy capacity and affective expression—can exist side by side, and do so in really well-rounded, gifted human beings. It may therefore be assumed that sum *C* is not inversely related to fantasy, but merely *unrelated* in itself to this area of functioning. Here Rorschach was perhaps unwittingly going beyond any systematic knowledge he could have been able to acquire, and by positing a relationship between *M*, sum *C*, and their behavioral correlates that could only be expressed by rather complex mathematical functions and tested by statistical treatments far beyond his ken. Simple attempts to correlate Rorschach introversion with questionnaires concerning social and thinking introversion have yielded negative results, but this may in part reflect limitations of the questionnaires involved (81, 93, 104). If attention is paid to specific characteristics of behavior presumably exemplifying inner life, considerable support exists for Rorschach's linkage of the introversive experience balance, and particularly *M* alone, with fantasy. In the area of cognitive attitudes and problem solving, for example, Rosenthal (80) has reported clear-cut differences in the approach to solution of the Katona match stick problem of otherwise equated groups of introversive and extratensive normals. The introversives thought longer about the task and thus had longer reaction times, while the high sum *C* subjects manipulated the problem sticks far more frequently. Thus, the contrasting experience types appear to reflect different modes of approaching the problem situation. The word *different* is important for one cannot say "superior" or "inferior" in this connection inasmuch as Rosenthal's groups were *equally proficient* in solving the problem. This finding suggests that, as Barron (4) has pointed out, we may be dealing with differing life styles which cannot be ranked as favorable or unfavorable except in relation to a highly specific cultural or intellectual demand. A similar result was obtained in a recent study by Singer and Opler (95). A group of Irish-American schizophrenics, who were more introversive on the Rorschach than a corresponding Italian sample of patients, failed to obtain superior Porteus Maze Test Quotients despite the fact that they were considerably more restrained and apparently planful in their mode of performance.

Barron (4) investigated correlates of *M* alone by developing a new series of all black ink blots standardized in a fashion so as to yield a threshold score for tendency to see human movement. A group of Air Force officers who showed low thresholds for perceptions of humans in motion were described in the following terms by psychologists who had observed them in a variety of interview, social, and stress situations: "1. Highly cathects intellectual activity; values cognitive pursuits. 2. Gets along in the world as it is; is socially appropriate in his behavior. 3. Is introspective; concerned with his self as object; frequently self-aware. 4. Has high degree of intellectual ability." Officers with a high threshold for *M* responses, on the other hand, were described in the following terms: "1. Has narrow range of interests. 2. Allows personal bias, spite, or dogmatism to enter into his judgment of issues. 3. Prefers action to contemplation. 4. Is rigid; inflexible in thought and action." Despite this impression created by their behavior, these *M*-disposed officers did not actually prove more intelligent or imaginative on a series of formal tests than the officers with high thresholds for *M* response. Thus Barron concludes that *M* may tap "thoughtfulness" as an intellectual *disposition* rather than as an ability. However, since the officers with high thresholds for perceiving *M* were generally described in clinically less "flattering" terminology, e.g., "rigid, inflexible, allows bias, spite, or dogmatism to enter into judgment of issues," there still is the possibility that an extreme lack of *M* tendency may indicate a liability for effective functioning.

A study by Barrell (3) with a design rather similar to Barron's also led to results linking Rorschach *M* tendency with assessment ratings of "broad interests, imaginative and independent minded." Significant positive correlations between *M* (with the effect of total responses partialed out) and a combined score for the Miller Analogies Test and the Primary Mental Abilities word fluency subtest emerged for Barrell's sample of Veterans Administration trainees, suggesting that some association between M and achievement measures of abstraction and ideational productivity does exist. One feature of Barrell's study was his finding that a distinction between $M+$ and $M-$ could be made since much of the correlation with intellectual variables occurred for the $M+$ response. As is plain from the summary of studies thus far, there has been little consideration in research for the form level of the M response as such, although certainly important differences in clinical interpretation often hinge on the form level of M. There seems to be a serious neglect in the literature of studies dealing with the qualitative characteristics of the experience type, as a matter of fact. Such studies could include, from a structural standpoint, the form level of the movement and color components and, from a dynamic standpoint, the actual content of these percepts.

The evidence linking the M response alone with various measures of imaginativeness or fantasy capacity is by this time quite convincing. One obvious avenue to test this linkage has been by correlating Rorschach M with various measures of fantasy disposition drawn from the Thematic Apperception Test or similar story-telling techniques. Thus, one may attempt an over-all rating of story originality or develop a more quantitative scheme such as scoring transcendent items, e.g., the number of characters, incidents, or emotions not actually depicted in the stimulus card but introduced into the story by the subject. Both types of analysis have yielded consistently positive correlations with M and $M:$ sum C (32, 33, 44, 61, 66, 84, 87, 93, 98, 106). Although data bearing on M alone clearly relate it to fantasy disposition, the results for $M:$ sum C are somewhat equivocal. In several studies (32, 33, 66), introversive experience types yielded clearer correlations with fantasy than extratensive scores. At the same time, in other studies (87, 93, 98), sum C showed either no correlation with fantasy measures or a positive one. The various components of sum C as well as the many qualitative complexities attendant on color reactions (86) seem to confuse the picture in study after study, since no investigator has been able to effect a thorough comparison of all types of scoring and weighting of color or of the movement and color relationships. There seems little doubt, however, that introversive or high-M subjects with introversively or ambiequally dilated experience types show greater fantasy disposition in story-telling activities than do low-M subjects, and are also more likely to show greater originality in associations (84), greater cognitive complexity in perception of persons (8), and more planfulness and time perspective (98). A study by Gibby et al. (27) which compared hallucinated with deluded psychotics found, contrary to Rorschach's original reports, significantly more M in the former group and more FC and total C in the latter group. The extremely low frequency of M limits generalization since both groups are decidedly extratensive in their experience types.

A highly significant feature of fantasy disposition is, presumably, the willingness to introspect and to face up consciously to problems and difficulties, or at least to attempt a solution by ideational means rather than by somatization, direct motor activity, or repression. To this extent a dilated or moderately introversive experience type should prove an asset in beginning psychotherapy. Recently Temerlin (101) selected two groups of patients in psychoanalysis who were apparently equated in all respects except that one group showed "flexible, productive behavior" in the first 20 sessions of psychotherapy, associating freely, taking responsibility for work at their treatment, etc., while the second group was "rigid, unproductive, blocked often, and was unwilling or unable to express the content of awareness, passively describing experiences in an affectless manner." Although specific Rorschach data were unfortunately not available, Temerlin found that the "productive" group showed considerably more variability in the perception of motion in an autokinetic situation, i.e., they could see movement more frequently. Temerlin attributes this motion perception to a "tolerance for experiencing self." Barron's (4) M-disposed officers were more frequently described by assessors as "more self-involved," whereas Shatin (87) found that Rorschach M was also associated with willingness to give open expression to unpleasant feelings in stories on the Thematic Apperception Test. Further evidence on this point is forthcoming from a study by Singer et al. (98), who found in a group of schizophrenics that M was positively correlated with willingness to admit distress after a failure experience. Finally, Palmer (64), in an elaborate comparison of Rorschach experience types and Minnesota Multiphasic Personality Inventory responses, found that inventory items dealing with self-dissatisfaction and self-awareness were more characteristic of introversive subjects, whereas items involving self-satisfaction or lack of awareness characterized extratensives.

It seems clear that introversiveness is very likely linked with self-knowledge, or at least conscious tolerance of distress or difficulty, perhaps because the person who has the capacity or disposition for fantasy has at his disposal a means for experiencing the difficulty without necessarily having "to take arms against a sea of troubles and, by opposing, end them." Clinical experience suggests that the extreme of this capacity is perhaps as maladaptive as its absence or as total extratensiveness; excessive rumination and resort to the ideational leads to inaction and gradually increases anxiety instead of coping with it. A clinical study of the origin of intellectuality presents some stimulating treatment of this possibility (42).

It appears that to some extent the tendency to deal on a fantasy level with conflicts or frustrated wishes serves as a temporary "experimental action" discharging small quantities of energy in a controlled and potentially productive manner. Unless this mode of response is reinforced, however, either by eventually leading to satisfaction of the original wishes or, perhaps, by yielding other socially acceptable rewards (prestige, approval of friends and family, creative achievement), the marked resort to constructive fantasy seems to wither away. This appears to be the case in certain precocious but disturbed children (47) and in schizophrenic children (102). It can be observed clinically in many schizophrenic adults who show considerable fantasy and obsessive rumination early in the course of their illness (with corresponding high M or dilated experience types), and who then, as they find no relief, settle into a chronic torpor or passive hospital adjustment with much sleeping and a decline in fantasy. The same trend appears demonstrable in nonpsychotics who have been blocked in their motor activity by illness. Murawski (61) found considerably more Rorschach movement responses in a group of subjects who were immobilized by physical illness but who retained hope of recovery of motion than in a similarly immobilized group who had no expectation of recovery. Wittkower (117), describing tuberculous adults, reported that enforced bed rest leads to heightened fantasy at the outset but this declines in time. Quite recently, Richards and Lederman (76), using Levy's movement blots, found that children physically handicapped from birth or soon after showed significantly *less* vigorous activity in their movement percepts than children who became handicapped after a considerable period of normal motility.

One final aspect of the introversive experience type is in the area of artistic achievement or creativity. Here is a complex problem that merits separate consideration. To some extent clinical experience and a variety of researches suggest that creativity or originality is greatest in persons with dilated experience types, as Rorschach found. It is this dilation-coarctation dimension rather than introversion-extratensiveness which appears to be crucial. To the extent that story-telling on the Thematic Apperception Test may be considered a measure of creative productivity or originality in associations, there is some evidence cited above (p. 239) that bears on this point. But what of evidence based on a life pattern of achievement? To what extent does the introversive ratio reflect a creative interest in people or a more general creativity expressed, say, in achievement in manipulating nonhuman symbols as well? Shakespeare, Dostoievsky, or Hugo were men whose minds must have teemed with vivid imagery of human interaction, and yet they themselves were often vigorously active. If some celestial Rorschacher examined these men and found few or no M and no indication of a dilated M : sum C ratio, the whole significance of the experience type would be called into question. Would that be the case, however, if Beethoven's Rorschach yielded no M or even few C responses? Certainly Beethoven's must have been a rich and vibrant inner life, but it was at the very least so full of sound as to leave much less room for human imagery than might be expected in a novelist's fantasy. Roe (78) found that physicists show more m than the psychologists, who tended to be most productive of M and of sum C as compared with other scientists. Her study, however, yielded evidence which suggests that a knowledge of ideal Rorschach patterns played some role in their reactions. Too little is known as yet to provide a definitive answer on this point.

Clinical experience has suggested some support for Rorschach's view that both M and sum C must be fully developed for optimal human functioning. It is possible in our society or in Western civilization generally that an individual with many M and low sum C could function effectively as a creative artist or as a specialist in some profession or skilled vocation. It seems less likely that this could be the case for someone with no M and a great many CF or pure C responses. But neither extreme would necessarily represent an individual living to his fullest potential as a person. The grossly introversive person might prove to be essentially detached and distant in his interpersonal relations, and even if he were to form a close human relationship, it might be still marked by an element of deliberation that would limit its development. The grossly extratensive person might be capable of passion and great warmth but little stability and little sense of direction, which could only lead to painful human relationships. Schachtel (82, 83), for example, has demonstrated in brilliant fashion the various complex facets of human interaction and creativity which may be gleaned from both human movement and color responses. The type of experimental research cited in this chapter scarcely touches on many of the issues raised by Schachtel or other astute observers of human nature who have used the Rorschach blots as their adjunctive tools. Yet, however trivial in themselves may seem tasks like slow writing or verb definition, they are theoretically consistent with the more general and subtle interpersonal behaviors with which clinicians deal, and they serve, in addition, to point out research models which by successive approximation may gradually test clinical hypotheses and elaborate on our scientific comprehension of the Rorschach.

SOME THEORETICAL CONSIDERATIONS

A theoretical formulation suggested or supported by the empirical data summarized in this chapter must remain sketchy at best, because so little of the research on Rorschach concepts has been addressed to theoretical problems. The relationship of Rorschach's experience type to Jung's introversion-extraversion *attitudinal* continuum has been re-examined recently by Klopfer (39) and Bash (5). It seems clear that Rorschach's M : sum C ratio is similar in many ways to the final formulation by Jung. In *Analytical Psychology*, introversion-extraversion represent extremes of a general personality orientation which interact with two other general dimensions—the *functions* of thinking-feeling and sensation-intuition—in the definition of any given response pattern characteristic of an individual. Both Rorschach's and Jung's conceptions of intro-extraversion unquestionably represent powerful and comprehensive schemata for evaluating the manner in which individuals experience their world. They provide the psychologist with a useful reference frame for interpreting and organizing the complexities of overt behavior as well. Jung, however, unlike Rorschach, stressed the principle of *complementarity*, which indicated that, if an introversive orientation is not overtly apparent, it is unconsciously present. Jung's conceptions have a certain power in reflecting a comprehensive picture of personality *structure* in contrast with *dynamics*. Failing precise operational definitions of the *function* dimensions, it is difficult to relate the theory of *Analytical Psychology* to the data thus far summarized.

Bash (5), in an ingenious manner, has sought, however, to test the theory of *complementarity* in the experience type. Subjects to whom Rorschachs had been previously administered were exposed to 200 consecutive presentations of card IX, and were instructed to offer a response for each exposure. Sequences of 50 responses were scored for M : sum C. It was found that introversives on their original records gradually reversed their experience types to a decidedly extratensive ratio, whereas initial extratensives gradually became markedly introversive. Ambiequals showed no change. This remarkable result in a very simple experiment bears repetition, particularly with the view of clarifying the basis for the reversal. It might be argued, for example, that the introversive subjects, having given so many M responses, had nowhere else to go, if they wished to vary their reaction, but to color. However, keeping stimulus characteristics (118) of the blot in mind, a simpler explanation than Bash's may be possible. While the Jungian constructs remain at a rather high level of abstraction, it might indeed be worth while to sample a variety of human performances which lend themselves to inclusion within the definition of the various Jungian functions, and then, if possible, to obtain some method for tapping conscious and unconscious manifestations of these functions and for evaluating the introvert and extrovert mode of utilizing each function. This suggests a rather grand factor analytic design, and, in some respects, is not too different from the program being carried out by Eysenck (16, 17).

The Jungian concepts, although certainly suggestive for comprehending the experience type at the level of a general typology, appear to be extremely limited in one respect, however. They do not afford, except possibly for the case of symbolic content analysis (59), a suitable basis for answering the crucial questions concerning *the linkage of specific determinants of ink-blot response to specific behavioral tendencies.* As a matter of fact, no theory has succeeded in this connection, and there is still a considerable gap between studies analyzing the stimulus properties of the blot (2, 14, 118) and those studies which attempt to relate a certain form of perceptual behavior to personality variables (74, 82, 83, 86, 112). The effectiveness of a theory in dealing with Rorschach data depends on whether it provides a rigorous basis for understanding the linkage of motor activity, affectivity, and fantasy to motion perception, and whether it affords some conception of the etiology of these functions, their developmental aspects, and the nature of individual differences. In addition, the theory must offer some explanation for the association of human movement perceived in ink blots with fantasy and motor inhibition, and for the association of color with motor responsiveness and affective expression. It must also account for the movement:color ratio as representing a complex dimension of human variation. Although no single theory seems capable at present of meeting these criteria, there has recently been a confluence of thought from psychoanalytic ego psychology, developmental psychology, and cognitive psychology, which appears to be opening the way for the development of a formulation incorporating the Rorschach experience-type data (35, 82, 86, 92, 114). Perhaps the greatest progress in this respect has come in connection specifically with the human movement response. At the perceptual level, Werner (112) and Werner and Wapner (114) have made important strides through the medium of their concept of the vicarious functioning of sensory and motor processes, which are linked by body tonicity. Their theory provides an important clue to the linkage of motion perception with inhibition of overt movement, which is essential in comprehending the origin of the M response. At the level of perception and motor activity, this theory has been specific enough to be tested and supported in several studies. Meltzoff, Singer and their co-workers (58, 94), for example, have found that Rorschach movement responses increased immediately after periods of motor inhibition. Werner's theory as yet does not fully specify the implications of this sensory-tonic vicariousness for fantasy and more general personality dimensions, however, nor does it provide sufficient basis for understanding why *human movement* rather than *animal* or any other type of movement on the Rorschach should be most closely related to motor inhibition.

Psychoanalytic ego psychology, as first expounded in Chapter 7 of Freud's *Interpretation of Dreams* (25), and subsequently developed in its application to thought by Rapaport (70), suggests some possibilities for specifying the origin of movement and color responses and their general significance. The central concept in Freud's theory of the shift from primitive, diffuse, wishful, primary-process thought and perception to a secondary process characterized by organization, reality groundedness, planfulness, and abstraction is that of *delay*. Thought develops in effect when the child is compelled to defer immediate gratification, either because it is impossible of attainment or because a more valued gratification is desired. In the course of the delay, the motor impulses already oriented towards action in the direction of the gratified object must be checked. Thought, which Freud termed "experimental action" (24), intervenes to sustain the child by discharging smaller quantities of energy, presumably through fantasy of the reward or planning directed towards obtaining it. Here Werner's theory seems to supply a specific bridge to explain how checked motor reactions find a vicarious expression in illusory motion perception or imaginal movements.

Learning to defer gratification, with an attendant resort to an imaginal or conceptual level of behavior, is a tremendous step in maturation. By freeing the organism from the spatial and temporal limitations of immediate perception and motor response, it makes possible mastery of the future and of countless new environments, while, as Freud has so acutely noted, some sustaining satisfaction is possible, since the image or name of the reward is present in the course of the fantasy or planning activity. In this process must lie the origin of an awareness of self and of a self-concept, since the delay of gratification and the fantasy clearly differentiates the organism from the immediate environmental situation. This differentiation, once effected, partially alters the perceptual field of the child and makes possible more self-directed responses. These responses unquestionably form the basis for a symbolism and an organization of behavior, which becomes part of the Freudian "ego" or Mead's (55) and Sullivan's (100) "self-system."

Because learning opportunities, family and cultural demands, and constitutional dispositions differ, children undoubtedly vary tremendously in their rate and extent of development of motor inhibition, fantasy tendencies, and sense of self. The Rorschach experience type and specifically the M response may well represent a unique if crude method of estimating these individual differences in motor inhibition, fantasy, and self-differentiation.

The specific element of human content in the M response must still be explained, however. Here the psychoanalytic theory of identification, as delineated in an intensive survey by Lair (43), provides some clues. The delay between arousal of a need and its fulfillment may be sustained by fantasy about the parent who will bring relief. To the extent that a certain consistency in delay with assurance of the eventual coming of the parent is part of the life pattern of the child, the parental image in fantasy becomes a temporary source of satisfaction and, perhaps later, in itself an instrumentality by means of which the child, through imitation of this image, learns to master other frustrating situations. In family constellations which are characterized by considerable emphasis on deferment of gratification, but with the ultimate promise from parental figures of reward, fantasy of humans must undoubtedly be enriched. A dependency on fantasy about humans seems to be fostered in this way, particularly if parental figures are relatively loving and rewarding. Lair (43) has attempted some formulation of the role of a benign parent in the learning of language and symbolic thought. Two studies (87, 97) have offered some evidence that neurotic and schizophrenic subjects who show relatively numerous Rorschach M responses describe parental figures in TAT stories as more nurturant or less rejecting than do patients with few *M*. Constitutional or cultural factors aside, therefore, a given family constellation may make for the development within a child of a pattern of behavior characterized by relative ease of delayed gratification, identification with parental goals and behavior fantasy, a heightened awareness of self-other or self-environment distinctions, and increased planfulness, introspectiveness, and concern with human relationships. The pathological extreme of this pattern may be occasioned by a parent-child relationship that so emphasizes control of motor response and dependence on the adult, or the adult's image, for gratification that it renders the child impotent for direct action or expression of affect. Fantasy, introspection, and self-responses are the only things the child can count on without the parent, and he grows to feel that all direct action or motor activity will reveal him as inept or inexperienced. An outcome of such a childhood pattern may be an individual with lopsided introversive experience type, whose color responses are few or absent, and who is clinically characterized by extensive obsessional preoccupations, withdrawal, gross conscious concern about inferiority and insecurity, and considerable inhibition in acting upon sexual or aggressive desires. Individuals in this group may function effectively in certain spheres of intellectual activity and prove extremely creative in their thought about human relationships or in poetic and dramatic imagery, but they continue to be blocked in intimate human contacts of a direct sort (42). This clinical formulation suggests a concrete exemplification of the general theory of delay and fantasy development. It remains to be seen, however, whether systematic research will support such characterizations. Suggestive possibilities are present in some data obtained by Opler and Singer (62, 95), who compared schizophrenic subjects coming from cultural backgrounds which differed in their relative emphases on impulse control and maternal influence. Irish patients, whose parental constellations and cultural milieu favored delay, showed themselves to be more given to fantasy (Rorschach *M*, TAT imaginativeness) and delay (time estimation, voluntary slowness of writing, ward cooperativeness and absence of assaultive behavior) than a corresponding sample of Italian patients. In symptomatology and case histories, the Irish emphasized excessive impulse control and obsessional or religious delusional preoccupations, compared with the Italian patients, whose histories revealed more open antisocial or acting-out behavior, more sexual activity of all sorts, and more hypochondriacal bodily rather than interpersonal preoccupations in their delusions.

Let us now consider the sum C term of the experience-type formula, its origin, its perceptual basis, and behavioral implications. The whole question of the relationship of color and affect is beyond the scope of this chapter; the problems involved have been covered by Fortier (21), Rickers-Ovsiankina (74), Schachtel (82), and Shapiro (86 and Chapter 7 of this book). The common core of theory linking the various points of view concerning the relationship of color to affect and impulsivity appears to emphasize the relatively immediate impact of color, which evokes what Schachtel has called a "passive" reaction, Rickers-Ovsiankina, a response "involving less complex processes of organization and articulation," and Shapiro, following Rapaport's theory of affect, a process involving "less delay." Certainly the developmental theory of Werner (113) concerning hierarchic levels of integration in perception and motility from diffuse and syncretic response to more complex, differentiated, and articulated reactions has provided both a viewpoint and data which afford a basis for comprehending why pure C or CF responses may be associated with impulsivity, egocentricity, and immaturity in general. Several questions remain unanswered by this formulation, however. Recent studies have questioned the specific issue of whether it is the color *per se* or rather the diffuse, poorly articulated, nature of the response which is associated with diffuse or hasty motility or affect (89, 115, 116). Even Shapiro, who has carried the concept of delayed discharge in relation to color a step further by delineating three types of passivity in response to color, has not indicated whether shading or black and white reaction differ in this respect from chromatic reactions. Does a diffuse $C'F$ response carry a different behavioral import than a CF? The theoretical basis for a distinction between these response tendencies does not seem apparent as yet, at least with a specificity that can explain the *perceptual* basis for the distinction.

The second problem raised in the linkage of color to affect by means of a "delayed discharge" theory is how to distinguish between M and C. If M represents the outcome of a long period of development in the personality of the capacity to free the individual from the pressure of immediate drives, and if FC in effect represents a similar example of this development, we are faced with the necessity of explaining why we differentiate between the two responses and between records with high sum C and those with no M. Indeed, Wittenborn (115, 116) has, on an empirical basis, questioned the association of FC with CF and C, and has claimed that his data support only a distinction between presence or lack of perceptual control. No simple solution seems forthcoming at present. Although Rorschach made it clear that movement and color measured different functional dimensions, he also took an important step by indicating the close association between affectivity and motility. The question as to how color and human-movement responses to ink blots come about and how they come to be linked to different personality dimensions persists as long as we cannot demonstrate a distinction between the behavioral correlates of the two types of responses.

A recent study by Singer, Wilensky, and McCraven (98) may point up the difficulty of an attempt to derive a comprehensive theoretical basis for the M:sum C ratio. A large battery of tests including the Rorschach and various behavioral situations were administered to a group of 100 schizophrenic patients. The tests and behavior samples were chosen because it was felt that most of them would have relevance to a dimension linking fantasy capacity with inhibited motility, planning, lack of impulsivity, or delaying capacity in general. Factor analysis of the matrix of intercorrelations yielded four factors. Factor A's heaviest loadings were for Rorschach M, Barron's Human Movement Threshold, Porteus Maze Test Quotient, Downey's Motor Inhibition Test, and rated cooperativeness with ward routine. This factor clearly links Rorschach M with a capacity for delay in the motor sphere. Factor B showed highest loadings on measures of productivity and aspiration. Factor C had highest loadings from FC, C', CF, R, and FM, as well as aggressiveness, uncooperative ward behavior and diffuse energy level in ward behavior. Factor D resembled factor A since its high loadings were from M and Barron's M-threshold, but here the other tests with appreciable loadings did not involve control of motor activity, but seemed to reflect imaginativeness, introspectiveness and lack of external interests.

Consideration of these results suggests tentative support for Rorschach's view of the experience type with its two dimensions. Factor A may clearly be termed a "delay" factor, and it resembles a similar result obtained in a factor analysis by Foster (22), using different behavior samples with the Rorschach ink blots. Factor C seems definitely to represent a pressure for outward living which might be termed "emotional surgency," and which again parallels a finding by Foster. Indeed, a second-order factor analysis reveals an inverse linkage between factors A and C, which seems in accord with Rorschach's uniting M and C in a common ratio while insisting that they still represented different functional dimensions. At the same time, the very high loading of C' on factor C, although supporting Piotrowski's

(67) empirical interpretation of C' as associated with acting-out tend-encies, complicates the picture somewhat in so far as it may be appro-priate to make a distinction between chromatic color and black-grey reactions. The emergence of two separate M factors, one linking M with motor inhibition, the other with introversion and imagination, is also puzzling. It may perhaps reflect a pattern peculiar to pathology, since the sample was made up of severely disturbed patients. Never-theless, it remains possible that the linkage of fantasy, control of hos-tility, and motion perception is far more complex than any description thus far attempted would suggest. Unfortunately, in this study and in most described in the literature, it was not possible or not planned to consider in detail the various nuances of M or sum C, and to incor-porate a specific M:sum C measure in the matrix.

A Tentative Theoretical Formulation of the Experience Type

In attempting a brief formulation which will incorporate Rorschach's experience type within a more general framework, the author hopes chiefly to provide a good target for experimental sniping. The basic tenet of this chapter has been that experimental and theoretical exploration in the Rorschach method is not only possible but genu-inely interesting, and fruitful not only for the practical purpose of validating a clinical tool but also for generating hypotheses about the nature of human personality.

To begin with, it is postulated that two dimensions of variation in human behavior exist at birth which have relevance for the concept of the experience type. These dimensions may well be considered aspects of a basic temperament relatively built into the constitution and modifiable only within limits by subsequent learning. One dimen-sion might be termed "capacity for internal experience," and it may be reflected in speed of assimilation of visual percepts, general tend-ency for rapid formation of associations, general intelligence, and capacity for development of imagery. Subsequently, it may be re-lated to ease of language development. The other dimension might be termed "activity" or "motility" and includes rapidity of autonomic arousal, a constitutional factor suggested by Wenger's work (109, 110, 111), rapidity of movement, and a low threshold for affective re-sponse. In crude terms, it may be that every child differs in the amount of energy available for expression along these dimensions, or in the differentiation and sensitivity of the organ systems or neural patterns relevant to these dimensions. It seems likely that differences in gross quantity of energy exist so that some children show marked development along both dimensions whereas others show little in one or both. It seems reasonable to suppose that just as some persons are put together in such a way as to enhance full and long employment of their physiques, others are born already possessing the potential capacities for richer use of imaginal and affective resources in interpersonal relationships.

To some extent, these dimensions together may well represent what Maslow (53) has termed "the expressive component of behavior." The inner-living dimension would certainly represent a scale along which the autonomous ego functions, described by Hartmann (31), would vary for each person. The rewards and frustrations of life are then brought to bear upon each child, and accident and parental attitude undoubtedly affect this behavior along each dimension. Parental emphasis on delay or routine may afford opportunity for fantasy development in some children and may reward such development, thus increasing its emergence as a conflict-free area in which the child finds considerable satisfaction and even practical use. In children initially lacking this possibility, but pressed for delay, other mechanisms may develop, e.g., somatization. Close parental ties may also enhance this development. In the sphere of affect or motility, parental demands for rapid response and for affective interchange may prove too much for the phlegmatic child, enhancing conflict and, as the emotional response sought is not forthcoming, leading to rejection by parents. The hyperactive sensitive child whose parents cannot tolerate timidity or aggression may be forced to suppress his affective potential by whatever means available. Affectivity would thus become part of the conflictual sphere of the ego, subject to a variety of defense mechanisms, one of which might be, in a child with fantasy potential, intellectualization or withdrawal into daydreaming. Cultural values will come into play here from the peer group and the school situation, thus enhancing further development along one or both of these dimensions. In a family setting in which open emotionality is acceptable and in which warmth enhances the value of adaptive affectivity, one might expect moderate control of motility and expression of feeling but little denial or repression.

Some outcomes of various family constellations may be sketched briefly. Given an individual already possessing constitutional potential for introversive living, with the concurrence of a close relationship with parents in a family where the mother is often nurturant and fosters identification with order or with ideal values ("Be a good boy for mother"), a highly developed inner life characterized by respect for mental process, deferment of gratification, fluidity of imagery, planning ability, and concern with human problems and human interaction may develop. An individual of this sort may well choose an occupation in keeping with this pattern [as Roe's (78) data suggest], but if circumstances lead to other work, humanistic interests may persist. Such a person might still prove to be cold, reserved, and distant in his direct interchange with others, and might win respect but perhaps not love. Sexual activity could perhaps be mechanical or characterized by extreme inhibition, while at the same time the introversive development might enable the individual to write sensual poetry or to empathize deeply with the experience of lovers. If, however, in such a person, the family constellation had perhaps more balance with a pattern permitting affective expression and encouraging motility, both potentialities might be developed and lead to the richness correlated with the dilated experience type.

Since at least in our society the influence of the mother temporally precedes that of the father, one might speculate on a chronological sequence of identification patterns necessary for optimal development of both M and C dimensions. An early experience with a reasonably nurturant mother who emphasizes control and delay may aid in fantasy development and ego formation through identification and imitation. For fullest development of the affective and action capacities, it would appear that, at least for a male child, some identification with the father subsequently reinforced by peer-group association is necessary. The father who moves about, works at chores, shows interest in sports, swears and expresses open hostility on occasion as well as affection, and can tolerate these tendencies in the child, offers a model for development of affective and motor spontaneity. As a matter of fact, the term "spontaneity" may perhaps involve separation of activity in the ideational and affective dimension—a markedly introversive individual may be capable of clever ideas and original thoughts or wit which can be put on paper, without having, however, much capacity for emotional responsiveness or motor freedom. Someone lacking such inner potential, but developed in the motor-affect area, may prove to be warm, sympathetic, and easily moved, and may be capable of great freedom of movement or bawdy but winning humor. Of course, translating these generalizations to the M:sum C ratio of a Rorschach protocol, it should be kept in mind that quality and content of the component responses in each ratio term would obviously require consideration in this connection.

Combining Rorschach data bearing on these two dimensions into a common ratio can now be seen as a method for tapping potentialities and capacities for spontaneity in two great spheres of human variation—the ideational and the affective. Other dimensions undoubtedly exist and are of equal importance for clinical purposes, e.g., anxiety level, masculinity versus femininity, reality orientation, etc. The M:sum C ratio, if it can be perfected, and really rational rather than arbitrary weightings could be made available, may tell us much of the gross patterns of fantasy, affectivity, and motility, and of the spontaneity potential in ideation and affect of the individual. A rich development in one sphere may afford evidence of potentiality for effective and satisfactory living even when there is minimal or disturbed development in the other sphere. Important differences between people which are often attributed to specific dynamic conflicts or distortions may in part be a reflection of gross temperamental differences represented by strikingly different experience types. Rorschach's suggestion that the M:sum C ratio be applied to ascertaining the suitability of marriage partners is worth some empirical consideration in this connection. As Barron (4) has suggested, the M type may represent not so much a distinctively *effective* mode of adjustment as a *style of life*. It is interesting in this connection that the psychologists who assessed the high-M individuals in Barron's study and who felt them to be more intelligent, may well, if Roe's (78) data are valid, have been M types themselves. The experience type, by reflecting the balance between developments in two crucial areas of human behavior, appears to go beyond expressiveness. however, to provide important clues to two major spheres of human life, two great dimensions of human variation along which we may observe the fulfillment of man's potentialities for thought and feeling.

BIBLIOGRAPHY

1. Ainsworth, Mary D.   Problems of validation.   In: Klopfer, B., Ainsworth, M., Klopfer, W., and Holt, R.   *Developments in the Rorschach technique* Yonkers: World Book Co., 1954, Chapter 14.
2. Arnheim, R.   Perceptual and aesthetic aspects of the movement response. *J. Pers.*, 1951, **19**, 265–281.
3. Barrell, R. P.   Subcategories of Rorschach human movement responses: A classification system and some experimental results.   *J. consult. Psychol.*, 1953, **17**, 254–260.
4. Barron, F.   Threshold for the perception of human movement in inkblots. *J. consult. Psychol.*, 1955, **19**, 33–38.

5. Bash, K. W.   Einstellungstypus and Erlebnistypus: C. G. Jung and Herman Rorschach.   *J. proj. Tech.*, 1955, **19**, 236–242.

6. Beck, S. J.   *Rorschach's test.*   New York: Grune and Stratton, 1946.

7. Bieri, J., and Blacker, E.   External and internal stimulus factors in Rorschach performance.   *J. consult. Psychol.*, 1956, **20**, 1–7.

8. Bieri, J., and Blacker, E.   The generality of cognitive complexity of people and inkblots.   *J. abnorm. soc. Psychol.*, 1956, **53**, 112–117.

9. Blechner, Janet E.   Constancy of Rorschach movement responses under educational conditioning.   *California J. Ed. Res.*, 1953, **4**, 173–176.

10. Blechner, Janet E.   Constancy of Rorschach color responses under educational conditioning.   *J. exp. Ed.*, 1954, **22**, 293–295.

11. Block, J.   A study of affective responsiveness in a lie-detection situation.   *J. abnorm. soc. Psychol.*, 1957, **55**, 11–15.

12. Brower, D.   The relation between certain Rorschach factors and cardiovascular activity before and after visual-motor conflict.   *J. gen. Psychol.*, 1947, **37**, 93–95.

13. Dawo, A.   Nachweis psychischer Veränderungen gesunder Frauen während der Menstruation mittels des Rorschach Versuches.   *Rorschachiana*, 1952, **1**, 238–249.

14. Eckhardt, W.   An experimental and theoretical analysis of movement and vista responses.   *J. proj. Tech.*, 1955, **19**, 301–305.

15. Eichler, R.   A comparison of the Rorschach and Behn ink-blot tests.   *J. consult. Psychol.*, 1951, **15**, 186–189.

16. Eysenck, H. J.   *Dimensions of personality.*   London: Routledge and Kegan Paul, 1948.

17. Eysenck, H. J.   *The structure of human personality.*   New York: John Wiley, 1953.

18. Felzer, S. B.   A statistical study of sex differences on the Rorschach.   *J. proj. Tech.*, 1955, **19**, 382–386.

19. Finney, B. C.   Rorschach test correlates of assaultive behavior.   *J. proj Tech.*, 1950, **14**, 15–30.

20. Ford, Mary.   *The application of the Rorschach test to young children.*   Minneapolis: University of Minnesota Press, 1946.

21. Fortier, R. H.   The response to color and ego functions.   *Psychol. Bull.*, 1953, **50**, 41–63.

22. Foster, A.   The factorial structure of the Rorschach test.   *Tex. Rep. Biol. Med.*, 1955, **13**, 34–61.

23. Freud, S.   *The ego and the id.*   London: Hogarth, 1923.

24. Freud, S.   Formulations regarding the two principles in mental functioning.   In: *Collected Papers. Vol. IV.*   London: Hogarth, 1946, 13–21.

25. Freud, S.   The interpretation of dreams.   In: *Standard edition of the complete psychological works. Vol. V.*   London: Hogarth, 1953, 339–628.

26. Gardner, R. W.   Impulsivity as indicated by Rorschach test factors.   *J. consult. Psychol.*, 1951, **15**, 464–468.

27. Gibby, R. G., Stotsky, B. A., Harrington, R. L., and Thomas, R. W.   Rorschach determinant shift among hallucinatory and delusional patients.   *J. consult. Psychol.*, 1955, **19**, 44–46.

28. Goldfarb, W.   Psychological privation in infancy and subsequent adjustment.   *Amer. J. Orthopsychiat.*, 1945, **15**, 249–254.

29. Goldfarb, W. Rorschach test differences between family reared, institution reared, and schizophrenic children. *Amer. J. Orthopsychiat.*, 1949, **19**, 624-633.

30. Goldman, A. E. Studies in vicariousness: degree of motor activity and the autokinetic phenomenon. *Amer. J. Psychol.*, 1953, **66**, 613-617.

31. Hartmann, H. Comments on the psychoanalytic theory of the ego. In: *The psychoanalytic study of the child. Vol. V.* New York: International Universities Press, 1950, 74-96.

32. Hays, W., Gellerman, S., and Sloan, W. A study of the verb-adjective quotient and the Rorschach experience-balance. *J. clin. Psychol.*, 1951, **7**, 224-227.

33. Herman, J. A study of some behavioral and test correlates of the Rorschach experience type. Unpublished doctor's dissertation, New York University, 1956.

34. Hertzman, M., Orlansky, J., and Seitz, C. Personality organization and anoxia tolerance. *Psychosom. Med.*, 1944, **6**, 317-331.

35. Holt, R. R. Implications of some contemporary personality theories for Rorschach rationale. In: Klopfer, B., Ainsworth, M., Klopfer, W., and Holt, R. *Developments in the Rorschach technique. Vol. I.* Yonkers: World Book Co., 1954, Chapter 15.

36. Holtzmann, W. H. Validation studies of the Rorschach test: Impulsiveness in the normal superior adult. *J. clin. Psychol.*, 1950, **6**, 348-351.

37. Hunter, Mary. Responses of comparable white and Negro adults to the Rorschach test. *J. Psychol.*, 1937, **3**, 173-182.

38. Klein, G. S., and Schlesinger, H. J. Perceptual attitudes toward instability: Prediction of apparent movement responses from Rorschach responses. *J. Pers.*, 1951, **19**, 289-302.

39. Klopfer, B. Rorschach hypotheses and ego psychology. In: Klopfer, B., Ainsworth, M., Klopfer, W., and Holt, R. *Developments in the Rorschach technique. Vol. I.* Yonkers: World Book Co., 1954, Chapter 16.

40. Klopfer, B., and Margulies, H. Rorschach reactions in early childhood. *Rorschach Res. Exch.*, 1941, **5**, 1-23.

41. Kris, E. On preconscious mental processes. *Psychoanal. Quart.*, 1950, **19**, 540-560.

42. Kupper, H. L. Psychodynamics of the "intellectual." *Int. J. Psychoanal.*, 1950, **31**, 85-94.

43. Lair, W. S. The psychoanalytic theory of identification. Unpublished doctor's dissertation, Harvard University, 1949.

44. Lane, Barbara M. A validation test of the Rorschach movement responses. *Amer. J. Orthopsychiat.*, 1948, **18**, 292-296.

45. Ledwith, Nettie. Rorschach responses of elementary school children. Paper read at meetings of the American Psychological Association, Cleveland, 1953. *Amer. Psychol.*, 1953, **8**, 385 (abstract).

46. Leiman, C. J. An investigation of the perception of movement on the Rorschach inkblots. Unpublished doctor's dissertation, University of Kentucky, 1951.

47. Levi, J., and Kraemer, Doris. Significance of a preponderance of human movement responses in children below age ten. *J. proj. Tech.*, 1952, **16**, 361-365.

48. Levine, M., Glass, H., and Meltzoff, J. The inhibition process, Rorschach *M*, color responses, and intelligence. Paper read at Eastern Psychological Association meetings, Atlantic City, 1956.

49. Levine, M., and Meltzoff, J. Cognitive inhibition and Rorschach human movement responses. *J. consult. Psychol.*, 1956, **20**, 119–122.

50. Lewin, K. *A dynamic theory of personality.* New York: McGraw-Hill, 1935.

51. Luria, A. P. *The Nature of human conflicts.* New York: Liveright, 1932.

52. Mann, L. The relation of Rorschach indices of extratension and introversion to a measure of responsiveness to the immediate environment. Unpublished doctor's dissertation, University of North Carolina, 1953.

53. Maslow, A. The expressive component of behavior. *Psychol. Rev.*, 1949, **56**, 261–271.

54. Matarazzo, Ruth G., Watson, R. I., and Ulett, G. A. Relationship of Rorschach scoring categories to modes of perception induced by intermittent photic stimulation—a methodological study of perception. *J. clin. Psychol.*, 1952, **8**, 368–374.

55. Mead, G. H. *Mind, self, and society.* Chicago: University of Chicago Press, 1934.

56. Meltzoff, J., and Levine, M. The relationship between motor and cognitive inhibition. *J. consult. Psychol.*, 1954, **18**, 355–358.

57. Meltzoff, J., and Litwin, Dorothy. Affective control and Rorschach human movement responses. *J. consult. Psychol.*, 1956, **20**, 463–465.

58. Meltzoff, J., Singer, J. L., and Korchin, S. J. Motor inhibition and Rorschach movement responses: A test of the sensory-tonic theory. *J. Pers.*, 1953, **21**, 400–410.

59. Mindess, A. Analytical psychology and the Rorschach test. *J. proj. Tech.*, 1955, **19**, 243–253.

60. Misch, R. C. The relationship of motoric inhibition to developmental level and ideational functioning: an analysis by means of the Rorschach test. Unpublished doctor's dissertation, Clark University, 1954.

61. Murawski, B. The perceptual and imaginal effects of immobilization: a clinical study. Unpublished doctor's dissertation, Harvard University, 1954.

62. Opler, M. K., and Singer, J. L. Ethnic behavior and psychopathology: Italian and Irish. *Int. J. soc. Psychiat.*, 1956, **2**, 11–23.

63. Palmer, J. O. Rorschach's experience-balance: The concept, general population characteristics, and intellectual correlates. *J. proj. Tech.*, 1955, **19**, 138–145.

64. Palmer, J. O. Attitudinal correlates of Rorschach's experience-balance. *J. proj. Tech.*, 1956, **20**, 208–211.

65. Piaget, J. *The language and thought of the child.* New York: Harcourt, Brace, 1932.

66. Pickering, W. D. A comparison of predominant verbal levels on the Thematic Apperception Test with the Rorschach experience-balance. Unpublished doctor's dissertation, University of Pittsburgh, 1950.

67. Piotrowski, Z. A. A Rorschach compendium, revised and enlarged. *Psychiat. Quart.*, 1950, 24, 543–596.

68. Piotrowski, Z. A., and Schreiber, M. Rorschach perceptanalytic measurement of personality changes during and after intensive psychoanalytically

oriented psychotherapy. In: *Specialized Techniques in psychotherapy*. New York: Basic Books, 1951.

69. Rabinovitch, M. S., Kennard, Margaret A., and Fister, W. P. Personality correlates of electroencephalographic findings. *Can. J. Psychol.*, 1955, **9**, 29–41.

70. Rapaport, D. *Organization and pathology of thought*. New York: Columbia University Press, 1951.

71. Rapaport, D. On the psychoanalytic theory of affects. *Inter. J. Psychoanal.*, 1953, **34**, 177–198.

72. Rapaport, D., Gill, M., and Schafer, R. *Diagnostic psychological testing*. Vol. II. Chicago: Year Book Publishers, 1946.

73. Rickers-Ovsiankina, Maria. Studies of the personality structure of schizophrenic individuals. I. *J. gen. Psychol.*, 1937, **16**, 153–178.

74. Rickers-Ovsiankina, Maria. Some theoretical considerations regarding the Rorschach method. *Rorschach Res. Exch.*, 1943, **7**, 41–53.

75. Rickers-Ovsiankina, Maria. Prognostic Rorschach indices in schizophrenia. In: *Review of diagnostic psychology and personality exploration*. Bern: Hans Huber, 1955, **3**, 246–254.

76. Richards, T. W., and Lederman, Ruth. A study of action in the fantasy of physically handicapped children. *J. clin. Psychol.*, 1956, **12**, 188–190.

77. Rioch, Margaret J. The use of the Rorschach test in the assessment of change in patients under psychotherapy. *Psychiatry*, 1949, **12**, 427–434.

78. Roe, Anne. Analysis of group Rorschachs of psychologists and anthropologists. *J. proj. Tech.*, 1952, **16**, 212–224.

79. Rorschach, H. *Psychodiagnostics*. Bern: Hans Huber, 1942.

80. Rosenthal, M. Some behavioral correlates of the Rorschach experience-balance. Unpublished doctor's dissertation, Boston University, 1954.

81. Royal, R. E. An experimental investigation of the relationship between questionnaire and Rorschach measures of introversion. Unpublished doctor's dissertation, University of Pittsburgh, 1950.

82. Schachtel, E. On color and affect. Contributions to the understanding of Rorschach's test. II. *Psychiatry*, 1943, **6**, 393–409.

83. Schachtel, E. Projection and its relation to character attitudes and creativity in the kinesthetic response. Contributions to the understanding of Rorschach's test. IV. *Psychiatry*, 1950, **13**, 69–100.

84. Schumer, F. Some behavioral correlates of Rorschach human movement responses. Unpublished doctor's dissertation, Yale University, 1949.

85. Schmidt, B. Reflektorische Reaktionen auf Form und Farbe. *Z. Psychol.*, 1936, **137**.

86. Shapiro, D. Color response and perceptual passivity. *J. proj. Tech.*, 1956, **20**, 52–69.

87. Shatin, L. Rorschach adjustment and the Thematic Apperception Test. *J. proj. Tech.*, 1953, **17**, 92–101.

88. Siipola, Elsa. The influence of color on reactions to inkblots. *J. Pers.*, 1950, **18**, 358–382.

89. Siipola, Elsa, and Taylor, Vivian. Reactions to inkblots under free and pressure conditions. *J. Pers.*, 1952, **21**, 22–47.

90. Singer, J. L. The Behn-Rorschach inkblots: A preliminary comparison with the original Rorschach series. *J. proj. Tech.*, 1952, **16**, 238–245.

91. Singer, J. L.   Perceptual and environmental determinants of perception in a size constancy experiment. *J. exp. Psychol.,* 1952, **43**, 420–427.

92. Singer, J. L.   Delayed gratification and ego-development: implications for clinical and experimental research. *J. consult. Psychol.,* 1955, **19**, 259–266.

93. Singer, J. L., and Herman, J.   Motor and fantasy correlates of Rorschach human movement responses. *J. consult. Psychol.,* 1954, **18**, 325–331.

94. Singer, J. L., Meltzoff, J., and Goldman, G. D.   Rorschach movement responses following motor inhibition and hyperactivity. *J. consult. Psychol.,* 1952, **16**, 359–364.

95. Singer, J. L., and Opler, M. K.   Contrasting patterns of fantasy and motility in Irish and Italian schizophrenics. *J. abnorm. soc. Psychol.,* 1956, **53**, 42–47.

96. Singer, J. L., and Spohn, H.   Some behavioral correlates of Rorschach's experience-type. *J. consult. Psychol.,* 1954, **18**, 1–9.

97. Singer, J. L., and Sugarman, D.   Some Thematic Apperception Test correlates of Rorschach human movement responses. *J. consult. Psychol.,* 1955, **19**, 117–119.

98. Singer, J. L., Wilensky, H., and McCraven, Vivian.   Delaying capacity, fantasy, and planning ability: A factorial study of some basic ego functions. *J. consult. Psychol.,* 1956, **20**, 375–383.

99. Stein, M. I., and Meer, B.   Perceptual organization in a study of creativity. *J. Psychol.,* 1954, **37**, 39–43.

100. Sullivan, H. S.   *An interpersonal theory of psychiatry.*   New York: Norton, 1953.

101. Temerlin, M. K.   One determinant of the capacity to free-associate in psychotherapy. *J. abnorm. soc. Psychol.,* 1956, **53**, 16–18.

102. Thetford, W. N.   Fantasy perceptions in the personality development of normal and deviant children. *Amer. J. Orthopsychiat.,* 1952, **22**, 542–550.

103. Thetford, W. N., Molish, H. B., and Beck, S. J.   Developmental aspects of personality structure in normal children. *J. proj. Tech.,* 1951, **15**, 58–78.

104. Thiessen, J. W., Favorite, L., and Coff, P.   An investigation of the relationship between clinically-observed emotional behavior in children and Rorschach test indicators of emotional response.   Paper read at the Eastern Psychological Association meetings, Boston, 1953.

105. Thornton, G. R., and Guilford, J. P.   The reliability and meaning of Erlebnistypus scores in the Rorschach test. *J. abnorm. soc. Psychol.,* 1936, **31**, 324–330.

106. Vernier, Claire, and Kendig, Isabelle V.   Analysis of the relationship between various measures of creative productivity in two projective tests. *Amer. Psychologist,* 1951, **8**, 349 (abstract).

107. Vernon, P. E.   The significance of the Rorschach test. *Brit. J. Med. Psychol.,* 1935, **15**, 199–217.

108. Weber, C. O.   The relation of personality trends to degree of visual constancy correction for size and form. *J. appl. Psychol.,* 1939, **23**, 703–708.

109. Wenger, M. A.   Some relationships between muscular processes and personality and their factorial analysis. *Child Develop.,* 1938, **9**, 261–276.

110. Wenger, M. A.   The stability of measurements of autonomic balance. *Psychosom. Med.,* 1942, **6**, 94–95.

111. Wenger, M. A.   A study of physiological factors: The autonomic nervous system and the skeletal musculature. *Human Biol.,* 1942, **14**, 69–84.

112. Werner, H.   Motion and motion perception: a study on vicarious functioning.   *J. Psychol.*, 1945, **19**, 317–327.
113. Werner, H.   *The comparative psychology of mental development.*   Chicago: Follett, 1948.
114. Werner, H., and Wapner, S.   Toward a general theory of perception.   *Psychol. Rev.*, 1952, **59**, 324–333.
115. Wittenborn, J. R.   A factor analysis of Rorschach scoring categories.   *J. consult. Psychol.*, 1950, **14**, 261–267.
116. Wittenborn, J. R.   Level of mental health as a factor in the implications of Rorschach scores.   *J. consult. Psychol.*, 1950, **14**, 469–472.
117. Wittkower, E.   *A psychiatrist looks at tuberculosis.*   London: National Association for Prevention of Tuberculosis, 1949.
118. Zubin, J.   The non-projective aspects of the Rorschach experiment: I. Introduction.   *J. soc. Psychol.*, 1956, **44**, 179–192.

CATEGORIES OF ANALYSIS: CONTENT

We come next to a theme of the utmost importance, the distinction Freud established between what he called "primary processes" and "secondary processes." It was perhaps his most fundamental contribution to psychology.

ERNEST JONES

10

by *Robert R. Holt*
and *Joan Havel*

A

METHOD FOR ASSESSING
PRIMARY AND SECONDARY PROCESS
IN THE RORSCHACH [1]

When Rorschach gave us his test—his blots, his way of administering the experiment, as he called it, and interpreting the results—he also left us a system of scoring the responses. Essentially, this was a way of abstracting from a complex performance four or five important dimensions—dimensions which hundreds of Rorschachers since have found most useful. Hermann Rorschach was perfectly open in pointing out the intuitive and heuristic nature of these scoring categories. One of the first points he made in his monograph was that the theoretical basis of the test was almost nonexistent.

Since Rorschach's death, other hands have worked to expand and perfect the scoring, but mostly this has meant increasing its differentiation and making explicit the criteria for assigning particular scores. Attempts to work out a theoretical rationale of the test, or to construct

---

[1] The first part of this chapter has been reprinted with some revisions from an article that appeared in the *Journal of projective Techniques* (8). We wish to express our indebtedness to Dr. Roy Schafer, whose book (17) has been stimulating and helpful in the development of the point of view expounded here, and who has contributed useful criticisms of the manual that embodies our scoring system.

new scoring systems on a theoretical basis, have been few indeed. Although the majority of workers have followed Rorschach in working within the framework of some kind of psychoanalytic theory in their thinking about personality, only rarely has this led to attempts to set up new ways of scoring the test.

THEORETICAL BACKGROUND

This chapter reports an attempt to develop one such supplementary method. It is based on classic psychoanalytic theory, and is limited specifically to the problem of finding operational definitions for the concepts of primary and secondary process. It is remarkable that these are among the least known and least well-understood of Freud's concepts, considering the basic place they hold in his theory, and the fact that his account of them was first published 60 years ago, in *The Interpretation of Dreams*. The reason probably is that the seventh chapter of that book, where the concepts are introduced and most fully expounded, is about the hardest to understand of all Freud's output, and until recently no good translation was available (3).

Psychoanalysis popularly has the reputation of being a voluntaristic, antirational theory, one that portrays thought as the plaything and creature of man's impulses. Actually, of course, Freud did *not* deny that logical, rational, realistic, and efficient mental processes exist, or even that they make up a great part of conscious mental life, a part which his therapy aimed to enlarge. He grouped them under the conceptual heading *secondary process*. The term *secondary* was a warning, however, that another type of thinking preceded genetically and had priority for our understanding of unconscious processes. In his studies of neurotic patients, he found that their dreams and symptoms were not the random coughs and sputters of a faulty engine, but intelligible and highly meaningful products of a peculiar kind of mental operation. This he called the *primary process*. He found evidence of its working in slips of the tongue and other errors, in jokes, in the thinking of primitive people, of children, of persons under extreme stress and strong affect, and in the creative processes of artists. It disregards considerations of time; logical contradictions abound. When the primary process holds sway, ideas shift about, lose their identities through fusion or fragmentation, become concrete and pictorial, and are combined and associated in seemingly arbitrary or trivial ways. The course of thinking and remembering is dictated by the instinctual drives, while realistic considerations are disregarded and the distinction between wish and reality is lost. Truly, the picture of a mind wholly in the grip of the primary process deserves the image of the "seething cauldron," which Rapaport (14) has used to describe it.

One needs only to imagine such a state of affairs to realize that it is an ideal conception rather than the description of an empirical possibility. Just as the rational man of the enlightenment was an ideal type never to be encountered, neither was his opposite, the id incarnate. In much of what Freud wrote about these concepts, it is fairly clear that he did not think of them dichotomously, but as defining the extremes of a logical continuum. Any actual thought process, even that of a baby or a deteriorated schizophrenic, has to be located somewhere in between the two poles. Rapaport (14), Hartmann (7), and Kris (12) are quite explicit about this way of viewing primary and secondary process.

Out of the many points that might be made in discussing these concepts, we want to emphasize three.

1. The more primary the thinking, the more it is organized and compelled by drives. In contemporary psychoanalytic ego psychology, motives are conceived of as a hierarchy, ranging from the most uncontrolled libidinal and aggressive urges to the most controlled and relatively autonomous drive derivatives, such as interests, values, highly socialized desires, and the like. As we go higher in this schematic structure, originally raw, blind urges are increasingly tamed by countercathectic controlling structures, so that the energies are transformed—in Hartmann's term (7), *neutralized* or sublimated. A motive belonging anywhere in this hierarchy can get control of a train of thought, so it follows that the less neutralized the drive that dominates thought and the closer its aims are to those of the original instincts, the more primary will be the mental process.

2. Primary thinking can be recognized not only from its preoccupation with instinctual aims but also by certain peculiar *formal* characteristics. These include autistic logic instead of straight thinking, loose and nonsensical types of associative links, and distortion of reality in numerous ways. But the most notable formal deviations of primary thinking were described by Freud as the mechanisms of the dream work. *Condensation* is a process resulting in the fusion of two or more ideas or images. *Displacement* is a shift of emphasis or interest from one mental content to another (usually a less important

content in terms of relevance to conflict or instinctual aims). *Symbolization* is the replacement of one idea or image by another, a concrete visual presentation which may have various formal features in common with what is being symbolized but which disguises the latter's dynamic significance. All of these mechanisms may be used defensively, since they produce changes that usually conceal the original meanings of the material on which they exert their effects. Thus, in the formation of dreams, they work over the dream thoughts and transform them in ways that make these dynamically "hot" materials acceptable to the censoring influence of the superego.

On the next higher level of generalization, in terms of the libido theory, the essential operation in all of these mechanisms is the *free mobility of cathexis*. According to Freud, every active idea has an energy charge, or cathexis, attached to it. This cathectic charge is ultimately derived from one of the drives and motivates thinking, which could not proceed without some cathexis of the ideas. In the secondary process any particular idea's cathexis is *bound* to it. A thing is reliably itself; an orderly, stable, realistic view of the world becomes possible. In the primary process, on the other hand, the aim is to re-experience situations of gratification by the most *direct methods* possible, even if it means arbitrarily pushing ideas and percepts around so that contact with reality is lost. In energy terms, this means that an idea and its cathexis are easily parted.

The operations of condensation, displacement and symbol-formation are by no means confined to the production of dreams and neurotic symptoms. They are conspicuously present in the language of schizophrenics; indeed, schizophrenia has been described (perhaps too glibly) as a state in which conscious mental life is dominated by the primary process instead of the secondary. Any weakening of the ego's controlling forces may result in the emergence of primary thinking—in reverie states, under the influence of drugs, in slips of the tongue, humor, and so forth.

(3.) The final point we want to underscore about the primary process has to do with humor and other enjoyable sides of life. It is one of mankind's great gifts to be *able* to abandon reality voluntarily for a little while; to shake free from dead literalism, to recombine the old familiar elements into new, imaginative, amusing, or beautiful patterns. Among modern psychoanalysts, Ernst Kris has been particularly interested in the functioning of the psychic apparatus in artistic creativity and humor. He has pointed out the fact that the ego of a mature and healthy person can at times relax, abandon secondary-process standards in a controlled and reversible way, and *use* the freedom and fluidity of the primary process productively; this he calls *regression in the service of the ego* (12). A person who is not asleep and dreaming may therefore fragment and recombine ideas and images in ways that flout the demands of reality on either of two bases: because he cannot *help* it, due to a temporary or permanent ego-weakness, or because he *wants* to, for fun or for creative purposes, and is able to because he is not too threatened by his unconscious drives. Thus, the third point is that we find primary thinking in conscious subjects either out of strength or out of weakness. In the former case, it is more likely to appear in a playful or esthetic frame of reference, accompanied by pleasant affect. If, on the other hand, primary thinking breaks through the usual defenses uninvited and unwanted, the subject may feel anxious or threatened and is likely to act defensively.

But why should the Rorschach test performance lend itself to analysis in terms of primary and secondary processes? If one accepts the idea that thought processes may be arranged in a continuous series from the most primary to the most secondary, we can apply these concepts to *any* sample of mental activity, though we know that anything obviously primary in character is exceptional when we are dealing with people who are not psychiatric patients. Taking the Rorschach, however, is a situation with a number of more or less unique features that favor the emergence of primary modes of cognition. First of all, the subject is called on to produce a series of visual images. This is a preferred mode of operation for the primary process; without the requirement (such as the TAT imposes) to produce a connected narrative, there is less demand for organizing and synthesizing and less necessity for secondary-process thinking. Moreover, the ink blots offer complex stimulus configurations, richly enough varied to evoke and support almost any kind of image that may be latent in the viewer's mind, yet without actually and unmistakably representing anything in reality. By releasing the subject from the more stringent of ordinary requirements for logical thought organization, and by sanctioning, as it were, the emergence of any kind of ideational content, the test thus offers a means of assessing both the nature and extent of drive-organization of thinking, and its formal structure as well—the first two points made above about the primary process. We know, however, that subjects react to this test in different ways, and permit themselves different degrees of freedom in their responses. The test thus also offers a means of assessing the third aspect of primary cognition referred to above: the characteristic response of the person to the emergence of primary material into consciousness, or his characteristic defenses against its emergence.

We have found, however, that test records administered in the usual way often leave us in the dark about the person's reaction to the primary-process material emerging in his responses. Only part of the time do the subject's behavior (as noted by the tester) and his verbalizations indicate his inner feelings about what he sees and says. We therefore took up a suggestion of a colleague, Dr. Fred Pine, and added an additional question to the inquiry on each response: "How did you feel about it?" Sometimes it is necessary to expand on this simple question by explaining that the tester is interested in the subject's reactions to each thing that he saw in the blots, whether seeing it was pleasant, unpleasant or a matter of indifference. Such a direct questioning approach is accepted well by patients and research subjects alike, and it yields not only the information needed for rating the effectiveness of the subject's controls (*DE*, see below) but also often data of considerable clinical value. Of course, the answers given cannot always be taken at face value; clinical judgment cannot be eschewed when dealing with the primary process.

The objection might be raised: How can you speak of primary *process* when you have only a *product* to deal with? The point is well taken; but the process is an intervening variable that is not directly observable—we can infer it only from its products. A scoring system thus could either attempt to work with inferences to the hypothetical process (something that is difficult at best and impossible without extensive free associations), or one can stick to the product itself and concentrate on its properties of still retaining the hallmarks of the processes that produced it. We have followed the latter course, hoping by minimizing inference to attain greater reliability and usefulness.

We take it for granted, therefore, that displacement goes on even though it leaves behind no traces we have been able to recognize, and that other aspects of the primary process too are at work during the generation of many responses that are not scorable by the present system. Is this a loss? On the contrary, it is a gain, for theoretically we all use the primary process continually in our unconscious fantasies, and to penetrate to that level would thus not produce individual differences. It is, however, both theoretically and practically valuable to identify the extent to which *communicated products of thought* are allowed to retain the stigmata of their unconscious origins despite the mediating defensive and controlling structures from which they emerge.

THE SCORING SYSTEM

We will not go here into the history and development of the scoring method to be described. They have been reported elsewhere (8). At its present stage, the system consists of three groups of scoring categories, corresponding to the three aspects of primary thinking just discussed, and several rating scales which are applied to each response. The first group (Content Variables) has to do with evidences of drive domination in the content of the test responses; the second (Formal Variables), with deviations in response structure; and the third (Control and Defense Variables) with the subject's reaction to the emergence of material in either of the first two categories. The rating scales deal mainly with over-all aspects of the response, and represent an attempt to summarize and integrate the other scores.

Before presenting the scoring system in detail, we should like to make several points about the method as a whole. First, the system is intended as a research tool, not as a clinical instrument, and is perhaps better suited, at this stage, for use with groups of subjects rather than for individual analysis. It has not so far been applied to a sufficient number of records to warrant considering it as more than in an experimental stage. It is not intended to supplant existing scoring, but to supplement it.

Second, the system was constructed on the basis of records taken from adults—some in treatment and some not, but all well-educated and of a relatively high socio-economic level. Moreover, these subjects took the test with the awareness that they were being judged for a serious purpose—diagnosis, acceptance into professional training, or research. We have no way of knowing the limits of applicability of the system as presently constructed, either to subjects of different backgrounds or to subjects who take the test in a different setting.

Third, despite the title of this chapter, there are no categories specifically designed to measure the effects of the secondary process as such. In effect, we are concentrating on the lower portion of the primary-secondary continuum, leaving most of the secondary part of it undifferentiated. Partly the decision was one of interest, partly it is attributable to the relative unsuitability of the Rorschach as a test of the secondary process. For a differentiated account of secondary-process functioning, we must look to multidimensional tests of abilities and adaptiveness, intelligence tests like those of David Wechsler. Though secondary-process operations are involved in the control and defense categories we score, the emphasis is not on getting "measures" of the secondary process but on estimating the efficiency of these operations in coping with the primary-process aspects of responses. Thereby we are enabled to distinguish with some success between maladaptive and adaptive regression (regression in the service of the ego).

We have said nothing so far about the relation of the ideational and structural characteristics of primary thinking, nor is this a question we are prepared to answer at this time. It may be the encouragement given by the test to abandon modes of thinking grounded in physical reality that facilitates the emergence of drive-centered ideation, but it may also be that the pressure of drive material itself leads to structural distortion of responses. The fact that responses with (apparently) neutral content do sometimes contain formal deviations suggests, however, that the latter are caused by a weakening of the perceptual-organizing function of the ego, induced by the structure of the test. In some instances, it is true, deviations in each category occur together, but this is by no means always the case. The fact of such differences poses some interesting questions about the nature of primary thinking and its relation to personality structure, questions we hope may be approached through the application of the present scoring method.

CONTENT VARIABLES

We have made the assumption that *all* thought and perception are organized to some extent by drives as well as by the given required-ness of external reality and the logical structure of ideas. We thus ask, not whether a thought process involves drives or not, but the *extent* and the manner in which drives are involved in cognition. Other things being equal, the less neutralized (and the more instinctivized) is the energy of the drive, the closer does thought come to the primary-process pole.

The problem of scoring Rorschach content for primary process becomes then a question of establishing criteria by which the degree of neutralization of the motivating drive energy may be identified. We ask first, whether any relevance to an instinct derivative can be seen in a given response. Since taking the test is not a situation in which there can be any realistic striving for direct gratification of a basic drive, we assume that any drive imagery that occurs is not a part of goal-oriented behavior but rather evidence that the drive is organizing the response in a relatively "primary" way.[2] If reference to a drive is apparent in the content, we estimate its closeness to the original instinct—as manifested in the directness or "primitivity" of its aim —and then the extent to which the drive itself dominates cognitive processes, as against being subordinated or controlled by them.

Both ideas and affects may indicate drive tension. The system makes provision for scoring each, and thus has two major divisions: ideational drive-representations and affective drive-representations. Since the Rorschach is designed, however, to elicit ideas rather than affect, by far the greater number of the content categories are devoted to the former.

This heading, in turn, has three major subdivisions: drives with libidinal aims; drives with aggressive aims; and thematic indications of guilt or anxiety. The latter covers responses which we assume are reactions to instinctual threat, even when their libidinal or aggressive nature cannot be discerned.

Each of these subdivisions has two main sections, noted as "Level 1" and "Level 2." These represent two levels of closeness to the primary-process pole, as defined by several criteria. One of these has to do with a "primitive-civilized" dimension: the more the type of drive expression described or implied is socialized and discussion of it is appropriate to communication between strangers in a professional situation, the more the thinking concerned is felt to be secondary; we then score Level 2. Conversely, the more direct, intense, or blatant the drive expression, the closer it is to the primary process; the score given is Level 1. In a sense, we have here a control distinction built into the content scoring. We have found it easier to score the greater degree of neutralization of the Level-2 responses in this way, rather than to add additional control categories.

[2] Note that the special test-taking situation gives the Rorschach an advantage over a sample of cognitive functioning in a real-life situation. In the latter, drive-relevant imagery does not necessarily indicate drive-domination (primary process), but is, in fact, necessary for the realistic gratification of needs—the basic function of the secondary process. In the test situation, the subject is, of course, motivated (as, for example, by the desire to please the examiner, to show off, to get out of the hospital, etc.), but in terms of the Freudian theory of motivation followed here, these needs are rather remote derivatives of the two basic drives, which are not *directly* gratified thereby.

A second criterion has to do with the degree to which the response focuses on the drive-relevant organ. When a certain part of anatomy is seen in isolation, this is scored on the lower level if one or more of the following effects would result:

1. Placing such a part of the anatomy in the context of perception of a whole body (or a whole face) implies a more socially acceptable type of content, in the sense that it is, for example, more permissible in polite society to discuss a woman's figure than to speak specifically of her breasts.

2. Going from the part to the whole implies a change in the percept itself, such as the implications of the presence of clothing. There is no such implication as far as a penis is concerned; whether it is specified as being part of a complete man, or seen by itself, clothes would not be present, whereas if breasts are seen as part of a total figure, there is an implication that the woman is clothed unless it is specifically stated that she is not.

3. Finally, it must be considered to what extent a particular body detail forms a "good gestalt" in itself—to what extent is it natural to see it as a unit in isolation? Lewis Carroll had this in mind and made deliberate use of it in the passage where Alice saw the smile without the Cheshire cat.

In addition, Level 1 includes a good many pathological fantasies, which differ from simple, direct references to the form of instinctual gratification in question in that their "blatancy" is probably a function of defensive exaggeration. Perhaps, also, Level-1 responses combine aggression and sex more often than might be expected in any "original" conditions of direct instinctual gratification.

The set of content scores, as it stands, represents a compromise between what we thought, on theoretical grounds, should be included and what we found, on the basis of several groups of records, had to be included. It is one of several ways of classification that were considered and tried out on a group of cases. This one was retained because it seemed to cover most completely what we considered indications of drive tension in the particular records studied. We make no claim for its completeness, and consider it still open to revision.

It will be seen that in the first portion—drives with libidinal aims—emphasis seems to have been put on bodily channels of expression rather than on psychological derivatives of drives: thus, "mouth" rather than "helplessness." This is not because we consider the first more primary, but because the ink blots lend themselves more readily to images of concrete objects than to descriptions of feeling states, and because the latter raise many theoretical problems. We have not entirely neglected such derivatives, but it will be noted that we have not included all types of content that might be used by the clinician in his interpretation of the drive aspects of personality, particularly the more remote, inferential, or higher order drive-representations. We have tried, as much as possible, to stay close to the most obvious kinds of scorable content and to reduce the numbers of *inferences* necessary for the scorer. Nonetheless, we anticipate many disagreements about both inclusions and exclusions in this portion of the system.

A word about the symbols used to designate the categories: Just as it is convenient to say FC [3] instead of writing out *form-color*, so, too, the scoring categories introduced here need a set of convenient symbols for use in scoring. We first used a set of arbitrary number-letter combinations, but the number of categories grew so large that it became very difficult to memorize them. Consequently, we turned to the set of abbreviated designations that appear in the margin by each category. The numbers 1 and 2 refer to Levels 1 and 2; the letters are abbreviations of key words in the category name. Thus, $L\,1\,O$ means Libidinal content, Level 1, Oral; $Ag\,2\,A\text{-}O$ means Aggressive content, Level 2, Active, from the point of view of the Object. In the Formal categories, C (except in $C\text{-}sym\,1$, color symbolism) stands for Condensation ($VC\,1$ = Verbal Condensation, Level 1; $C\,f\text{-}p\,1$ = Condensation, fused percept, Level 1). The abbreviations for Control and Defense categories are (we hope) self-explanatory, except for the Sequence variables: $S\,M\,1\text{--}0$ means Sequence, Modification of percept from Level 1 to unscorable; $S\,C\,2\text{--}1$ means Sequence, Change of percept from Level 2 to Level 1. All of the scores have been summarized for ready reference in Table 10.1.

Ideational Drive-Representations: Drives with Libidinal Aims [4]

Level 1 (crude, direct, "primitive" expression of drive)

$L\,1\,O.$ *Oral:* Mouth; lips; tongue; breasts; udders of a cow—score when seen in isolation.

---

[3] For explanation of standard scoring symbols, see Appendix, pp. 441 ff. [Editor].

[4] This is a condensed version of the actual *Scoring Manual*. For reasons of space, we have had to omit many examples of scored responses and some explanatory material. The same is true for the presentation of the formal, control, and defense portions of the scoring system.

TABLE 10.1. Summary of Primary- and Secondary-Process Variables

Content Variables	Formal Variables (Formal Aspects of Content)

Ideational drive-representations:
L.   Drives with Libidinal Aims:
  L 1.   Level 1—*L* 2.   Level 2
    O.   Oral
    A.   Anal
    S.   Sexual (phallic-genital)
    E-V. Exhibitionistic-voyeuristic
    H.   Homosexual (sexual am-
        biguity)
    M.   Miscellaneous libidinal
Ag.   Drives with aggressive aims:
  Ag 1.   Level 1—*Ag* 2.   Level 2
    P-S.   Potential-subject
    P-O. Potential-object
    A-S. Active-subject
    A-O. Active-object
    R.   Results (object)
Anx.   Anxiety and guilt about drive ex-
      pression:
  Anx 1.   Level 1—*Anx* 2.   Level 2
Aff.   Affective drive-representations

C.   Condensation (image fusion):
  C f-p 1.   Fusion of two separate percepts
  C i-e 1.   Internal-external views
  C p-f 1.   Partial fusion
  C u-p 1.   Unrelinquished percepts
  C-co 1 or 2 Composition
  C a-l 2   Arbitrary linkage
  C a-c.   Arbitrary combination
    C a-c i 2. Impossible combinations
    C a-c u 2. Unlikely combinations
Arbitrary combinations of color and form:
  FC arb 1.   *FC* arb, or *CF* arb.
  FC̸ 2.   *FC̄* and (in some cases) *F/C,*
            C/F, etc.
Do 2.   *Fragmentation*
Imp 2.   *Impressionistic response*
Trans 1. *Fluid transformation of percept*
Visual representation of the abstract:
  C-sym 1 or 2. Color or shading symbolism
  S-sym 1.   Spatial relation symbolism
  I-sym 1 or 2. Concrete image symbolism
ML 1.   *Loosening in conceptual organization*
         of memory
Au Lg 1. *Autistic logic*
DW 1.   *DW responses (including DrD, etc.)*
Ctr.   Contradiction:
  Ctr A 1.   Affective
  Ctr L 1.   Logical
  Ctr In. 2. Inappropriate activity
V.   Deviant Verbalization:
  VS 2.   Verbal slips
  VP 2.   Peculiar verbalizations
  VQ 1.   Queer verbalizations
  VC 1.   Verbal condensation
  VI 1.   Verbal incoherence; confusion
Au El 1 or 2. *Autistic elaboration*
S-R 1.   *Self-reference*
F-Msc 1 or 2. *Miscellaneous formal aspects*

TABLE 10.1 *(Continued)*

Control and Defense Variables

S. Sequence: recovery:
  M. Modifying percept—*C.* Changing percept
    1–0. Level 1 to unscorable
    2–0. Level 2 to unscorable
    1–2. Level 1 to Level 2
  S M R. Sequence: Modification, Rationalization (+, −)
S. Sequence: regression:
  M. Modifying percept
    0–1. Unscorable to Level 1
    0–2. Unscorable to Level 2
    2–1. Level 2 to Level 1
  S C 2–1. Changing percept (Level 2 to Level 1)
Delay:
  Inh. Inhibition
Reflection on response:
  Isp. Introspection (+, −)
  Crt. Criticism of response (+, −)
R. Remoteness:
  R-min. Minimal remoteness
  Remoteness in person
    R-eth. Main figure different from S in ethnic group
    R-an. Main figure an animal
    R-pl. Main figure a plant
    R-ia. Only inanimate objects or abstract concepts are involved
    R-dep. Persons depicted (as in a painting)
  R-geo. Remoteness in geography
  R-tm. Remoteness in time
  Remoteness in level of reality
    R-fic s. Reference to specific fictional character or context (+, −)
    R-fic n. Nonspecific fictional, supernatural, mythical, etc., character (+, −)
    R-fan. Explicit fantasy or dream (+, −)

Cx. Context (+ successful, − unsuccessful):
  Cx C. Cultural context
  Cx E. Esthetic context
  Cx I. Intellectual context
  Cx H. Humorous context
Pathological defenses:
  Va—. Vagueness of percept
  Prj—. Projection of responsibility
  Neg. Negation (+, −)
  Eu—. Euphemism
  Minz—. Minimization
  Obs—. Obsessional defense
  Den—. Attempted denial
X. No defense

Ratings of Total *R*esponse:
  DD. Defense-demand of response
  DE. Effectiveness of defense

Do not score: Lip print (scored as Level 2).

Sucking, nursing, or other activities that point to a passive taking-in or expectation of food: "Hungry birds waiting for mother to bring something to eat"; "animal, sucking from this red part."

L 1 A. *Anal:* Score any reference to excretory organs, defecation, or feces.

Buttocks—score when seen in isolation.

L 1 S. *Sexual (i.e., phallic-genital):* Genitals—score whether seen in isolation or as part of a person or animal; indirect references to sexual organs. ("Womb" is frequently given as equivalent to vagina; score here unless clearly indicated that reference is only to uterus.)

> *Do not score:* "Pelvis" unless given with some reference to sexual organs; if the reference is to internal sexual anatomy, score under *L 2 M.*

Any reference to a sexual act.

L 1 E-V. *Exhibitionistic-voyeuristic:* Any specific reference to nudity when this is a spontaneous elaboration of the response.

L 1 H. *Homosexual (sexual ambiguity):* Uncertainty, ambiguity, or changing mind about sex of genitalia (even when unintentional): "Some more of a body [S had been talking about genitalia]—I don't know if it's man or woman"; "some sort of symbol—phallic—not phallic, sexual—guess I'd say vagina."

Male and female sex characteristics seen on the same figure: e.g., "Men with breasts"; note that such responses will also get formal scores (Composition, *C-co* 1).

(Uncertainty about sex of figures on card III is not infrequent; if this arises because both breast and penis are seen, score here; if the figures are identified specifically as men but are seen with breasts, also score here; if, however, the S is uncertain about the sex of the figures because they look as if they might be men but also have breasts and therefore might be women, then score under *L 2 H.*)

L 1 M. *Miscellaneous libidinal:* This is a left-over category, intended to catch responses that are relatively infrequent but that have some of the same qualities as those described above.

For example: menstruation; birth; urine.

Level 2 (controlled, indirect, "socialized" expression of drive)

L 2 O. *Oral:* Mouth; lips; tongue—score when seen as part of a person or animal *and* unduly emphasized (either by description or by activity involving mouth). Enumeration among several body parts is not sufficient. If in doubt, do not score.

When the pink areas in card X are described as figures smoking pipes, chewing bubble gum, etc., and there is more than the simple statement that they seem to be holding something in their mouths, the response may be scored here.

Breasts—score when seen as part of person *and* emphasized (either by description or by manner of presenting). Enumeration among several body parts is not sufficient. If in doubt, do not score.

Stomach—either external as in "fat bellies," or internal as in "stomach and esophagus." Do not score when seen as part of a whole figure.

Kissing—when described as activity of either people or animals; also score "animals rubbing noses."

Eating or drinking—when described as activities of either people or animals; also include here active attempts to get food *unless* the emphasis is on its destructive aspect (as biting or tearing) in which case $L\,2\,O$ is given a minor (parenthetical) score and $Ag\,2\,A\text{-}S$ the major score.

Cooking; cooking utensils; containers for food or drink.

Food—score when seen in isolation or as part of larger response; a response that describes eating and also depicts a food object (e.g., "Dogs, going to eat these two pieces of liver") is, however, scored only once under this category.

$L\,2\,A.$ *Anal:* Buttocks or corresponding region around the anus— score when seen as part of a person or animal (this is to be scored whenever specifically pointed out since it does not figure in usual descriptions): "Ducks—standing with their hind ends out"; "woman—one leg—fanny."

Rear view of a person or animal—score unless the designation is given as justification for the absence of features.

Disgust attributed to figure seen: "Bugs Bunny—disdainful look— like he smelled something bad."

Mud; dirt—either alone or in context of larger response: "Bug in a mud-puddle."

These last two types of response have a somewhat different character than those previously considered, referring not to drive zone, activity, or object but rather to derivatives of drives. They are included here largely because their symbolic meaning is quite clear and they occur quite rarely.

L 2 S. Sexual: Score here oblique, socialized, or aim-inhibited references to sex or sexual contact: "Bride and groom standing here, holding hands."

L 2 E-V. Exhibitionistic-voyeuristic: References to the concealing function of clothes—this includes responses that point to a failure of concealment (as in the first two examples below) and clothing that conceals or is associated with sexual parts: "Two cavemen—don't seem to have many clothes on"; "woman with transparent dress"; "brassiere"; "corset."

Eyes—score whether seen in isolation or as part of a person or animal provided there is emphasis on the act of looking: "Monster-eyes —seem to be looking"; "peering child—curiosity"; "a profile, but looks like the eye is looking this way" (this last is a borderline response; it was scored here because the awareness of the eye of the figure was so valent it led to a contradiction within the response).

Do not score: References to eyes when the eye is used as a vehicle for expressing anger or disapproval ("grotesque mask—fierceness of the eyes"; "wild horses—eye has an angry look about it"; these are scored *Ag 2 P-S*); references to looking without elaboration and without mention of eyes; nor "eyeglasses"; "goggles."

Masks (score also *Neg+* and *R-dep*).

Also score if the blot offers little perceptual support for the response (e.g., the eye is unusually distorted in shape) or if the eye is otherwise notably emphasized, without specification of looking. "A figure [usual center, card I] with eyes [upper middle bumps] and hands up here."

L 2 H. Sexual ambiguity: Uncertainty or ambiguity about sex of person or animal; if the uncertainty is brought out only in response to inquiry about the sex of the figures seen, note on scoring sheet as *weak:* "Not too much difference—looks slightly more feminine"; "could be either—I thought men, but could be women."

Do not score: Changing mind about sex of figure ("A man—no, it's a woman"); contradictory descriptions, including both male and female characteristics ("Powerful figure—warlike—witch or something").

Men wearing women's clothing and vice versa, or with other nonanatomical attributes of the other sex: "Two men—holding ladies' handbags."

Reversal of the sex usually attributed to a figure—score *weak*. This applies primarily to the following responses:

Card I, center detail—should be female;

Card IV, whole—should be male;

Card V, side detail—reclining figures should be female;

Card VII, whole or upper detail—should be female, either the
popular or reversed ("Dancing girls").

In addition, the popular human figures in cards II and III should
be seen as of the same sex as the subject.   There are a few other
areas with a fairly strong pull for one sex, but none is very frequently
given.

Do not score: For areas without strong pull for either sex, like the
popular "witch" or "clown" detail on card IX or the "children
blowing bubble gum" on card X.

L 2 M. Miscellaneous libidinal: What the following rather motley
group of responses have in common is that they are somehow libid-
inally tinged, though at a distance.

Internal sexual anatomy: "Uterus"; "Fallopian tubes"; "female organs where the eggs are"; "pelvis (?) what the doctor would see up
inside making a pelvic examination."

Embryos—either human or animal.

Reflections—score only when given with definite narcissistic implications (e.g., admiring self in mirror); self-admiration attributed to
figure.

Do not score: Reflections when given as rationalization for symmetry or when there is no emphasis on the act of looking at one's
own reflection.

Drives with Aggressive Aims

Responses are scored here according to whether they refer to preparation for or potentiality for a hostile or destructive act (potential
aggression), to the act itself (active aggression), or to the aftermath
of destructive action or processes (results of aggression).   The first
two of these categories are further subdivided according to whether
the person, animal, or thing of the response is the *subject,* initiating
or carrying out the aggression, or the *object,* against which it may be
or is being directed.   In case both are included in the response, score
for subject; thus: "A bully hitting a terrified child" would be scored
Ag 2 A-S. It is possible for a response to include only the object of
active aggression, so categories *Ag 1 A-O* and *Ag 2 A-O* have been
included, but such responses seem unlikely to occur very often.   For

the most part, the "subject" categories represent fantasies with a sadistic slant, "object" categories those with a masochistic slant, but such a distinction could probably not be supported with complete consistency.

Level 1. Level 1 categories are to be used conservatively. They are meant to include only the most blatant, uncontrolled expression of drive tension, and rarely occur except in psychotic records.

Ag 1 P-S. Potential—subject: Vivid sadistic fantasies which portray events *about* to happen. Most of the examples we have found are oral-aggressive in nature, but in principle any other kind of imminent primitive destruction can be scored.

"Cannibalistic" responses (score a parenthetical *oral, L 1 O*): "Bared fangs"; "something with snapping jaws—there's his hot breath coming out to get you"; "yawning, grasping mouth—going to bite off this part." The following is scored *L 1 S*, with a minor *Ag 1 P-S* score because of the unconcealed nature of the implied fantasy: "Vagina with little hooks."

> *Do not score:* Teeth, even when seen in isolation, are scored *Ag 2 P-S.*

Ag 1 P-O. Potential—object: "Frightened figure—menaced, nightmarish."

Ag 1 A-S. Active—subject: Primitive annihilation of object: "Witches, tearing a woman apart"; "worms—look as though they're scratching the eyes out of that face."

Ag 1 A-O. Active—object: "Sharp instrument going through the penis"; "vagina—it's going to burst, and it does—drops, like a volcano"; "profiles—being silenced, pushed to keep their mouths shut—mouths smashed."

Ag 1 R. Results: Aftermaths of sadistic, violent action; of necessity these are all on the *object* side.

Mutilated persons or animals (compare these with the "do not score" examples below): "Animal—looks like it's been in a horrible fight—all torn up"; "body without a skin; I see the blood—the lungs would be raw and red."

> *Do not score:* "Butterfly—wings cut off, wings shredded"; "insect, holes in wings, pieces torn out"; "animal, after it had been slaughtered." (These are all scored *Ag 2 R.*)

A mutilated object or plant could also be scored here, but only when the response implies the effects of really ferocious action.

Level 2

Ag 2 P-S. Potential—subject: Verbal hostility—this is "potential" in the sense that it warns that aggression may erupt through the motor apparatus: "Ladies—beginning to say nasty things"; "people, arguing, swearing at each other"; "animals—growling."

Aggression limited to facial expression: "Ogre—facing you—with anger"; "evil women—stern, indignant, annoyed"; "professor—smirking at the stupidity of his students" (*weak*); "eyes—they're furious."

Persons or animals stalking or about to attack—this generally implies physical tension, an effortful holding-back from aggressive action: "Men on horses, waiting to attack"; "two lions—not exactly as if ready to leap" (the denial of intent does not save the response from being scored; the denial is scored as a control variable, *Neg—*).

Frightening or potentially dangerous people, animals, or objects: "Witches—claws—could be doing a diabolic dance"; "teeth"; "soldier"; "Ku Klux Klan figure"; "bullet"; "spear"; "lions."

> *Do not score:* Spiders; octopi; rats—unless there are affective verbalizations or other comparable indications that the subject finds them frightening or extremely distasteful; thus, *do* score: "poisonous spider"; "rats—look kind of horrible to me."

Ghosts; witches; giants; dragons; monsters—all the frightening creatures of childhood fairy tale and fantasy. Psychoanalytic studies have shown that these are usually projections of sadistic impulses.

The following are also scored, though they represent borderline cases: "Evil-intented people—conspiring sorcery"; "witch—aggressive and protective"; "vampire"; "scorpion."

Also score: "Dogs—want to get at each other, but tied"; "bears— know they can always fight back any aggression" (these are also borderline cases; what marks them as "potential" is the implication of inhibition—in the first case an external one, in the second, more internalized—of the aggressive act itself).

Volcanoes—score here unless S makes it clear that he sees it in the process of eruption; the score is then *A-S*.

Ag 2 P-O. Potential—object: Frightened or threatened persons or animals: "Figure—silenced—kind of frightened"; "people—looks like they're scared of each other."

Defensive objects: "Shield"; "armor"; "fortress walls."

Ag 2 A-S.   *Active—subject:* Any physical conflict between people or animals, even when rationalized as playful; "fighting" without further specification: "Animals—pulling—both trying to get it"; "ducks, having a playful tug-of-war"; "witches—two more boosting them into a kettle."

A hostile act against a passive recipient, or against an unspecified recipient; if the actor is not seen, however, score *A-O.* "Eagle—another one pushing him down the rocks"; "bull's face, charging."

Bombs bursting, fires, explosions; volcanoes when seen in the process of eruption; abstract concepts of violence (e.g., "war").

Ag 2 A-O.   *Active—object:* Victims of any of the kinds of active aggression in *Ag 2 A-S*: "An unhappy person—looks like he is being bawled out"; "barbs going into people."

Ag 2 R.   *Results:* Blood (include even "blood smear on a microscope slide").

Injured persons or animals—compare these examples with those given in *Ag 1 R*, mutilated persons or animals: "A deformed foot" (scored here, even though the deformity may not have been the result of a specific injury); "insect, holes in wings, pieces torn out."

Persons or animals with parts missing—this is to be scored whenever mentioned, even though there is no implication of a hostile act and the S appears to be only carefully describing the card: "Woman's body —no head"; "dog—nothing missing except the tail."

Dead persons or animals: "Chicken, it's dead; their legs are up after they're killed"; "swans—looks like their throats are cut."

> *Do not score:* Lifelessness when described only in response to inquiry as a rationalization for absence of movement.

"Embryo split open," or "cerebellum, cut and laid open"; even though these are dissection operations, they should be scored as *weak.*

Broken objects, aftermath of bombs, fires, explosions, volcanoes: "Mushroom cloud of the A-bomb" (S denies seeing the actual explosion); "blackened trees after a forest fire."

Anxiety and Guilt about Drive Expression

These categories are intended to catch responses indicating a (nonspecific, diffuse) projection of instinctual danger or superego punishment. Common to all these responses is an explicit or implied feeling of helplessness (either in the figure seen or in the beholder). Do not score when any *Ag* (aggression) categories can be scored.

Note: These scores do *not* purport to pick up all aspects of the Rorschach that indicate anxiety, and thus do not furnish a useful measure of anxiety. Anxiety is considered here only so far as its presence hints at unverbalized threats that libidinal or aggressive impulses may break into awareness.

Level 1

Anx 1: The responses scored here belong essentially to the world of nightmares. They include projection of feelings of utter helplessness and are essentially pathological fantasies. They differ from the object (masochistic) aggression categories in that the dangers are not specified or are quite impersonal: "Three heads, frightened they might fall into this crevice—helpless"; "man—tied, helpless, falling into space, helplessly." The latter response carries an implication that the man is the victim of hostility, but the emphasis is so strongly on helplessness in a situation of impersonal danger that it is scored here.

Level 2

Anx 2: Similar to the above, but on a more socially acceptable level: "Pagoda god—peaceful evilness . . . he looks helpless, like he's being posed." (This last is a complicated response in which the image represents both a threatening and threatened object—on the whole, however, it qualifies for an anxiety score, since the threat implied in the word "evilness" is rather remote and nonspecific.)

Figures or objects in states of precarious balance: "Someone falling"; "a pile of rocks, about to topple over"; "a machine to catch you if you fall."

Devil; Satan; Mephistopheles—any of the personifications of the punishing superego in religion and mythology.

"Abstract" dangers: "Preachers warning that the last day is coming"; "hell"; "the inferno"; "mankind in flight."

Affective Drive Representations

Aff 1. As Rapaport has pointed out, the psychoanalytic theory of affects is not in a very satisfactory state of clarity (15). The relationship between the amount and kind of affect present and the primary or secondary nature of thinking particularly needs clarification. Certain statements by Freud support the position that affective elements in thinking are stronger the more primary it is, but this does not necessarily mean that all manifestations of strong affect make the accompanying thought processes primary.

Nevertheless, if the subject produces a display of affect instead of responding to the card with an image, it seems arguable that this affect is part of a primary thought process. We score under this category only those instances where a clear display of affect is indicated either in the verbalization or in the behavior of the subject as recorded in the protocol, and when the affect is *not* merely an expression of anxiety about inability to satisfy the tester's (explicit or assumed) demands.

"It just gives me a weird feeling" (with no response). "All I can say is a mess—do you want associations?" Score this response as *weak,* because the affect is not very clearly expressed in the verbalization. Of course, if there were notes indicating unmistakable affect in the subject's voice, expression, or demeanor, a full score could be given as long as no image was produced.

Do not score: "It just doesn't look like anything" (weeps). Here the affect is clearly enough present, but apparently linked to the experience of failure, and *not* an expression of an underlying drive or a direct reaction to it.

FORMAL VARIABLES

Primary-process thinking was first defined in terms of certain formal characteristics. In considering how these might appear in responses to the Rorschach, we thought first of the formal characteristics of dreams—condensation, displacement, and symbolization. But there is obviously a considerable difference between Rorschach thinking and dream thinking. The Rorschach, being anchored in consciousness, provides only a very crude equivalent of the dream process. We thus had to derive the scoring categories from the unique situation presented by the test. The formal categories refer both to the perceptual organization of a given response and to the thought process that underlies giving it. They are an attempt to measure deviations from the logical, orderly thinking grounded in experience with the real world that characterizes the secondary process. We would like to emphasize again that these categories should not be taken evaluatively. Although some of them we have learned to recognize as clearly pathological (for example, the contamination response), this was not the basis for their inclusion here. The abbreviations indicate the classification of each category as Level 1 or Level 2. These formal variables represent formal aspects of content rather than the formal, perceptual-structure scores of location and determinants with which they should not be confused. Note, however, that they include a couple of the latter.

Condensation (Image-Fusion)

One characteristic of the secondary process is the binding of cathexis to idea, aiding the maintenance of an orderly and stable image of the outside world. In this group of categories, we classify what seem to be results of the fluid shifting about of images and ideas that characterizes primary-process thinking. Image-fusion refers to the inability to keep images separated in the way demanded by a realistic view of the outer world. Seven varieties of image-fusion have been distinguished below. In the first four, the fusion comes about when more than one idea arises with respect to a *single area* of the card *and* there is a failure of at least a temporary suppression of all but one. In the last three, the fusion comes about between *adjacent areas* and there is difficulty in delimiting a single percept. This distinction is not a clear-cut one; *C-co* seems to present a borderline category.

C f-p 1. *Fusion of two separate percepts:* Here overlapping images are fused into a single percept. This includes the conventional contamination response, also those that might be scored only "contamination tendency." Such responses will appear rarely, especially in the records of patients who are not hospitalized for psychosis. "Vampire; the bat is a vampire—wiles of the vampire in action, allure of the woman so to speak . . . symbolic of the bat in action using the woman as bait" (card V—bat is the whole card, woman the entire side area).

C i-e 1. *Internal-external views of something:* This is scored when both external and internal body parts are pointed out on a given figure in a way that is realistically impossible. Do not score for responses of X-rays or skeletons unless part of the external anatomy or clothing is also seen. "Could be part of a woman's breasts with a bow in between . . . this might be the lungs . . . she might be wearing the bow around her neck."

C p-f 1. *Partial fusion of two separate percepts:* Two percepts are seen in the same area, and S is unable to make up his mind between them. Usually the conflict between the competing percepts is discernible in the response. "Here we have what appears to be a French motif—French poodle—trimmings of the poodle or trimmings of the female . . . brassiere . . . high-heeled shoes."

Do not score: "The body of a frog or some animal leaping—could be a deer with legs like that, only the body is too fat for a deer." This response is too close to the usual, "This looks like X—well, no, it looks more like Y," or "An X—or even better, a Y." It does not have the idea of *simultaneity* of meaning.

C u-p 1. *Unrelinquished percepts:* The S expresses a preference for one percept but is unable to relinquish the other. The uncertainty is expressed in the form: "It looks like X, but it's really Y."

"It's supposed to be something in the cat's mind—but to me it looks like a ball of yarn."

C-co 1. *Composition, Level 1:* Parts from two or more percepts are combined to make a new, hybrid creation. Score only when the composite image does not have some existence in a common cultural reality: "Witches—they seem to have tails for some reason"; "men with breasts"; "a rabbit with bat's wings."

Persons or animals with more parts than necessary (e.g., "A two-headed lobster") are to be scored in this category; but note the score as *weak*. The following response also gets a *weak* score: "Looking at this front leg of the insect, it appears to have the shape of a woman's leg" (note that S does not say: "An insect with a woman's leg"; nevertheless he does not keep the two responses clearly separate in his manner of presenting them).

Do not score: "Animals with hats on."

C-co 2. *Composition, Level 2:* Composite images that actually exist in mythology, art, etc. "Hindu statue with all those arms"; "man with wings—Icarus"; "the two-headed eagle of the imperial Russian coat of arms"; "centaur"; "Pegasus."

C a-1 2. *Arbitrary linkage of two percepts:* This score is given for two subclasses of responses (which need not be separately scored). In both, the underlying assumption seems to be: Two areas of the blot are touching, therefore they cannot be separated and the description of what they represent must take this relationship into account. Similar reasoning underlies the next category, *Arbitrary Combinations;* what distinguishes the present group of responses is the feeling of physical attachment, of stickiness between the percepts, and the partial loss or diffusion of object identities.

In the first type, two distinct objects are seen—often in corresponding areas on opposite sides of the blot—but they are perceived as physically joined in an arbitrary way: "Women, sort of stuck together" (card VII—attached at lower center); "heads of lions—no sense to why they're joined" (card III—top detail).

Do not score: "Two witches holding onto a centerpiece"; "dogs balancing something on their noses."

In the second type, S has difficulty in separating one fairly distinct percept from an adjoining area, seen as some kind of vaguely defined mass in which it is embedded, or the like: "Some sort of flying animal —held back by this mass here, because it seems attached" (card VI— animal is top detail, mass is rest of card); "rat or mouse, trying to climb—being held back—in some sort of morass . . . I don't know what it is, a live thing, it's active" (card VIII).

C a-c. Arbitrary combinations of separate percepts: Two separate but contiguous percepts are placed in some kind of meaning relationship that violates reality. Responses that might be acceptable if kept separate are reported as being in impossible, or implausible but possible, combinations. The first includes those that violate the laws of physical reality; the second violates reality in a less absolute sense, since it is to be scored for combinations that could conceivably occur, though they are unlikely to.

C a-c i 2. Impossible combinations: There are three principal types to be looked for here: First, combinations in which the impossibility derives from a discrepancy of size (almost always from taking the relative sizes of things in the blots very literally, or from disregarding them); the second arises from putting things together that do not occur together in reality. The first two examples illustrate the first two types. The third type comes from mixing natural and supernatural frames of reference (thus, witches or devils are not scored on these formal variables unless seen in contemporary or realistic settings). "A prairie dog climbing on a butterfly"; "two animals holding a bridge in their mouth."

C a-c u 2. Unlikely combinations: "Totem pole—animals hanging on it with their feet up"; "ducks—standing on ducks"; "a vulture with a crown."

Do not score: Combinations that may reasonably be expected to occur in reality (e.g., "women holding big pocketbooks").

Responses combining percepts which, though reasonable, are out of proportion, but not as grossly as in the prairie dog–butterfly response above, are to be scored as improbable combinations, *weak:* "Bears–not doing something sensible–climbing a tree" (card VIII) (note that this combination is not scored if the animal is smaller and does climb trees in the manner depicted); "witches studying a crystal ball" (card IX–witches in orange, ball is center white); "French butlers tearing a crab apart" (card III).

Arbitrary Combinations of Color and Form

We assume that arbitrary combinations of color and form are a special kind of condensation in which fusion takes place between two modalities rather than within one; they are therefore kept separate from the first group of responses.

FC arb 1. *FC arb or CF arb:* "Red bears"; "a sheep–I don't know why it should be green, but it is."

F¢ 2. *FC̄ and (in some cases) F/C (or C̄F, C/F):* Although these types of responses are a good deal less primary in their implications than the *FC arb* response, they are to be scored if S mentions a color that is unnatural for the percept described, even though negated (*FC̄*) or rationalized more or less convincingly (*F/C*). Responses of these types in which the form element is vague and nondefinitive occasionally occur, in which case they would be scored here.

Note that not all *F/C* or *C/F* responses are included, for example, colored maps. If various organs of the body are described as being in assorted inappropriate colors, as they appear in a medical-book picture, score *weak*. If the inappropriate color is explained in terms of an animal's having fallen into a tub of dye, or being seen in light reflected from a fire or sunset, score here (adding the relevant successful or unsuccessful control category).

FC: "A monkey, except that it's the wrong color–who ever saw a blue monkey?" (Whenever *FC̄* is scored here, score also *Neg–*, under *Control and Defense.*)

F/C: "Two wolves circling a fire–the light from it makes them look red."

Do not score: "Clouds in a sunset sky" (card X–pink areas). In general, cloud responses are not to be scored, save where the color is really unlikely, as in the case of the green areas on card IX: "Green clouds. (?) Well, clouds are any color in a sunset" (scored *C/F*). Even in this last case, do not score if the entire card is seen as sunset cloud formations of various colors.

Do 2. Fragmentation: Just as the free mobility of cathexis and the failure of ideas to maintain fixed identities in the primary process show up in condensation, so, too, they may logically result in the breaking up of natural perceptual units. It is assumed (a little shakily) that what most people see in the blots as a unit—a whole human figure, say—corresponds to an image the integrity of which secondary-process thought should respect. Thus, when a *Do* response occurs, this unity has been arbitrarily broken up; only a part is reported where most Ss see a whole. Possibly experience will force us to a different rationale for this type of response; meanwhile, it is to be considered a formal manifestation of the primary process.

"Head" (card III—popular—rest of figure not seen); "a paw of an animal" (card VII, hand of the popular, which is not given).

Imp 2. Impressionistic response: In the records of some Ss who have a poor capacity for delay (usually hysterical women), there occur responses that are based on partial or fragmentary *qualities* of the blot, only a portion of what usually is used to make up a response. The impressionistic response is usually given as "a feeling."

"Something belonging to an aquarium, that's the feeling I get. (?) Color—green, and also middle part—colors fading into one another"; "get the feeling of a horizon, depth . . . (?) gives me the feeling of horizon, blue leading into green."

Trans 1. Fluid transformation of percept: Anyone who gives more than one response to a card in the same area sees the same thing as having two different meanings. Ordinarily, however, these are kept quite separate, and the secondary-process property of thought identity is maintained. A person may, on the other hand, describe an experience in which one thing turns into another under his very eyes, so to speak. The subtle difference between these two experiences carries along with it the connotation of magic or of the violation of reality; there is something of the "unrelinquished percept" about this.

"An Indian with a hide over him [further description]. Now he's beginning to transform; as his hide droops down, it becomes two enormous feet"; "a map . . . now it's sort of breaking up; the two upper things are puppies . . ."; "rats climbing a tree . . . now the whole thing has turned into a flower." (Inquiry: "The whole center was the tree but it quick-like turned into a flower.")

Do not score: "When I first looked at these, they looked like doctors in surgical outfits in conference. The more I look at it, they look like men in uniform. They work in another planet." Notice that S does not describe a process of transformation before his eyes, and that he is just shifting his interpretation of what is essentially the same response—men in some kind of uniform.

Visual Representation of the Abstract

We assume that the dream-work mechanism of symbolization is represented in the Rorschach by this type of responses. The S attempts to represent an abstract idea, an activity, or an "object" that cannot be readily represented by a specific form. In the examples below, the words in italics are the "abstract" elements scored.

C-sym. *Use of color or shading to stand for an abstract idea:* Two kinds of color symbolism are here distinguished, following the logic that divides *C-co* into Levels 1 and 2: the idiosyncratic is considered more primary, the conventional being scored Level 2. Note that, although this is usually scored for chromatic color, achromatic color or shading may also be used to symbolize something.

C-sym 1. *Color or shading symbolism, Level 1, idiosyncratic:* "The red reminds me of *prostitution*"; "the red possibly as *nature in the raw*"; "a *concert*—the colorfulness and weirdness—I thought of a concert as colorful—I think of Walt Disney."

C-sym 2. *Color or shading symbolism, Level 2, conventional:* There is a commonly used, culturally shared repertory of stereotyped conventional meanings of color: blue is depression or coldness, green is envy or inexperience, purple is passion, yellow is cowardice or peril, red is anger, stop, or heat, etc.

"Dogs—their noses are pushed up together—because of the red I think of *violence*" (note the difference between this and a response in which the red is seen as blood and the S draws the inference of fighting—such a response would not be scored); "a green face, *green with envy.*"

S-sym 1. *Use of spatial relations to stand for an abstract idea:* "Dogs —this [upper red] is the *idea they want to get at each other*"; "*intercourse*—or union—I didn't think of a specific picture, everything is just united"; "I get the impression the yellow things are *feminine* because these [penis, a previous response] seem to project onto them." (The last two responses are given major scores on *Autistic Logic*.)

I-sym 1. *Use of an idiosyncratic concrete image to stand for an abstract idea:* "Rats—symbolic of the nibbling away of the good green earth—of the *good by the evil* so to speak"; "two men, a little drunk, over a punchbowl—the red bow tie represents *gaiety*."

Do not score: "Phallic symbol"; "the top part is symbolic of trees, earth, grass" (this is another way of saying "it looks like"); "doves —doves represent peace and love and tranquility" (this is an associative "aside"); "dictatorial figure—very powerful father symbol." Score *I-sym* 1 *tendency* for these.

I-sym 2. *Use of a conventional image symbol:* "The bow gives a feminine touch"; "an explosion, somewhat atomic, could represent anger."

ML 1. *Loosening in conceptual organization of memory:* Falsely equating a concept with a conceptually related but not identical one: "Bat, the winged bat, a bird, and I hate bats." (Also *VP 2*.)

Au Lg 1. *Autistic logic:* The failure of thinking to follow a logical course is one of the hallmarks of the primary process. Although autistic thinking is implicit in many of the responses described above, this category is reserved for responses cast in a syllogistic form and in which the reasoning used is fallacious. What distinguishes these responses is the implication of logical necessity, the subjective feeling of "it must be."

"Everything's so small it must be the insectual kind of thing"; "skunks—a small portion of the picture indicates to me it's a small animal"; "snakes. [How much of the card represents the snakes?] I don't know, because when they coil around they're endless"; "ice cream—it looks like it's melted because the colors are warm."

The *Po* (position) response is a subtype of autistic logic. It is to be scored strictly.

DW 1. *DW responses (including DrD, etc.):* This kind of response, sometimes called "confabulation," is a wild generalization or a jumping to conclusions about the identity of a larger unity on the sole basis of a minor part; the result is *always* an *F* −. Implicitly, it too could be regarded as involving autistic logic. Thus, in the classic example of "cat" for card VI "because of the whiskers," the implied syllogism is: cats have whiskers, this has whiskers, therefore this is a cat. Since there is no way of knowing that any such process goes on, this category has not been combined with *Autistic logic.*

Ctr. Contradiction

Illogical thinking leads to contradiction, which is tolerated in primary thinking. Scored here are both affective and logical contradictions, including activities inappropriate to the figures seen. The former are likely to go unrecognized by the S, the latter not necessarily so. Do not score when the S is explicitly aware of and uncertain about which of two conflicting interpretations to give; see "do not score" examples below.

Ctr A 1. Affective contradiction: Score both affective aspects of regular responses and affective responses to the cards themselves. Usually, a good deal of fluidity is necessary for such responses to come about. In the examples below, the element scored is italicized.

"*It's pretty*—I don't see much—it gives me a feeling of fur, that's why I said gorilla . . . *I see horrible things*—bats, gorillas, vampires, bugs. . . ." "*Something very beautiful* about the whole card—I don't know what it is but I like it—*nothing really unpleasant* . . . my first impression, *ugly*—spiders, possibly blood—only thing *a bit unpleasant*— the colors are sort of dirty." (Despite the esthetic frame of reference, S is clearly referring to a pleasant-unpleasant dimension.) "Witches —could be a *diabolic dance* or chanting their chants—*a very pleasant picture*—could be music and love and enjoyment." (What is contradictory here is the affective comment juxtaposed to the content of the response.)

Ctr L 1. Logical contradiction: Score for assigning incompatible or inappropriate qualities to a given percept: "Old maids, but they look very young"; "pagoda god—a peaceful evilness"; "a powerful figure— aggressive and protective" (these are all scored *weak* since the concepts described are within the realm of possibility).

Do not score: "Little old men cherubs"; here the incompatible attributes are subsidiary to the process of composition (which should be scored instead). Note that the opposing qualities in the above examples do *not* come from the creation of a composite image with incompatible aspects: scoring the latter in addition to composition would be superfluous and misleading: "Two people —either in a dance or representing sorrow—I can't tell"; "a hand— I don't know if it's authority or frightened." These are alternations of which the S is explicitly aware, and they are clearly changed interpretations. In scored examples, S speaks as if both terms of a contradiction could be simultaneously true.

Ctr In 2. *Inappropriate activity* (impossible—*i*, or unlikely—*u*): Here the contradiction is expressed in terms of verb rather than adjective, so to speak. It is to be scored when people, animals, or objects are seen in an activity inappropriate to them.

"People, flying through the air"; "a witch with her thumb out, hitch-hiking."

Do not score: Animals in humanlike activity when this occurs in the realm of fact (e.g., dancing bears).

If the activity is rationalized by reference to cartoon or fairy tale it is still scored here—the context of the response is accounted for by the control variables.

V. Deviant Verbalization

This category includes all examples of autistically distorted language, as distinct from distortions of either the content or structure of thought. Here we follow Rapaport (16) very closely, borrowing some of his examples.

VS 2. *Verbal slips:* Slips of the tongue occur occasionally and are all scored here. (Conceivably, a slip might be Level 1, but none has been encountered so far.) Include here *both* slips followed by self-correction (e.g., "A plant growing up a tree; these are its tentacles— no, I mean its tendrils"; score also S M 2–0) and uncorrected slips and malapropisms.

"A butterfly . . . these are the *antlers*"; "bats are supposed to sleep, *standing* upside down"; "something in a cave, the *icicles* hanging down"; "something you see in bio lab—the embryos, *in* a child"; "but-terfly . . . these *receptacles,* feelers."

Do not score: "A batterfly—I mean a butterfly; it also looks like a bat"; score VC 1 and S M 1–0.

VP 2. *Peculiar verbalizations:* These are instances of linguistic usage that are autistic enough to sound odd, recognizably not idiomatic, and not a function of group membership, unfamiliarity with English, or the like. At the same time, there is a quantitative distinction between the "peculiar" and the "queer"; compare the examples given.

"Part of a lady's vagina"; "a fine dog—noblest of all dogs." Notice the inappropriateness of both examples, which still do not deviate very markedly from common modes of speech. The former is unnaturally stilted and strangely specific for someone who is presumably embarrassed to mention such a thing. The latter has a flowery rhetorical flavor, quite out of keeping with the test situation, though acceptable in another context.

VQ 1. *Queer verbalizations:* "A twat—I don't get the same sensation as if it were real"; "a crab, I was hoping for an octopus"; "twins, placed in the position of birth . . . for research study of two animals being born simultaneously or of a Siamese nature"; "artistic design of fly's foot." In some of these examples, the queerness comes largely from the inappropriateness of the response as a communication in a professional situation; in others, because the stiltedness goes so far as to be very noticeable. In general, however, queer verbalizations show a failure to maintain an appropriate set in talking about what one sees —appropriate to the subject matter, to the relationship between S and tester, or to S's level of actual knowledge.

VC 1. *Verbal condensation:* The portmanteau word. Do not score all neologisms, only those in which the contaminating elements can be discerned.

"Diaphragram" (condensation of diagram and diaphragm).

VI 1. *Verbal incoherence; confusion:* When the course of associations is extremely autistic, the connections being omitted or being made on entirely idiosyncratic grounds, the result is a use of words that fails to communicate and becomes incoherent. It is extremely unlikely to occur except in schizophrenia, organic psychoses, or other gross interferences with the secondary process.

"Desert pictures, shadow pictures—you lift up your hand in desert pictures"; "a bundle of love, how do you like that for an answer, wrapped up in endearing young charms—dementia praecox."

Au El.   Autistic Elaboration

This category largely overlaps with what Rapaport (16) and Schafer (17) call "confabulation." Since this last term is ambiguous, it is being replaced with the present one, though otherwise we follow the discussion in *Diagnostic Psychological Testing*, Vol. II, pp. 329–330, 333–334. In general, score this category when the subject elaborates a response in a bizarre, unrealistic, or otherwise deviant manner, if the deviation has not been already taken care of by another formal category.

Au El 1. Level 1: "Aztec figure—stone-like, an idol figure . . . hips, legs, some sort of symbol—sexual, I guess I'd say vagina . . . here a dinosaur figure—now they're fighting over this woman, because of the sexual symbols—horrible—frightened—and she can't talk, her mouth is closed"; "two bears out for a good time . . . Russian bear with the red significant—might be gaily chasing each other around while— possibly we do the same thing in this country—might be a merry dance of what's to come—bear against bear—nothing symbolic; people gaily parading around while blood is being spilled" (also *VI 1*). The above examples are both long and loosely associative, but autistic elaborations need not be so; see the following examples (from Rapaport): "The white streak reminds me of the wide, powerfully flowing Mississippi River" (card VI); "two women, they have their genital organs together."

Au El 2. Level 2: Occasionally it happens that a response is autistically elaborated but not in as extreme a way as the above examples. Score thematic elaboration that involves a good deal of "transcendence" (Weisskopf), but without any other signs of primary process: benign fantasy, but a good deal of it.

"Two bunnies, looking at each other. They've noticed each other and turned their heads to look each other up and down, as if to say, 'Well, who are *you?*' And soon they'll scamper on about their business, wondering where the other came from."

S-R 1. Self-Reference

Though primary-process thinking is generally very egocentric, not all self-references are thereby primary. Score here only indications that S feels the test or the thing seen has (in an unrealistic and essentially magical way) reference to him personally.

"My family"; "insect crawling toward me."

Score the following kinds of self-references as *weak:* "Two people arguing—that reminds me of my problem . . ."; "caterpillars just like we had in our garden in Texas"; "a design in ink—I used to make these when I was a boy." Do not score such responses if they appear only on inquiry.

F-Msc1 or 2. Miscellaneous Formal Aspects (may be Level 1 or 2)

Score here the very occasional formal indications of primary process that are not classifiable under the above categories.

Synesthetic responses: Responding to color as if to another sense modality ("the blue reminds me of the thin clear scent of boxwood hedges"), score Level 1.

Deliberate molding of reality to fit a preconceived idea: "This looks like two ladies (card VII), sort of seem to be kissing each other. Not exactly kissing, but their lips are puckered." (Score Level 1; note S M 1–2. Each is seen quite correctly, but S, in effect, molds the reality of the card by seeing them as in contact when they are really an arm's length away.)

"Color projection"—attributing chromatic color to achromatic blots (Level 2).

CONTROL AND DEFENSE VARIABLES

The following categories are scored only in conjunction with responses that have received scores on either content or formal variables. The use of these categories seems to represent an attempt on the part of the subject to contain the material, implying some awareness (not necessarily conscious) that the response needs to be justified or defended against (see DD, below). Some of these ways are obviously more satisfactory than others: thus, the control implied by a "successful introspection" or an "esthetic context" score seems more adequate than that involved in "negation" or "projection of responsibility." A few of the categories may represent not so much control as evidences of its failure, while the elaboration in others may be more imaginative than defensive. One problem that arises, therefore, in the use of the control scores is the interpretation of the categories that are scored; see below, discussion of DE—the effectiveness of defense.

S. Sequence: Recovery

Score when relatively primary material is followed by more secondary. Note that several distinctions are made here: modifications of percept are distinguished from sequential replacement, and in both cases *degrees* of recovery are differentiated.

M. Modifying percept: The basic percept remains the same, but it is modified or elaborated in a way that makes it more secondary.

S M 1–0. *Level 1 (content or formal) to unscorable:* [5] "Men with breasts—no, jackets."

S M 2–0. *Level 2 to unscorable:* "Dogs—the red makes me think of violence—no, they're playing"; "bird without a head—well, a small one."

S M 1–2. *Level 1 to Level 2:* "Face—looks like a penis in the mouth, or rather a candy stick"; "a bloody head, looks like it's been flayed—or could be a savage, painted to go on the war path."

S M R. Rationalization without modifying percept: Sometimes a response begins in an unpromising way with an instinctual content or a formal bizarreness; the S then seems to catch himself and add details (either in the way he verbalizes it, or additional perceptual elements, or both) which he hopes make it more acceptable or more plausible *without* changing the level on which it is scored.

Successful—*S M R+*: "A woman dressed in only a corset, being pulled in opposite directions by two men. It's a satirical dance—she's fat and dowdy but is pretending to be in danger of assault from these dashing, cloaked figures."

Unsuccessful—*S M R−*: "The costumes of the Klux Klan—and he's eating an ice-cream cone." Here S apparently tries to soften the aggressive implications of the Ku Klux Klan figure by a homey touch, but the incongruous ice-cream eating leaves the response unrationalized and unsuccessful.

C. Changing percept: The original, more primary response is not modified but relinquished and replaced by a more secondary one; this may or may not be a conscious and deliberate substitution, and need not be given to the same area.

S C 1–0. *Level 1 (content or formal) to unscorable:* "Phallic symbol—more like a finger."

S C 2–0. *Level 2 to unscorable:* "Lions; they look more like statues of poodles."

S C 1–2. *Level 1 to Level 2:* "Buttocks" (card VIII, lower detail) followed by: "These could be lionesses trying to dance on one hind leg" (Level 1 content, to Level 2 formal).

[5] The term "unscorable" should throughout be construed to mean "not scorable in terms of the present system."

S.   Sequence: Regression

This category follows the model of recovery exactly except that the changes are in every case from less primary to more primary. (The term "regression" is used here only in its systematic sense, with no implication of retrogression or topographical regression in the psychic apparatus.) Again, changes may take place within the context of one response, or in the sequence from one response to another. There is one difference, however: when S goes from an unscored response to one that is scorable on either formal or content grounds, no control score is given. This category applies, thus, only to instances where a person gets started on a response that is scorable and "digs himself in deeper" by following it with another that has even stronger primary-process implications; or to such changes within a single response. Strictly speaking, it is a failure of control that is scored under this category, rather than a type of defense.

M.   Modifying percept: Note that even though the response starts out as unscorable, if S makes a modification that brings it within the province of one of our categories, it is scored here.

S M 0–1.   *Unscorable to Level 1.*

S M 0–2.   *Unscorable to Level 2.*

S M 2–1.   *Level 2 to Level 1.*

S C 2–1.   *Changing percept:* This includes only going from Level 2 to Level 1. In such a response, the score applies to the earlier of the two responses.

Delay

Inh.   Inhibition: When the scorable aspect of a response, or the entire response, emerges only in inquiry, the inhibitory control that delayed the primary aspect is signalized by scoring the present category.

Reflection on Response

Isp.   Introspection: This is scored when S makes a clear attempt to remove himself from the response by observing or thinking about his own thought processes or feelings, or attempting to explain how his associations came about. Do not score unelaborated remarks that S saw the same thing on a previous administration. Note: *Rarely* to be scored from inquiry.

Successful—*Isp*+: "I've had two impressions which are quite contradictory, but the second seems to be dominant, so I'll mention it first." Notice the ease and naturalness of the introspective attitude here, as compared with the more fragmentary and questionable attempt in the unsuccessful example.

Unsuccessful—*Isp*—: "Profile, here's the mouth—like it would receive it; before, seemed like it would hurt it—that's my conflict."

Crt. Criticism of response: This score is given when the S verbalizes his awareness that something is wrong with the content or organization of his response, especially its unrealistic aspects.

Successful—*Crt*+: "*It isn't sensible* to think the penis is on top of the woman, but it looks like it"; "bears—*not doing something sensible*—climbing a tree"; "feminine symbol—*it doesn't look natural.*"

Do not score: Criticism that is clearly focused on the blot, or criticism of the poor fit between concept and percept (see also below).

Unsuccessful—*Crt*—: Score if the criticism is inappropriate, exaggerated, directed against an acceptable response, or otherwise unnecessary and defensive.

R.   Remoteness

Under this heading, we apply to the Rorschach essentially the same notions that Tomkins introduced for the TAT (19, pp. 78–82). When an unacceptable impulse is expressed in a response, it may be made more acceptable if S puts distance between himself and the response by making the latter remote in time, place, person, or level of reality. An *R*-score is given to every response for which a content score has been recorded. In addition, any *R*-score from *R-geo* on *may* be scored for formally deviant responses when the remoteness has any relevance to the formal quality scored.*

R-min. Minimal remoteness: The response involves *persons* (or parts of persons) *here* and *now*, implicitly or explicitly *existing* in reality. Assume that time, place, etc., are close unless it is stated or clearly implied otherwise. In addition, "food," "feces," "blood" and other human bodily products are all scored *R-min* unless it is clear from context that they are animal.

One or more of the following (*R-eth* through *R-fan*) may be scored for any one response.

* See pp. 218 ff. of this book [*Editor*].

Remoteness in person:

R-eth. Score when persons in the response are different from S in *ethnic group* only: Negroes, Indians, etc.

R-an. Main figure of the response is an *animal* rather than a person.

R-pl. Main figure is a *plant.* "Tree stumps blackened by a forest fire."

R-ia. Neither persons or animals are involved, real or unreal: *inanimate* objects and/or actions. "Explosion"; "pile of rock falling over"; also *abstract concepts:* "destruction"; "death"; "hell."

R-dep. Persons are involved, but are seen as *depicted* in a painting, drawing, statue, etc. "Puppets"; "caricature of two old maids"; "fountain with sculptured angels"; "mask."

R-geo. Remoteness in place (geography): Score for all explicit geographical remoteness, and also if clearly implicit: "Wounded Russian bears"; "African cannibals"; "cannibals around a pot" (remoteness in place is still clearly implied in the latter formulation); "two spacemen fighting on Jupiter."

R-tm. Remoteness in time (past or future): "A duel between two knights" (here remoteness in time is clearly implied); "tyrranosaurus jaws"; "two men of the future shooting disintegrator rays at each other."

> *Do not score:* "Witch"; "devil"; "dragon"; etc. The flavor of the past may cling to such concepts as these, but they are to be scored *R-fic* unless it is clearly specified that they are "ancient" or the like.

Remoteness in level of reality: Each of the categories below is further divided into successful (that is, appropriate) and unsuccessful attempts to achieve this kind of remoteness.

R-fic s. Reference to a specific fictional character or context: Successful (+): "Mephistopheles"; "Li'l Abner eating a pork chop"; "the Inferno"; "boy in the Campbell soup ads, his tongue sticking out."

Unsuccessful (−): "Rabbit with wings—à la Bugs Bunny"; "witches from Macbeth, boosting two other witches into a kettle."

Note that in both of these responses, the primary process element is not adequately accounted for by the fictional reference.

R-fic n. Nonspecific fictional, supernatural, mythological, or similar character or context: Successful (+): "Menacing man from Mars"; "witches"; "ghost"; "monster"; "devil" (but "the Devil" or "Satan" are *R-fic s*+); "hell"; "a scene on some strange planet."

Unsuccessful (−): "People—this is the rump, phallic symbol—they look like gremlins"; "the Last Judgment . . . dinosaurs guarding the throne of God." The dinosaurs spoil the otherwise adequate supernatural context.

R-fan. Characters or context are from dream or explicit fantasy: To be successful, this kind of distance must involve a clear recognition by the S that what he sees is "only imaginary," i.e., he is making something unrealistic acceptable by explicitly pointing to its fantastic nature. Thus, *R-fan*+ is an indication of good reality testing.

Successful (+): "Frightening figures like you'd see in a nightmare"; "someone's imagination of what a disease germ must look like."

Unsuccessful (−): "A scene out of a dream sequence in a movie—a couple of snakes eating out a rabbit's eyes, two boys eating these lollipops—here [yellow, card X] they are urinating. . . ." S gets carried away by an autistic fantasy, beyond his stated frame of reference.

Do not score: Responses that are clearly fantastic and delusional without any distance. If the S gives no indication that he does not wholly accept his unrealistic premises as true, a response like the following is not scorable here: "Representation of the System that is out to get me."

Context

This refers to the setting in which the response is presented and by which the S presumably attempts to "explain away" or make more acceptable the primary-process aspect of his response. Four kinds of context are distinguished below. They are scored as being either successful (+) or unsuccessful (−) in dealing with the content or formal element involved in the response. A given context is considered successful when the explanation or justification it provides for the response is sufficient to cover its deviant elements and to make the total response acceptable as a communication. It is considered unsuccessful when it only partly explains these elements or when it is essentially irrelevant to their presence in the response, or when it entails forcing or straining after control.

Cx C. Cultural context: A response that is otherwise implausible, shocking, or in other ways unacceptable may be made more or less appropriate as a communication by explaining the questionable aspect by reference to a ritual, custom, occupational role, or other social reality.

Cx C+: "Cavemen— they don't seem to have any clothes on"; "Ubangis with a shield"; "soldier with a gun."

Cx C−: "Cobras ready to attack, like taking part in a ritual."

Cx E. Esthetic context: This covers appropriate references to either artistic or literary activities or productions.

Cx E+: "A frightened figure like Alice in Wonderland"; "figure, the head is upside down—as in a Chagall painting."

Cx E−: "Series of paints squeezed on the card"; "men having a playful tug-of-war—like theatrical figures."

Cx I. Intellectual context: This includes reference to scientific fact or technical knowledge.

Cx I+: "Phallic symbol"; "prostate and *vas deferens.*"

Cx I−: "Animals coming out of Dante's Inferno—red, the fire is reflecting."

Cx H. Humorous context: This is meant to catch those responses in which there is playful or fanciful elaboration of content, where S uses humor appropriately or creates something amusing.

Cx H+: "Two people, with both male and female organs—guess you could say they're ambisextrous."

Cx H−: "Blackboard that hasn't been cleaned properly—some kid running out of paint, smudging everything up [laughs]."

Do not score: Responses in which the only humor implied is the fact that the thing seen is supposed to be a cartoon or a caricature.

Pathological Defenses [6]

Va−. Vagueness of percept: This is to be scored *only* when the S *complains* after giving a response that he does not really see it, or he sees it indistinctly. This kind of "marginal" perception seems to be a

---

[6] The minus sign after the symbol for this and the following pathological defenses indicate the weakness or failure of the defensive effort.

form of evasion, an abdication of responsibility for producing the response. Or in some cases it may be an anxiety-induced disorganization of perception, with clouding of consciousness and withdrawal.

Do not score: For percepts of indefinite form, nor for vaguely seen percepts about which the S does not complain.

"I get a glassy *feeling—doesn't appear to be any shape—*like a goblet" (note the inappropriateness of this comment: the goblet was actually of good form and well seen—IX, center white); "dogs, kissing—*I don't see it, but it suggests it.*"

Do not score: "I can't figure out what these two little things are; they don't seem to take on any image. About the only thing they would be is pincers on a lobster." Here the vagueness is verbalized first; it lacks the covering-up or undoing quality of the scored examples.

Prj—. *Projection of responsibility:* Score when S openly denies that he is responsible for giving the response, and says, in effect: "The response is in the card, not in me." Score only when clear-cut. Also include cases in which the response is attributed to another person (see the last example).

"A woman's body. (?) It's obvious, anyone could see it"; "maybe this is supposed to be something in the cat's mind"; "my kid would tell me I saw a wolf."

Neg. Negation and undoing:

Neg—: This is scored when the content or formal element is presented in negative form: "It's not X" or, "It's not X, it's Y."

"Two animals drinking water—*but not hateful";* "animals—*not exactly as if ready to leap";* "female organs—*nothing exciting about them"* (here the denial is not of the content but of its importance).

Do not score: "Men having a playful tug-of-war." It is perfectly possible for a tug-of-war to be playful, even though there is a certain amount of contradiction in the relation between the adjective and the noun. But there is a difference between saying that people are *friendly* and denying that they are *unfriendly;* only the latter form is scored here. Also *do not score:* "Snarling skunks . . . no, it doesn't look like skunks." Sometimes S will defend himself against the original idea in a way resembling negation but not quite identical with it. He may attribute "good," "nice" qualities to something threatening that slipped by his defenses, trying to decontaminate or purify it; e.g., "A lion—a nice, gentle one." *Also do not score:* "A quiet panther." (The attribute does not constitute a clear denial.)

Neg+: Sometimes the negation of an impulse is built right into the response in such an integral way that it must be considered a successful defense.

"Mask"; "blind man"; "broken spear" (*Neg+* applies only to the *L 2 E-V* and the *Ag 2 P-S*, not the *Ag 2 R* in these responses); "virgin."

Eu—. *Euphemism:* A closely related type of defense is the substitution of a "genteel" or roundabout word for a direct one. There are many socially shared words and phrases to enable us to talk about various facts of life without having to soil our lips with the real names of things.

"Two men having a little misunderstanding" (inquiry brings out that S sees them as fighting); "a woman with a big fanny" (also many other such terms); "a man's private parts."

Minz—. *Minimization:* Under this heading fall attempts to control (chiefly content) deviations by two main devices: seeing them in tiny areas (as small as the "arrowhead" *Dd* on card II or smaller), and in the concept itself, introducing modifications or qualifications that have the effect of making the threat a literally small one:

"A *baby's* arm and fist"; "a lion *cub.*"

Obs—. *Obsessional defense:* Score doubting, vacillation, obsessional "worrying" of a percept, or indecision about it. Score if there is the equivalent of two waverings between possibilities: also anything clinically considered obsessive, *except* that it must be clearly more than what is usual for S on nonscored responses.

"I can't quite tell whether it's a bat or a butterfly—in some ways it's more like a bat, but then in others it's more a butterfly"; "should I try for more responses or should I stop here? I can give you more, but maybe you're getting tired"; "two men—perhaps waiters bringing a tray, but that isn't a very good tray—they could be 18th century dandies bowing to each other, or even cowboys, with those high-heeled boots, but then that wouldn't account for this business" (breast area). Also, meticulous description of the blot taking into account minute differences between the two halves.

Den—. *Attempted denial:* Score attempts to retract a response or deny that it was ever given: "Two lions, or beavers. [Did the lions seem to be doing anything?] I didn't *say* lions—I said beavers"; "a penis—no, no, don't write that down, it really looks like a snake instead"; "two cloaked figures, holding knives"; in inquiry, S cannot find knives, and finally says: "I couldn't have said knives, there aren't any there."

GENERAL RATINGS OF TOTAL RESPONSE

DD. Defense Demand of Response

Under this heading, the shock value of the response is to be rated: the degree to which the very nature of the underlying idea, or (in the case of the formal variables) the way it emerges, demands that some defensive and controlling measures be undertaken in order to make the response a socially acceptable communication. (Note that we do *not* try to score differently for each S; criteria are *general*.) Scores at the upper extreme will usually be given to blatant, Level-1 sexual or aggressive *content*, but formal aspects also make varying demands that the "craziness" of the conception be concealed or explained away. In part, this rating represents an elaboration of the Level 1–Level 2 distinction.

1. *No apparent need for defense:* Here fall responses that contain aspects of the primary process only implicitly, or references to matters that would hardly be noticed if referred to at a polite tea party; e.g., food; *Do.*

2. *Slight need for defense:* The content and structure of the responses rated at this level are only slightly unusual in conversation, and arouse only slight degrees of tension. Also, any response containing both Level-2 content and Level-2 formal scores must be rated at least 2; e.g., "animals fighting"; verbal slips.

3. *Moderate need for defense:* The content and formal deviations here scored are at a level that might cause moderate tension or social embarrassment if they occurred in conversation. Also, any response combining Level-1 content and Level-2 formal, or Level-2 content and Level-1 formal must be rated at least 3; e.g., "buttocks"; impossible combinations.

4. *Considerable need for defense:* The level here is set by the example of sexual organs. It is possible for most people to refer to such things in a doctor-patient setting, but it is not permissible in ordinary conversations. Also, any response combining any kind of Level-1 con-

tent and Level-1 formal material must be rated at least 4; e.g., genitals; *DW*.

5. *Great need for defense:* Shocking ideas which could under no circumstances be introduced into a social conversation without extensive controls and defenses. Such responses are almost pathognomonic of psychosis, since they imply both a serious breach of judgment in order to be mentioned, and the availability to awareness of ideas that are usually kept unconscious; e.g., "two men eating a dead body"; autistic logic.

6. *Greatest need for defense:* Sometimes it happens that a response contains content that would be rated 5 and also formal deviations that are at the 5 level. The result is about as much primary process and need for defense as can be packed into a single response; responses rated 6 occur exclusively in psychotic records. (For an example, see under 6a, *DE*.)

DE.   Effectiveness of Defense

Each response that contains any scorable content or formal element is to be rated on the effectiveness of controlling and defensive measures in reducing or preventing anxiety, and making a successful, adaptive response to the examiner's demand to interpret the blots.

In making this rating, keep the following three elements in mind: (1) The form accuracy and organization of the response; [7] (2) expressive behavior and any other indications of threat or enjoyment, from the protocol and the affect inquiry; and (3) the nature of the particular control categories scored (if any). In addition, consider also unscored aspects of defense: indications of defensiveness, evasion, or disruption, various kinds of rationalizations, and slight changes in the form level (for better or for worse) when the primary process aspect of the response is introduced. Use all of your clinical sense!

Note that two types of ratings are given, distinguished by the letter *a* following the *undefended* type. An *undefended response* is defined as one that lacks any control and defense category except *R-min* and/or the sequence categories ($S M R+$ or ($-$) not included). It is as-

---

[7] We use the system for scoring form level devised by Martin Mayman (unpublished) in which Fo = ordinary; Fw = weak; Fv = vague; Fs = spoiled form accuracy. The scoring of *DE* could be adapted to any other differentiated set of form-level scores, however, like Klopfer's rating technique (11).

sumed that if someone is quite mature and unthreatened by the primary process, he may feel no need to defend a response containing a good deal of it; therefore, the lack of any scorable defenses is not considered a detriment if the response is in other respects successful.

1. *Completely successful control and defense, in a successful response:* Good form level ($F+$ or Fo); no disturbance, if any affect, it is positive; only "good" control and defense categories; response is a perfectly acceptable communication, with no deviations of language.

In general, responses rated in the top categories (5 and 6) of *Defense Demand* will hardly ever be rated at the top here—it would constitute a very unusual achievement.

"Here I can also see the outlines of a man—gangster-type individual with hat brim over his eyes. [Inq.] Looks like a gangster in one of those English stories they show over TV." Card VI, D $F(C)+$ H; $Ag\,2\,P\text{-}S$; $R\text{-}fic\,n+$, $Cx\,E+$. (DD: 2)

"Top here helps give the impression of the cloud of an atomic bomb." Card IX, position $\vee$; D $F+$ $Expl.$; $Ag\,2\,A\text{-}S$; $R\text{-}ia.$ (DD: 2)

1a. *Highly successful response, undefended:* Above description applies, except that no control and defense category is scored other than $R\text{-}min$ or S (sequence)—except $S\,M\,R+$ or ($-$), which is considered a conscious effort at defense. *Note:* Not to be scored for otherwise successful responses rated 5 or 6 on DD.

"A woman's sexual organs—here are the lips, the opening, even this little hole back here could be the anus. [Inq.] The color and shape." Card II, $Drs\,FC+$ Sex; $L\,1\,S$ ($L\,1\,A$); $R\text{-}min.$ (DD: 4)

2. *Successful control and defense:* Like 1, except that response does not meet full specifications in *one or two* respects of the following: Form level may be Fv *if* form is subordinate to another determinant or $Fw+$ (*not* $Fw-$, Fs or $F-$, however); mild signs of discomfort may be present; D scores may include one of the unsuccessful types if successful ones are also present.

The content and formal scores listed above as precluding a rating of 1 may be rated 2 *if* they are well defended and in all other respects meet the criteria for 1. ("Well defended" means that one of the $+$ controls is scored or, if not, that two or more of the other, nonminus, controls are scored and no minus control.)

"Vaguely an African devil mask. [Inq.] There's a vaguely facial aspect of this part which made me think of the . . . think of as a face, it's sort of ominous-looking, that's why I thought of the African devil mask." Card I, *Ws F+ Mask; Ag* 2 *P-S: Cx C+, Isp+, R-dep, R-geo* (*Va* tend.); (*L* 2 *E-V*): *Neg+* (also rest of above defenses). (*DD:* 2)

If S clearly liked it instead of finding it "ominous," and if it lacked the complaint of vagueness, it would have been given a 1.

2a. Successful response, undefended (same relationship as 1*a* to 1; not on quite as high a level as 1*a*): If a response is undefended, it may contain anything with *DD* of less than 5 as long as the form level is *F+*, or *Fo*, or *Fw+* if accompanying affect is neutral or positive.

"Woman's figure with wings—in between two objects." Card I, *W M+ H-Obj.; C-co* 1: *R-min.* (*DD:* 3)

3. *Only moderately successful control and defense:* The "difficult" content and formal categories are more likely to occur here; the defensive efforts generally have to be more extensive or effective if such material is present than if more innocuous material is used, which is acceptable with less efficient defenses. For the latter, the response must still be reasonably defensible and acceptable as a communication. Form level may be *Fv* or *Fw*−; if it is *Fs*, the response must be relatively *good* in other respects, and *F*− is still unacceptable at this level. Signs of serious disturbance are not allowed; but control scores may be relatively poor as long as the total effect is not bad.

"This looks like some kind of animal. [Inq.] This looks like an animal—with a fang . . . [kind?] It doesn't look like a fox—or a wolf." Card IX, *D Fs Ad; Ag* 2 *P-S: Neg*−, *R-an, Inh.* (Usual *human* head; *DD:* 2)

3a. Ditto, undefended: "Might be two figures hanging from some objects. Might say it represents the human figure without heads." Card VII (∨), *W F+ H; Ag* 2 *R, C a-c u* 2: *R-min.* (*DD:* 2)

The form level is acceptable though at the bottom of what could be called *F+*; apart from the primary aspects, the response suffers only from its lack of the expected *M*, the vagueness of "some objects," and the long delay (70 seconds) before it was given as the first response, suggesting disturbance.

4. *Relatively unsuccessful control and defense:* Poor responses with one or two strong saving features, or generally mediocre attempts with some weaknesses. *D* scores may range from predominantly successful *with* some unsuccessful aspects, to predominantly unsuccessful with some successful aspects (depending on other aspects of the response). *Note:* Fairly good responses may be scored 4 if accompanied by strong disturbance; see especially affect inquiry.

"It's a sort of a butterfly; it looks like it got caught in something—cut his wings and messed 'em up. Looks like it's trying to fly. I think the wings will grow back and get well again—unless he dies of starvation. Looks like a nice butterfly." Card I, $Ws\,FMo\,A\,P$: $Ag\,2\,R$ ($L\,1\,O$): R-an, $Neg-\,wk$; $Au\,El\,2$: X. (DD: 3)

This is an example of mediocre defensive efforts with a weakness in the attempted restitution, which collapses with the starvation fantasy (an example of *thematic elaboration* rather than a percept).

4a. *Ditto, undefended:* "This looks somewhat like a penis." Card I, usual side wing: $d\,F\,-\,Sex$; $L\,1\,S$: R-min, $S\,C\,1$–$0\,wk$ (followed by an Fv response). (DD: 3) The sequence has minimal defensive efficacy, the Fv being followed by another Level 1 response. And the form level is so poor the response must be counted unsuccessful.

5. *Unsuccessful attempts at control and defense:* Always accompanied by some signs of considerable discomfort and defensiveness (direct or indirect). Form level may range from Fo to $F-$ (but if it is fairly good, other features must be worse); there usually will be no very positive control scores.

"This looks like a six-figured structure of animated things—maybe not humans—two heads holding up green figure and green holding up orange. I can kind of visualize a head and nose and several pairs of arms joined together in center. Kind of a strange figure. [Inq., orange?] Not human, like just figures like you'd see in a comic book somewhere [laugh]. (?) Each one is holding the next one up. (?) I don't know—just looks that way" [laugh]. Card IX, $W\,Fs$ (M tend.); C-$co\,1$ ($VP\,2$): $Cx\,H-\,wk$, $Crt+\,wk$, R-$fic\,n-$. (DD: 4)

Note in addition to the general inadequacy of the controls, the signs of disturbance (embarrassed laughter).

5a. *Unsuccessful responses, undefended:* Responses that meet the general criteria for 5, but have no control scores (or virtually none).

"This one looks like a spider, and it must have lost its feelers—you know, it's having a hard time moving around. That's what it looks like; he's—looks like he's got in a fight or something with some other bug, because he's got all things dripping down from him. He'll most probably die. [Inq.] And he must have got in a fight with a bigger bug or something, and he lost his feelers. (?) Way I figure it out, a spider has more legs, but he must have lost it . . . (?) Trying to get in safe spot so other bugs won't eat him up, protect himself. [Die?] He'll have a hard time getting that food—not unless he has a storage of it—and from losing all that blood." Card IV, $W FM - A$; $Ag1R$ ($L1O$): R-an; $VP2$, $Au El2$: X. (DD: 4)

The remoteness of person is the only defense, and it seems of negligible value in relation to the greatly elaborated aggressive fantasy; in addition, the autistic elaboration is undefended, as is the peculiar verbalization.

6. *Disorganized responses with only pathological attempts at defense:* All but the last two of the examples given under *Au El* 1 are rated 6. Rarely found except in psychotic records.

6a. *Ditto, undefended:* "It looks like an insect, on two parts of it, and looks like somebody's chest. [Inq.] That doesn't look like an insect; it looks like part of a body (?) 'cause it looks like part of a man's chest. And it looks like he has some kind of a disease, with two insects inside . . . [What's happened inside?] He's in the hospital." Card VIII, $W Fs At$, A; $Ag 1 R$ ($Ag 1 A$-O); $C f$-$p 1$, $Au El 1 wk$: R-min ($S M$ 0–1? *Inh?*—not clear; perhaps neither). A rare example of DD: 6, because either formal or content scores alone would have been rated 5.

RELIABILITY AND VALIDITY

In brief outline, this is the system we have worked out for scoring Rorschach records for the primary process and how it is handled. Obviously, such a detailed system is cumbersome until it is thoroughly learned, but even then, scoring is not a quick affair. It is necessary to scrutinize each remark of the subject quite carefully and weigh it against many kinds of standards. What evidence is there that such a system can be reliably scored, and that the scores are valid, i.e., lead to verified predictions about the behavior that is theoretically to be expected?

Reliability

Our preliminary efforts to check scorer agreement show that many individual categories are difficult to score reliably, but when these are combined in certain over-all indices, agreement is excellent. Two independent scorers rated 1,089 responses given by a mixed group of 30 women; the proportion of responses per record with Level-1 primary process (formal plus content) as scored by one rater correlated .97 with the same index as scored by the other. Similar indices of Level-2 primary-process materials and total (Level 1 plus Level 2) yielded coefficients of observer agreement of .98. It is true that these judges [8] had worked with the senior author for about a year, scoring many records and discussing disagreements; one should not assume that these coefficients are a function of the scoring system alone. Nevertheless, we think that these reliability figures encourage the use of the system in quantitative research.

Validity

In the course of his Ph.D. dissertation (4), in which he used the present Rorschach scoring system to predict individual differences in reaction to perceptual isolation, Leo Goldberger devised a useful method of combining the scoring summaries to come up with a measure of *adaptive versus maladaptive regression*. The procedure is essentially as follows: Make up a rank order of a group of subjects, according to their total per cent primary process, weighting Level-1 responses especially. Take the lowest ranking subject on the "amount" measure and put him near the middle of a new rank order—just above a line indicating the mid-point if his primary-process responses have high *DE* scores and just below it if the effectiveness of his defenses is poor. Take the next lowest man in the amount rank order and put him above the first one if he had good *DE*, below if he had poor *DE*. Continue thus until you come to the top subject on the first variable, the one with the greatest amount of primary process in his Rorschach; again depending on his *DE*, he will be either the highest or the lowest ranking man in the new rank order. Note that high ranks go to subjects with a lot of primary process without threat and well controlled (the mature or adaptively regressing subjects); near the middle will be the constricted subjects who produce very little primary process of any kind; and at the bottom of the rank order will go the uncontrolled subjects who cannot prevent a good deal of primary-process material from breaking through, disrupting the response process and causing the mobilization of pathological defenses and anxiety.

In Goldberger's study (5), carefully screened male college students were paid to "spend a day doing nothing." For eight hours, they lay on a comfortable couch in a semisoundproof room, hands gloved and encased in cardboard gauntlets, eyes capped with translucent halved

[8] Reeva Safrin and Anthony F. Philip, Research Assistants at the Research Center for Mental Health.

ping-pong balls, and ears covered by padded earphones through which a random, "white" noise was continually piped. They were asked to lie quietly and to talk occasionally to describe what was going through their minds; they were fed lunch and were taken to a nearby toilet by the experimenter without any change in the inputs to eye or ear.

In such a situation, the most adaptive responses were to lie quietly, to allow primary process to enter conscious thought (as in daydreaming) without being threatened by it, to spend some of the time in undisrupted secondary-process thinking, to take advantage of residual opportunities for self-stimulation, to enjoy oneself, to speak freely and have vivid imagery. These reactions (as rated reliably from the tape-recorded protocols by two judges) formed a positively intercorrelating cluster, which, in turn, correlated .50 with the measure of adaptive versus maladaptive regression (a predicted result, significant with 14 cases at the .05 point). Most of the components of this syndrome also correlated equally significantly with the Rorschach measure, which was scored independently and without contamination (see Table 10.2). It is especially interesting that the amount of time spent in sleep correlated .65, which is significant at the .05 level (two-tailed test). Sleep has been cited by Hartmann and Kris as an example par excellence of adaptive regression, and it surely was one of the most agreeable ways for a subject to pass the time.

The same subjects were extensively tested and interviewed, the following data finally being worked up and integrated on each of them: autobiography, interview, Wechsler-Bellevue,[9] Rorschach, and TAT. Two staff members of the Research Center for Mental Health made independent analyses of this material on a case, and expressed their evaluations in the form of Q-sort ratings on 180 items covering six major areas of personality (motives; affects and inner states; characteristics of thought processes; defenses; identity and self-attitudes; interpersonal relations). These variables in turn were intercorrelated and reduced to 55 intercorrelating clusters of meaningfully related items, which were finally correlated with certain Rorschach measures. Correlations with these clusters, and with a number of objective test scores are presented in Table 10.2.

The correlated aspects of personality listed in Table 10.2 form a fair approximation to the description of the personological matrix in which regression in the service of the ego is found according to

9 It was not possible to give this test to all S; all, however, were given the Ohio State Psychological Examination, a good group test of intelligence. It correlated only .17 with adaptive versus maladaptive regression.

TABLE 10.2. Measures of Personality That Correlate with Rorschach Measure of Adaptive versus Maladaptive Regression

Rank Order Correlations	Personality Measures Correlating with Rorschach Measure	N
	Effective, Intraceptive Thinking Versus Hypermasculine Practicality	
.59 *	Q-sort cluster: Feminine, intraceptive versus masculine, extraceptive style and outlook	15
.71 †	Q-sort cluster: Communicates ideas clearly and effectively, in colorful yet appropriate language; versus S's thinking is blocked, inhibited	15
.74 †	Barron-Welsh Art Scale (2) (measure of complexity of personality;)	14
−.55 *	Masculine Identification Scale, Dynamic Personality Inventory (6)	14
−.55 *	Political value; Allport-Vernon-Lindzey Study of Values (1)	14
−.48	Economic value; Study of Values	14
−.55	Rating of Path of Life 11: Active somatotonic mastery, Paths of Life (12)	12
.45	Unimpaired secondary-process thought, isolation study	14
.54 *	Controlled primary-process thought, isolation study	12
.46	Exploration and self-stimulation, isolation study	14
	Freedom from Self-Directed Aggression	
−.54 *	Q-sort cluster: Depressed, self-blaming	15
.68 *	Q-sort cluster: Overcompensation versus turning against self	15
−.52	Manic scale, MMPI	14
	Emotional Balance and Free Affect	
.56 *	Q-sort cluster: Balanced, flexible emotional control versus low anxiety tolerance	15
−.64 *	Rating of Path of Life 10: Stern Spartan self-contro'	12
−.50	Unpleasant affect, isolation study	14
47	Pleasant affect, isolation study	14
	Positive Oral Traits: Kindliness and Dependence	
.52 *	Q-sort cluster: Sympathetic and respectful, accepting and fatherly	15
.53	Ranking of Path of Life 3: Nurturant love of others	11
.69 *	Rating of Path of Life 13: Submissive (masochistic) dependence	12

* Significant at the .05 level, two-tailed test.
† Significant at the .01 level, two-tailed test.
Note: All other correlations are significant at the .10 level, two-tailed.

Schafer (18). The correlation coefficients are not impressively large, for the most part not even being highly significant, but they are in the right directions. A word of caution, however: Incomplete but largely negative preliminary results from a group of college girls of the same age suggest that these correlations may not hold up in different samples, but may, in some as yet unknown way, be specific to unknown parameters of the present group of college boys.

On the whole, we feel encouraged to believe that our scoring system does provide an approximate measure of adaptive versus maladaptive regression, one that can and (we hope) will be improved. Sensitive and experienced clinicians have doubtless been making similar judgments for years using the Rorschach, but it has not been possible previously to specify a reasonably teachable and objectively scorable technique for making the vital distinction between primary process that serves the ego's adaptive purposes in humorous, scientific, and artistic creativity, and primary process that invades the ego to its detriment as a result of decompensated defenses and cognitive controls. If the genius and the madman are akin in that the thinking of both shows more evidence of the primary process than the ordinary man can tolerate, it is the effectiveness of their controls and defenses that will distinguish them.[10]

BIBLIOGRAPHY

1. Allport, G. W., Vernon, P. E., and Lindzey, G. *The study of values* (rev. ed.). Boston: Houghton Mifflin, 1951.
2. Barron, F. Complexity-simplicity as a personality variable. *J. abnorm. soc. Psychol.*, 1953, 48, 163–172.
3. Freud, S. *The interpretation of dreams.* (James Strachey, trans.) New York: Basic Books, 1955.
4. Goldberger, L. Individual differences in the effects of perceptual isolation as related to Rorschach manifestations of the primary process. Unpublished doctoral dissertation, New York University, 1958.
5. Goldberger, L., and Holt, R. R. Experimental interference with reality contact (perceptual isolation): method and group results. *J. nerv. ment. Dis.*, 1958, 127, 99–112.
6. Grygier, T. *The dynamic personality inventory.* Sutton, England: Banstead Hospital Management Committee, 1955.

[10] *Note:* Dittoed copies of the complete manual describing the scoring system are available through the Research Center for Mental Health, to interested research workers who are willing to share their findings with the senior author.

7. Hartmann, H.   Comments on the psychoanalytic theory of the ego.   *Psycho-anal. Study Child,* 1950, 5, 74–96.
8. Holt, R. R.   Gauging primary and secondary processes in Rorschach responses.   *J. proj. Tech.,* 1956, 20, 14–25.
9. Klein, G. S.   Need and regulation.   In: M. R. Jones (ed.), *Nebraska symposium on motivation, 1954.*   Lincoln: University of Nebraska Press, 1954, 224–274.
10. Klein, G. S.   Perception, motives and personality: a clinical perspective.   In: J. L. McCary (ed.), *Psychology of personality, six modern approaches.*   New York: Logos Press, 1956.   Pp. 121–200.
11. Klopfer, B., Ainsworth, Mary D., Klopfer, W. G., and Holt, R. R.   *Developments in the Rorschach technique, Vol. I.*   Yonkers: World Book Co., 1954.
12. Kris, E.   *Psychoanalytic explorations in art.*   New York: International Universities Press, 1952.
13. Morris, C., and Jones, L. V.   Value scales and dimensions.   *J. abnorm. soc. Psychol.,* 1955, 51, 523–525.
14. Rapaport, D.   *Organization and pathology of thought.*   New York: Columbia University Press, 1951.
15. Rapaport, D.   On the psychoanalytic theory of affects.   *Int. J. Psychoanal.,* 1953, 34, 1–22.
16. Rapaport, D., Gill, M. M., and Schafer, R.   *Diagnostic psychological testing. Vol. II.*   Chicago: Yearbook Publishers, 1946.
17. Schafer, R.   *Psychoanalytic interpretation in Rorschach testing.*   New York: Grune and Stratton, 1954.
18. Schafer, R.   Regression in the service of the ego: the relevance of a psychoanalytic concept for personality assessment.   In: G. Lindzey (ed.), *Assessment of human motives.*   New York: Rinehart, 1958.
19. Tomkins, S. S.   *The Thematic Apperception Test.*   New York: Grune and Stratton, 1947.

THE
TEST
PATTERN

Then boldly stirs imagination's power,
And shapes these formless masses of the
*hour.**

JOHANN WOLFGANG GOETHE

11 | by Roland Kuhn

SOME

PROBLEMS CONCERNING

THE PSYCHOLOGICAL IMPLICATIONS

OF RORSCHACH'S

FORM INTERPRETATION TEST

Since Hermann Rorschach's death, research on his form interpretation test has concentrated almost exclusively on statistical studies (7). We should, however, understand clearly what can be achieved by statistical methods. They lead to the use of certain "signs," [1] the meaning of which is either based on conventional procedure or has been derived from rather superficial relationships between indices. The validity of such signs may be established through the use of statistics, but statistical methods alone can never give us psychological understanding of inner relationships, nor the reason why a certain "sign" is considered indicative of a particular psychological characteristic. It is well known that Rorschach himself used and reported in addition to statistics quite different methods (7, pp. 181–213), based chiefly on theoretical considerations. This kind of approach lends itself well to further development as demonstrated, e.g., by the research of Binder on chiaroscuro (1) [2] and by that of the author on "mask" responses (6).

* Translated by J. C. Hüttner.
[1] The term sign is used here in the phenomenological sense of Edmund Husserl (5, pp. 23–105).
[2] See Chapter 8.

319

Our ideas regarding the psychological nature of the Rorschach method will be presented in two parts. Part I will illustrate our testing procedure with the analysis of an individual case. Part II will attempt to throw new light upon the theoretical problems involved in the interpretation of certain test categories.

PART I

The method involves repeated spaced administration of the Rorschach by different examiners. This procedure has proved to be especially useful when the examiners were of different sexes. The theoretical underpinnings of results obtained by this method are too involved to be covered here. Neither does space allow us to take up possible objections that might be raised in regard to the technique itself. Our objective is merely to demonstrate on a single case how the method is to be applied and what kind of information it may yield. It is perhaps appropriate to mention here that we have been using this method for many years on a great number of cases and that our conclusions could be supported by numerous other examples.

The following summary of anamnesis is intended to provide background information regarding the subject's problems, past experiences, and the apparent interrelations between these experiences. The information has been gathered in the course of a prolonged psychiatric treatment, most of it by the patient's psychotherapist, a woman psychiatrist.

Summary of Anamnesis and Psychotherapy of W. E., Born 1934
(compiled by Verena Gebhart, M.D.)

Family history. The patient comes from a middle-class family. The father has an economically secure position as clerk in a business firm. Both parents belong to the Methodist church. There are five children in the family, three brothers and two sisters. The patient is the second, and her sister is the youngest in birth order. On the paternal side of the family there were several cases of depression which, however, did not require hospitalization. The father is described as serious. All members of the family are said to be somewhat peculiar, the patient's younger brother being particularly poorly adjusted.

Personal history. The patient's intellectual level is above average. Her physical development was normal but her personality showed peculiar characteristics even in early childhood. As a small child she used to be excessively preoccupied with fairy tales and was hyperemotional in her reactions to the world around her. It is also reported that when the family went out for Sunday walks she used to walk behind the group, mumbling and talking to herself. She took no liking to work, yet once she started a task, she went about it in a slow but systematic and conscientious fashion. In grammar school she had no particular difficulties. Her performance was uneven: poor in arithmetic but above average in verbal facility. She always got along easily with her schoolmates and was well liked. While the patient was in the fourth and fifth grade, her mother had to go out and take a job. During this period the children were cared for primarily by the grandmother, a person of extreme strictness and exactitude. Under her rule the patient became disorderly in her behavior and began to stay away from home after school. It was with great effort and after the second attempt only that she succeeded in being admitted to a secondary school. The subject in which she failed completely was arithmetic. In the secondary school she had good teachers and seemed to be getting along well; she enjoyed reciting poetry and showed signs of artistic talents, especially in singing.

It was during her third year in secondary school when the first episode of depression occurred. This was, in all probability, precipitated by the sexual experiences she had with her father: for a period of several months, he used to come into her bedroom almost every night and, thinking she was asleep, he would touch her body. This stopped only when it was finally discovered by the patient's mother. In the same year she started to go out with a boy. Once she was beaten by her father for coming home very late at night where upon she locked herself into her room for two days and remained there until the door was forced open. From then on there were increasing difficulties and the patient wished to get away from home as soon as possible. She had two jobs as domestic help in the French part of Switzerland, one for three and the other for four months. In both places she did well in the beginning; her letters home were full of enthusiasm of how well off she was. Soon, however, she began to neglect her work, failed to get up in the morning, and became disgusted with everything, so that finally she had to be dismissed. The parents wanted the patient to return home and stay with them, but she expressed the wish to become an actress or receive training in voice. The parents did not consent to this. Finally it was agreed that the patient would go to Geneva to be trained as a baby nurse. The following year of studies and training-on-the-job is said to have gone quite well. She had to work rather hard, had little time to go out, and led a respectable life. In addition to this one-year training, she was required to complete two half-years of practicum. During this period she became acquainted with girls who liked to go out in the evenings. The patient joined them and went to dances where she met young men. She found pleasure in dancing, smoking, and being in male company. It was then that she had her first intimate relationships with men. At the end of her practicum year she went on a vacation trip with her boy friend, letting her parents believe that she had to stay on the job for a few more days.

The patient began her employment as a baby nurse in England. During her 18-month stay in that country she worked at three different places. Her first job, which she held for six months, she quit from one day to the other because she was not allowed to go out with her friend in the evening. Then she took a job in a hospital; here she enjoyed complete freedom after working hours and became rather promiscuous in her conduct. One of her boy friends was a Negro. Toward the end of her stay in England, the patient did not work at all for several months. At that time she had many friends, was associated with so-called bohemian circles, and posed as a model. Finally, she became pregnant, had an abortion, and, a few days later, returned to her home in Switzerland. At home she felt tired and sick and did not get along anymore in her environment. For a while she worked as a substitute for vacationing personnel in a hospital. Later she took a job with a doctor who was an acquaintance of her parents. First she liked the job, but half a year later, after she had to be reprimanded because of unrestrained behavior and neglect of her duties, she resigned and returned home. There she fell into a dejected mood, complained of feelings of uselessness and of being a complete failure in life, and expressed guilt over her immoral conduct. She found no consolation in religion either, and felt desperate and helpless. It was then that she first attempted suicide. One night she hid a razor blade in her bed, intending to cut her wrist. The blade was discovered and taken away in time by her mother. The patient reacted to her mother's interference with a severe crying spell, insisting that she did not want to live any longer. From then on she felt very depressed and did not want to work. She quarreled with her sister and threw objects at her. Finally, she made a second suicidal attempt (two months after the first), this one by the use of gas. This attempt was almost successful and led to her hospitalization. It was in the hospital that we first met the patient. She gave the impression of a very sick person. Soon she was transferred to a mental institution. There she received psychotherapy and drug treatment, and by the end of 2½ months improved sufficiently to be discharged and sent home. Since then she has been working in a home for the crippled. There her condition keeps fluctuating between fair and severely depressed. Her spells of depression, which are particularly pronounced on days preceding the onset of the menstrual period, are characterized by complaints of difficulties in thinking, complete lack of motivation and, in the morning, a lack of desire to get up at all. During these depressed periods she sleeps poorly, dreams a lot, and also often simply takes off to meet one of her male acquaintances. Symptoms as severe as the ones just described occur, however, only when the patient is not under medication. Her work is said to be satisfactory although she has considerable difficulties in keeping things in order. Her neglect of order and neatness is most marked in her room, but it also shows in her dealings with the children. She is liked among her co-workers because of her friendly and cooperative attitude.

Themes from Psychotherapy

According to the patient, her mother has been very strict with her and has shown partiality in favor of her brothers. The patient reports having felt inferior to her brothers. She has no clear recollection of her childhood relationship to her father, in particular, during the period prior to his sexual advances to her. It seems that he actually showed little interest in the way his children were brought up. The patient always thought of him as a rather insignificant figure; nevertheless, she recalls that once, after having failed on an examination in the secondary school, she was depressed by the idea of having inflicted disgrace upon her father.

The patient states that, although as a small child she was very orderly and conscientious, she was still in her childhood when she became disorderly. She adds that she is simply unable to adjust to any rules or routine and that she cannot see the sense in adhering to order or in keeping within limits. She seems to relate this attitude to her artistic interests and to her tendency of indulging freely in esthetic experiences.

The patient complains of compulsive masturbation. Ever since she became sexually aroused by her father's nightly visits to her bedroom she sought satisfaction in masturbation now and again. Patient reports that her sexual relationships with men were not gratifying until she once experienced complete satisfaction in intercourse with a Negro. Perverse sexual practices she finds repulsive. Her esthetic orientation seems to play a considerable role in her sexual life, even though she insists that serving as a model had no sexual connotation for her. She has always found pleasure in looking at beautiful bodies and even in secondary school was fond of paintings of nudes. She also liked to observe herself nude in the mirror (this was said to have been the case before the occurrence of the sexually arousing episodes with her father) and liked to swim in the nude. She realizes that there is something wrong with her sense of shame. This was confirmed by her mother who noticed that the patient had been indulging, especially lately, in obscene talk about her sexual relations and about her abortion. Also, she is said to have remarked that she did not care about people's opinion of her.

The Rorschach Protocols

Protocol A   Date: April 9, 1956   Examiner: Dr. Verena Gebhart

Time 4:55 P.M.

I. 1. "This is a bat, a distorted one . . ."	W	$ChF+$	A	P^3
2. "Or a butterfly . . . , at any rate, it is a small animal."	W	$F+$	A	P
II. 1. "This, too, could be an animal but I don't know what kind . . ."	W	$F-$	A	
III. 1. "These are two people lifting something."	W	$M+$	H	P
IV. 1. "Bear skin hung up, rug . . ."	W	$F+$	A	P
V. 1. "This one could be a bat."	W	$F+$	A	P
VI. 1. "This is a fish, disemboweled, or perhaps an eel, something of that sort. . . ."	W	$F-$	A	
VII. 1. "Little Mickey-Mouse-like animals, two of them are horses or bunnies or something."	D	$F+$	A	
VIII. 1. "Two sea lions climbing on rocks of some sort. . . ."	D	$F+$	A	P
IX. 1. "This one is rather abstract, I can't make anything out of it. . . ."		Description Failure		
X. 1. "Crystals."	W	$ChF, CF+$	$N/Cryst.$	

Time 5:06 P.M.

[3] For explanation of scoring symbols, see Appendix, pp. 441 ff. [Editor].

The Rorschach Protocols (Continued)

Protocol B   Date: May 2, 1956   Examiner: Dr. Verena Gebhart

Time 5:55 P.M.

I. 1.	"A butterfly."	*W*	*F*+	*A*	*P*
2.	"It could also be a pattern produced by cutting folded paper . . [?] it doesn't represent much, it is only these corners here which are cut out so far."	*W*	*F*−	*Obj.*	
3.	"It could also be an island. . . ."	*W*	*F*−	*Geo.*	
II. 1.	"My first guess would be—little animal. I don't know, there is again this division in the middle and the two sides are the same."	*W*	*F*−	*A* Symmetry	
III. 1.	"Two persons lifting something, they look exactly alike and the motions they go through are exactly the same."	*W*	*M*+	*H*	*P*
IV. 1.	"This could be the skin of a bear, as a rug, . . . spread out."	*W*	*F*+	*A*	*P*
V. 1.	"I see here a bat."	*W*	*F*+	*A*	*P*
2.	"Could also be a bone, with flesh around it, the light parts are the bones. . . ."	*W*	*ChF*−	*At*	
VI. 1.	"Snake skin, may be the whole thing had been a snake."	*W*	*F*−	*A*	
VII. 1.	"Here I see two Mickey-Mouse figures."	*D*	*F*+	*A*	
2.	"But it could also be a few snowballs put together."	*W*	*ChF*−	*N/Snow-ball*	

[Interruption: examiner on the telephone for two minutes.]

VIII. 1.	"This, too, is an animal, a sea lion or something, the underwater world."	*D*	*F*+	*A*	*P*
2.	"Crystals or something."	*D*	*ChF, CF*	*Pl*	
3.	"Or animal in a jungle."	*W*	*FCh*−	*A, N*	
IX. 1.	"Ink wiper (i.e., a cloth that has been used for cleaning ink pens) [?], because of these colored blots neither of which seems to represent anything specific."	*W*	*ChF, CF*−	*Obj.*	
2.	"This here strikes me as funny; it looks like a vein that connects something; one should think of some living creature but I don't see anything in here."	*Dd*	*F*−	*At*	

The Rorschach Protocols (Continued)

Protocol B   Date: May 2, 1956   Examiner: Dr. Verena Gebhart

Time 5:55 P.M. (*Continued*)

X. 1. "Here are two caterpillars [middle green]."	D	F+	A
2. "It could be also the inside of man, here the esophagus [middle grey] but I cannot remember well . . . , recollect any more how it looks inside. . . ."	D	F−	At

Time 6:14 P.M.

Protocol C   Date: June 6, 1956   Examiner: Dr. Roland Kuhn

Time 5:24 P.M.

I. 1. ". . . I see it as a butterfly [turns card repeatedly]."	W	F+	A	P
II. > [Covers up lower half]. . . . "I don't see anything in this one. Uh . . . "				Failure
III. 1. "Here I imagine a human being who is lifting something."	W	M+	H	P
> 2. "One could also imagine the . . . the white part as being the sea and the black ones islands . . . and . . . [And?] sort of inlets and fjords."	Ws	F−	Geo.	
IV. 1. "Here I imagine a bear skin."	W	F+	A	P
V. 1. "Here I see a bat."	W	F+	A	P
VI. "Uh . . . [puts down card]. . . ."				
1. "The top only [covers rest with hand], I imagine, could be some type of fish."	D	F−	A	
2. "Covering up this part here [lower part of upper lateral projections], I see some sort of a fowl, a type of pigeon [very unusual response, the head—the grey that surrounds furniture leg, the tail—remaining part of upper lateral projection]. I cannot make anything of the whole."	Dd	F−	A	
VII. 1. "Here I see a little Mickey-Mouse-like animal, running away [right half of blot]."	D	F+	A	

The Rorschach Protocols (*Continued*)

Protocol C   Date: June 6, 1956   Examiner: Dr. Roland Kuhn

Time 5:24 P.M. (*Continued*)

VIII.   [Sighs]. . . .

> 1. "Here I see a polar bear or something   D   F+   A   P
of that sort."

∧ 2. "This here [center part] too, I noticed   Dd   F−   At
one could say a bone, well, I don't
know, some sort of a . . . , [Hm?]
yes, a bone structure, I don't know
how should one say. . . ."

     3. "Or it could be a caterpillar. This   Dd   F+   A
color combination I haven't noticed
before . . . , the orange fading into   Color Naming
the red and the grey into the blue,

IX.   I don't see anything" [rather quick   Failure
reaction]. [Shakes head.]

X.   [Shakes head] "I don't see anything."   Failure

Time 5:46 P.M.

Note: Card III was seen as figures cut out of paper and set off against a white surface. The patient conveyed the impression that she saw more in the cards when previously tested by Dr. Verena Gebhart. She also remarked that in a previous session she did respond to the last card, but she felt her response was silly and therefore did not want to repeat it. As regards the test as a whole, the patient began to wonder whether the responses she gave in the previous sessions had been thought over carefully enough. She could give no definite answer to the examiner's question as to whether this time she felt more inhibited than during the previous testings. She did say, however, that this time she felt differently than in the previous sessions.

Summary of Scores for Protocols A, B, and C

	A	B	C
Total time, minutes	11	19	22
Time per response, seconds	66	63	120
Number of responses	10 (2) *	18 (7) *	11 (3) *
Failures	1	0	3

* Figures in parentheses refer to the number of responses on the last three cards [Editor].

Summary of Scores for Protocols A, B, and C (Continued)

Location	A	B	C		Determinants	A	B	C
$W+$	6	4	4		$F+$	5	6	6
$W-$	2	8	0		$F-$	2	6	4
Ws	0	0	1		M	1	1	1
D	2	5	3		FCh	0	1	0
Dd	0	1	3		ChF	1	2	0
					ChF, CF	1	2	0
	10	18	11		CF	0	0	0
						10	18	11

Content	A	B	C		Miscellaneous	A	B	C
A	8	9	8		Popular	6	5	5
H	1	1	1		Color naming	0	0	1
At	0	3	1		Description	1	0	0
Pl	0	1	0		Symmetry	0	1	0
N	1	1	0					
$Geo.$	0	1	1					
$Obj.$	0	2	0					
	10	18	11					

Quotients and Percentages	A	B	C
Experience balance	1:1	1:2	1:0
$F+\%$	71	50	60
$F\%$	70	67	91
$A\%$	80	50	73

Before we go into the interpretation of the three Rorschach records, a few things should be mentioned. The first protocol was obtained on the very first day of examination and treatment, i.e., immediately after the suicidal attempt, and in a state of depression. Protocols B and C originate from one and two months later respectively, and were taken while the patient was under treatment; they were obtained after a marked improvement in the patient's clinical condition had taken place. During the interval between the second and third testing, there was hardly any change in the clinical picture.

Our discussion of the test material will be oriented primarily toward a comparative analysis of the three records. This analysis is not planned to be exhaustive; we shall merely demonstrate with a few examples of how such a comparative analysis may be done. As background for the analysis it is pertinent to remember that the first and second protocols were taken by a female examiner whereas the third record was obtained by a male examiner.

Setting aside the first record produced while in a state of depression, we note that when the sex of the examiner differs from that of the subject the total number of responses goes down markedly and the number of responses on the last three cards diminishes to the extent of becoming suggestive of color shock. This finding is at variance with the norms at our institution based on a large number of cases. According to these data, the number of responses is lower when examiner and subject are of the same sex than when the sex differs. Particularly on the last three cards an increase in responses is to be expected. We have then a deviation from the norm here which, by itself, is already indicative of some disturbance in the patient regarding her relation to men.

Considering the content of the Rorschach responses, it is of interest to note that certain content categories tend to reoccur from record to record on cards different from the ones on which they occurred previously. One could, indeed, speak of certain individual content categories as having a tendency to shift from one card to another. Other contents, again, seem to be fixed to certain cards. The shifting of some contents as well as the card-bound behavior of others are probably controlled in part, and in part only, by qualities of the particular ink blot; partly they appear also to be influenced by psychological factors. In the case of our patient, however, the role of the psychological factors cannot be readily investigated and demonstrated. Therefore, in this paper we have to content ourselves with merely mentioning the above phenomena as ones which deserve attention in the longitudinal study of Rorschach protocols.

Now let us discuss the individual content categories as they occur in the records of our patient. There is one human-movement response in each of the three protocols (on card III). Comparison of the verbal formulations of these responses reveals that: (a) in the first and second protocols, where patient and examiner were of the same sex, the response is in terms of two figures, whereas in the third record, where patient and examiner were of different sexes, the response comprises one figure only; (b) in records A and B the patient speaks of "persons," whereas in record C she calls the figure "a human being." These differences, which could hardly be attributed to chance, found their parallels in some of the patient's animal responses. In the second protocol she saw two caterpillars on card X; in the third record a similar response was given to card VIII, but only one caterpillar was seen. To card VII both record A and record B contain the response of two Mickey-Mice; in record C, however, there is only one Mickey-Mouse and even this one is seen as running away. There is one response that does not fall in line with the aforementioned pattern: on card VIII, the two sea lions of the first protocol diminish to one already in the second record. Then, in the third record, the sea lion turns into a polar bear.

Also interesting is the disappearance of the "crystal" response in the last record after having occurred in both of the two preceding protocols. Similarly, all shading and color responses vanish in the third record; instead, a space response, not present in record A or B, makes its appearance in record C. The number of whole responses is lowest in the last protocol, i.e., even lower than in the first record which was produced in a state of depression. Furthermore, not until record C does a tendency towards small detail responses become clearly manifest. The first protocol does not contain any Dd responses at all; the second has one, and the third, in spite of a decrease in the number of responses as compared to record B, shows as many as three small detail responses. Finally, it merits notice that responses the content of which would fall under the category of inanimate objects appear in the second protocol only.

In order to gain more insight into the inner dynamics of the changes that occurred from one record to the other, one should also consider the patient's failure in responding to some of the cards. In record B, which was produced in a state of marked clinical improvement, there were no failures. Interestingly enough, in record C which, too, originates from a period characterized by improvement but was obtained by a male examiner, the patient failed to respond to as many as three of the cards. It is of particular interest to scrutinize the responses given in previous sessions to cards to which she failed to respond at the third testing. One may thus state that the patient displayed in her interpretations more freedom and spontaneity when the examiner was of the same sex, and that she experienced her task as different and more difficult when tested by a person of the opposite sex.

The question may be raised whether the differences between the records B and C, and in particular the signs of disturbance in record C, were not merely the result of the patient's trust and confidence in the first examiner who also was her therapist, and her unfamiliarity with the second examiner. The role of the factor of familiarity or unfamiliarity with the tester can hardly be doubted. It is to be emphasized, however, that to a certain extent the response patterns considered by us as the salient features of protocols obtained under same-sex conditions already made their appearance in the first record, i.e., before a relationship of trust and confidence had time to develop. We are referring here primarily to those human and animal responses discussed above which were featuring two figures each. These response patterns underwent significant modification in the third record where patient and tester were of different sexes. Thus it seems we are dealing here with a factor that is sex-determined.

This finding undoubtedly has not one but several possible diagnostic meanings. It is entirely conceivable, for instance, that because of her previous sexual experiences the patient is so inhibited in her associations with men that she no longer can conceive of a free interaction between a man and a woman and, consequently, tends to withdraw into herself. Thus, when confronted with a male examiner, she selectively perceives *one human creature* on the Rorschach, instead of seeing *people* in relationship and interaction with each other. Such an explanation of the dynamics would imply that the patient's Rorschach protocols are primarily determined by her life style and by specific past experiences. One may, however, go one step further and postulate behind both her Rorschach responses given to a male examiner and her deviant, promiscuous social conduct the same source, namely, a deep-seated disturbance in her relation to men. This, again, may have been brought about by past experiences, especially by the patient's relationship to her father.

The Rorschach data by themselves will hardly enable one to decide in such a case which one of the several possible assumptions regarding the underlying dynamics is correct. The test findings will, however, be of invaluable service in pinpointing the crucial problem area which then can be probed into and clarified in the course of psychotherapy. Moreover, there is evidence that the Rorschach is apt to foster insight into problems that remain undisclosed for a considerable length of time even in intensive psychotherapy. The present case is a good example of how extremely difficult it is to penetrate by means of therapeutic interviews the inner layers of personality which hold the answers to questions regarding the underlying dynamics: psychotherapy of almost a year's duration has not yet succeeded in clarifying the psychodynamics of the patient's pathology. It has been revealed in the course of treatment that the patient believes herself to be suffering from a constitutionally determined disturbance which has led to her inability to become attached to a man for a substantial length of time. She is fully aware of her promiscuous tendencies and sees them as a consequence of her inability to establish genuine emotional relationships with men. A psychological explanation of her conduct and her disturbance in the interpersonal sphere could so far not be formulated.

PART II [4]

To gain a better understanding of the psychological problems involved in the Rorschach test, it is of primary importance to develop some definite and precise concepts. This constitutes an admittedly difficult task. Let us choose, for example, the whole (W) responses. By inspecting Rorschach's own writings (7, p. 54) and those of some of his co-workers, a clear picture of the real meaning of whole responses may be obtained. According to Rorschach, whole responses are related to "richness of associations," "marked availability of visual memory images," "active striving," "goal directed striving toward global comprehension," "tendency to combine details into a meaningful whole." Rorschach already noted that W responses must be further differentiated (7, pp. 37–41). In keeping with these suggestions as well as with Furrer's research (3), we currently classify the whole responses in the following way:

[4] The major part of the remainder of this chapter has been reprinted (revised and translated) from R. Kuhn, Grundlegende statistische und psychologische Aspekte des Rorschachschen Formdeutversuches, *Rorschachiana*, 1953, I, pp. 320–333.

1. Simple whole responses of good form; also called "primary" or "abstract." The entire blot is taken in by one glance and simultaneously interpreted as a whole.

2. Combinatory whole responses of either good or poor form (in Rorschach's sense).

3. Primitive, undifferentiated whole responses (W CF and W ChF).

4. Confabulatory whole responses (DW and DdW).

5. Other whole responses with poor form accuracy ($WF-$).

However, when attempting to apply these categories to the interpretation of an individual record, one may encounter certain difficulties. As an example, we might review the case of a hypomanic psychopath, who is an inventor, confidence man, and gambler. On the Rorschach he has 23 W out of 39 R. He does indeed show the expected comprehensive memory for visual images, specifically in the form of complex planning. Although his hypomanic temperament may be regarded as a form of lively activity, it would hardly be appropriate to speak here of goal-directed striving toward global comprehension since he lives merely for the moment at hand, displaying the most amazing skill in forgetting the burdensome problems of his swindler's career. Thus, he manages to sleep undisturbed despite his heavy debts and the constant threat of imprisonment for fraud. In trying to apply to this case the psychological meaning of combination of details into a whole, it turns out that this interpretation fits the builder and inventor aspects of his behavior very well, but fails in characterizing the swindler, who is completely incapable of relating and integrating his various activities. Still the inventor and swindler are united in this one person. Considering the distribution of his whole responses into 14 primitive undifferentiated W, 2 $W-$, 6 simple W, and 1 combinatory $W+$, one cannot help but wonder why his pathological lying is not expressed in the form of confabulatory responses.

Inspection of carefully examined and clinically thoroughly studied cases, such as the one briefly referred to above, reveals many unsolved problems concerning the interpretation of whole responses on the Rorschach. Although there is a good deal of validity in the standard interpretations of whole responses, our knowledge in this area is too schematic, and conceptually insufficiently clarified. Different, possibly more crucial, factors might well be obscured by our traditional categories and interpretations.

Any theory concerned with "wholes and parts," and this is what we are dealing with here, may be readily conceived of in terms of Plato's and Aristotle's ancient differentiation between "pan" versus "holon," "compositum" versus "totum," or the "sum" versus the "configuration." So far, the most significant contribution to these problems has been made by Husserl, who contrasted the sum as "a whole, consisting of independent parts," against the "genuine whole, consisting of dependent parts" (5, pp. 223–293). This distinction may be illustrated by two responses to card I of the Rorschach test. The response "slag" (scored as $W ChF$) obviously refers to the subject's perceiving a whole with independent parts, similar to the ancient philosophers' notion of the gold nugget. Any given piece of slag may be divided, and each separate part will represent a complete whole just as the original one does. It is quite a different matter when a human face is perceived on that card. The parts of a human face, such as eyes, nose, mouth, can never represent the face in and of themselves; in other words, the whole response of a human face consists of (inter-) dependent parts.

Rather than simplifying, however, the problem of whole responses on the Rorschach test, the foregoing considerations appear at first to introduce further complications. For instance, the DW, DdW, and certain $W F-$ responses are probably much more complex than we thought. This, however, will not be discussed here. It may merely be suggested that once a whole response has been identified in the manner described above, Rorschach's "combination of details into a whole" may be further differentiated. In the case of a whole with clearly independent parts, such as the "slag" response cited earlier, we are dealing with a "striving toward totality" (*Totalisierungsbestreben*), tending to level and to simplify. Such an orientation may express itself in a number of ways, e.g., in the form of a generalized mood. Conversely, W with dependent parts suggest a tendency for structuring, a capacity to apprehend and follow the inherent laws of the given configurations (*Gestalten*). In the case of the inventor discussed above, the predominance of primitive whole responses, i.e., those with independent parts, suggests a tendency to make superficial judgments, sweeping generalizations, and purely visual combinations of parts, but also the ability to perceive parts by themselves—all of which brings us closer to a better understanding of the clinical picture.

There is a close relationship, statistically as well as psychologically, between whole responses with dependent parts, on the one hand, and movement responses, on the other. Both of them are determined not so much by the shape of the blot as by structuring from within.[5] Animated movement does not consist of a piecing together nor of a linking of independent parts. In effect each movement response constitutes a sequence, and thus includes both the movement immediately preceding it, and the one which follows. Goethe, impressed by a dancer's pose in a picture, wrote: "The beautiful fluidity of movement in transition which we admire in such artists has here been arrested for one moment, permitting us to visualize past, present, and future simultaneously and by this very experience we transcend earthy limitations"[6] (4, p. 378). Living motion, then, is also a whole, specifically one consisting of dependent parts, to the extent that its organization in time is experienced as the essential feature. Rorschach's $W M+$ responses may thus be regarded as an intricately organized space-time entity, i.e., a whole consisting of interdependent parts. By reacting with this type of response, the subject reveals a rather specific capacity of the human mind.

To go a step further, the question arises as to the how and why of man's capacity for structuring perceptions in space and time. It appears that a cue to the problem may be found in man's experience of the temporal totality of human existence including death itself. Consistent with this reasoning is the increase of $W M + H$ responses during adolescence, a period when thoughts concerned with death seem to be quite common. Furthermore, there is some evidence that immediately following an encounter with death, children tend to produce many $W M + H$.[7] To be sure, the awareness of the finality of life may manifest itself in more than one way. For instance, profound inner and/or outer restlessness and discomfort may occur. In such cases, the production of $W M + H$ responses would be correspondingly reduced.

To throw further light upon this complex issue, it might be helpful to recall Rorschach's original definititon of movement responses. According to Rorschach, as we know, a scoring of M is acceptable only if the movement is not just "associated," "seen," or "demonstrated"; rather it must be "sensed" (*erfühlt*) by the subject (7, pp. 14–25). This was precisely the reason why Rorschach limited the use of the M score to responses involving humans and just those animals which are perceived in humanlike motion. It would only confuse matters if this

---

[5] These ideas were developed by A. Weber in "Ueber Bewegungsdeutungen," lecture given at meetings of Zurich Psychiatric Association, Summer 1941.

[6] Editor's translation.

[7] Personal communications by A. Friedman and A. Weber.

definition of Rorschach's were ignored. Rorschach's "kinesthetic perception" occurs when the overt manifestation of a kinesthetic impulse is inhibited, a state of affairs for which Binswanger coined the felicitous expression "taming" (*Bändigung*) (2, p. 24). The amount of active demonstrating made by a subject is therefore inversely related to the *M* quality of his interpretations; in extreme cases demonstrating or describing might actually replace the process of interpreting (1, p. 45 ff.). The restraining impact of fright or surprise upon spontaneous mobility is a common observation. It was left to Rorschach's genius, however, to highlight the phenomenon that during a state of being stunned or tamed, movement impulses set the perceptual world into motion, as it were; hence, the movement responses on the test. On the basis of these considerations, the relationship between *M* and creativity (*schöpferische Gestaltungskraft*) may be derived without difficulty, since "creating" (*gestalten*) actually means "bringing to life." Of course, this should not imply the idea that initially we are surrounded by dead objects, which are later set in motion by us through some kind of mysterious "psychic energy." Rather, the creative person at first glance perceives his environment as animated and moving. This experience he can direct either into artistic endeavor or into esthetic enjoyment. Such creativity is revealed by genuine movement responses on the Rorschach. The *M* responses do not by themselves, of course, provide a cue whether this form of creativity leads to artistic productivity or merely suggests the capacity for esthetic enjoyment. An interesting sidelight of the above considerations is the observation that people who produce *W M*+ responses may under the impact of grief display increased creative activity. We cannot go into all the complicated ways which bring this about, and which may contribute to a person's awareness of the finiteness and totality of human existence. This awareness, in turn, has an inhibiting effect on free spontaneity. Such a person will not react with agitated unrest to experiences of the transitoriness of life. Some one who would react in that restless manner deprives himself of the possibility of perceiving the world in motion, and would, therefore, not see movement on the Rorschach plates.

Furthermore, a way of life which is governed by awareness of the finiteness and totality of human existence is also determined by developmental factors. If a subject with several genuine *W M*+ *H* responses on the test reports a happy childhood and gratitude to his parents for the many pleasant experiences provided for him, indicating that because of this he can meet any crisis with inner strength and comfort, he is in effect telling us of the high value he places on the past and on the sequential aspects of his existence. Such a value system appears to be closely related to $W M + H$ responses. Conversely, this kind of historic emphasis with respect to a person's life pattern (*Daseinsform*) may also give rise to neurotic developments. This observation is well in accord with the frequently voiced hypothesis regarding the intimate link between M responses and unconscious forces.

These examples were given to demonstrate the method here suggested for the interpretation of Rorschach protocols. It is in a true sense a psychological method. Its aim is to give an adequate description of experiences and their structural patterns, which, going beyond the experiences themselves, reveal the hidden interrelationships of these experiences. Such a method furthers the formulation of clear-cut concepts. It relies, on the one hand, on experience analysis (*Erlebnisanalyse*) and, on the other hand, on empirically established material. A single case may be studied by comparing the test findings with psychological material that has been obtained from other sources. This cross validation results in an increasingly accurate personality picture of the individual. By studying a concrete case through such analysis, it becomes apparent how much closer we get to an understanding of the psychological foundations of the Rorschach test by this approach rather than by that of theoretical speculations, particularly since the latter involve coming to grips with some of the most complex philosophical writings. Nevertheless, the meaningful integration of statistical and psychological methods in Rorschach research ultimately depends on just such philosophical considerations. This was illustrated by our examples. As Rorschach had already observed, the M responses correlate positively with $W+$ responses (7, p. 60). Although admittedly very incomplete, our attempts at elucidating the psychological significance of these two Rorschach factors make their statistical relationship appear plausible.

At this point it seems appropriate to take up Rorschach's usage of the term "introversion," which he closely relates to the M factor. This is a difficult task since Rorschach did not succeed in defining the concept unequivocally. A comparison of his discussions of this concept as given in different places reveals a rather vague, if not contradictory, picture. In addition to *Psychodiagnostics*, one should consult Rorschach's other publications, such as his article on reflex hallucinations (8) and his studies on the behavior of sects (9). One thing becomes fairly certain: Rorschach's concept of introversion has something to do with "inner life," "inner creativity," and an "orientation of interest toward intrapsychic life rather than the outer world" (7, p. 60 ff.). Furthermore, Rorschach does not conceive of introversion as a fixed state, but rather as a highly dynamic process. The latter point is brought out more specifically in his construct "experience type," where introversion is described as a shifting from the outer world to the inner, and "extratension," described as the reverse (7, pp. 69–83).

In line with the above discussion, the problem of introversion in the Rorschach test perhaps may be further clarified. If we follow Rorschach's ideas regarding the relationship between introversion and M responses, then introversion must also be related to the holistic longitudinal aspects in a person's existence. An interpretation of existence along these lines cannot depend, however, on merely traditional, inadequately understood "signs," nor on toying with arbitrary notions and vague concepts; in short, it cannot spring from commonplace "hearsay" from which so many derive their philosophy of life, or from their "psychodiagnostic" interpretations—with or without benefit of ink blots. Such an approach would obscure the test's intrinsic potential for revealing that aspect of living which cannot be understood in terms of the outer world, but which is concerned with the awareness of one's own existence. With his concept of introversion Rorschach attempted the difficult task of describing this particular aspect of human existence and thereby probably made his primary, most unique contribution. Only those individuals, however, will be able to follow Rorschach here who in their own life are capable of perceiving it in perspective and perhaps even of realizing the potentialities of their personal existence. In other words, the problems of the Rorschach test are closely linked with the existential problems of the person who does the testing and interpreting. Again and again the "hearsay" of everyday life tends to obscure and disguise the deeper awareness of one's own existence as manifested in the test. It is our responsibility to safeguard and, if possible, to advance further this kind of awareness, which has provided the access to Rorschach's most fundamental discoveries. This requires constant vigilance on the part of all serious Rorschach workers, who are called upon to join in the fight against the ever-present obfuscations of convenient, commonplace talk.

In conclusion, a further example may illustrate our approach to the interpretation of M responses. A young thief's Rorschach protocol of 21 responses shows 5 $W+$, no $W-$, no DW. The experience type is 4 $M: OC$. The $F+$ is 87%, and the animal percentage is 57. The content of the M responses is as follows: card II–(1) "Two clowns"; card III–(1) "Again two men"; card X–(2) "Here two human figures with heads" [red and grey]; card X–(3) "Here again, shaking hands" [central blue]. In order to arrive at a psychological interpretation of these M responses, the subject must be further questioned. Then it turns out, that the responses should actually read: card II–(1) "Two clowns with white, powdered faces, fooling around together"; card X–(2) "Two knights in iron helmets, their faces covered by visors, arms drawn up, jousting together"; card III–(1) "Two men, talking to each other, carrying two bags or baskets in their hands"; or, "Two women, who won't have anything to do with the skeleton, making a rejecting gesture."

Each of these three M responses are closely related to experiences and fantasies which are highly significant to the subject's "inner" life history. The youth has a severe corpse phobia. He is chiefly afraid of the corpse's pallor. In this connection there is pronounced fear of death. He tries to hide his anxiety from himself and from others through overt demonstrations of his masculine prowess in sports, and also through his fantasies. For instance, he imagines that he and the other young fellows of his village, masquerading in white sheets, will stage a "ghost patrol" or "wild chase" on horseback at night. Thus, by assuming the role of death, he is trying to frighten others. The white-faced clowns have the physiognomy of corpses; they are disguised, one cannot tell who or what they are. The helmeted knights are also fantasied as masked men, playing a game of life and death, similar to the game our subject plays in his sports contests and in individual fights. His fantasies always center around gaining or losing, the highest stake being life itself. His thefts too are such longitudinally multidetermined "games," which, psychiatrically speaking, have to be viewed as neurotic behavior.

Even from these brief sketches, it should become apparent how closely the M responses are related clinically to unconscious material and, psychologically, to considerations of time perspective, particularly to the problem of finality of life which confronts every human being in one form or another. It is this struggle with his fate that makes man escape into illness or seek relief from anxiety in conventional life patterns, unless he accepts the alternative of facing the impenetrable forces of existence and thus attains maturity and independence.

BIBLIOGRAPHY

1. Binder, H.   Die Helldunkeldeutungen im psychodiagnostischen Experiment von Rorschach. *Schweiz. Arch. Neurol. Psychiat.*, 1932–1933, **30**, 1–67, 233–286. Reprinted, Bern: Huber, 1959.
2. Binswanger, L., Der Fall Juerg Zuend. *Schweiz. Arch. Neurol. Psychiat.*, 1947, **58**, 1–43.
3. Furrer, A.   *Der Auffassungsvorgang beim Rorschach'schen psychodiagnostischen Versuch.* Zurich: Buchdruckerei zur Alten Universität, 1930.
4. Goethe, J. W.   Der Tänzerin Grab. *Collected works. Vol. 10.* Leipzig: Inselverlag.
5. Husserl, E.   *Logische Untersuchungen. Vol. 2.* Halle: Niemeyer, 1913, part 1.
6. Kuhn, R.   *Maskendeutungen im Rorschach'schen Formdeutversuch.* Basel: S. Karger, 1954.
7. Rorschach, H.   *Psychodiagnostik.* Bern: Huber, 1937, 3rd ed.
8. Rorschach, H.   Ueber Reflexhalluzinationen. *Z. ges. Neur. Psychiat.*, 1912, **13**, 357–400.
9. Rorschach, H.   Zwei schweizerische Sektenstifter. *Imago*, 1927, **13**, Sonderheft, 395–441 (posthumous).

*Each thinker, however, has dominant habits
of attention; and these practically elect from
among the various worlds some one to be
for him the world of ultimate realities.*

WILLIAM JAMES

12 | by Lois and Gardner Murphy

HERMANN RORSCHACH

AND PERSONALITY RESEARCH

I

The intimate relation between Hermann Rorschach's personality and the test which bears his name has often been forgotten in our attempt to devise a modern comprehensive test program based upon the utilization of ink blots. Even in the case of Alfred Binet's ingenious development of intelligence tests, much depends upon Binet's time, place, and culture, and much upon his own personality; but in the fifty years which have passed since his first tests, psychometrics has become almost an impersonal endeavor, a general branch of psychological science. Nothing of the sort has yet occurred in the domain of personality testing. The unique genius of Murray (12) is evident in the Thematic Apperception Test; the Picture Frustration Test (15) eloquently bespeaks some of Saul Rosenzweig's insights; the Draw-A-Person of Karen Machover (11), the Lowenfeld Mosaic (10), and the Szondi (17) tests are still essentially "sonnets" or "essays" in the literary style of individual psychologists. The Rorschach, because of its power, range, depth, and subtlety is to a still greater degree an expression of the man who made it.

This point can easily be forgotten, as one attempts to square Rorschach findings with those from psychoanalysis. For Rorschach, though an analyst, was working primarily within the European conception of the biological and psychological structure of personality as it obtained in the scientific and literary expressions of the 19th century, as Henri Ellenberger's beautiful little biographical sketch (4) makes clear. Rorschach had been preoccupied through all his medical training and his early years of institutional and private practice with problems of personality dynamics which had been widely recognized by philosophers and medical men long before the dawn of psychoanalysis; he was concerned as much with the deeper creative aspects of personality as with those of immediate clinical import. He thought of himself as striving to cut through a forest of difficulties to the achievement of a brief, yet subtle representation of personality structure, as given to a very large degree by constitutionally grounded trends of development. At the same time he saw, as few were capable of seeing in his day, that this biological continuity is a biosocial continuity as well, and that the cultural world of the individual makes its permanent mark upon the developmental pattern. He had, then, a biosocial definition of personality in which psychoanalytic dynamics was one, but only one, of a number of contributing viewpoints.

It is also important to remember that he worked alone, having few friends or colleagues, and almost no intellectual stimulation in the world in which he moved. He had indeed a few intimate professional friends, such as Dr. Emil Oberholzer, who worked on Rorschach's "posthumous case" and presented it to the world, and who made himself for many years the primary avenue of information concerning the nature of Rorschach's life and work. There were his students, especially Dr. Behn, from whom Rorschach derived much inspiration, essentially along lines which he had himself laid down, but had not had the capacity to follow through until this response of a junior colleague gave him inspiration and direction. With these notable exceptions, Rorschach lived his brief life largely in his own intellectual world, deriving his inspiration from books and, above all, from reflection. How utterly out of line he was with the cultural atmosphere of the day is shown by the fact that almost no copies of the book were sold in the first few years, the publisher having bitterly reproached himself for taking on such a hopeless venture, and Rorschach in his last months having no comfort whatever from the sense of any intellectual response to his work. The impact of Rorschach's own personality is realized in such a context to be a major factor in the unique way in which unstructured visual materials were first used as personality test materials, a full fifteen years or more before Sanford (16) and others realized the possibilities of these unstructured materials for what came soon to be called "projective testing" (5).

This solitary position of Rorschach and the fact that he saw so much more than his contemporaries will serve in some degree to explain the extreme tentativeness and modesty of his formulations. He had something very concrete to offer, knowing that it was the concrete that might possibly win some ultimate acceptance and that he could not in any sense enforce his broad philosophical scheme upon his contemporaries.

II

This situation, together with his biosocial orientation, made him eager to make clear at every point what the specific determining circumstances of the test response might be. Thus, some aspects of the test are most likely to vary in response to specific influences, for instance, the conscious effort of the individual who is being tested. Rorschach (14) noted that many W imply affect and volition beside associative engrams, i.e., will; this might be a conscious or an unconscious will to produce.[1] W can be increased only when conscious willing is abetted by individual dispositional tendency (14, p. 66). One could hardly ask for a more comprehensive conception of the way in which constitutional factors, long-range developmental factors, and immediate situational factors interact in the production of a response. In contrast, he noted responses over which the will had little control. For example, the reduction of the animal per cent, the increase of originals and of human movements could not be effected by an effort of the will, unless the dispositional tendency towards such pattern of responses was already present. On the other hand, the $F+\%$ and the clarity of perceptions and of associative processes, the ability to control and discipline the logical function (sequence and apperceptive type), and the ability to form stereotyped associative sets (revealed in animal per cent) did respond, he noted, to conscious volition (14, p. 66 ff.). Here again, however, one is immediately reminded of "wide individual variations," the fact that, even in their most explicit and thoroughly understood forms, the general principles of personality development did not yet suffice for the specification of the quantitative

[1] For explanation of scoring symbols, see Appendix, pp. 441 ff. [Editor].

variations from person to person. There still remained unexplained "individual variations" (14, p. 66).

From these passages follows a discussion of the general role of learning in the environment as contrasted with constitutional talents; the factors just mentioned show a prominent contribution from learning, while percentages of whole, movement, or original responses are mainly the expression of abilities inherent in the disposition of the individual. Conscious effort may indeed produce modifications in percentages of these attributes primarily conceived to be inborn, yet the effect of effort or set, although at first sight appearing to be successful, may actually injure the function which is being expressed. Human movement, for example, may be increased, but at the expense of injury to the response, the reason lying simply in the fact that it is unconscious emotional energy rather than conscious effort that is normally expressed through these responses (14, p. 65).

Similarly, the effort to "improve" performance, such as the tendency to good form, may indeed produce a measurable increase in $F+\%$, but will at the same time produce a reduction in human movement and whole responses, and a loss of quality in the apperception type. Together with this will go an increase in the number of animal responses and a decrease in original and color responses, again with "large individual variations" (14, p. 66). In other words, Rorschach observed that changes in responses in one area involved related or balancing changes in other areas; no dimension could be changed without affecting other dimensions. The intensely empirical character of the work is evident here as elsewhere. This matter of interdependence of personality aspects came generally to be recognized in the 1930's under gestalt-theoretical influence, but, for Rorschach at his time, it was an empirically evident proposition which burst upon him and demanded emphasis. Even with the best sophistication of 1960, we are still bewildered by this conception that nothing can be changed without changing everything else at the same time. It is basically alien to the thought forms which have come down from 17th century mechanics and a 17th century geometry appropriate for its own period, but today are out of line with biological and, especially, with psychosocial modes of analysis. Rorschach's thinking is still far ahead of our contemporary capacity for conceptualization. We have not yet found suitable quantitative techniques for the study of dynamic phenomena which, in this manner, resolutely refuse to display that atomic isolation and simplicity of character which would be so convenient for our traditional modes of quantitative thinking.

Another large area of contemporary psychology concerned with perceptual and cognitive functions to which Rorschach early gave much attention was the factors of temporary mood, set, or attitude, the factors which could be classed neither with sheer constitution, on the one hand, nor past learning, on the other hand. Of course, mood has its own biosocial history, but often it has to be dealt with as it appears, and its effects have to be traced out, even though we may have the gravest difficulties in defining its origins. For Rorschach nothing was more important than to note the difference between stable characteristics in the person and those which varied with mood or attitude, often side by side with consciously directed attention or will, as already noted.

Mood may, for example, exert a prominent effect upon form perception, sequence, human movement, and color (14, p. 93 ff.). Depressed moods typically tend, for example, to improve form perception and to increase rigidity of sequence. At the same time, whole responses may become less frequent and apperception type poorer; variability may decline; there may be fewer originals, but more animal responses; color may disappear altogether and human movement be reduced. In depressed moods, moreover, factors determined by an increase in control of associations are most accentuated. Those factors which depend on emotionally charged energy of associative activity and on freedom of association are reduced. On the other hand, elation and similar moods may likewise be defined in relation to a wide variety of characteristic responses. The moods themselves require analysis and their own vocabulary. There is, for example, a distinction to be made between the manic, the hypomanic, the elated, and a mood of sheer "good humor."

Of special philosophical importance in grasping the nature of personality is Rorschach's conception of variability *within* one's own characteristic mode of response, as well as variability from person to person. The tendency to vary from one's own norm and from one's own way is as basic to personality as is the maintenance of a special position or stance in comparison with other persons. There are different *ranges within which different individuals might vary.* Such variability is related, of course, to the extent of operation of both volition and mood, as already considered. Volition and mood are themselves expressions of varying positions on a curve of variability within one's own characteristic or normal response. Yet each person may vary more in one area of expression than in another, depending to some degree upon the anchorage or limiting effect of constitutional factors, certain capacities being conceived to be more definitely fixed by constitution than others.

III

From all these considerations it is evident that it was very far indeed from Rorschach's thought to believe that a single Rorschach test told the whole story of individual make-up, or that it defined the person's capacity to move in one direction or another from an exhibited norm, or that it revealed in a sort of X-ray fashion the basic constitutional make-up, or that it displayed simply the attitude, set, or learning processes operating within the person; or indeed that it manifested any of the other clichés which have been attributed to the Rorschach test. As we reread his work, what we observe is a thoughtful, imaginative, subtle craftsman, sensitive to human beings, a poet and philosopher concerned with the reaches and depths of individuality, a psychoanalyst, a practical hospital doctor, and a traveler; we also see a man of the world living in a little out-of-the-way institution where he either worked or dreamed as he saw fit, now plodding with difficulty, now bursting forth with seven-league boots, mastering a conception of the richness of human individuality and, in the span of a few years, creating an amazingly subtle, yet incomplete and unsystematic, sketch for the development of a study of the ways in which individuality is reflected in the structuring of semi-structured visual materials.

There are, therefore, two ways of responding to his challenge. One is to revere him, read him, love him, and use him as one would Shakespeare, Goethe, Whitman, or Emerson, adapting him freshly day-to-day to new tasks, and never dreaming of any disloyalty in remaking and passing beyond the instrument which he left to the world. The other is to standardize him, codify him, make him basic, fixed, eternal, hallowed, a foreign body from 1921 stuck in the moving tissues of today's development. Both methods are all too human, and both will certainly continue to be tried. A third possibility would be to develop from his original conception new methods of testing which embody his rich awareness of the dimensions of personality to be tested through visual perception of unstructured forms, utilizing along with his experience that of the years which have followed since the time of his first publication. In doing this, one would regard as the permanent thing about Rorschach's contribution its embodiment of a conception of personality, its empirical spirit, its objective and quantitative aspects integrated with a subtle intuition, and its conception that, through many approaches made at the same time, one may begin, but only begin, to get some glimpse of the total structure of personality. It is by using Rorschach in this tentative way, by studying and applying his conception of human individuality, its levels, its interrelations, its dependence upon culture, the situation, and the mood and will of the individual that the Rorschach worker of today may best enrich the personality conceptions of classroom and clinic. It is not because Rorschach devised a test that his position will remain revered in psychology; it is because his test is the embodiment of a sensitive, exploratory, original view of human individuality, unfinished but capable nevertheless of being measured, the measures interrelated, moment by moment, as the demands of life change. It is because the Rorschach test is the expression of a profound conception of personality that it is important in psychology today.

But the Rorschach is not only a clinical test but also a basic instrument in personality research. The assessment of personality necessitates (a) clear conceptualization of the tendencies within a person and the ways in which they may be interrelated; (b) the development of instruments to detect and, if possible, measure these tendencies and their interrelations. Whether we regard personality as a self-sufficient ordered whole with internal structure which can somehow be tapped by an instrument applied to the periphery, or whether we regard personality as an interaction of organism and environment in which our task is to observe the back-and-forth flow between inner and outer, the first task is to conceptualize what the processes are that can be reached through assessment instruments. This necessitates some sort of working conception of what are meant by personality tendencies and the mode in which such tendencies are interrelated.

In terms of that unique interaction of biological growth and individual learning processes which gives the developmental picture of a person, we seem driven to a conception of *levels*. The following are some of the more influential of the doctrines of levels that have guided modern work upon personality structure:

1. The evolutionary view pictures human individuality as dependent upon a very broad base of biological continuity derived from those common organic processes which we share with all living things, processes which have to do with growth, differentiation, integration, and adaptation. From such a point of view, one retains the older basic

primordial functions along with those which arrive in differentiated form at each new level. There is, for example, a superposition of central nervous functions upon the older biochemical forms of communication within the living system. When the differentiated central nervous system is capable at last of developing symbolic functions, the more primitive reflex functions still remain. There is thus an ever-developing proliferation of new functions superposed upon the old, but never replacing them. This will make especially useful for us Hughlings Jackson's conception that the most *recently arrived* and the most *complex* evolutionary functions are the most *individuated* and the most sensitive and, therefore, the most *vulnerable* to stress or pathology.

2. A somewhat similar conception is that of Heinz Werner (19), who asks us to imagine, in both race history and individual life history, a development from (*a*) a diffuse or global stage through (*b*) a differentiated or individuated stage into (*c*) an integrated stage in which the individuated parts now find new structure. Werner's conception can legitimately be grafted upon the Hughlings Jackson conception as it relates to individual development. It may be applied to each specific system of functions within the individual—perceptual, motivational, motor, etc.—and it may, moreover, be applied to the development of fresh contacts with new features in the environment which we learn to perceive or to cope with; new adjustment processes may be conceived to pass through the same stages from global to individuated to integrated.

3. A third conception, that of Kurt Lewin (9), having much in common both with the Jackson system and the Werner system, uses spatial representation in which life space as a whole undergoes differentiation here and there, until differentiated parts are capable of interacting in a total. But instead of emphasizing the phylogenetic or ontogenetic problems as central issues, it prefers in general an "ahistorical" approach, dealing with short time spans rather than long ones, making it relatively easy to take account of momentary regressions or returns from higher to lower levels and that process of "dedifferentiation" in which there is a loss of the integrated in favor of the individuated (stage 2 noted above), or a loss of the individuated in favor of the earlier global patterns.

All these ways of thinking make it possible for us to regard personality structure more or less in pyramidal terms, as involving a broad base, consisting of the primitive raw stuff of human nature with its phylogenetic built-in basis in organ systems and their ingrained tendencies to respond in specific ways (all this remains as a base while differentiated functions develop), and through the later interaction of these differentiated processes, integrated wholes may be observed.

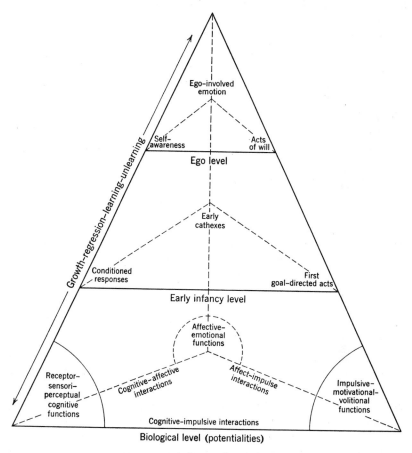

Fig. 12.1. A Personality Schema.

As already noted, the learning process assists in both differentiation and integration, so that the three-level system may be applied as well to learning sequences as to growth sequences; the typical individual history comprises an intimate mingling of growth and learning, or, indeed, a single process from which learning and growth may conveniently be abstracted for analysis. Following Werner, we may likewise conceive of structures within structures, so that different functions, such as form perception, rhythm perception, language, locomotion, can all be conceived to go through their own cycles of development while still remaining very dependent upon one another and upon the basic rhythms of life as a whole. With all its inadequacies, then, the conception of levels gives a schema with both spatial and temporal attributes and very suggestive clues to functional interdependence, which may be used to guide us in developing instruments to make contact with the various functions and their modes of interrelation within the person and within the organism-environment interaction processes which constitute his personality.

Implicit in the doctrine of levels is the conception that every kind of organ can be viewed in developmental terms and that every psychological process likewise undergoes development. It would follow, therefore, that the phenomena of perception, of motivation, or of learning are to be found at all levels in the developmental structure, and that there are, so to speak, horizontal relationships between the various psychological functions at each level. There is, for example, a relation between perception and motivation at the lowest level, and there is likewise a relation of perception and motivation at the highest level. (Fig. 12.1.) If we proceed, therefore, to slice horizontally at a given level, we have a system of interrelationships which will undergo transformation, but not disappear, as we move up the pyramid.

IV

This rough schema may be used as a sort of scaffolding for the preliminary classification and organization of findings about personality. It emphasizes (*a*) levels, and (*b*) the interdependence of functions. What now are the implications for the development of a suitable personality test? It would certainly seem that in any complete study of personality we need at each moment to sample all processes at all levels. We need, for example, to have some knowledge about perceptual, imaginative, memorial, motivational, and volitional phenomena, as they exist in their undifferentiated or primitive form, and also knowledge regarding all these variables as they appear at higher levels. For example, at the adult perceptual level, we need to know the residues of the more primitive perceptual functions, the mode of development of individuated perceptual responses, and the present functioning level of the person in terms of integral perceptual responses.

It will hardly be necessary to explain to the reader of this book that Rorschach's test is redolent with the problem of levels and, likewise, with the problem of interdependence; but a few examples may be useful. The Rorschach test distinguishes between levels two and three, in which the "large detail" is typically a response to a component already analyzed out from its context in what we have called "stage-two behavior," and the integral response often appears in highly structured interpretations ordinarily classed as "wholes." The concept of global or *undifferentiated* response is, of course, not fully developed by the Rorschach method, though some "poor" wholes may give us a suggestion of this, and many color responses representing the flow of affect, with no use for either form or movement, may also come close to the stage-one process. The concept of differentiation and integration is particularly well brought out in the form-color category, and the concept of sequences through the three stages is frequently almost exactly what is involved in some of the succession patterns, such as W to D to d when followed by a new whole at a higher (articulated) level.

It is remarkable that the conception of fundamental personality regions (cognitive, affective, impulsive) and their interrelations should have been so fully developed at a time when perception was generally thought of almost solely in terms of a knowledge function rather than an affective and impulse function. Rorschach understood that perception might give clues to these other psychological dimensions. The phenomena of impulse control and many of the motor phenomena so essential for the understanding of refined adaptation to the environment are not fully grasped in the Rorschach scheme; but he *did* understand that one function could be used as a clue to all others related to it, just as he understood the developmental sequences and hierarchical structure of personality organization. And there can be no doubt that these ways of thinking, built into the Rorschach test, have contributed powerfully, through clinical and research work, to the development of modern personality theory. The Rorschach is the constant and eloquent reminder of *levels* and of *interdependence* in a visible and commanding form too cogent to allow either rejection or evasion.

V

We come now to the question of sampling the tendencies of personality. This is a question that must be answered if a test is to be expected to tap the aspects of an individual's personality in such a way as to give a sound over-all picture. The problem is immensely difficult. If we allow ourselves to tap the residues from, let us say, only three developmental levels, not taking into account the co-existence of separate functions which move at different rates, undergo stoppage and fresh accelerated movement at different times, and even if we allow ourselves only ten different personality functions to be sampled at each level, we shall need at least thirty scores to be derived from one testing instrument. But if the reliability of each score is not unity, and a single test item cannot give us a pure representation of the function, uncontaminated and free from all possibility of misinterpretation, we shall need many more. This is a formidable order. Can we perhaps determine the more important components and leave the rest out of the picture, hoping that by seeing the more important components and concentrating on the relation between them, we may somehow get the major structural outline of the personality? On all these questions of sampling personality functions through tests, clinical and experimental research has been focused from time to time, as in the work of Rapaport (13), Witkin (20), and others; but it can hardly be asserted that we have any test elements with the desired reliability of scoring, or that we understand the interrelations between observed test responses well enough to be able to sample this whole universe of personality dispositions.

This is one of the reasons why there is grave doubt as to the soundness of the many statements we currently hear about a test which is to reveal the "total personality." In terms of sampling of personality attributes, the problem appears to be insoluble. Of course, if it can ever be demonstrated that there really are a few cardinal attributes which pool their contributions in some definable way, it may be possible to derive a fairly good prediction regarding those attributes which depend upon these major components or their most important interactions. But even this more modest objective is very far from realization.

We fall back, therefore, necessarily to another line of defense and ask ourselves whether it is possible, by ignoring developmental levels, to invent devices which will, in fact, sample personality *at the present time.* If we use three test items to tap a function, fifteen responses would give us fairly uncontaminated information about five functions. If we could get twice or three times this number, we might get some rough preliminary picture of those functions which are ready, so to speak, to push themselves forward into our field of observation and have no need to hide from us.

But here we might have a brainstorm and grasp a new possibility. We might contrive methods by which a single response to our procedure will give us information about *several* kinds of things, several levels, several functions, at once. It seems altogether remarkable that, in point of fact, Hermann Rorschach had this brainstorm and grasped this technical point in the logic of personality analysis forty years ago. Just as he grasped the requirement set by the theory of levels and the theory of the interpretation of personal characteristics, Rorschach saw that by using ten cards, allowing multiple response, and scoring in three columns, he could extract an extraordinary amount of sampling information about personality functions and their interrelations. Twenty responses can give enormously more information than twenty items passed or failed on a linear measure of some simple cognitive skill. The strength of the test was chiefly in its applicability for effectively understanding the problem of sampling the many functions which enter into the personality structure. Hand in hand went the understanding that the time pattern, the sequences, the response emerging only at the time of the inquiry, and the ratios of frequency of one kind of response to frequency of another kind of response gave a rich network of facts about interrelationships of function, in that the number of items of information was far greater than the number of responses made.

VI

At the same time, this attempt to do so much involved a weakness in terms of the ultimate understanding of the basic dimensions being measured, by virtue of the very fact that by sampling so much with so little one gets involved in contamination, in problems of low reliabilities which cannot be explained away nor fully understood without cleaner measures of the separate functions. It became evident even in the 1930's that it would be worth while to separate out the various functions which enter into a Rorschach response in terms somewhat different from those which Rorschach had himself conceptualized. One can, for example, empirically analyze movement responses and their relations to other kinds of responses without assuming that movement is a pure or even a fairly safe clue to introversiveness or a rich inner life. One may study movement in its relation to various other Rorschach categories and in relation to many other types of clinically significant functions, as known through other approaches (see Chapter 9). In the same way, one may disentangle for study in the perception laboratory a great many of the components formulated by Rorschach, conceptualizing them or factoring them, ad lib.

The next step beyond this series of manipulations carried out with responses to the original Rorschach cards, or the Behn (23), Harrower (6), or Levy (21) or other (3, 22, 24) series of cards, is to invent one's own semistructured visual materials, deliberately choosing the materials so as to get a relatively simple or even, if possible, one-dimensional range of responses. This would permit measurement in the sense in which a psychometric examination involves measurement, and, at an ideal level, it might permit a disentangling of basic personality dimensions comparable to the disentangling involved in the Thurstone Primary Mental Abilities Test (18) as an approach to basic capacities.[2]

It is not a function of this chapter to describe the directions in which such investigations may move. It is evident by now that the original Rorschach test was successful largely because, in its time and place, it did an extraordinary variety of rich, interesting, challenging, and valuable things for clinicians, some of which they were ready to do and some of which they only learned to do a decade or more after Rorschach's death. His wisdom and imaginativeness established a high level which other workers have seldom again climbed. As in so many brilliant creative expressions of genius, much was left in poorly defined form. A foothold was nevertheless provided for any great successor to climb to a new height.

We might, in a certain sense, lament the fact that the Rorschach method became a standard procedure some 25 years ago, just as one might regret that the Stanford-Binet and later the Wechsler became standard, standardizing the imperfections along with the positive contributions. Those refinements which preserve what Rorschach was aiming to do, those improvements which make it possible to assess the

---

[2] Wayne H. Holtzman (7), for example, has extended the test so that there are 40 ink blots, indeed two parallel forms each using 40 ink blots, sacrificing number of responses and certain sequential variables in order to gain greater psychometric precision with regard to all the remaining variables. This is done by having the subject give one, and only one, response per card. Results are promising with respect to the preservation of the original meaning of the variables, at the same time increasing the reliability to about .90.

dimensions which he saw in personality and to do a more consistent and reliable job, will certainly be used more and more in the next decade or two, and all this is to be welcomed. What is, however, to be feared is that the technical skills may overwhelm and becloud the original vision. We have been surfeited in the last decade by refinements aimed primarily at doing highly specialized jobs with highly specialized groups of patients for highly specialized purposes. The basic conception of a way of sampling the rich fluid and growing structures of personality can hardly be said to have benefited by this. Seldom has the Rorschach test been used as a way of throwing light upon the fundamental conceptualization of personality. Seldom has any well-thought-out theory of personality been systematically tested by the use of Rorschach material. *Seldom, indeed, has the Rorschach been used as a personality research instrument in the serious sense.*

This seems altogether extraordinary. There has never been a time in the history of psychology when perception research has been as eager, as vivid, as far-ranging as it has in the period since World War II. If one thinks of the amazing developments from Innsbruck with reference to form perception (8), the extraordinary development and influence of the work of Ames (2), the rich proliferation of understanding with regard to the biology of perception, especially the cortical projection functions involved in visual perceiving, or if one looks at the developmental studies having to do with animal and human perceptual functions at various stages and in various kinds of environments, or at the interrelations between perception, on the one hand, and motor and affective phenomena, on the other hand—as shown in sensory-tonic theory (19), in need theory, or in any of the thirteen major theories of perception reviewed in the recent book by Allport (1)—one is amazed to see the Rorschach work progress like a side stream, unaware of the mighty current of a new river flowing nearby. Here and there, as reported in some of the other chapters of this book, one may note comparisons of Rorschach functions with those of perceptual functions derived by other methods, particularly those of the laboratory. For the most part, however, the clinicians appear to go on refining their procedures rather than seeing the broader implications of the study of perception for the understanding of personality. The younger generation of clinicians who know their clinical as well as their experimental methodology may manage to prepare the great canal which will enable these streams to meet, and we shall have a psychology of perception which is big enough to do the huge job waiting to be done.

While they are doing this, they will add to our knowledge about the relations of perception to personality structure. For example, whether *perception*, rich as it is, *is* a big enough portion of the individual to reveal what personality assessment calls for is still not clear. It is conceivable that from the Rorschach a projective test can gradually be made, not too long nor too complex for everyday clinical practice, which will give us purified representations of the various personality dimensions which can be caught by such a procedure, and which, at the same time, will give a picture of memory and imagination, volition and impulse control, values and value conflicts, rhythms, styles, vortices and cadences, aspirations and despairs, consummations and frustrations, broad enough to pass reasonably as a picture of a person. The Rorschach test is still the best effort we have in this direction.

BIBLIOGRAPHY

1. Allport, F. H. *Theories of perception and the concept of structure.* New York: John Wiley, 1955.
2. Ames, A. *An interpretive manual for the demonstrations in the Psychology Research Center, Princeton University.* Princeton: Princeton University Press, 1955.
3. Barron, F. Threshold for the perception of human movement in inkblots. *J. consult. Psychol.*, 1955, 19, 33–38.
4. Ellenberger, H. The life and work of Hermann Rorschach (1844–1922). *Bull. Menn. Clin.*, 1954, 18, 173–219.
5. Frank, L. K. Projective methods for the study of personality. *J. Psychol.*, 1939, 8, 389–413.
6. Harrower, M. R. (Harrower-Erickson), and Steiner, M. E. *A manual for psychodiagnostic inkblots.* (A series parallel to the Rorschach blots, with accompanying psychodiagnostic inkblots.) New York: Grune and Stratton, 1945.
7. Holtzman, W. H. Objective scoring of projective techniques. In: Bass, B. M., and Berg, I. A. (eds.), *Objective approaches to personality assessment.* Princeton: D. Van Nostrand Co., 1959.
8. Kohler, I. Experiments with prolonged optical distortions. *Proc. XIV intern. Cong. Psychol.*, Montreal, June 1954. Amsterdam: North Holland Publ. Co., 1955.
9. Lewin, K. *A dynamic theory of personality.* New York: McGraw-Hill, 1935.
10. Lowenfeld, M. *The Lowenfeld Mosaic Test.* London: Newman Neame, 1954.
11. Machover, K. A. *Personality projection in the drawing of the human figure: a method of personality investigation.* Springfield: C. C. Thomas, 1949.

12. Murray, H. A. *Explorations in personality.* New York: Oxford, 1938.
13. Rapaport, D., Gill, M., and Schafer, R. *Diagnostic psychological testing* (two volumes). Chicago: Year Book Publishers, 1945.
14. Rorschach, H. *Psychodiagnostics,* 4th ed. New York: Grune and Stratton, 1949.
15. Rosenzweig, S. A test for types of reaction to frustration. *Amer. J. Orthopsychiat.,* 1935, **4,** 395–403.
16. Sanford, R. N. The effects of abstinence from food upon imaginal processes: a preliminary experiment. *J. Psychol.,* 1936, **2,** 129–136.
17. Szondi, L. *Experimental diagnostics of drives.* New York: Grune and Stratton, 1952.
18. Thurstone, L. L. Primary mental abilities. *Psychomet. Monogr.,* No. 1, 1938.
19. Werner, H. *Comparative psychology of mental development* (rev. ed.). Chicago: Follett, 1948.
20. Witkin, H. A., et al. *Personality through perception.* New York: Harper, 1954.
21. Zubin, J., and Young, K. M. *Manual of projective and cognate techniques.* Madison: College Typing Co., 1948 (Levy blots).
22. Zulliger, H. *Der Diapositiv-Z-Test. Ein Verfahren zur psychologischen Untersuchung von Gruppen.* Bern: Hans Huber, 1948.
23. Zulliger, H. *Der Behn-Rorschach Test.* Vol. I—text, Vol. II—tables. Bern: Hans Huber, 1952.
24. Zulliger, H. *Der Tafeln Z-Test. Ein abgekürztes Rorschach-Verfahren für individuelle psychologische Prüfungen.* Bern: Hans Huber, 1954.

PROBLEMS
OF
SCIENTIFIC
APPRAISAL

13 | by Jules D. Holzberg

RELIABILITY

RE-EXAMINED

Assessing Rorschach reliability is a long-standing problem that has been perplexing and challenging to the clinician as much as to the experimentalist. In spite of much serious research directed toward determining the reliability of the Rorschach, the problem is by no means resolved, although it is the author's conviction that significant strides are being made in moving toward a resolution. It is a strange irony that the most significant contributions to the resolution of this problem have not emerged from research systematically designed to test the reliability of the Rorschach, but rather from research designed for other purposes, particularly validational studies.

There exist wide divergences in attitudes among psychologists toward the problem of Rorschach reliability. To some clinicians as well as to the bulk of experimental psychologists, the insistence is that the Rorschach must be considered like every other method of personality assessment and, therefore, must meet the *same* criteria of reliability according to traditional methods that are imposed on other instruments. A second group of psychologists, and they represent a fairly substantial number, insist that the problem of assessing reliability of the Rorschach is quite inappropriate for the purposes for which the Rorschach is being used in clinical practice and research. Thus, Symonds (41) has stressed that the concept of reliability loses importance when the purpose of the technique of personality assessment is not so much to measure as it is to describe. Vernon (45), in a similar vein, argues that the Rorschach is analogous to a play technique in that it is not a test in the usual sense of the word but a means of obtaining insight into the personality. Some have stressed that the variable errors which psychometric reliability disregards may, from the point of view of personality diagnosis, be of great significance interpretively (30, 31). Thus, from this vantage point, the issue of reliability is not a major concern.

A third attitude would ignore reliability *per se* and would stress validity of the Rorschach as the major concern, on the assumption that validity implies the presence of fundamental reliability. This position has been stressed by Piotrowski (33) who stated, ". . . the Rorschach method can be subjected to measures of reliability only after its validity has been established." McClelland (27) has emphasized that reliability has been overstressed in American psychology. His orientation is that the culture out of which American psychology has grown and developed is one which has emphasized traits such as regularity and dependability in the personality of its individuals, and this cultural emphasis has led to the stress in psychology on the concept of reliability of psychological instruments. He too would prefer to see reliability pursued through validational research. This emphasis on the search for evidence of validity as *prima facie* evidence of reliability has been challenged by Hertz (13). She states that the validity of an instrument may be greater than its reliability and observes that a high degree of validity may be demonstrated by comparing Rorschach interpretations of an individual with outside clinical data, yet the reliability of these interpretations when compared with each other may not be high because different aspects of the personality may be emphasized by different interpretations.

A fourth attitude, and one with which the author is identified, stresses the fact that the Rorschach must, indeed, meet the criteria of reliability that are imposed on other measuring instruments, but that the methods for assessing reliability must be specifically adapted to the peculiarities of this unusual technique of personality study. Sargent has stated: "Questions of reliability and validity cannot be casually dismissed simply because the statistical treatment which serves for the simpler, more rigid measures of mental and emotional traits are unsuitable" (35, p. 435).

If one agrees that the Rorschach should meet reliability criteria, the problem of the degree of reliability is posed. Jahoda et al. have offered their solution:

> There is no simple answer to the question of what is a satisfactory reliability. It depends upon one's purpose. If one wishes to distinguish pre-

cisely among a group of people who are similar in the characteristic being measured or if one hopes to find close relationships between variables, it is necessary to have highly reliable measuring instruments. If one wishes only to distinguish between people at the extremes or to determine whether a relationship exists, high reliability in the measures is not so necessary (18).

THE HOLISTIC NATURE OF THE RORSCHACH

The special peculiarity of the Rorschach, which distinguishes it from psychometric methods of personality assessment, is its holistic nature. As Munroe has stated, ". . . the Rorschach is the first really extensive effort to apply 'objectively' in diagnosis and in research those holistic principles to which psychology at large does at least give lip service today. The familiar methodologies of psychology, especially of psychometrics, date from a more 'atomistic' era" (29, p. 37). This peculiarity of the Rorschach presents a problem not merely for those interested in the study of reliability but for all research with the Rorschach. Here is a psychological assessment instrument that yields no single total score which is characteristic of methods in the field of psychometrics. Instead, there emerges as the end result of the use of this method a nonquantitative protocol diagnosing an individual personality. The problem posed is that of how to study the personality synthesis that emerges as the end product of the Rorschach method rather than to study a conglomeration of isolated parts which has been the frequent practice in much of the research in the field of reliability as well as with other research involving the Rorschach. To those who have been interested in a psychology that has meaning for the study of the individual human being, there has been an inclination to disregard such problems of reliability out of the recognition that these problems were being studied on a meaningless level, unrelated to the holistic nature of the Rorschach. Their attitude has been that conventional statistical comparisons of isolated test items have destroyed the total pattern on which the individual diagnosis of personality is based.

It has been on this peculiar facet of the Rorschach that much of the research pertaining to reliability has floundered. Hertz has, however, insisted that there is a need to study the consistency of parts of the Rorschach on the assumption that the establishment of the reliability at this level yields evidence that has significance for the instrument as a whole. However, this is subject to serious question, since it is evident that subparts of a test such as the Wechsler-Bellevue Intelligence Scale possess low reliabilities and yet the total test has acceptable reliability.

A number of methods have been developed to cope with this peculiar facet of the Rorschach, among these being the use of the psychogram, rating scales, and matching techniques (26). The psychogram, which contains the quantitative statement of the major scoring categories in the Rorschach, has become the basis for a number of research studies which have been reluctant to utilize individual Rorschach variables in isolation. This is obviously an improvement over the use of individual scores, but even this has serious limitations. Much that goes on in the examining situation is grist for the mill of the clinician concerned with personality study. He observes many cues which cannot be written down explicitly and, consequently, do not appear in the psychogram. Thus, such factors as perseveration of content, the subject's style of speech, his manner of examination of each blot, etc., do not become recorded in the psychogram.

The second method that has been introduced into research with the Rorschach in order to take into account its holistic quality has been the use of rating scales of selected parts of the record, i.e., capacity for acting-out behavior, potentiality for therapeutic involvement, etc. Although the rating method has not been used primarily in reliability studies, a vast number of studies utilizing the Rorschach as a measuring instrument have used rating scales of specific variables and have demonstrated successful reliability for these ratings.

The most significant research development, and one which has been applied with some success in the study of reliability, has been the use of the matching technique. The matching method has been defined by Vernon as ". . . a method for establishing quantitative relationships between qualitative aspects of personality" (44, p. 149). He has stressed this method as a means of comparing whole Rorschach records in contradistinction to correlational methods which are usually applied to the comparison of isolated Rorschach variables. Matching can be used at several levels: matching two sets of protocols from the same subjects, matching the protocols with their interpretations, or matching interpretations of the same subjects made by different examiners. Although this is clearly a less artificial method for capturing the holistic quality of the Rorschach, there are a number of problems related to the use of this research tool. These are:

1. The complexity of the material to be matched is an important condition affecting results. The number of elements that are involved

in the Rorschach are so numerous and varied that it becomes a difficult task for the judge to be able to grasp the total Rorschachs of different individuals in order to relate them to their mates.

2. The experience and skill of the judges comprise a second condition affecting the results of matching. Clearly, differing results will be obtained from individuals who are less experienced with the Rorschach than those with greater experience. This introduces the problem of the confusion between the role of the judge and the role of the test in the reliability findings.

3. Another factor determining the success of matchings is the length of time spent in the study of records. This is in part related to the complexity of the Rorschach but, unless there is sufficient time to comprehend the totality of the Rorschach protocol, there is likely to be greater unreliability introduced into the matching experiment.

4. The heterogeneity of the Rorschach protocols is another condition affecting success in matching. As the Rorschachs of the subjects involved are less unlike one another, the more difficult the task of matching becomes and the greater the degree of unreliability.

THE MEANING OF RORSCHACH RELIABILITY

When one talks of reliability as it pertains to the Rorschach, there is need to clarify more precisely what is meant. Is it the consistency between different judges in their *scoring* of the same protocols? Is it the consistency of the subject's *responses* to two or more Rorschach examinations? Is it the consistency between different judges in their *interpretations* of the same Rorschachs? Is it the consistency of one judge in his *scorings and/or interpretations of the same Rorschachs on two or more occasions?*

If our concern is with the consistency of the subject's responses to the Rorschach, do we refer to *temporal consistency* (test-retest), *consistency of performance on two forms of the test* (equivalency), or do we refer to the subject's *internal consistency* on a single administration of the Rorschach (split-half)? Each of these clearly have different psychological meanings.

It is evident that the practice of applying the single term "reliability" to all of these issues is indefensible, and it is our purpose in the remainder of this chapter to focus on the specific types of reliability enumerated above. In doing so, it should be noted that there will still remain considerable ambiguity, for it is evident that reliability, of whatever kind, cannot be generalized too freely for there is lack of information on relative reliabilities for groups differing in age, diagnosis, social background, etc. This is true not alone for the Rorschach but also for almost all psychological tests, psychometric as well as projective.

CONSISTENCY OF SCORING

This aspect of reliability of the Rorschach has received minimal treatment to date. It is evident that the similarity of scores, training, and ideological identifications with Rorschach authority determines how two judges will score. What little research is available suggests that, as individuals are oriented to the same scoring system, there will be higher consistency in their scoring. Sicha and Sicha (38) had 300 responses scored by five Rorschach investigators and the results showed a high percentage of agreement (70 to 82%). This occurred despite the fact that there were differing criteria that were undoubtedly applied in determining the scores, inasmuch as the individuals doing the scoring were identified with different systems of scoring. Hertz, as reported by Vernon (45), reports that there was 93% agreement between two scorers in the scoring of 11,000 responses. In this instance, there had been prior agreement on scoring between the scorers. These results suggest that, as such prior agreement occurs, the reliability is increased.

CONSISTENCY IN SUBJECT RESPONSES [1]

Temporal Consistency (Test-Retest)

A number of investigations have studied the temporal consistency of subjects on the Rorschach, but here, as with other areas that will be reported, there are conflicting results. Typical of these are the studies

[1] The attempt here is not so much to survey completely the research done in the area of Rorschach reliability but primarily to focus on the limitations of methodology employed in the various aspects of the study of reliability. A number of historically significant studies and reports will not be reviewed because, although they are of some *relevance* to the reliability problem, they are not *pertinent* to it, because they usually involve a second administration of the Rorschach under conditions different from the first administration (7, 8, 22, 34) or they are not supported by statistical evidence for claims made (2, 47).

by Ford, Swift, and Kerr who studied relatively young children in terms of test-retest reliability. Ford (6) reports reliabilities of the determinants ranging from +.38 to +.86 based on a one-month interval of retesting. It was the author's conclusion that, since the reliabilities of tests at the preschool level tend to be lower than the reliabilities of these same tests when used with older subjects, the results with the Rorschach are striking. On the other hand, Swift (40) in her analysis of the test-retest reliability of the Rorschach with children found that reliability of individual-scored items in retests after a short interval of time was only fairly satisfactory and, after a longer period of time (10 months), was quite unsatisfactory. Swift identifies a number of factors working against reliability, i.e., the small number of total responses, the low frequency of responses in many scoring categories, and the variability in the attention span and interest of her subjects during the retest situation. Kerr (21), similarly, found low reliabilities after one year of retest with children. Here, as with a number of other studies, there is the question as to how much of the changes were due to real personality changes occurring in the children and how much to the unreliability of the method. Troup (43), utilizing a matching technique, presented six judges with the task of matching the psychograms with their retest mates. A coefficient of contingency of +.94 is reported. Holzberg and Wexler (17), in order to force unreliability, used an "unpredictable" population (schizophrenics) and found fairly good reliabilities for individual Rorschach variables on test-retest. In addition, there was excellent agreement in matching the psychograms of both testings.

A number of conditions which are required for the use of test-retest reliability cannot be said to be present when applied to the Rorschach.

1. It cannot be assumed that personality data can be reproduced exactly from one testing session to another. There is evidence to support the thesis that changes in the set of the subject will affect certain aspects of his Rorschach performance (9, 36, 37); changes in the nature of the testing situation, similarly, can produce changes in Rorschach performance (22, 25); and, where different examiners are utilized, there is the problem of the effect of examiner personality and other characteristics on the Rorschach performance of the subject (24).

The giving of changed content on a retest does not necessarily reflect the unreliability of the Rorschach. The individual Rorschach examination, in a sense, has built within it a test-retest situation in that the initial part of the test is a free association (the test) whereas the conclusion of the examination consists of an inquiry (the retest). It is not unusual that, during this inquiry, different or additional responses will occur. The coming about of different or additional responses from test to retest may well have the same significance as the production of different or additional responses in the inquiry; i.e., as the subject becomes more familiar with the blots and with the total Rorschach situation, certain integrations of perceptions and associations may occur that would ordinarily not occur during the initial contact with the cards.

2. It cannot be assumed that the object of study, the personality of a subject, is unchanging. Significant aspects of the personality change through time in response to internal and external factors. This issue is particularly related to the ages at which testing occurs and the length of time between testings. The younger the age at which test-retesting occurs, the greater is the expectation of change. Similarly, the longer the time interval between testings, the more change may be anticipated. Macfarlane and Tuddenham have stated it this way: "Although a subject's test performances at different times should be congruent with each other in the sense that they reveal the more central and enduring dimensions of personality, they should not be expected to show statistical reliability because the subject himself may have changed" (26, p. 39). Swift has stated that, "Once the ambiguous material has been organized in a certain way, there is a tendency for this organization to interfere with subsequent attempts at reorganization, even when the factor of pure repetition is not present (that is, where the individual does not try consciously to repeat what he said before)" (40, p. 209). This has been described even more succinctly by Kelley: ". . . if at the time of the second test there is any memory, conscious or subconscious, of the earlier responses, then certainly the mental operations being performed at the second taking are not the same or even similar in kind to those performed at the first taking" (20, p. 80). Swift (40) found that an average of 47% of the responses given to the first testing were remembered by her preschool children after 30 days, and presumably this percentage would even be higher in the case of adult subjects.

This does not merely mean that memory for the first testing will bring about the same responses. For certain individuals, the memory of the first testing may bring with it a desire to change responses in order to be "different" at the time of the second testing.

A number of ingenious attempts have been made to avoid the pitfall of the memory factor in test-retest reliability. Kelley, Margulies, and Barrera (19) utilized a series of subjects who had received electroshock therapy and had developed complete amnesia for the first testing. These patients were free from confusion resulting from shock when they were readministered the Rorschach some two hours later. For the most part, the psychograms remained unchanged and the diagnostic impressions were the same. Griffith (10) tested several patients with Korsakoff's syndrome, a disorder characterized by severe memory defect. These patients seemed to have a complete lack of recall for the first Rorschach testing that occurred 22 hours previously. The findings here were that the test-retest protocols were very similar, the original autistic content remained, and the reaction times were not significantly altered.

Equivalence Reliability (Equivalent Forms)

The use of equivalent forms of a test to determine the consistency of performance of subjects has long been a standard approach to the establishment of reliability in psychometrics. This method has been utilized with regard to the Rorschach, even though there has been considerable difficulty in developing a truly comparable or equivalent set of ink blots. A number of attempts to create such sets have been made, and the comparison of results on these as compared to the Rorschach has shown the same variable results as were found with the test-retest method.

Swift (40) utilized a form of the Rorschach devised by Behn (the Behn-Rorschach) for retest after an interval of one week in her study with preschool children. Most of the scoring categories showed high reliability coefficients, but a number were strikingly low. Her conclusion was that the differences in the two sets made the Behn form *not* a completely equivalent set to be used in clinical practice. Singer, again utilizing the Behn, found that the ". . . group profile on the Behn would be almost identical with that on the Rorschach . . . the two tests seemed in this study to elicit in general the same number and type of responses" (39, p. 241). McFarland (28) showed that his modification of the Rorschach and his modification of the Behn correlated significantly with one another on all of the six variables that he considered. Similar findings were reported by Buckle and Holt who state: "The resulting similarity is not only one of similarity in scoring category, but is often a complete identity between actual responses given to the two blots" (3, p. 491). Eichler, again comparing performance on the Behn and on the Rorschach, found that: "In general, the Behn showed substantial agreement with the measures obtained by the standard Rorschach" (5, p. 187). However, on further analysis, he was able to show that the Behn tended to encourage the production of certain responses that did not occur as frequently on the regular Rorschach.

In general, findings relating performance on the Rorschach and the Behn series of ink blots support the general thesis of similarity of response, although there are sufficient differences as to arouse concern about this measure of reliability of the Rorschach.

Can the method of equivalence be considered appropriate when applied to a technique like the Rorschach? Clearly, the method of equivalence is less affected by memory and practice than is the method of test-retest but it is a questionable assumption that a subject taking the second form of the test is not in some way affected by the first form. In a task like the Rorschach, its novelty is a factor in affecting responses. Repetition, even with a second set of blots, destroys this novelty. Perhaps of greater significance is the assumption that the two forms are equivalent.

A psychometrician constructing a true-false achievement test can be reasonably sure of achieving equivalence between its alternate forms, because all subjects are set to respond to the same aspect of each item [that is, to its correctness] and because the items in each form can be renderd comparable with respect to difficulty and content. In an unstructured projective test, different subjects are free to respond selectively to different qualities of the stimulus material. The projectivist may not always be able to specify all the aspects of his test to which a subject might conceivably respond (26, p. 40).

Another issue posed by Buckle and Holt pertains to the problem of developing equivalent sets which, if they become truly equivalent, may well end up being the same set.

The logical implication of endeavors to provide closer equivalence in the alternative form by figural similarity, leads in the end, to an exact reproduction of the original form. As complete equivalence is approached, the validity of the alternative form for retest is thereby weakened. When a subject is re-tested with an alternative form of the test the same responses are likely to occur, both because the subject "recalls" them from the first test, and also because the similarity of the visual perceptual field tends to induce similar mental sets (3, p. 492).

Internal Consistency (Split-Half)

The split-half technique, long used in psychometric testing to establish one form of reliability, i.e., internal consistency, has also been used in the study of the Rorschach with, again, conflicting results. Thornton and Guilford (42) report contradictory findings in their split-half study. Vernon (46) found low split-half reliabilities for all of the Rorschach variables except the number of responses. He suggested the need of control for the number of responses if one was to utilize this method appropriately, based on his observation that reliabilities were higher for records of more than 30 responses. A major research effort, which contradicted the results of Vernon, is that of Hertz (12) who—although she presently rejects the split-half method as applied to the Rorschach (11)—did utilize it successfully and demonstrated that the odd-even cards in 100 records of junior high school students produced split-half correlations for Rorschach variables which range from .66 to .97 with an average of .83. More recently, Ford (6), in her study of young children, found that her split-half reliabilities were comparable to those of Hertz. Wirt and McReynolds (48) found an average correlation of .85 for the three groups they studied.

Clearly, the split-half technique eliminates the disadvantages of the other two methods of reliability insofar as it has no practice effects and makes no assumptions regarding changes in personality over the course of time. However, it does make the significant assumption that the Rorschach can in some way be divided into two equal halves, which is the basic condition involved in the split-half technique. Clearly, this condition cannot be met with the Rorschach where the blots vary in formal configuration, color, shading, etc. It is apparent that some cards in the Rorschach are more suggestive of certain content, such as humans as opposed to animals. Other cards are organizable in a particular perceptual mode such as wholes as opposed to details. Some cards have a "pull" for both humans and wholes, or animals and details, or some combination of these four variables, and these are only four of a much larger number of variables on the Rorschach. It is not probable that the ten ink blots can be separated into two equal halves such that there will be represented in each half the same opportunity to "pull" for all the Rorschach variables. Furthermore, the fact that the cards consist of five grey and five color cards requires that any splitting of the Rorschach into two halves would end up in unequal distribution with regard to this variable.

However, this position with regard to split-half technique on the Rorschach is challenged by Orange who states:

> Contrary to the contention . . . that the factor of differential stimulus-import on the Rorschach renders employment of split-half techniques theoretically impracticable, the establishment of extensive reliabilities in this study precipitates the challenging conclusion that organizational functions in perceptual behavior are self-assertive despite changing stimulus-configurations (32, p. 228).

Another condition for the appropriate utilization of the split-half technique is that the test must be of sufficient length so that when it is split, there will not be an inadequate sampling of behavior. This condition cannot be met in the case of the Rorschach because of the low incidence of certain categories which, when split, would contribute to low reliabilities, and this inadequate sampling of many factors in the Rorschach cannot be compensated for by statistical operations to correct for its length. Unlike psychometric tests to which the split-half technique has been applied, the number of responses in the Rorschach is not determined by the examiner who brings with him a list of test items. Rather, the number of responses is determined exclusively by the subject.[2]

CONSISTENCY OF RORSCHACH INTERPRETATION

Although the question of whether the Rorschach consistently elicits similar responses from the same subjects has been subjected to considerable research, as described in the previous sections, the question of the extent to which independent analysts agree with each other in the interpretation of the same Rorschachs has received only minimal treatment. To some Rorschach workers this has been the most critical reliability problem since it is the interpretation of the Rorschach that is used clinically. However, it is here that one deals with the most difficult aspect of the reliability problem inasmuch as the basic data are the nonquantitative personality descriptions prepared by the psychologist.

One of the classic attempts to study the degree of agreement between independent Rorschach workers in their interpretation of the same case was conducted by Hertz and Rubenstein (14) who claim reliability for the test as a whole. Hertz, Beck, and Klopfer did blind

---

[2] From a statistical point of view, this criterion applies equally to reliabilities of the test-retest or equivalent-form type.

interpretations of the same Rorschach record. A comparison of the three interpretations obtained showed a high degree of agreement among the Rorschach experts. This is based, however, on only a single case and is far from a crucial test of the reliability of Rorschach interpretation. Of concern here would be whether the same degree of agreement could have been obtained by individuals with less experience with the Rorschach. A close examination of the three interpretations did show a number of disagreements, which disagreements were nevertheless all valid. In the case of one instance, the emphasis was on the depressive features of the case; in the second, the excitable and extrovertive features were stressed; and in the third, emphasis was put on the conflict with regard to the feminine role. All of these emphases were checked against other clinical data and were verified. This poses one of the genuine problems in the study of the reliability of interpretations, since it is possible for judges to emphasize different aspects of the record, and yet all of these aspects may be valid.

The really crucial investigation on the reliability of interpretations was that done by Krugman (23). Independent interpretations of 20 Rorschach records were prepared by two Rorschach workers. These were presented to three judges in four groups of five pairs. All identifying references were removed. The three judges made a perfect score in matching, showing that two Rorschach workers are able to interpret a record very similarly. The same judges also rated the degree of agreement between the two interpretations. Essential agreement was shown in 89.6% of the interpretations, fair agreement in 10%, and approximately equal amounts of agreement and disagreement in .4%. Krugman further studied the reliability of the Rorschach by securing matchings of 25 scored Rorschach records with their interpretations. Six judges achieved an average coefficient of contingency of .872. Clearly, these are impressive results, supporting the thesis that interpretations of Rorschachs can be very reliable. However, there is need for further research that will attempt to replicate this experiment in order that there may be greater confidence in the findings.

There are a number of special problems concerned with the study of the reliability of interpretations of the Rorschach. Clearly, one issue is that no single authentic interpretation of the Rorschach is possible. In the study by Hertz and Rubenstein, referred to above, three outstanding Rorschach workers, although agreeing in essentials, disagreed in certain features, and yet each was valid. Clearly, clinicians may devote attention to different phases of the Rorschach in their interpretations, partly as a function of their training, partly as a function of the purpose for psychological referral, and yet the analyses, although differing, may nevertheless be valid.

Perhaps this is another way of saying that there can never be a complete interpretation of the Rorschach, since an interpretation of a personality is the function, in part, of the background, training, competence, and psychological understanding of the interpreter. It is here that we must emphasize that unlike psychometric instruments, the Rorschach method cannot be isolated from the interpreter, the Rorschach and the psychologist being one integral methodology. To be sure, this has led some to complain that one confounds the interpreter with the test, but there is much feeling that it is this aspect that represents the great strength of the Rorschach as a personality assessment instrument (30).

It should be stressed that differences in interpretation may also be a function of the conceptual scheme in which one operates with the Rorschach. Thus, there are psychologists who are essentially "sign oriented," whereas others develop their personality analyses on the bases of hypotheses that are formulated, tested, and then refined in the light of data as they emerge in the analysis of the Rorschach. Such differences of approach may well lead to different emphases in the interpretive write-up of the case (15).

One aspect of consistency of interpretation that has not been subjected to any systematic scrutiny has been that of the consistency of the same Rorschach worker in his interpretations of the same Rorschachs. Here, of course, we are dealing again with problems of memory which would mean that the interpretations would have to occur at significant intervals of time. With the recognition of the importance of the background and psychological sophistication of the psychologist as a factor in the interpretive process with the Rorschach, it is quite likely that self-consistency or reliability of interpretation may yield low correlations principally because of the maturing process of the psychologist as a function of his experience. This by no means is a reflection on the instrument, but merely is a recognition that the deepening of one's understanding of personality, dynamics and psychopathology will be reflected in more penetrating interpretations of techniques such as the Rorschach.

PERCEPTUAL AND CONCEPTUAL CONSISTENCY AND RORSCHACH RELIABILITY

In a recent provocative paper, Dorken (4) has suggested that much recent research, which has varied the stimulus properties of the blots only to find remarkable consistency of the subjects in their perform- ances on the regular and altered blots, far from yielding data which invalidate the Rorschach offers evidence of the basic perceptual con- sistency of the subject. His thesis, extended, is that the Rorschach is reliable inasmuch as alterations in its perceptual qualities do not alter the responses of subjects: "The strength of the individual's char- acteristic mode of perception, whether he is normal or mentally dis- ordered, permits a surprising degree of variance in the formal aspects of the test material before response is significantly altered" (4, p. 101). This thesis has been emphasized by others such as Brosin and Fromm who similarly state that a considerable degree of variation in the field ". . . will still elicit similar responses [since there is] a wide range of possibility for recognition of similar configurations" (2, p. 5). In his thesis, Dorken does not deny that each blot of the Rorschach has stimulus value that has some influence on response, but "This in- fluence, however, must be relatively less than that of the individual personality structure, otherwise there would be insufficient divergence of response between individuals to provide any basis for the differen- tial evaluation of personality" (4, p. 103). Baughman similarly sug- gests this same approach in his analysis of his research:

Many of the measures that we make of perceptual behavior in the Rorschach test appear to be primarily dependent upon processes inherent in the perceiver . . . rather than upon properties of the stimulus (1, p. 163).

The data are clear and impressive in their demonstration that the major dimensions of perceptual behavior in the Rorschach task remain remarkably constant even though marked alterations are made in the stimulus attributes. . . . The fact that perceptual behavior is so minimally affected by major changes in stimulus characteristics should make us feel more secure in our use of such techniques for personality evaluation (1, pp. 161, 163).

These attitudes, it seems to the author, are not wholly satisfactory. To the extent that color, shading, figure-ground qualities, etc., are variables that are used in the interpretation of the Rorschach, failure to show alterations in responses while varying these stimulus condi- tions poses a serious problem for the validity of these interpretations.

Furthermore, this hardly seems to be an answer to the problem of reliability. This becomes the earlier argument in reverse, i.e., instead of validity presuming reliability, the absence of validity presumes reliability. This argument is not particularly impressive.

I do believe that it is possible to extend Dorken's argument one step further, and stress that perceptual and conceptual consistency in *differing* tasks does hold out hope of providing a more reasonable basis for assessing the reliability of the Rorschach. In a study done by McFarland (28), he was concerned with the consistency of verbal responses to a series of differing perceptual and conceptual tasks. Using four tasks, i.e., a modified Rorschach, a modified Behn, a picture title test, and an object recognition test, McFarland was able to demonstrate that subjects respond consistently to all of these tasks in terms of the number of responses, the range of interpretations, and the frequency with which responses are given to different stimuli. McFarland here demonstrated certain consistencies in perceptual and conceptual behavior between the Rorschach and these other tasks. If we look upon the other tasks as being forms of perceptual and conceptual tasks which are alternate to the Rorschach, it is the author's thesis that research of this type can become the basis for demonstrating the essential reliability of the Rorschach.

Another study in this same vein which the author believes is a demonstration of the reliability of the Rorschach is that of Holzberg and Schleifer (16) who related the performance of subjects on the color-versus-noncolor cards of the Rorschach to their performance on a number of perceptual and conceptual tasks in which color was introduced as a variable. In this research, they were able to demonstrate a significant degree of consistency in behavior insofar as the subjects' responses to color are concerned. This would be another demonstration of the use of other perceptual and conceptual tasks as alternate forms for purposes of determining the consistency of subjects' performances on the Rorschach and in other perceptual and conceptual operations.

CONCLUSIONS

The problem of the reliability of the Rorschach is a many-faceted problem. This chapter has stressed that the Rorschach must, like all instruments of study, demonstrate its reliability, but that it should demonstrate it through methods which take into consideration the peculiar characteristics of the Rorschach. It has furthermore been stressed that the concept of "reliability" has multiple meanings, and that there are a number of reliability problems as they pertain to the Rorschach as there are with all instruments of personality study. It has also been emphasized that the traditional methods of assessing psychometric reliability are inappropriate to the Rorschach, and it is felt that the most fruitful approach to the reliability problem is through the study of perceptual and conceptual consistency, and comparing performance on the Rorschach with other perceptual and conceptual tasks, with these other perceptual and conceptual tasks being looked upon as alternate forms.

While such research on the ultimate reliability of the Rorschach proceeds, the Rorschach will continue to be used by trained clinicians who recognize its unsettled reliability status. Such ambiguity that does exist will encourage the clinician to utilize complementary sources of data from test batteries, case histories, and interactional data from the clinical testing situation. He will continue to think in terms of probabilities rather than certainties in his formulations of personality from the Rorschach (15).

BIBLIOGRAPHY

1. Baughman, E.   A comparative analysis of Rorschach forms with altered stimulus characteristics.   *J. proj. Tech.*, 1954, 18, 151–164.
2. Brosin, H. W., and Fromm, E.   Some principles of gestalt psychology in the Rorschach experiment.   *Rorschach Res. Exch.*, 1942, 6, 1–15.
3. Buckle, D., and Holt, N.   Comparison of Rorschach and Behn inkblots.   *J. proj. Tech.*, 1951, 15, 486–493.
4. Dorken, H.   Psychological structure as the governing principle of projective technique: Rorschach theory.   *Canad. J. Psychol.*, 1956, 10, 101–106.
5. Eichler, R.   A comparison of the Rorschach and Behn-Rorschach inkblot tests.   *J. consult. Psychol.*, 1951, 15, 185–189.
6. Ford, M.   The application of the Rorschach test to young children.   *Univ. Minn. Inst. Child Welf. Monogr.*, 1946, No. 23.
7. Fosberg, I. A.   An experimental study of the reliability of the Rorschach psychodiagnostic technique.   *Rorschach Res. Exch.*, 1941, 5, 72–84.
8. Fosberg, I. A.   Rorschach reactions under varied instructions.   *Rorschach Res. Exch.*, 1938, 3, 12–38.
9. Gibby, R. G.   The stability of certain Rorschach variables under conditions of experimentally induced sets: I. The intellectual variables.   *J. proj. Tech.*, 1951, 15, 3–26.
10. Griffith, R. M.   The test-retest similarities of the Rorschachs of patients without retention, Korsakoff.   *J. proj. Tech.*, 1951, 15, 516–525.

11. Hertz, M. R.   Current problems in Rorschach theory and technique. *J. proj. Tech.*, 1951, **15**, 307–338.
12. Hertz, M. R.   The reliability of the Rorschach ink-blot test. *J. appl. Psychol.*, 1934, **18**, 461–477.
13. Hertz, M. R.   Rorschach: Twenty years after. *Rorschach Res. Exch.*, 1941, **5**, 90–129.
14. Hertz, M. R., and Rubenstein, B. B.   A comparison of three "blind" Rorschach analyses. *Amer. J. Orthopsychiat.*, 1939, **9**, 295–314.
15. Holzberg, J. D.   The clinical and scientific methods: synthesis or antithesis? *J. proj. Tech.*, 1957, **21**, 227–242.
16. Holzberg, J. D., and Schleifer, M. J.   An experimental test of the Rorschach assumption of the impact of color on perceptual and associative processes. *J. proj. Tech.*, 1955, **19**, 130–137.
17. Holzberg, J. D., and Wexler, M.   The predictability of schizophrenic performance on the Rorschach test. *J. consult. Psychol.*, 1950, **14**, 395–399.
18. Jahoda, M., Deutsch, M., and Cook, S. W.   *Research methods in social relations.*   New York: Dryden, 1951.
19. Kelley, D. M., Margulies, H., and Barrera, S. E.   The stability of the Rorschach method as demonstrated in electric convulsive therapy cases. *Rorschach Res. Exch.*, 1941, **5**, 35–43.
20. Kelley, T. L.   The reliability coefficient. *Psychometrika*, 1942, **7**, 75–83.
21. Kerr, M.   Temperamental differences in twins. *Brit. J. Psychol.*, 1936, **27**, 51–59.
22. Kimble, G. A.   Social influence on Rorschach records. *J. abnorm. soc. Psychol.*, 1945, **40**, 89–93.
23. Krugman, J. E.   A clinical validation of the Rorschach with problem children. *Rorschach Res. Exch.*, 1942, **6**, 61–70.
24. Lord, E.   Experimentally induced variations in Rorschach performance. *Psychol. Monogr.*, 1950, No. 64.
25. Luchins, A. S.   Situational and attitudinal influences on Rorschach responses. *Amer. J. Psychiat.*, 1947, **103**, 780–784.
26. Macfarlane, J. W., and Tuddenham, R. D.   Problems in the validation of projective techniques.   In: Anderson and Anderson (eds.), *An introduction to projective techniques and other devices for understanding the dynamics of human behavior.*   New York: Prentice-Hall, 1951.
27. McClelland, D. C.   Toward a science of personality psychology.   In: David and von Bracken (eds.), *Perspectives in personality theory.*   London: Tavistock, 1957.
28. McFarland, R.   Perceptual consistency in Rorschach-like projective tests. *J. proj. Tech.*, 1954, **18**, 368–378.
29. Munroe, R. L.   Considerations on the place of the Rorschach in the field of general psychology. *Rorschach Res. Exch.*, 1945, **9**, 30–40.
30. Munroe, R. L.   The use of projective methods in group testing. *J. consult. Psychol.*, 1948, **12**, 8–15.
31. Mursell, J. L.   *Psychological testing.*   New York: Longmans, Green, 1949.
32. Orange, A.   Perceptual consistency as measured by the Rorschach. *J. proj. Tech.*, 1953, **17**, 224–228.
33. Piotrowski, Z. A.   The reliability of Rorschach's Erlebnistypus. *J. abnorm. soc. Psychol.*, 1937, **32**, 439–445.

34. Rabin, A. I., and Sanderson, M. H. An experimental inquiry into some Rorschach procedures. *J. clin. Psychol.*, 1947, 3, 216–225.
35. Sargent, H. Projective methods. In: Pennington and Berg (eds.), *An introduction to clinical psychology.* New York: Ronald, 1948.
36. Schachtel, E. G. Subjective definitions of the Rorschach test situation and their effect on test performance. *Psychiatry*, 1945, 8, 419–448.
37. Schafer, R. *Psychoanalytic interpretation in Rorschach testing.* New York: Grune and Stratton, 1954.
38. Sicha, K., and Sicha, M. A step towards the standardization of the scoring of the Rorschach test. *Rorschach Res. Exch.*, 1936, 1, 95–101.
39. Singer, J. The Behn-Rorschach inkblots: a preliminary comparison with the original Rorschach series. *J. proj. Tech.*, 1952, 16, 238–245.
40. Swift, J. W. Reliability of Rorschach scoring categories with preschool children. *Child Developm.*, 1944, 15, 207–216.
41. Symonds, M. *Adolescent fantasy.* New York: Columbia University Press, 1949.
42. Thornton, G. R., and Guilford, J. P. The reliability and meaning of Erlebnistypus scores in the Rorschach test. *J. abnorm. soc. Psychol.*, 1936, 31, 324–330.
43. Troup, E. A comparative study by means of the Rorschach method of personality development in twenty pairs of identical twins. *Genet. Psychol. Monogr.*, 1938, 20, 461–556.
44. Vernon, P. E. The matching method applied to investigations of personality. *Psychol. Bull.*, 1936, 33, 149–177.
45. Vernon, P. E. Recent work on the Rorschach test. *J. ment. Sci.*, 1935, 81, 1–27.
46. Vernon, P. E. The Rorschach ink-blot test. II. *Brit. J. med. Psychol.*, 1933, 13, 179–205.
47. Wertham, F., and Bleuler, M. Inconstancy of the formal structure of the personality: experimental study of the influence of mescaline on the Rorschach test. *Arch. Neurol. Psychiat.*, 1932, 28, 52–70.
48. Wirt, R., and McReynolds, P. The reliability of Rorschach number of responses. *J. proj. Tech.*, 1953, 17, 493–494.

14 | by Jesse G. Harris, Jr.

VALIDITY: THE SEARCH

FOR A CONSTANT

IN A UNIVERSE OF VARIABLES

A METAPHORICAL VIEW OF THE PROBLEM

There is a touch of shadowy humor in present-day apperceptions of Rorschach methodology. On the horizon of this field of phenomenological vision, one finds the vanguard of the ink-blot movement still engaged in the generation-old conflict of intuitive versus empirical, clinical versus experimental, European versus American, and holistic versus atomistic. With little hope of emerging victorious, the dedicated Rorschach legion seems gradually to have adopted the strategy of incorporating its antagonist's ego ideal—the concept of validity.

The task of assimilating validity and of treating this operationally definable concept as if it were a new projective stimulus has not been an easy one for Rorschach methodologists. It has required a frequent repetition of the anticipatory statement that intuitive hypothesis making constitutes the first stage in the development of any science. But with the inadvertent assistance of a test constructionist named Guilford who once stated that "In a very general sense, a test is valid for anything with which it correlates" (25, pp. 428–429), the feat has been accomplished. Validity, that once proud emblem of psychologists who aspired to be pure scientists, can now be apperceived as a fuzzy verbal-perceptual entity, to be avoided, attacked, distorted, free-associated to, philosophically intellectualized about, constructively utilized, or outrightly rejected. It can be defined and redefined with enough

380

abstruseness and intragroup subjectivity to elicit a wry smile even from the most sober of logical positivists.

The disciples of Hermann Rorschach were by no means the first group to have struggled with the concept of validity. For centuries, courts of justice had puzzled over data which they obtained about human beings while employing the concrete, prosaic approach of direct interrogation. Operating like modern-day pencil-and-paper testers on the assumption that the best way to find out something about a man is to ask the man himself or someone who should know him, these agents of justice had been baffled by the responses to their simple requests for "the truth, the whole truth, and nothing but the truth."

Then, too, in the formal history of tests and measurements, the American successors of Binet had parted with their intellectual dignity long enough to climb aboard a merry-go-round of exhaustive reasoning about validity. In presenting all conceivable evidence for the statistical acceptability of their favorite instrument, the followers of Terman had managed to correlate intelligence-test results on children with, among other things, the ratings of teachers whose variable judgments the test results originally were supposed to replace.

Although such preliminary work on the circular interpretation of validity had already been done, it remained for the masters of Rorschach terminology to add the circumferential touches of global logic. Somewhat less methodical, but possessors of no less superego, the Rorschach thinkers early distinguished themselves in their analysis and synthesis of the problem of validity. It was their lasting contribution to the science of testing to introduce more background in philosophy than the intelligence testers had ever dreamed of, and to unveil far more talent for elevating their style of reasoning about validity to the level of an art.

Paradoxically, the world of psychology would have been deprived of much of this newly acquired prerogative to perceive and to think intuitively, had a chorus of experimental psychologists not arisen to deprecate the amoeboid movements of the ink-blot specialists and, on occasion, to hail down the oppressive authority of statistical probabilities. For in this resounding denunciation of ink-blot methodology, all psychological man's archetypal fears of being swallowed by a sea of unknown relevant and irrelevant psychological variables could be dramatized in a single professional gesture, and could be interpreted accordingly.

As familiar a note as the exhortations of reformers may strike for those of us who have been interpreting Rorschach protocols on the closed wards of medical institutions, the content of what these critics say should not go unheard.

It is permissible for a psychological technique or test to be as complex, or as esoteric, as its author chooses. The irony of the ink-blot development is, in fact, that a man-made tool, created to simplify our understanding of human nature, has thus far proven much too complex to be understood adequately by its users. But while there may be no limit to the complexity of the instrument itself, the tools and rules by which one decides whether the technique should be formally recognized as a proven method of scientific endeavor should not be obscured in the shadow of appeals either to complexity or to clinical usefulness. It is to reflect on the present status of the Rorschach method and its potential as an instrument of science that this chapter is written. The following discussion will include neither a defense nor a denial of the effectiveness of the Rorschach technique in the clinical setting; it will endeavor instead to analyze what the author regards as the fundamental causes of the several failures to demonstrate experimentally the validity of the method.

THE LANGUAGE OF THE SUBJECT

It is a universally acceptable principle of scientific method that definitions of any kind should be as simple as possible and should possess a meaning common to all users. Translating this appeal for clarity and for agreement on definitions into the language of semiotic, the philosophers' new behavioristic science of signs, we might apply several basic concepts regarding signs to the Rorschach method of investigation.

In the words of Morris (38, pp. 81–82):

> The process in which something functions as a sign may be called semiosis. This process, in a tradition which goes back to the Greeks, has commonly been regarded as involving three (or four) factors: that which acts as a sign, that which the sign refers to, and that effect on some interpreter in virtue of which the thing in question is a sign to that interpreter. These three components in semiosis may be called, respectively, the *sign vehicle,* the *designatum,* and the *interpretant;* the interpreter may be included as a fourth factor. These terms make explicit the factors left undesignated in the common statement that a sign refers to something for someone.
> . . . The most effective characterization of a sign is the following: S is a sign of D for I to the degree that I takes account of D in virtue of the

presence of S. Thus in semiosis something takes account of something else mediately, i.e., by means of a third something.

When elaborated into a language system, this fundamental relationship of semiosis may be analyzed at three levels of abstraction: syntactics, semantics, and pragmatics. Syntactics is concerned with the relations between signs, the rules of formation and transformation of statements. The signs may be a part of any arbitrary self-contained system of language, such as algebra, symbolic logic, English grammar, or contract bridge. Semantics is the science which deals with the relations of signs to objects. It determines the rules by which signs or systems of signs may serve as the adequate representations of objects or of the relationships between objects. Pragmatics, the third area of exploration, is concerned with the usage of signs, i.e., with the relations of signs to their interpreters. The subject matter of pragmatics would include reactions to signs, and the influence of needs or past experience on the selective utilization of signs. This would not involve a commitment of the science of signs to any psychological theory of behavior.

Applying the concepts of semiotic to the Rorschach procedure, we should distinguish between (a) the ink blot as a sign vehicle to be interpreted by the subject, and (b) the subject's verbal report and nonverbal behavior as a collection of sign vehicles to be interpreted by the examiner.

To grasp fully the implications of syntactics for the language network of the subject who looks at a Rorschach card, we might assume that the individual lives in a mythical, speechless society in which the language consists entirely of abstract or concrete drawings of objects. To converse in this graphic language, a member of the society must be able to define implicitly, or through substitution, all basic (or primitive) terms, such as curves, angles, colors, and textures. He must know also the significance of symbols which indicate the relations between signs (e.g., change of position or distance between parts). Although the mute citizen may find these graphic symbols to be very arbitrary, such as a semicircle to indicate roundness or an arrow to represent change of position, he must be in possession of a set of rules by which he can interpret the formation and transformation of all statements.

If this language is to have anything to say about the world of objects, the user must have available a second major set of rules by which he can accept a drawing or hieroglyphic as the representation of a class of objects. This latter set, the semantical definitions, would include the rules by which the arrangement of spatial relationships or the sequence of pictures conveys an empirical meaning (e.g., \\|// means inanimate movement, or ////) five claw marks, means aggression). Depending on the conventions agreed upon, the rules of adequate representation (i.e., semantical rules) might permit either abstract or highly concrete reproductions, such as lifelike portrait paintings.

Although the nonmythical subject who views the Rorschach card is able to describe his operations in the words of English grammar, these higher level verbalizations should not obscure the fact that he is dealing primarily in a language of visual images, with unstated syntactical and semantical rules.

If the subject looks at card I and reports "a bat," that portion of the ink blot which he uses becomes the sign vehicle, the class of objects called "bats" is the designatum, and the verbal response and all accompanying unverbalized and nonverbal behavior comprise the interpretant. How the subject might respond to a real bat is not a matter of concern in this immediate semiotic relationship, since all but a few psychotic patients would be aware that these pictorial symbols have no reference to concrete objects within the context of psychological testing. But how an odd-shaped blot of ink comes to serve as the sign of a bat is a matter of central importance not only to the science of signs but to Rorschach methodology as well.

The essential qualities which a spot of ink must possess in order to serve as a sign vehicle for a bat may vary with individuals. After all, the task of assigning perceptual labels to ambiguous masses is not one for which there is a long common history of verbalized experience among the members of any sample of a population. If we say, however, that a subject has accurate percepts, as we do in Rorschach interpretation, we are implying that semantical rules do exist for the application of perceptual signs to objects, and that this subject is conforming reasonably to such rules.

If the subject produces elaborate verbal accompaniments to his response either during the free association or during the formal inquiry, it becomes exceedingly difficult, or impossible, for us to determine whether he is verbalizing about the qualities of his percepts as signs, or about well-learned word associations as signs of the "bat." In other words, we are in doubt as to whether it is the subject's associations between perceptual attributes or his associations between words that are orderly and conventional. He may be telling us precisely what he sees, or he may be reeling off verbal associations to a concept suggested by the blot. It is difficult to make this distinction in the movement response, in the obvious FC, FC', or Fc [1] response for which no color or texture is reported, in the confabulatory response, and in the psychotic stream of thought which follows the report of a percept. The problem begins to mock the examiner when it reaches the extreme instance in which a patient with visual hallucinations fails to produce unequivocal psychotic material in response to any of the ten cards.

It is thus apparent that, when we score and interpret Rorschach data in the traditional manner, it is impossible for us to make a clear distinction between the subject's language of percepts and his language of words. As soon as we ask the subject to state what he sees or why he sees what he reports, we are inviting him to contaminate the information on percepts which we plan to use in our primary interpretation of data. We are left with the eternal question of whether our proddings were too directive or whether the subject actually saw more or less than what he reported.

Since the source and accuracy of the information on Rorschach scoring categories are matters of consequence to the user of the data, how might a research investigator attempt to isolate perceptual responses from the accompanying verbalizations? It has occurred to the author to try a more structured procedure for collecting data on ink blots. One might explore in a systematic manner the unstated rules by which a person accepts an ink blot as the representation of a class of objects. An experiment of this type would make use of a series of thirty or forty cards, on each of which is printed a small ink blot. The set of ink blots would represent graded composite variations in shapes, textures, and colors—step-by-step distortions of a single indisputable figure of a bat. As each card is presented in random order to the subject, he would be asked to rate the blot (e.g., 1 to 5), as to the degree to which he finds the blot to be an acceptable representation of a "bat."

After having collected normative data with respect to ranges of variation along each of the scoring dimensions, and on specified populations, the examiner would be able to test the extent to which an individual subject departs from established, though unstated, semantical rules in matching a blot to his concept of a class of objects. This experimental approach is in some ways similar to the methods employed by Bousfield [2] and his co-workers in their studies of the clustering of word associations. Bousfield, for example, has developed stable

---

[1] For explanation of scoring symbols, see Appendix, pp. 441 ff. [*Editor*].

[2] Bousfield, W. A., 1959. Personal communication.

results on the responses of college students to such a question as "To what extent does the word 'short' make you think of the word 'tall'?" The question is answered on a seven-point rating scale from "not at all" to "very strongly." It has been found that the mean rating obtained for a given word pair in this structured task correlates highly with the percentage of occurrence of the second word as a free-associate of the first word in a separate task.

It should be experimentally possible to develop normative data on ink blots in a similar manner and for a variety of noun and possibly verb (i.e., movement) concepts. Such an approach should provide abundant information on the extent to which a subject reserves color for special types of concepts, regards it as a distraction, or uses it indiscriminately for many concepts. Whatever hypothesis about color (or any other determinant) the interpreter of the test data chooses to employ, he may hope to find greater support for his statements regarding the meaning of the subject's use of this determinant than he can obtain at present from the three, or four, or fewer color responses produced in an individual record by the free-associational method of Rorschach procedure. To the extent that sufficiency of data contributes to the reliability of scores on any type of test and to the certainty of statements which are made about those scores, the accumulation of information in quantity on an individual subject becomes a matter of considerable importance for problems of validity.

The objection to such a hypothetical experiment would be raised that the totality of the responsiveness by free association to the Rorschach cards is lost, while the difficulties of compiling normative data would remain. In addition, the experiment would involve an introduction of the problem of selecting and sorting noun and verb concepts on which to build single series of experimental ink blots. The fact is, however, that validity continues to be a major problem for the Rorschach technique, and we are engaged in a never ending search for new ways of obtaining information on consistency of responsiveness and dependability of our interpretations. If we are to investigate the most fundamental problems of validity, it seems wise to violate some of our sacred assumptions that the Rorschach test has meaning only when administered and interpreted as an organic whole. The proposed experiment would be an attempt to isolate some of the variables and to obtain information in sufficient quantity, with due consideration for economy of time and effort, to enable an interpreter to make statements with confidence about the subject's usage of form, color, texture, or possibly even movement. Location and organization would not be investigated with these unitary blots, but might be explored by a similar rating procedure on sets of cards which contain both discrete and partially adjoining areas, large and small.

At present, our only recourse is to ask the subject who happens to report "a bat" on card I what it is about the card that suggests a bat. In view of our inability as interpreters to distinguish clearly between a "pure percept" and words associated to the percept, it would be an equally sound procedure to ask the same subject in what ways the ink blot does *not* look quite like "a bat" (or any other percept that he reports). Such a procedure would demand of the noncommital or noncritical subject a thorough analysis and report of his percepts. Although such an experimental approach would probably eliminate most movement responses, it would provide information on other determinants, and particularly on the subject's awareness of perceptual incongruities.

In the opinion of this contributor, the spade work on validation of the Rorschach method should consist of a search, via unrestricted experimentation of the type outlined, for the rules by which vague percepts may serve as sign vehicles of objects. At the level of the subject's language this is a problem in semantics, or, as another school of thought might have it, a problem in the ultimate reduction of operational definitions. It is not necessary that researchers in this area concern themselves with perception as a biological process, but it is of utmost importance that they learn something about the language and rules of usage of percepts.

Nor is it necessary to attempt to consider in one experiment the influence of needs on the utilization of this language of percepts, or the reactions of the subject to the percept or concept of "bat," once the latter has been admitted by the subject's own rules of usage. His reaction may be one of many, such as intellectual satisfaction at a job well done or fear of strange, winged creatures. An ink blot may, in fact, evoke an intense reaction, such as rejection of the card, or "Oh, how gruesome!," without the subject's being able to verbalize what it is about the blot that troubles him. That is, he is unable to conjure up a semantical rule by which he can utilize this blot as a reasonable facsimile of an object in his world. Such reactions and needs should be handled as separate problems—apart from the essentially cognitive meaning functions of this graphic language.

Restating this position, the first major problem on validity calls for a deciphering of the rules, if such exist, by which a person for whom major personality and situational variables have been independently specified can accept vague percepts as signs of objects. How much will he require, and how much discrepancy will he allow in each of the determinants?

After having investigated some of the rules of usage of this language of percepts, the researcher who is deeply concerned over the absence of experimental foundations for his instrument will secondarily begin to ask questions about performance in a totally unstructured ink-blot task, such as the Rorschach test, in which interpersonal variability and uninterpretable static are at a maximum. After he has found some consistency in the patterns of usage of this language by an individual, he may then proceed with some feeling of scientific legitimacy to a study of free-associational tasks in which it is doubtful that entirely satisfactory measures of reliability and validity will ever exist. At this point he may begin to speculate euphorically about the second-order problems of validity.

THE LANGUAGE OF THE INTERPRETER

Ascending now to this higher level, we might ask how the interpreter of the Rorschach protocol uses the verbal and nonverbal information with which the subject has supplied him. We are no longer concerned with ink blots as sign vehicles of objects, but rather with the subject's responses as sign vehicles of his personality. We now incorporate as a problem in the syntactics and semantics of scientific language what formerly was a problem in pragmatics at the level of the subject's performance. That is, in what way does the usage of a lower-level common language of words and percepts reveal to the scientist the needs, habits, and reactions of an organism?

At this point, within the realm of syntactics, we come to grips with the arbitrary rules of language of Rorschach purists. Shall we employ only perceptual behavior, or shall we include also verbal associative behavior and nonverbal behavior, and our own inferences about non-verbalized behavior? And within the category of "pure perceptual behavior," shall we distinguish between "structure" and "content" of percepts?

It is not always easy to define a response at the level of syntactics, but it is far more difficult to define one semantically. An inspired intuition or a formal vote can determine whether a smiling face or an explosion should be classified as an inanimate movement response; but only a careful study of the conditions under which this word combination occurs or fails to occur can tie this datum to a stable, or knowably unstable, referent in personality. At the level of syntactics the user of sign vehicles may free-wheel as arbitrarily as he chooses. If he does not like his own or someone else's signs, definitions, or deductions, he may shift gears, alter either his definitions or his rules of inference and produce a new set of deductions. But when the psychologist as scientist decides to make his system of signs isomorphic with the world of objects, i.e., when he proposes to link his system of language legitimately to the human personality, he must defer to the authority of natural occurrence.

It is in this relatively unknown area of the relations of Rorschach sign vehicles to facets of the subject's personality that the interpreter and the critic of the interpreter, alike, have acquired a facility in stating clichés as if they were solemn pronouncements of eternal truths. One may hear now the echo of many different voices proclaiming that the interpretation of the elements of the Rorschach protocol cannot be considered alone; each element derives its meaning only from the total configuration.

When prediction at the global level breaks down and offers, as it often does in experimental literature, no more dependable prediction statistically than that from the elemental level, one hears a second, still louder, imaginary voice.

The prediction failed because the Rorschach test is a highly complex instrument, the worth of which cannot be assessed by usual methods of test validation. Since the Rorschach method is clinically valuable and contributes information about persons not available through other channels of interpersonal communication, the users of the Rorschach technique need not concern themselves with such matters as experimental demonstrations of reliability and validity.

Equally enshrouded in verbal certainty is the more rigid critic, the keeper of the keys to the scientific kingdom. He believes that, since the reliability and validity of the Rorschach test have not been adequately demonstrated in a large number of studies, the predictions and descriptions made from this test deserve no more respect than fortune telling or phrenology, and should be abandoned by intellectually self-respecting psychologists.

It seems unnecessary to adopt either type of reasoning. It is no great mystery that the Rorschach protocol in many formal studies fails to describe or to predict accurately the behavior of an individual. Considering the number of independent probabilities which enter into the interpreter's analysis of a single response sequence and our present limited knowledge of each of these probabilities, it is more of a miracle that an accurate prediction can sometimes be made in the individual case.

As an illustration, let us suppose that a man looks at card I, rotates the card slowly 180°, smiles, completes the turn of 360°, and at the end of 40 seconds reports, "a bat." He immediately turns the card face down.

There are several estimates of probability which the interpreter must make, either implicitly or explicitly. He must decide in this case on the most probable meaning of (a) rotation at a slow rate; (b) a smile; (c) a long reaction time; (d) a single popular response; (e) immediate termination on producing the response; and (f) the absence of all other known forms of relevant or irrelevant behavior, such as a request for permission to turn the card, a remark that the blots are symmetrical, a qualifying phrase such as "it seems to be . . . ," or a psychotic verbal commentary. For purposes of simplicity, we shall assume that no important additional information is elicited during the inquiry.

For this single response, "a bat," which alone would have been recorded in a multiple choice or a group Rorschach test, the interpreter must integrate all available behavioral information. He does this by assigning tentative meanings to each of the behavior fragments (a) through (f). He then interrelates them and stands prepared to alter each of his interpretative hypotheses as he examines further responses throughout the test. As he proceeds, he properly invokes the gestalt principle that "the whole is more than the sum of its parts."

It is only when he later attempts to extract the meaning of his single variables from the total synthesis that his logic seems elusive. Guided by the converse of the familiar gestalt rule concerning parts and wholes, he comes out with a formulation such as the following:

$$P_1 \neq W_x - (P_2 + P_3 + \cdots P_n)$$

where W and P signify whole and part respectively, and subscript x signifies an unknown to the extent that the whole exceeds the sum of its parts.

Although the part is now not equal to the inferred whole minus the sum of the remaining parts, its meaning is to be established from the stated relationship. Since the two inductive leaps which have been made in this global interpretation sound, in everyday language, very much like pulling oneself up by the bootstraps, it is no wonder that Rorschach analysis sometimes arouses the suspicions of academicians.

It becomes the task of the interpreter who wishes to answer his critics to examine the elements which entered into his over-all assessment and the steps of reasoning by which he arrived at his global description or prediction. On embarking on this task, he soon encounters serious problems of empirical reference. What meaning can he assign to each of the behavior fragments (*a*) through (*f*)? Some of the probable meanings are as follows:

(*a*) *Slow rotation of the card:*
1. S is searching.
2. S is threatened, either by the content of the card, by the test, by E, or by the clinical setting.
3. S refuses to be hemmed in by what he perceives as inhibiting rules of administration.

(*b*) *Smile:*
1. S sees something humorous.
2. S is free-associating to something humorous.
3. S is reacting with a smile to threat perceived in the card, in E, or in the clinical setting.
4. S is expressing his disdain for the task or for the examiner.

(*c*) *Latency of response:*
1. S is slow by temperament.
2. S is tense or anxious.
3. S is depressed.
4. S is disturbed specifically by the dark gray color.
5. S is cautious.
6. S is intellectually slow in organizing.
7. S feels intellectually inadequate and wishes to please E.
8. S feels threatened by what he sees.
9. S is contemplating the dishonesty of his proposed report of his percepts to E.
10. S is outrightly negativistic or hostile to the task or to E.

(*d*) A *single popular response with form alone as a determinant* ("a bat"):
1. S perceives conventionally (i.e., he applies semantical rules in a conventional way in deciding whether a percept may serve as an appropriate sign vehicle for a class of objects).
2. S lacks higher order intellect or originality.
3. S is either consciously or unconsciously avoiding other percepts.
4. S is aggressive.

5. S reveals phobic qualities in his perception.
6. S exerts minimal energy.
7. S sees other things but is cautious in reporting.
8. S responds in this manner only in a new situation.

(e) *Immediate termination following the response:*
1. The card is unpleasant.
2. S is satisfied with his production.
3. After achieving some measure of success, S is afraid to expose himself to a possible subsequent failure.
4. S is being negativistic.

(f) *Absence of other forms of behavior* (e.g., bizarre associations):

Although it may be assumed that many of these hypotheses, particularly those in category (f), are automatically eliminated by the interpreter in the clinical setting on the basis of his skill and experience, this clinical reasoning does nothing to establish the validity of the individual hypotheses that he uses. The list of hypotheses about each fragment of behavior might be lengthened by the clinical intuition of the interpreter or by a polling of the opinions of a group of interpreters, but until it has been established empirically that any one or all of these meanings do apply in some individuals, no single statement of probability can be considered definitely valid. Only after it has been determined that a fragment of behavior can actually have all the meanings which are used in stating a most probable meaning do we begin to have a solid basis of scientific validity at this level of interpretation of the subject's behavior.

However self-evident the validity of these individual hypotheses may seem to the experienced examiner, they have not been adequately tested. Meer (35) has shown, for example, in an investigation of color shock, that mean reaction time and mean form level of the first response produced vary considerably from card to card for a group of subjects. If the interpreter uses reaction times in his evaluation without regard for such differences between cards, or without benefit of experimental demonstration of the personality correlates of differing reaction times to particular cards, his inferences cannot be regarded as sound. As an informal illustrative study, it might prove to be quite surprising for the examiner to check his hypotheses on experimental subjects by asking them at the conclusion of card I why they responded so slowly (if they know), or why they did or did not rotate the card.

If this naive approach of direct interrogation seems unthinkable to the user of the Rorschach technique, the same objective might be accomplished by having the subject perform on independent but similar perceptual tasks, as suggested by Holzberg on reliability in Chapter 13 of this book. The response-response correlations thus obtained would permit inferences of broader generality regarding the behavior fragments under consideration in this individual subject.

Many users of the Rorschach cards prefer to avoid the many difficulties inherent in speculation about nonverbal material by limiting the number of variables to the major scoring categories. The primary analysis of data by such a procedure is based on the psychogram of determinants (i.e., scores derived from actual percepts), on the location and on the content of responses, with only secondary, if any, utilization of nonverbal behavioral fragments. In the framework of this discussion, such an interpreter would concentrate on category (d) —the report of the percept—and would group his responses according to their common properties before stating tentative hypotheses. He would subsequently state his hypotheses in terms of the presence, absence, relative frequency of occurrence, and quality of responses in the various categories of determinants, location, and content. Depending on his orientation, he might then make use of a supplementary analysis of sequence of responses.

The interpreter who proceeds in a piecemeal, response-by-response fashion operates implicitly in much the same manner as soon as he reaches the point of assigning a tentative hypothesis to category (d)— the "bat." He treats this percept in the context of several hypotheses— location, form, achromatic color, texture, movement, and content. By the time he has examined the final response in the protocol, he may have decided that the first response—the "bat"—had something important to say about all six, or possibly only three, of these scoring categories, for which there are known, statable hypotheses regarding personality correlates.

The single response used in this way serves as a composite example of several classes of description. The problem of classification and identification is not unlike that faced by the student of archeology who, for an informal quiz, is asked to identify a small fragment of red pottery bearing an unusual black design. The student conjectures that the original vessel was produced by one of ten different ancient societies, probably by one of three. If allowed to inspect a few more pieces from the same object, he would probably be able to narrow it down through accumulation of evidence for shape, color, texture, design, and utility, to only one society. By a comparable process of reasoning, the interpreter of a Rorschach protocol narrows his description to one of many constellations of hypotheses regarding needs or behavioral traits. Since the single response, like the fragment of pottery, provides too few clues as to the identity of its producer, it becomes a logical necessity for the interpreter to derive a meaning for this single element from the empirical hypotheses concerning the major scoring categories of location, determinants, and content.

Although there is some disagreement among schools of Rorschach interpretation as to how this categorization should be done, there is also much common ground. One school may insist that animal movement be dealt with separately, or that animated human faces be included in the category of inanimate movement responses. Another school may refuse to treat three-dimensional vista as a scorable entity. Still another school may point to the usefulness of its statistical norms for popular responses, even though no subclassificatory norms are presented for age, sex, independently determined levels of intelligence, or socio-economic background. The difficulty of obtaining such normative data is obvious, but the inappropriateness of the logic which rests on a single general set of norms is equally undeniable. In spite of differences of opinion on the definitions of categories, however, there is little question among users of the test as to the interpretative significance of form qualities, location, white space, human movement, and gradations of texture and color as partially independent scorable entities. The extent to which such scoring categories are truly independent is a problem for factor analysis, which will be discussed later.

Additional problems arise when the eclectic interpreter attempts to assign a hierarchical order of priority to the Rorschach determinants while scoring his main responses and his additional responses. In the free-associational response "Costumed clowns all in bright colors enacting a sword fight," does human movement logically assume dominance over all other determinants, or is the determinant first mentioned of most importance? If another subject says, "A yellow flower shaped very much like a rose," does one school of scoring have more authority than another in assigning an FC instead of a CF?

Although these problems may seem far from minor ones to the interpreter who is employing his favorite hypothesis on color or human movement, they are of equal or greater consequence to the researcher who is utilizing frequency counts on the major scoring categories in his experimental design. The scores obtained would make a difference in a factor analysis, or in studies on empirical validity involving single variables, or for that matter possibly even global assessments. Whatever the type of experiment or clinical study, the scores would make a significant difference to the Rorschach interpreter who believes that he is dealing in "pure percepts" and, after eliminating all extraneous behavioral information such as rotation of the card and smiles, deals in quasi-quantitative global Rorschach analysis in its most refined form.

Whether an interpreter begins his analysis and synthesis with a study of relationships among responses in the several scoring categories, or whether he proceeds in a response-by-response fashion, utilizing all available verbal and nonverbal cues, he ultimately asks questions about the occurrence of a single response within a behavioral context or sequence. When the examiner asks himself why a subject who gave several conventional responses failed to see the animals on card VIII, but reported instead the spire of the University chapel in the lower center of card VIII, he is compelled to deal with the problem of content. He may place little confidence in what he regards as the undisciplined free associations of psychoanalytically oriented interpreters, or he may feel that content by any theoretical interpretation is too undependable to provide solid raw data for primary interpretation. Nevertheless, content may be providing him with more clues to personality than he is able to appreciate, and content may also be the one category of data which cannot be investigated adequately by a nonfree-associational, structured type of experiment.

Within the past few years, Fisher and Cleveland (22) have written a series of articles, later summarized in a book, in which they have reported differences in Rorschach content between persons having, and those not having, specific somatic illnesses. Of importance in the subject's performance are the number of barrier (container, or boundarylike) responses and the number of penetration responses (disruption of the surface, channels between exterior and interior, or permeable or fragile qualities to surfaces). Although several questions might occur to the reader of their articles concerning the adequacy of their scoring system, the independence of their variables, and the nature of their correlations with personality traits, the technical features of these problems will not be elaborated in this context.

Fisher and Cleveland ignore the usual scoring categories of Rorschach interpretation and restrict their analysis to frequency counts of specific content. They report high scorer reliability, and, in terms of group performance, seem to be able to distinguish the pathological from the nonpathological groups. Although the information obtained does not permit prediction of a somatic ailment in the individual case, the method suggests that content of responses in a perceptually ambiguous task deserves more careful and controlled study than it usually receives.

The author has had a similar experience with content while attempting to distinguish severely airsick from nonairsick Naval Air Cadets by the Rorschach method. He found that, of a total of seven response categories used in a sign formula, content alone, of the single variables, distinguished reliably between the airsick and nonairsick groups—the former group producing a greater quantity of responses characterized by "unhealthy" content (e.g., smoke, explosions, blood, etc.).

Although such single-variable studies of content do not attempt to deal with the individual Rorschach protocol as a configuration of responses, the work of Cleveland and Fisher does represent a channeling of efforts into a search for the physiological and personality correlates of high scores on their two categories of content. Whether the onlooker agrees with their dissection of the Rorschach configuration or not, the nature of their thinking seems rationally, if not entirely experimentally, sound. After having asserted a conviction regarding the value of content in their clinical observations of a free-associational perceptual task (i.e., the Rorschach task), they have been willing to define precisely a circumscribed portion of the total production, and have systematically searched for external correlates.

Their findings suggest that analysis of content has for too long been frowned upon by more conservative Rorschach thinkers, and that content might well serve as a topic worthy of serious, well-planned experimental investigation. The fact that content often seems unreliable in a configurational analysis in no way precludes the possibility that it may prove to possess as much, or more, interpretative significance and validity than the major determinants, when handled independently through properly designed experiments.

Summarizing this portion of the discussion, beginning with our analysis of a single response, "the bat," we have classified as elements the nonverbal behavior fragment and the single percept, the latter serving as the composite of several definable characterizing qualities (location, determinants, and content). We have, in addition, assigned elementary quantitative and qualitative status to each of the major scoring categories from which the single response derives its identity and meaning (i.e., location, determinants, and content). In other words, response X may possess properties A, B, C, D, E (e.g., color, shading, etc.); but response X may also contribute differentially to the magnitude of qualities embraced separately by categories A, B, C, D, and E. Thus, response X and scoring categories A, B, C, D, or E are viewed as interdependent elements.

These are the elements which many interpreters feel cannot be investigated independently of the total configuration. The conclusion seems inescapable, however, that the validity of interpretation of the single response which contributes to the total configuration derives in large measure from the validity of hypotheses which are anchored in the major scoring categories. If the meaning of a major determinant must be modified by the quantity or quality of one or more other major response categories, or if a single hypothesis must embrace several scoring categories, it should be conceded that at some point before the Tower of Babel reaches the clouds, some collection of sign vehicles must be circumscribed and stated as the definite sacrificial commitment of the interpreter. Once this small constellation of fragments or elements has been defined, the relevant hypothesis about personality should be put to exhaustive experimental tests and found to be either valid or invalid. If found to be invalid, then something is wrong with the semiotic sign collection, the hypothesis, or the precision of definition of the behavior being observed. The search for provable validity, from an experimental point of view, cannot be extended into the spirals of ever higher global reasoning; somewhere at lower levels a stand must be made. Without such a firm commitment and willingness to subject the elements to the destructive and constructive hazards of experimental investigation—and in the absence of convincing evidence for the validity of global interpretation, as most recently reported by Little and Shneidman (33)—the configurational interpretation of psychologists in the clinic will continue to receive severe criticism.

THE INTERPRETER AS ACTUARY

Beyond the point of establishing that a nonverbal behavior fragment, a single response, or a Rorschach scoring category can actually have one or a combination of several specific meanings, the interpreter does, and probably always will, deal in probabilities that one meaning is more applicable than another. From the known universe of meanings which a reaction time, for example, may have, the interpreter must select one as the most probable and combine it with the most probable meanings that rotation, smiling, "a bat," and immediate turning of the card face down all may have in this case.

Having integrated this information on the single response, the interpreter then proceeds to a higher level, comparing, contrasting, and combining the "most probable" generalization from the response to card I with responses to subsequent cards. From this set of generalizations, new probability statements must be made, providing at this highest level of interpretation a composite description of the individual. However implicitly actuarial it may or may not be, this is the nature of clinical description and prediction as it is today and as it may always be.

It is reasonable to assume that an interpreter alters the hierarchy of probabilities in preceding responses, and changes his frame of reference for succeeding responses, as he works toward the end of a Rorschach record. Insofar as such alterations occur, it is apparent once again that a behavior fragment, such as the smile on card I, derives its meaning, in part at least, from the total response pattern. This reasoning from whole to part, however, is based on the ultimate assumption that a universe of meanings for the behavior fragment has been, or ought to be, empirically established.

If the planners of programmatic research on validity of the Rorschach method begin at higher levels with the confident assumption that groundwork on the nonverbal fragments or on the major scoring categories is not really necessary, it means that the last threads of contact with the shores of empirical validation have been cut, and the entire Rorschach system of interpretation becomes a free-floating system of interesting semiotic signs and sign relationships. Statements made from the Rorschach protocol about the personality of a living organism then become abstract inferences which may be based on fact, intuition, or prejudice; they may be correct or incorrect, but they cannot be verified through the most liberal logic of test analysis. In such a situation, it becomes as difficult to predict the correctness of inferences as it is to foretell the exact spot at which lightning from a darkened sky will strike a dense forest.

The users of objective tests, which consist of aggregates of homogeneous items and which possess a known reliability, can afford to make bold predictions of a criterion at higher levels of empirical generality. They may do so with the expectation that the test should correlate dependably with some outside criterion; or if it does not, they may usually assume that the test is measuring reliably some previously undefined hypothetical construct for which new response-response correlates must be found. In such a structured test, high reliability may exist for the total score, even in the absence of reliability for individual items or subtests. This occurs, for example, on the Stanford-Binet forms *L* and *M*, because the odd assortment of items are known to be highly intercorrelated, and, in accordance with the objective of the original construction of the test, the items are measuring essentially the same intellectual functions. A test which possesses such properties may be employed satisfactorily to establish the validity of an appropriate hypothetical construct.

The interpreter of a projective test, on the other hand, is dealing with an instrument for which there is boundless heterogeneity of stimulus material, acknowledged heterogeneity of responses within a single scoring category, minimal information on the intercorrelation of response categories, and highly unsatisfactory measures of reliability. Since the projective tester has created this unfortunate situation for himself in order to clarify his understanding of human nature, it remains for the tester to reason his way out of his difficulties without sacrifice of acceptable logic.

If the Rorschach expert could make predictions dependably at the global level in experimental studies, he would already have opened a new era in projective testing. The fact that, in a formal investigation, he is sometimes able to describe a personality accurately from a blind or partially blind analysis, and sometimes not, leaves the burden of proof for validity squarely on the shoulders of the user of the test.

The most recent report on a large-scale study of validity is by Little and Shneidman (33). In their enumeration of negative findings for clinical tests, the authors follow in the tradition of the well-known investigations of graduate students in clinical psychology by Kelly and Fiske (29) and of success in flying by Holtzman and Sells (27). Little and Shneidman set out to investigate congruencies among personality descriptions made by 48 highly qualified clinical psychologists from four tests (Rorschach, Thematic Apperception Test, Make a Picture Story Test, and Minnesota Multiphasic Personality Inventory —with 12 judges assigned to each test), and by 23 psychiatrists (plus one clinical psychologist) from anamnestic data. The 12 patients were drawn equally from the psychotic, neurotic, psychosomatic, and psychiatrically normal diagnostic categories. The judges were asked to describe the patients by performing the following interpretive tasks: assignment of diagnostic labels, ratings of adjustment, *Q*-sort items, true-false factual items, and true-false inferential items. All judges performed the same tasks, thus minimizing, as much as possible, the problem of defining the criterion.

Without adding the ameliorative effect of critical comments concerning the design of the experiment made by the authors themselves, the findings on the blind analyses of each of these four clinical tests can best be summarized in the authors' own words:

. . . the results of the analyses for four frequently used psychological tests did not yield the kind of positive correlations [either betweeen judges or between tests and anamnestic data] that would gladden the hearts of psychological test proponents.

The results are even somewhat more distressing when one considers the magnitude of correlations even when they were significant (33, p. 26).

Until accuracy of prediction at higher levels has been demonstrated through replication of controlled studies on a great variety of subjects—if this can ever be accomplished—there is little justification for transcending obstacles by assuming, as some interpreters have done, that validity need not presuppose reliability. In the author's opinion, this position is tenable only if it is rephrased to read that "validity need not presuppose a formal demonstration of reliability."

It is conceivable that a test might possess a reliability for which no satisfactory measure has been developed. Such a state of affairs cannot be presumed to exist, however, unless valid predictions are regularly being made from the test. If such predictions or descriptions have not been achieved in carefully controlled studies, the quest for reliability should continue. This does not imply that the tester must measure only stable traits, unvarying with time or circumstance. It does imply, however, that, if the examiner is to report such characteristics of the individual as impulsivity or emotional lability, his diagnostic instrument must be able to indicate such features, either on more than one occasion or from several different observational measurements within a single test session. Otherwise, neither test nor tester is rendering a professional service.

Without basic research on the reliability and empirical meaning of the elements, or small combinations of elements of ink-blot behavior, global interpretation will remain a highly refined game of induction and deduction, largely at the level of syntactics. There will always be new intuitions followed by new definitions and new rules of inference, all of which will constitute an interesting self-contained system of sign relationships. There may even be a high degree of scorer-interpreter reliability to indicate that two individuals of comparable ability and experience can learn to use the same language in the same way. But if this system of sign relationships does not require solid ground legs at the level of empirical reference, studies of validity will continue to be a hit or miss affair; now a nonreplicable prediction on improvement with shock therapy at the .05 level of significance for a selected group of patients, then a prediction at the .40 level on the presence of constructive utilization of emotional potential in a sample of nonclinical subjects of average intelligence.

That is not to say that higher order problems of validity will automatically be solved by experimental groundwork on the elements but that, without such basic research, the riddles of the variable validity of more global interpretations cannot be expected to be solved.

SUFFICIENCY OF DATA

Every interpreter of a Rorschach protocol who is at all conventional employs some form of configurational analysis. He does this regardless of whether he chooses to work out an elaborate statistical scheme such as that provided by Cronbach for three elements (18), or operates instead in the customary implicit, informal manner. An intermediate, less data-bound approach, would be represented by the factor analytic work on *The Six Schizophrenias* by Beck (11) and Molish and Beck (37). These investigators have Q-sorted a large sample of traits on the basis of their over-all impression of the individual's Rorschach responses.

Regardless of whether the combination is done quantitatively or qualitatively, however, a fundamental assumption must be made that each element used in an interpretation has been drawn from an adequate body of data. If a statement is to be made about the personality correlates of the human-movement response, two M responses may not be a sufficient number to distinguish reliably this individual from one who produced no M responses. This would be true in an interpretation which conceived of the test protocol as a universe of information about the individual, as well as in an analysis which treated the test data as a collection of single measurements to be compared or contrasted with group norms or universal norms. These several viewpoints on the universe of data have been discussed previously by Rosenzweig (40).

For any of the approaches, however, whether oriented to intraindividual or interindividual variability, it is desirable to collect several manifestations of the response tendency which enters as a single variable into the global equation. This is particularly true in an ink-blot test, since the analysis of data requires a translation of the language of percepts, in addition to a direct observation of verbal and nonverbal behavior.

The production of a large number of responses within a particular Rorschach scoring category may possess a clear-cut interpretative significance for a given protocol, but the absence of responses in this scoring category in another protocol may possess no more specific meaning than a low score on an anxiety questionnaire. Equally low scores may be achieved on the latter test by the individual who experiences a minimal amount of anxiety and by the person who consciously or unconsciously denies his anxiety.

By a similar process of reasoning, a high score on the Rorschach test may in nearly all cases point to high intelligence (as conventionally tested), but a low score on M or an absence of M responses may provide minimal, if any, evidence for the level of general intelligence. This common clinical finding is supported by Altus and Thompson's (3) study employing the group Rorschach test on college students.

The demand for sufficiency of Rorschach data in no way ignores the possibility that an interpretation of a human-movement response may be modified by the quantity and quality of location and form responses produced by the same individual. Quite to the contrary, the possibility that one variable may be modified by the magnitude of another makes it even more desirable that statements made about response tendencies be based on more evidence for the individual's capacity to perceive human movement or to organize large areas than can be obtained from the voluntary production of from zero to three or four movement or whole responses.

The demand for sufficient data does question seriously, however, the notion that the individual responses which contribute to this pattern analysis must be treated experimentally only in the context of a longitudinal pattern in which they are dependent on each other in the sense of a response-response determinism. There is little question that some kind of psychic determinism underlies the subject's pattern of responsiveness; this does not imply, however, that the researcher should be permitted to seek basic principles of response productivity only after he has first succeeded in following intuitively a tenuous thread of causality in each new protocol. A person who looks at a blank white screen with 6 hours of food deprivation may report the following vague percepts in order: "cup—bowl—smiling face—ice cream—lake." The presence of a chain of apparently related associations need not conceal the possibility that a strong immediate drive is directing the production of responses on a statistical basis, nor should it prevent an experimental treatment of these percepts as if they were independent manifestations of the common strong drive. The fact that some interpreters of long experience place little confidence in sequence analysis in itself suggests that the individual responses need not be interwoven into the form of a short novel, such as the manifest content of a dream, in order to provide usable information for the global interpretation of personality or to provide manageable material for experimental study.

If the specialist in Rorschach technique can, for purposes of research on validity, temporarily part with his deep conviction that configurational analysis necessarily presupposes an elaborate sequential plot in test data, the implication is once again that research on experimental ink blots may open the doors to hitherto unknown principles of ink-blot interpretation. Such independent experimental work may tell him a great deal more about the subject's utilization of color, movement, and texture than he is able to determine from the ten cards and from the methods of clinical interpretation which he now uses.

REPRESENTATIVE SAMPLING OF RESPONSE TENDENCIES

Aside from the question of sufficiency of data, there is a fallacy in the generally accepted belief that the response pattern to the ten Rorschach cards represents a kind of absolute package of information from which a global interpretation of the subject's universe of response tendencies can be made. This fallacy of proportional representation of response tendencies in test data would exist, unfortunately, even in the case in which highly similar records were obtained on the same individual after an interval of two months or two years. In a remote way, the problem would be similar to that which arises in the construction of an achievement test in high-school mathematics. Such a test would be of questionable validity, from the point of view of item sampling, if it consisted of three times the number of problems in plane and solid geometry that were included from algebra or trigonometry. Statements made about the subject's achievement in geometry would be far more dependable than those made about his accomplishments in the other areas of mathematics. In our present ten Rorschach cards we have no way of knowing that we have presented the subject with stimulus materials which permit a representative sampling of the several facets of his personality, as revealed in response tendencies, although we treat scores on the experience balance and on other combinations of scoring variables as if such an assumption were sound.

The problem, which might be regarded as one of content sampling,[3] is illustrated in Figs. 14.1 and 14.2:

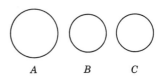

Fig. 14.1. Relative Strengths of Re-sponse Tendencies A, B, and C.

Fig. 14.2. Opportunity for Manifestation of These Tend-encies in Response to Ror-schach Cards.

The threshold or intensity of response is seen as a function of the strength of the response tendency and of the stimulus properties of the card. Response tendency B is pressing for expression with greater intensity than A or C. But since there is more ample opportunity from the structure of the stimulus figures for A to express itself, response

[3] The suggested similarity is not intended to imply an actual equivalence with content validity as it is known in achievement testing. The primary concern in achievement testing is with the sampling of content of a well-defined universe of items or subject matter; in the present instance, the problem is one of sampling a relatively unknown collection of response tendencies—tendencies, for example, to perceive movement, to utilize color, or to ignore determinants. It would be un-realistic to hope that any set of ambiguous stimulus materials could provide a perfect medium for the precisely quantitative seismographic recording of each of these interrelated tendencies within an individual protocol. However, once the response tendencies have been crudely detected by the so-called sign approach to personality testing, and after careful observation has led to an acceptable cate-gorization of response tendencies from which qualities of personality may be in-ferred, the problem then becomes one of altering the nature of the stimulus fig-ures in order to provide the best possible medium for recording the relative strengths of response tendencies. For example, one might proceed in the ap-parently undesirable direction of eliminating all cards with color, thus preventing the manifestation of a tendency to utilize color, or one might develop new sets of ambiguous stimulus figures which permit a relatively normal distribution, or at least a broad distribution, of color tendencies in a specified population of sub-jects. The emphasis gradually shifts from a "sign" approach to a "sample" ap-proach, as distinguished by Goodenough (24), since the larger problem of valida-tion eventually requires a transverse analysis of selected parts of the total sign collection as these parts appear within many different individuals. The trait or quality of personality, unknown at first, must be inferred from initial studies with a given body of projective test data; but once the quality has been accepted, it should be treated in further research by cross-sectional as well as by configura-tional analysis.

tendencies A and B may seem to the Rorschach interpreter to be of equal strength, whereas response tendency A, unfortunately, may seem to be of greater strength than C.

If one chooses to make a strong stand for global interpretation only at the expense of de-emphasizing or denying the need for knowledge of single variables or behavior fragments, is it reasonable to state that the ten ink blots we now use have, themselves, a fixed, absolute contribution to make to this high-level interpretation?

In our major example—"the bat"—we stopped at the end of the free association to card I. Any interpretation we might have made from the probability statements about each of these behavior fragments would necessarily have been of limited value.

If, on the other hand, we had accumulated data on the complete set of ten cards—free association plus inquiry—we would have classified our behavior fragments into categories, judged the relative magnitudes, examined the individual elements by sequential analysis, and made an over-all evaluation. If, in still a third instance, we had expanded our set of cards to twenty, we would have arrived at a new set of relative magnitudes for our scoring variables and a new global-II interpretation, which might have been quite different from the global-I interpretation.

Just as it is not at all to be expected that a small sample of behavior fragments would offer the same information about the individual as the whole Rorschach record, so it is seriously questionable that a record of ten cards would produce the same global interpretation as a set of twenty cards. Although we might seek new empirical hypotheses with the twenty-card set, these new statements need not be at all similar to the first set of hypotheses. There is simply no basis for assuming that the relative magnitudes we now use are not themselves a function of the arbitrarily chosen ratios of 3 chromatic: 2 black, red, and white: 5 black and white stimulus figures. At all levels—the behavior fragment as a single response, the ten-card set, and the twenty-card set—we are dealing with a limited amount of information. Despite the clinical interpreter's pride in his ability to generalize from a small sample of behavior, there is no absolute description of the total personality which can be derived from a single set of ten ink blots. It becomes then difficult to state that elements or single variables have no meaning apart from the total configuration, because the total configuration is never really known. In the absence of some kind of prophecy formula in Rorschach methodology, with which to predict the effect on stated relationships of lengthening the test through the utilization of many different sets of dissimilar blots, we cannot say what the true total configuration would be.

There are several ways to approach this problem of representative or proportional sampling of response tendencies in test data. One step in this direction would be to set up a structured (i.e., nonfree-associational) experiment employing separate sets of ink blots, each series representing a single object concept. This was suggested earlier in the discussion of the subject's language of percepts. It was proposed that the set of cards for a single concept (e.g., "the bat") consist of graded composite variations in form, color, shading, and possibly movement—step-by-step distortions of an indisputable representation of the specified object. The subject would be asked to indicate by ratings the extent to which a single blot in the randomly arranged series served as a reasonable representation of the object. A considerable body of information would be accumulated within a relatively short period of time on the subject's differential utilization of Rorschach determinants for different types of object concepts.

Although the particular concepts selected for representation in these sets of ink blots would be dictated initially by logical considerations on the part of the investigator, such an arbitrary procedure would still permit a sampling of usage of the various determinants for a variety of single concepts. In other words, one person might include color as a qualifying characteristic in the assessment of all concepts, another would make little or no use of color, while still a third person might use color only for concepts which in real life have clearly definable forms. In contrast to the usual procedure of obtaining evidence for the use of determinants secondarily from the responses which happen to be produced and which happen to be reported accurately as percepts, this experimental method would force the subject to commit himself, nonverbally, to a usage or nonusage of the determinant. It might also shed some light on the problem of complexity in color-form incongruity.

A second method of studying representative sampling of response tendencies—free-associational in nature—would be to develop independent sets of ink blots, each dealing specifically with only one of the determinants (form, color, shading, movement), or with content or organization. The subject would be asked to respond to each set of cards as he does to the Rorschach cards. A start in this direction has already been made by Levy (32) who has developed a set of painted cards conducive to the perception of human movement. Rust has utilized these cards in an elaborate study of the personality correlates of the human movement response (42, 43). As Piotrowski (39) has pointed out, however, the Levy method has shortcomings as a free-associational task, since the subject is asked to imagine people engaged in activities. A more satisfactory free-associational procedure for investigating human movement would be to ask the subject simply to report what he sees in a set of ink blots which possess an abundance of large and small areas perceived with moderate difficulty as human forms.

Taking still another free-associational approach to the problem of human movement, Barron (5) has been able to determine threshold values for the production of M by individual subjects on the basis of independently determined normative thresholds for a set of 26 experimental ink blots. Barron has also attempted to find personality correlates of these threshold values. Although it is apparent that procedures of this type introduce new sets of problems in experimental design, such methods might be used more widely to investigate the strength of response tendencies involved in other scoring categories of the Rorschach test.

Within the context of investigations of reliability, another type of experiment has shed some light on the problem of adequacy of sampling of response tendencies. Epstein et al. (21) constructed 100 ink blots which they assigned randomly to ten sets of ten blots each. They administered a separate set of the blots to their subjects during each of ten sessions, extending over a period of five weeks. The investigators limited the number of responses to three per card, and used several Rorschach scoring categories as well as one of their own in tabulating the responses. Although the reliability coefficients were below acceptable standards for individual prediction, all scores measured individual differences significantly beyond chance. The authors readily admit the disadvantage in time consumption inherent in any attempt to increase the reliability of a free-associational type of ink-blot test by increasing the number of cards, but they are convinced of the need for a demonstration of response consistency.

Moving one final step in the direction of measurement of response consistency, Starer (50) has used the kaleidoscope on patients who had previously given too few responses to the Rorschach cards. Although this rather informal experimental approach may seem to inject some angular wit into the contours of Rorschach thinking, it does have serious implications. There may be stable perceptual or intellectual organizational processes within the individual which manifest themselves in responses to a constantly varying stimulus. Although

Starer's primary analysis of responses to the kaleidoscope was limited to content, he did find much of the usual type of Rorschach content, and, as one might expect, a large number of geometrical designs. In addition, he found the use of color, movement, and many personalized associations.

It should be possible to follow up Starer's exploration by introducing curved as well as angular chips (if they were not already used) in the stimulus material of the kaleidoscope, and by constructing separate chromatic and achromatic instruments. Such innovations should provide information on the stability of relative magnitudes of the determinants, and on the consistency of production of particular types of content with increasing numbers of responses.

Studies of this type go beyond the work of Behn-Eschenburg (12), who has developed alternate (equivalent) forms of Rorschach cards, and Baughman (7, 8, 9), who has altered the stimulus characteristics of successive sets of Rorschach cards in an investigation of the independent effects on response data of each of the stimulus variables. Although some degree of consistency in the subject's responsiveness has been found in these studies, the previously mentioned investigations which employ randomly assigned, infinitely varied stimulus figures, or constantly varying stimulus materials (i.e., the kaleidoscope), constitute a broader search for consistency of response to ambiguous materials in general. Such work is much in line with the conviction of Holzberg that reliability for the Rorschach test should be sought in a variety of perceptual tasks which are similar to but not necessarily of ink blots in nature (see Chapter 13).

There is apparent in the work of any researcher who devotes his energies to problems of reliability on the Rorschach test a skepticism regarding the statements he makes from the test protocol in the clinical setting. He usually proceeds in his research on the assumption that unless he can eventually demonstrate a fair degree of consistency in the subject's responsiveness to a variety of stimulus materials, he should be prepared to conclude that the interindividual and intraindividual variability in human personality does not lend itself to adequate measurement by ink-blotlike tasks. Until he is able to find such consistency, he is unwilling to insist that his ink-blot method has the established merits of a solid technique of science, or that his intuitive, creative thinking is of the same order of cerebration that took place in the hypothesis-forming activities of Sir Isaac Newton. Prehistoric men, like schizophrenic patients, undoubtedly have observed many new relationships in nature; but what usually distinguishes a scientific from a nonscientific endeavor is the fact that the investigator not only has a strong conviction about the conditions under which the relationship occurs, and the conditions under which it does not occur, but that he also is willing to put his ideas to a test. Although the work of researchers on reliability may not possess a flavor of intuitive imagination, this is the kind of experimentation which may well determine the entire future of the Rorschach test.

TEST RESPONSES AS MEASURES OF PERSONALITY

At this point we have considered the language of the subject, the language of the interpreter, the validity of inferences from combinations of probability statements, the problem of sufficiency of data, and the problem of proportional sampling of response tendencies. We come now to the abstruse question of what it is that we are—or think we are—measuring. As White has viewed the task confronting us, "It is not unduly difficult to make up a personality test, but it is a gigantic undertaking to find out what it is worth" (55, p. 228). Although the foregoing discussion may raise some question about the ease of construction, there can be no doubt about the difficulty of validation.

The interpreter of the Rorschach protocol is dealing primarily with what we customarily designate as hypothetical constructs—needs or traits which cannot be observed directly, but which may be manifested in some form of overt behavior. Such properties of the organism as intellectual organizational capacity, sensitivity to inner stimuli, autistic fantasy, capacity for identification with others are but a few of the many constructs which are utilized, sometimes in different forms, in the several schools of Rorschach interpretation.

It is possible to avoid some of the problems of tracking down and defining experimentally these hypothetical constructs by adopting the view that demonstrations of validity must await the development of a satisfactory theory of personality. Slightly less comforting are statements that such validational work must await the development of a theory of perception, or that questions of the independence of the conventional scoring categories must be postponed until the factor analysts have learned how to define new factors.

Responsibility for the future development of a test cannot be disclaimed so easily. It is highly probable that theories of personality will always be constructed of molar variables, and that predictions made at increasingly molecular levels will be regarded as correspondingly more inaccurate or indeterminate. This was a fundamental assumption in the fragment-by-fragment analysis of the "bat" response. We were making statements at a molecular (or atomistic) level about specific behaviors in a specific testing situation. From a collection of such observations we attempted to generalize about a larger trait of personality which might influence behavior in many similar situations. We did not predict that a subject, if handed a new complex problem in printed or graphic form, would begin to rotate the piece of paper on which the problem was stated. The inference would have been made, if we had developed our logic further, that this fragment of behavior was guided in its expression by a larger, unifying trait of personality which might appear overtly in many different forms. It would have been our task as interpreters to select the larger trait from one of the following possibilities: unrestrained intellectual curiosity, intellectual inadequacy, indecisiveness, fear of tests, fear of examiners, fear of disapproval, general fearfulness, etc.

It has been only within the past six years that the method of inferring constructs from diverse observations and test performances, as exemplified in projective testing, has been recognized by specialists in test construction as a legitimate procedure of validation, both for the test and for the quality which it purports to measure. The term "construct validity," as introduced by the American Psychological Association's Committee on Psychological Tests (Technical Recommendations, 1954), and as later discussed in considerable detail by Cronbach and Meehl (20), was a logical development in the thinking of test constructionists who were dissatisfied with traditional views of "empirical" validity. The earlier formulations had usually assumed that a quality of personality as measured by a test could be defined adequately only by specification of one or more independent behavioral or test criteria. In many instances, the interest was centered entirely in the independent criterion, with only secondary emphasis on the nature of the odd, haphazard assortment of test scores which might prove to be good predictors of the criterion. The proponents of "construct validity" reasoned that validation of a test might involve primarily an accounting for the variance in test performance, as in factor-analytic studies, or a gradual accumulation of intercorrelations among many different criteria as methods of inferring the nature of an unobservable attribute of personality. As applied to the Rorschach technique, the element of test performance itself might be regarded as a behavioral derivative of a highly subjective life experience (e.g., autistic fantasy); and if one such behavioral derivative exists, many others presumably could be found from which theorists might establish the hypothetical quality of personality as an acceptable "construct." This is, in a way, similar to the statement in geometry that the locus of a circle can be determined from three points.

The task of construct validation becomes one of inferring a quality from a number of interrelated observables and then predicting additional related observables, or of predicting the interrelated observables (test behavior included) from a construct within a theory. The process may involve verification of individual hypotheses within a previously formulated theory or the building of a theory from very low levels of empirical law.

Unfortunately, the newer conception of validation has been misinterpreted by the defenders of some tests as providing an avenue of escape from the necessity of demonstrating empirically the significance of a construct within a theory or within a body of empirical laws. In projective testing, the incorrect conclusion would be that the term "construct validation" simply dignifies what the Rorschach specialist has been doing for decades—inferring constructs from many interrelated variables. What the Rorschach theorist sometimes fails to realize, however, is that his test does not have the properties necessary for establishing a form of factorial validity, and that, unless extensive correlation of Rorschach test behavior with external behavioral derivatives is accomplished for the individual constructs, one at a time, the system remains the free-floating body of syntactical sign relationships discussed earlier.

Bechtoldt (10, p. 628), reflecting on the general confusion regarding construct validity, despite formal clarification, and commenting on the excessively narrow interpretation of operational definitions and aversion to such terminology on the part of test specialists, has recently suggested that "The renaming of the process of building a theory of behavior by the new term 'construct validity' contributes nothing to the understanding of the process nor to the usefulness of the concepts." His argument is compelling when one considers that all forms of test validation involve, in the ultimate analysis, some form of operational procedure and definition, and that these methods have already been used in other areas of psychology to attempt to demonstrate the significance of a construct within a body of empirical laws.

Very little is known about the ways in which the postulated needs or traits which underlie test-response tendencies are manifested in a person's daily life. This question has been raised previously by Ainsworth.

Does a subject's "organizing ability" as sampled by his Rorschach performance extend to organizing the use of his time, organizing group activity, and organizing his thinking? Or does it merely refer to his ability to see relationships between various aspects of his perceived world? Or does it perhaps have no generalized significance beyond perception of the Rorschach material itself? (2, p. 408).

The answers to such questions await future systematic investigation. At present, our trait labels are of such broad applicability as to represent, in many instances, relatively nondifferentiating concepts. This is at once both a weakness and a legitimate defense for both projective techniques and personality theories. To possess adequate predictive power, a hypothesis or an observation on behavior must be sufficiently general; and yet, as it gains in generality, it usually loses in its capacity to differentiate individuals. It may be this very lack of capacity of major traits to distinguish one individual from another which sometimes helps to create the impression that statements made about a single individual by several different Rorschach interpreters possess little interpreter reliability, although possessing equal validity. The paradox may lie not in the definitions of reliability and validity but in the general nature of the traits which are being described. Each interpreter may emphasize different traits in his report, but for each trait which is delineated, heavily weighted, or omitted, some support could probably be found in the subject's behavior. On thorough critical analysis, however, the evidence from independent, unbiased observations or tests might well prove to be incapable of differentiating the individuals.

The same problem of generality of traits may show up as a decided advantage in validational studies which involve the matching of overall evaluations of Rorschach protocols with clinical descriptions, when this method is compared with other studies in which single variables on the Rorschach test are correlated with single traits of behavior. If the interpreter is afforded the opportunity to match his report with a clinical case description, he may succeed on the basis of one or two decisive accuracies in his holistic interpretation, whereas the rest of the report may in no way mirror the clinical description.[4] If twenty or more statements are made in a report about general traits, it is probable that in a collection of hypotheses of this size, at least a few

---

[4] It is also true, as has been pointed out by Cronbach, that "The judge may mismatch a very accurate prediction because just one sentence is contradicted by the criterion, or may match a very poor prediction with the criterion because one correct sentence gives him a clue" (16, p. 367).

of them in combination should enable the interpreter to narrow the problem of identification to a single individual. In terms of the cumulative frequency of hypotheses alone, the previously undetected gain in predictive power of more general statements about personality finally becomes apparent. It is unfortunate for workers who are engaged in an endless quest for validity that this vision of final success is more apparent than real.

Cronbach (16) has devised a modification of the blind-matching method which permits a more accurate assessment of the validity of single statements about the subject's personality. The judges are required to decide whether each statement on a list does or does not fit the person described in a criterion sketch. A procedure of this type may or may not produce results more favorable for the Rorschach test in a particular study, but at the very least, it reduces the number of contingencies inherent in a global-matching technique and leaves the interpreter with a clearer picture of the appropriateness of his evaluation. The major difficulty in this experimental approach, or in any trait-sorting procedure, is that of selecting a sample of descriptive statements about personality which are congruent with the theoretical orientation of the judge, in this instance, the Rorschach specialist.

It seems unlikely that we will ever be able to reduce the degree of generality of the personality traits which we customarily postulate. But we may be able to reach an alternative solution to the problem by defining our hypotheses regarding Rorschach data more precisely in terms of differential overt or covert responses to specific life situations. The major problem becomes that of making exhaustive investigations of individual personalities as they appear to other persons, within the home, in the place of employment, and in places of social or physical recreation. Although the traits which are guiding the individual's observable behavior in each of these situations may be very general, their nature, strength, and differential manifestation may be understood and defined more clearly by an accumulation of such response-response correlations.

A thorough experimental investigation of environmental variables might help to correct the frequently noted tendency of Rorschach interpreters to emphasize the pathological or negative side of personality. It would do so by focusing not only on the presence, absence, or magnitude of a trait but also on the actual need for that trait in the current life situation of the individual. Carrying the gestalt point of view to its logical conclusion, this would imply that the Rorschach configurationist of today is not showing due regard for the general formula to which he readily subscribes:

$$Behavior = f \ (Person \times Environment)$$

It may be found from such research on the interaction of Rorschach personality variables with environmental variables, for example, that the absence of creative organizational capacity is in no way a deficiency for an individual whose movements are limited to particular areas of society. This man may live a contented family life, he may complete a constructive, satisfying block of work each day in his occupational life, and he may be an active member of his community. He may also produce a most uncommendable "bug, bear, bat" type of Rorschach protocol. The absence of the trait of creative organizational capacity may be seen as a deficiency only by the Rorschach examiner himself, who by intellect, temperament, or middle-class academic background values such a trait above all others. Far more than other scientifically inclined intellectuals, the Rorschach interpreter may, himself, feel at home in the area of creative literary, philosophical speculation, encumbered as little as possible by what he perceives as the straitjackets of statistical, experimental reasoning.

The search for validity of personality description from Rorschach data seems, then, to require not so much the splitting apart of primary traits or tendencies into infinitesimal units, as a conservative retention of larger traits (which may change with the development of theory) and an empirical specification of the major environmental situations in which these traits usually express themselves. This alters the perspective from a need to Q-sort large listings of trait elements—for which the intercorrelations often have not been determined—to a search for the manifestations in different settings of a smaller number of major trait aggregates.

THE PROBLEM OF DEFINING AN INDEPENDENT CRITERION

As for the procedural aspects of experimentation, it is the earnest hope of every investigator who sets out to test an hypothesis linking Rorschach data to personality traits that he will be able to minimize the contamination of his data by irrelevant variables. He finds that to achieve this objective, the interpreters of protocols in his experiment must reach complete agreement with the independent observers or raters of the subject's behavior on the manner in which a trait is to be observed and described. They must agree also on the definition of the environmental setting in which the trait is to be observed. If these conditions have, indeed, been met, the test has an optimal opportunity to exhibit its merits as an instrument of prediction or description.

In practice, this ideal arrangement is rarely approximated. It may be necessary and, in fact, logical to obtain the ratings from friends or relatives of the subject, ward attendants, psychiatrists, employers, or fellow employees. These persons, even after careful instruction by the researchers, may not conceive of their task or of the traits which they are rating in the same way that the interpreters of the protocols are viewing the situation.

As the independent rater becomes more dissimilar to the interpreter of the protocol in ability, personality, or background, any true relationship which may exist between test data and criterion measure becomes attenuated through the intrusion of irrelevant variables. As the trait or performance criterion to be observed becomes increasingly complex to the extent that it becomes a measure of accomplishment in a life adventure—such as success as a salesman or success as a pilot—the picture becomes still more flooded with irrelevant variables. If such grandiose predictions do succeed with an instrument which is as vaguely understood as the Rorschach test, the researcher should consider the advantages of seeking membership in a society of mystics. If the prediction fails, the failure may or may not be the fault of the instrument. In this event, the ink-blot method has not been put to a fair test of its efficacy.

Although there always may be the temptation to display the dramatic, spectacular qualities of one's art or science, such ambitious experiments with extremely complex criteria are better left to tests for which some definite information on reliability and validity has already been obtained—at least at our present stage of limited knowledge of ink blots.

It is unfortunate for the development of research on the validity of the ink-blot method that much of the energy available for experimentation must be channeled into problems of practical importance in the clinical setting. There is little question, even among severe critics of the Rorschach method, that in a large percentage of the classical cases of the various psychiatric disorders, particularly schizophrenia, the Rorschach test provides rather clear-cut diagnostic evidence of the disorder. But when the problem of establishing a diagnosis from samples of deviant perceptual behavior merges, in a more heterogeneous population, into the task of determining the validity of inferences regarding the structure of personality in general, the spectacular effectiveness of clinical diagnosis from the Rorschach protocol becomes markedly reduced. It would be easy to cite a large number of studies which have taken either a configurational approach or a single-variable approach to the problem of diagnosis. However carefully each of these studies has been done, it is quite possible that discrepant findings would have been obtained in a different type of hospital or clinic in a different geographical location with a different staff of psychiatrists. This would be true even if the group of Rorschach examiner-interpreters were the same in all studies. It is well known that medical staffs as well as individual psychiatrists and psychologists differ greatly in their application of complex diagnostic labels, such as schizophrenia or character disorder, particularly when dealing with the broad band of borderline patients. This set of circumstances forces the investigator into the position of violating a fundamental assumption of his statistical analysis—that of random or representative sampling of the population of schizophrenic patients. The researcher in a single institution has neither random nor representative sampling of patients who bear, for example, the diagnostic label schizophrenia, and any conclusion which he reaches at the .05 or .01 level of significance, even with replication, tells only a limited amount about the ability of the Rorschach test to predict or to describe schizophrenia.

It cannot be repeated too often that prediction of complex criteria such as psychiatric diagnoses or success in an occupation should not be regarded as a fair indication of the general validity of a psychological instrument, unless that instrument was constructed to mirror the complexity of the criterion. Batteries of tests have, on occasion, been assembled for industry or for the military organization with just such a purpose in mind, but the Rorschach test was not designed, and cannot be properly employed alone, for the prediction of such complex criteria. If the Rorschach method is employed in such a manner, it suffers a needless loss in prestige each time it fails.

First of all, the prediction of performance in a life adventure usually presupposes the provable validity of hypotheses about single personality traits or trait patterns—a shaky assumption, indeed, for the Rorschach test. Secondly, the criterion must be exhaustively defined. The difficulties of this task have been carefully enumerated by Anastasi (4) and Cronbach (17), in their texts on tests and measurements, and by many other writers. This means that in addition to a general evaluation of the subject's personality in the abstract, the researcher must obtain adequate information on the general and particular demands for occupational and interpersonal behavior, and must have a knowledge of the expected and unexpected stresses of the job. He should know whether the behavioral traits can summate in a kind of qualitative multiple regression equation, or whether certain traits must be present to a minimal degree before any kind of success can be obtained.

Sometimes the experimental prediction must take into account aspects of the occupational endeavor which may not always be apparent to persons who are in a position to supply the information for an analysis of the criterion. Also, what the user of the Rorschach protocol may think represents a well-integrated personality for success in that occupation, may be markedly lacking in the clinically maladaptive features—particularly the trace of psychopathiclike aggressiveness—which sometimes seem necessary for final success in many life undertakings.

The criterion itself may change with time. The traits of personality which constitute effective leadership or so-called followership for a young cadet in the early phases of a military training program may not contribute to success when the demands for effectiveness in interpersonal relations of a particular type are intensified at higher levels of rank. Still more difficult for the researcher in another area is the problem of defining a criterion of success or improvement with time in psychotherapy. And yet researchers insist on creating a symbiotic relationship between the Rorschach test and psychotherapy—a relationship in which each measure presumably gains evidence for its validity from the other.

It is just such unrelenting research with exceedingly complex criteria that helps to provide abundant support for the negative appraisals of the Rorschach technique which appear so often in general literature on psychology. One need only turn to a text in introductory or developmental psychology to find uncomplimentary summary statements about the coveted Rorschach test, statements which are being presented regularly to successive classes of undergraduate students:

The conclusion here [in a study by Filmer-Bennett, 1955] was that, with our present state of knowledge, this [Rorschach] technique alone is not at all an adequate predictor of how a patient will react to treatment (41, p. 80).

Despite improvements in administration and interpretation, the Rorschach test in many instances probably gives a better picture of the examiner than of the examinee (36, pp. 491–492).

THE VARIABLE CONSTANTS

To the list of grievances of the many academicians who at times seem to develop their critical remarks from secondary or tertiary sources of opinion on the Rorschach method, we should add one final class of relative unknowns to the complex process of Rorschach communication. These are the possible variables which we uncritically assume to be constants. Some of them may ultimately prove to be constants; a few of them have been shown experimentally to be variables. To an unknown degree they all may serve to influence the subject's responses or, secondarily, the interpreter's report. Many of the variables have been discussed at length by Sarason (46). Since the Rorschach protocol serves as a source of information for controlled research or for a clinical report to a therapist who may have a direct influence on the subject's life, it is important that we know how much of the information transmitted in this chain of communication is an uncensored message from the inner recesses of the subject himself.

The schematic diagram, shown in Fig. 14.3, indicates the point of

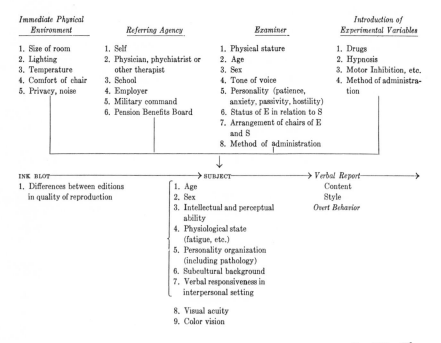

Immediate Physical Environment	Referring Agency	Examiner	Introduction of Experimental Variables
1. Size of room	1. Self	1. Physical stature	1. Drugs
2. Lighting	2. Physician, phychiatrist or	2. Age	2. Hypnosis
3. Temperature	other therapist	3. Sex	3. Motor Inhibition, etc.
4. Comfort of chair	3. School	4. Tone of voice	4. Method of administra-
5. Privacy, noise	4. Employer	5. Personality (patience,	tion
	5. Military command	anxiety, passivity, hostility)	
	6. Pension Benefits Board	6. Status of E in relation to S	
		7. Arrangement of chairs of E and S	
		8. Method of administration	

INK BLOT ⟶ SUBJECT ⟶ Verbal Report ⟶

INK BLOT	SUBJECT	Verbal Report
1. Differences between editions in quality of reproduction	1. Age	Content
	2. Sex	Style
	3. Intellectual and perceptual ability	Overt Behavior
	4. Physiological state (fatigue, etc.)	
	5. Personality organization (including pathology)	
	6. Subcultural background	
	7. Verbal responsiveness in interpersonal setting	
	8. Visual acuity	
	9. Color vision	

Fig. 14.3. The

intrusion of each of these variables. The reader should keep in mind that only those items listed under "Subject," items 1 through 7, and the items included in the class of "Experimental Variables," such as drugs, hypnosis, motor inhibition, etc., are recognized as legitimate and accountable variables by the interpreter of the Rorschach protocol.

Each person listed in the diagram—the subject, the examiner, the interpreter, the referring agent, and the therapist or researcher—participates in this process of semiosis, this "mediated-taking-account-of." At each stage, beginning with the ink blot as the sign vehicle of a class of objects, the message is altered as if it were a ray of white light passing through a complex series of fluid or prismatic media. What is often assumed to be a faithful transmission, through a single prism, of the coded description of an individual personality is seen here as a reflection, refraction, and scattering of message elements.

Neither researcher nor clinical interpreter can afford to be complacent about what may seem to him to be the negligible contribution of these variables. Although many of the variables may play a minor role in most cases, they may make a significant contribution in some

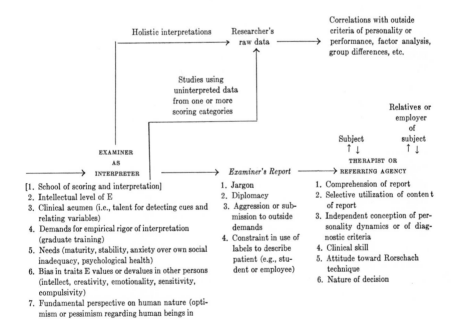

Variable Constants.

inconstant subjects, or in some untalented or insecure examiners or interpreters. In the absence of experimental information on many of the variables, we can make no final assumptions in a free-associational task of the type represented by the Rorschach test. The fact that responses to all tests are to some extent influenced by situational factors or by variability among interpreters in no way modifies the fact that the Rorschach technique, as probably the least structured of all tests, provides maximal opportunity for the operation of these variables.

Beginning with the stimulus card itself, there are differences in the ink coloring of successive editions of the Rorschach cards. Or at times, it does happen that an institutionalized patient becomes curious about stray grease spots on the card. The lighting in the room may be poor, the patient may be color blind, or he may have failed to bring his glasses from the ward. A small testing room, cramped and over-heated, or an inadequately sound-insulated cubicle may easily limit the patient's responsiveness.

With regard to the referring agency, it makes a difference whether the subject is voluntarily seeking professional assistance, or whether his career in military aviation or his governmental pension is at stake. It will make a difference for another subject in the military service, if he succeeds in gaining a transfer from a prison cell to a more comfortable hospital ward by convincing the inspecting physician and the Rorschach examiner that he is a very sick man. Although the Rorschach expert may express confidence that his evaluation will not be affected by such maneuvers, the problem proves to be a difficult one when the response configuration turns out to be an equivocal one.

The subject's perception of the test situation may influence his performance even though he has no premeditated intent to deceive the examiner. In one exploration of this variable Henry and Rotter (26) informed an experimental group of subjects that the Rorschach test was used to discover serious emotional disturbances, prior to presenting the standard instructions of Klopfer, while offering only the standard instructions to a group of control subjects. The investigators assumed that the responses of the experimental subjects would be comparable to those of other individuals who hold implicitly the same hypotheses regarding the significance of the test situation.

Experimental subjects produced a smaller total number of responses, a larger number of responses of high form level, and a larger number of popular and animal responses. These findings suggest greater conformity and stereotypy in the pattern of test responsiveness of persons who believe that their emotional stability is in question. The quality of caution or inhibition which the interpreter usually attributes to the basic personality structure of the subject, in some cases, may be caution only as a function of the test situation.

The examiner, also, may contribute to the alteration of the subject's message. A diagnostic tester who is pressed to keep another appointment or who has grown weary at the end of a long day of interviewing patients may not be aware that his temporary impatience is being conveyed subverbally to the subject as a cue not to burden the examiner with a large number of responses or elaborations during the inquiry. On the other hand, another subject, reacting to what he perceives as indifference on the part of the examiner, may force the attention of the latter by opening the floodgates of his own productiveness.

Significant differences among examiners in controlled experiments have been found by Lord (34), by Baughman (6), and by Sanders and Cleveland (44). Using a standard technique of administration, nine previously unsophisticated graduate students who were trained in Rorschach administration specifically for the experiment as examiners, and a separate group of 30 randomly assigned subjects (undergraduates) for each examiner, Sanders and Cleveland found differences among examiners on 20 out of 38 Rorschach scores. When those scores which correlated highly with the total number of responses were disregarded, the number of significant differences remained well beyond chance.

Dividing the examiners into high and low subgroups along four separate dimensions—(a) overt anxiety and (b) overt hostility, as measured by ratings obtained from the subject at the conclusion of the test; and (c) covert anxiety and (d) covert hostility, as determined from the examiner's own Rorschach record—the investigators found the following: Examiners who possessed high overt anxiety elicited from their subjects more general responsiveness (total R), more white space, and more color than those with low anxiety. In contrast, those examiners who scored high in covert anxiety evoked more hostile content, more passive trends ($Y\%$), and a larger number of human-figure and human-movement responses.

The subjects of examiners who were rated high on overt hostility produced a larger number of responses indicative of stereotypy and passivity ($A\%$, $Y\%$), and fewer responses of human and hostile content. The inverse was true of subjects whose examiners were high in covert hostility (i.e., less stereotypy and passivity, and more human and hostile content in the subjects' Rorschach responses).

Although the nature of such differences may vary with the type of examiners, the population of the subjects, and the design of the experiment, the evidence is convincing that we cannot regard the examiner as a constant.

The examiner plays still another role as interpreter in this system of communication. Regardless of his clinical ability, training, or professional experience, he may, as a part of his personal equation, have an affinity for such descriptive labels as neurotic, homoerotic, schizophrenic, passive dependent, hostile, or emotionally unresponsive to environmental stimuli. Willner (58) has reported differences among interpreters in a study in which he asked each of five Veterans Administration staff psychologists to rate eight out of the ten personality factors on the Multi-Dimensional Scale for Rating Psychiatric Patients (outpatient form) from Rorschach data. Although he did not describe his results in detail, he attributed the variability among interpreters to differences in personality.

If a longitudinal statistical study were made of the reports of individual interpreters through many years of professional work, it would probably be found that some Rorschach experts unconsciously seek evidence to justify the application of particular personality trait labels, quite apart from the methods of configurational analysis which they learned in seminars or devised on their own. The problem is not unlike that faced by the psychoanalyst who diligently attempts to maintain objectivity about the verbal and nonverbal productions of his patient. The analyst may be able to find Freudian symbols in places where the master would never have thought to look.

In his written report, the interpreter may specialize in minute interpretations which can be classified as Rorschach jargon, or he may deal in descriptive terms of such molarity that the analysis might well have depicted any symbol-using primate at any era of recorded history. The extent to which the Rorschach interpreter actually maintains communication with the therapist or other referring agent may, indeed, have far-reaching consequences for the patient. And since the medical clinic is the setting in which Rorschach testing finds its greatest application and, at present, its maximal effectiveness, it becomes necessary in a discussion of the validity of the test itself to extend this chain of communication all the way to the door of the therapist.

Experimentally controlled manipulations of the testing situation have been discussed previously by Schneider (47) and by Ainsworth (2), and will not be described in detail in this article. As an example of such studies, Singer et al. (49) found that motor inhibition resulted in an increase in the number of human-movement responses. In the same experiment, they failed to obtain confirmation for a second hypothesis which stated that a period of hyperactivity should be followed by a decrease in productiveness of M responses. Similar investigations in which drugs have been employed are of considerable interest, but should not be regarded as studies primarily of validity. There is little question that something different takes place in the functions of the perceptual, intellectual, and motor controls under the influence of even such innocuous fluids as ethyl alcohol; but information on changes in behavior of this kind contribute a limited amount to our search for consistency in Rorschach performance or to our quest for manageability of data.

Each of the variables listed in Fig. 14.3 could be considered a source of unreliability or invalidity in the use of basic data for purposes of research or for disposition of a clinical case. Each could serve as an independent problem for experimental investigation. In an area as fundamental to Rorschach technique as the nature of the inquiry, for example, Klingensmith (30) has studied the effects of using four different methods of structuring this part of the interview:

1. Free association.
2. "Is there anything else that gives this impression?"
3. "What else, in addition to the shape, if anything, helps you to see what you do?" The emphasis is on detailed report of percepts.
4. Explanations and printed definitions of Rorschach determinants.

Klingensmith found a gradual increase from conditions 1 to 4 in the frequency of occurrence of responses in a given scoring category. The increment varied, however, with the determinant. For example, while human movement emerged in the free association and showed no significant increase with levels of inquiry, shading, chromatic and achromatic color, and animal movement came out most readily under condition 4.

Although such research might be viewed by the defender of a particular variety of Rorschach interpretation as an ill-advised plan to undermine our faith in the basic principles of the test, it is our responsibility as users of the test to lift the heavy curtain and to accept these variables for whatever they may or may not contribute to our knowledge of the instrument.

FOR THE FUTURE, ART OR SCIENCE?

In the face of such a multiplicity of variables affecting the subject's responses—the basic raw material which must be fed into the patterns of responses before the interpreter can even begin to think about problems of prediction from probability statements or about factor analyses —the Rorschach worker cannot intelligently ignore the rapping on the door by the experimental psychologist. If he is at all concerned with the scientific merits of his instrument, he can ill afford to disregard the sometimes friendly and sometimes hostile pleas for a re-examination of the Rorschach test in academic and research institutions throughout the land. As far back as 1948, Thurstone (53), in a genuinely interested vein, made a request for bold new experimentation with ink blots.

It is no satisfactory answer to this recommendation to state, as has often been done, that validation of hypotheses and clinical application of the test go hand in hand. Validation and clinical use of the ten Rorschach cards have been going hand in hand for several decades; they have as yet produced only one illegitimate offspring named "Inconclusive."

There is very little concrete basis for making an optimistic prediction that a review of studies of validity, in which the ten Rorschach cards have served as the sole instrument of investigation, will be any different 25 years from now than they were when reviewed in 1954 by Ainsworth (2), or more informally by earlier and more recent authors. From each of these reviews it could be inferred that the Rorschach test had been shown by existing methods to be neither consistently valid nor invalid. A few hypotheses seem highly valid, but many others seem seriously questionable.

One need not be magnanimous to appreciate the fact that many highly intelligent, original thinkers have devoted the major part of their professional lives to the study of this instrument. It would be a grave understatement of their contributions to conclude that gaps in statistical knowledge or faulty designs of experiments—as most helpfully pointed out by Cronbach (19)—have rendered their many observations a matter of inconsequence. Anyone who has worked in a clinical setting is aware of the meaning of clinical acumen or sensitivity, whether it pertains to behavioral observation or to piecemeal analysis of data on projective tests. The empirical validity of hypotheses about test data is one matter, but the sensitivity to isolated cues concerning these hypotheses is another.

The most skeptical of users of the Rorschach cards would agree that the traditional hypotheses were not pulled out of thin air, nor entirely out of the personalized projections of the earlier interpreters. The traits of personality of which the Rorschach analysis speaks sometimes confront one with such startling clarity as to leave the statistically sophisticated interpreter in wonderment that these hypotheses are truly valid in some persons. The question of why these hypotheses do and why they sometimes do not hold cannot in good conscience be abandoned with the simple conclusion that the statistical probabilities involved are too staggering in complexity ever to provide a satisfactory answer. This explanation may satisfy an academic experimentalist who nurtures his status as a scientist too closely ever to permit himself to read an article on the Rorschach technique, but it does not provide comfort to the user of the test who is debating whether it would be profitable for him to invest his time in research on this instrument.

The ink blots as sign vehicles do seem to speak a language—one which we have not yet succeeded in translating. We have fleeting views of the many meanings of single percepts, but we do not yet know whether these signs are speaking a universal language or instead a language that has a very large number of dialects.

In the author's analysis of this problem, we make a serious mistake when we assume that the ten cards presently employed in the Rorschach test constitute the Rosetta stone by which this language will ultimately be understood. From all that we have learned about test construction in general, we cannot expect patterns of interpretation to be reliable or valid if too little information enters into the major variables which comprise these patterns. Two human-movement or three form-dominated color responses, or one reaction time to card VI, provide amazingly little information with which to make dependable statements about personality; and when the lack of dependability of statements about personality leads to a general questioning of the validity of the method, as is evident in current critical commentaries on the Rorschach technique, it becomes the intellectual responsibility of the users of this method to examine their fundamental assumptions regarding both stimulus materials and logical procedures of critical evaluation.

If the author's view of the field is in proper perspective, the postulate on which much Rorschach thinking and research seems to rest is that the ten stimulus figures originally designed by Hermann Rorschach provide adequate building blocks for the founding of a science which underlies ink-blot interpretation. It follows from this assumption that experimental work on non-Rorschach perceptual materials, if recommended at all, serves merely to verify conventional hypotheses or to provide new hypotheses to be incorporated in conventional interpretations. For example, since the empirical referents of the human-movement response have not been defined satisfactorily, independent research will clarify its many meanings; the clinical user of the test will then embody these findings in his analyses of individual test protocols. In this instance, the stimulus figures serve as a permanent constant while the modes of interpretation appear as variables.

A second, not unrelated, fundamental assumption concerns the desirability of unification of research efforts. Granted that the ten ink blots originally devised are not necessarily the best, they are productive ones; and if the interpreters are ever to develop a common language, they should talk about the same stimulus materials.

The pressure for such conformity in investigation becomes stronger as the decades roll by. The widespread conviction that research should be restricted to specified channels has been expressed formally by Korner:

> Instead of realizing that all of these techniques operate on the same principles and instead of exploring a few techniques thoroughly aiming at an integration between the tests and the body of personality theory, we are busy devising new gadgets which in each instance require new standardization and new validation (31, p. 619).

This statement was well intended as a deterrent to the proliferation of new marketable products which grapple in parallel fashion with the same problems that are being encountered in the Rorschach test. The task of providing evidence for the validity or invalidity of a projective test is an immense one, and there are few, if any, research-minded individuals who would advocate the introduction of a new ink-blot test for general use by the profession at the end of every five- or ten-year period. As a general philosophy, however, the implied request that experimentation on ink blots produce feedback of direct relevance to the Rorschach cards has self-destructive overtones. It is of utmost importance that experimental ink blots, which may have nothing at all to say about the Rorschach test, be used to ask new types of questions of fundamental significance to the validity of ink-blot methods. Some of the research proposals discussed earlier in this chapter could not be explored experimentally by a free-associational method. Other problems concerning consistency of response tendencies could not be investigated without new sets of blots.

Despite our knowledge that science takes giant steps forward through the discoveries of pure unrestricted research, the belief grows more firmly entrenched that permanent foundations for the method have already been provided by the 2500 or more studies already published on the ten original stimulus figures. The unfortunate aspect of this belief is that many of the earlier investigations, as well as a few of the more recent experiments, have been unable to withstand the waves of criticism which recurrently wash the shores of the Rorschach world. Two examples will serve to indicate the degree of precision employed in the specification of major variables in many of these studies.

In 1933, seventeen years after the advent of reasonably quantitative measures of intelligence, Vernon described the groups of subjects who provided data for his Rorschach norms, as follows:

My own results were obtained from the following three groups of students and adults:

I. Twenty-five male freshmen at Yale University, aged 17–19 years; an undistinguished group of about average intelligence and heterogeneity.

II. Forty-eight male students at Harvard College, ranging from freshmen to seniors, aged 16½–23 years. This group was, as far as possible, unselected in the statistical sense of the term.

III. Seventeen English subjects, of whom seven were women. This was a highly educated group, consisting for the most part of graduates of Cambridge University. They ranged in age from 20 years upwards, the median age being about 25 years. Owing to their small numbers, no attempt will be made to distinguish the sexes (54, p. 96).

That all errors of scientific analysis were not committed by an earlier generation of Rorschach investigators is apparent in the published report of Henry and Rotter (26), cited previously in this chapter. The authors explore the effect of informing an experimental group of subjects that the Rorschach test is used to discover serious emotional disorders. Experiments of this type, like all recent studies mentioned in this chapter in the section entitled "The Variable Constants," are usually regarded as having particular scientific merit because they demonstrate that something is wrong with Rorschach interpretation rather than right with it. One finds on reading the article, however, that, although E scored all records and was checked for reliability by a second scorer, the study nowhere states whether one or one dozen examiners administered the test. In view of the fact that the examiner is known to be a variable in the subject's production of Rorschach responses, one might feel justified in asking the authors to specify very clearly the control of this variable. Otherwise, the reader must accept the scientific merits of the experiment on good faith.

Few would question the earnest efforts or the conscientious reports of the earlier investigators or of the more recent ones, but, as times change, the nature of problems and of criticism in a developing science changes. What seems today to be a most penetrating analysis appears tomorrow as a naive observation.

In the realm of art—an area of acknowledged nonscientific endeavor —it is the privilege of collectors to specify the disposition of their treasures after their time. This has been done many times with the passing of generations. In Boston, an entire museum of objects of art has been left to society with the stipulation that, with the exception of living flowers, no object should ever be moved or replaced. There is little doubt in the mind of the visitor who spends a delightful afternoon in the Isabella Stewart Gardner Museum that such a collection of art treasures, by its very survival of time, will increase in its value to society.

In the realm of science, such an accrual of worth with the passing of time cannot be assumed. Wilhelm Roentgen was not disposed to state in his last will and testament that, henceforth, X-rays should be given in strict accordance with his specifications of film, machinery, and voltage. Alfred Binet could not demand that the items in future intelligence tests conform to his ideas of content, administration, or scoring. The concept of intelligence quotient had not even been introduced in his day.

And yet with a widespread plea for unification of Rorschach research efforts, together with a tacit assumption that the ten Rorschach cards constitute a fixed constant among peripheral developments in the field of perception, we tend to discourage the kind of pure research which can ever hope to crack through the labyrinthine shell of this system of semiotic sign relationships. There is an authoritarian tendency among the adherents of more formalized systems of Rorschach interpretation to assert that only highly sophisticated Rorschach workers can know the meaningful and relevant hypotheses, and to imply that experimental psychologists who tamper with the Rorschach test are like naive actuarial chickens scratching aimlessly for food in an unfamiliar barnyard. On more rational grounds, it would seem that the gains in perspective which could result from an open invitation to experimental psychologists to do what they will with ink blots of any kind would far outweigh the apparent loss of direction in a few ill-conceived, meaningless experiments with non-Rorschach materials.

Foremost among the unwelcome guests in the past have been the high-level statisticians. In the minds of most researchers in the area of projective techniques, however, there is little question that Cronbach (19) rendered an invaluable service when he presented his detailed criticisms of the statistical methods which had been applied to studies of the Rorschach technique prior to 1949. As the interested but growingly impatient adviser of Rorschach methodologists, Cronbach has offered a number of other constructive suggestions pertaining to treatment of data, previously mentioned in this chapter.

Less graciously received have been the factor analysts, whose complex operations sometimes appear more awe-inspiring than is justifiable. Like Rorschach specialists, the factor analysts have developed their own impressive-sounding jargon—matrices, rotations, second-, third-, and fourth-order factors. Whether one wishes to question the ability of these statisticians to define their newly discovered factors or not, the least that their methods can do for Rorschach enthusiasts is to point out the relationships between variables.

For several reasons, it is premature to engage in debates with researchers who have factor-analyzed the Rorschach test as to the implications of their conclusions. The number of factor-analytic studies reported in the journals is small; the samples of subjects have been limited in size and breadth; some of the Rorschach scores are restricted in degrees of freedom by other scores, particularly, in the opinions of some investigators, by R, the total number of responses; the distribution of scores within categories is highly variable. Finally, the statistical method itself is as much influenced by the many irrelevant variables listed in Fig. 14.3, and by other errors of measurement discussed previously, as would be true of any other quantitative or nonquantitative treatment of data. Factor analysis is not immune to the errors introduced by differences between examiners or differences between methods of administration. Nor can its conclusions fail to reflect the lack of representative sampling of response tendencies, which is probably inherent in every assessment of personality based on responses to the ten specially selected Rorschach cards.

Nevertheless, this higher order statistical method does have something to say about the nature of conventional scoring categories. Although a few of the earlier studies have been restricted in scope, as in the analysis of content by Sandler and Ackner (45), or of content and language by Hsü (28), a larger number of the investigations have made use of all the major scoring categories. The emergence of a factor for productivity in the factor-analytic studies of Sen (48), Wittenborn (59, 60), Adcock (1), Cox (15), and Williams and Lawrence (56, 57) has led to a recent divergence in technical procedures with respect to inclusion of R, the total number of responses, in the matrix. Two studies will serve to illustrate the differences in outcome by pointing out not only the presence or absence of a factor for productivity but also the limitations imposed on the generality of statements which can be made from a small number of studies about factors underlying performance on the Rorschach test.

Consalvi and Canter (14) factor-analyzed scores on the Rorschach test, the Wechsler-Bellevue Form I Vocabulary, and the Raven's Progressive Matrices of 45 normal adults of a broad range of intelligence, education, and occupation. They extracted four factors from the Rorschach data:

I. A general factor of intelligence which correlated highly with scores on the Wechsler Vocabulary Test and Raven Progressive Matrices, and with $M+$, $FK + Fc + Fk$, $W+$, number of content categories, and $FC + FC'$. High negative loadings were found on two Rorschach variables, $F\%$ and $A\%$. Further analysis of the loadings on this factor suggested to the investigators that whereas single Rorschach scores may not be adequate predictors of intelligence, a multiple regression equation based on $M+$, $W+$, $FK + Fc + Fk$, and number of content categories might prove to be of value. This finding lends partial support to the conviction of many Rorschach specialists that variables must be treated only in combination with one another.

II. A unique factor of low form dominance, which included both color and shading ($C + C'$, and $K + c + k$), as well as a factorial similarity among the high form-dominant and shading scores.

III. A productivity factor, minimally related to intelligence. The highest loadings were with R, D, and number of content categories.

IV. A movement factor which included both $M+$ and $FM + m$, as well as $W+$. The two movement subcategories were found to differ in the fact that M had a high loading on the intelligence factor, while $FM + m$ did not.

In contrast to the all-inclusive approach of Consalvi and Canter, it was the intent of Coan to reduce the sources of spurious correlation as much as possible (13). Coan chose to eliminate not only R, the total number of responses, but also location, since the number of whole responses in relation to the number of detail responses is necessarily limited by the stimulus properties of the blot. Using 12 determinants as variables and Wittenborn's 92 undergraduate protocols as data (59), Coan obtained seven factors which he defined from their highest loadings, as follows:

I. *Not clearly definable*, but may indicate intelligence, productivity, or originality (very high loading with *FC*).

II and VI. Low perceptual control (anxiety and passive submission to emotional impulses). The highest loadings for II are *K*, *FK*, and *CF*; for VI the loadings are *c* and *C*.

III. Sensitivity to inner stimuli (*M*, *FM*, *m*, *K*, *C'*).

IV. Inner control, empathy (*M*, *F*, *Fc*, *C'*).

V. Outer control, or controlled emotional responsiveness to the environment (*m*, *Fc*, *C'*, *FC*).

VII. Largely residual.

Even with such statistical refinements and with the consequent elimination of a factor for productivity, it is fairly obvious that the definitions of the various factors are derived in large measure from traditional hypotheses concerning the empirical meaning of Rorschach determinants.

Wittenborn and Glickstein have taken different positions concerning the significance of *R* in a matrix of Rorschach scoring categories. Glickstein (23) regards *R* as a common third variable and, accordingly, reanalyzes data from two of Wittenborn's studies, presenting new tables of partial correlation coefficients, with *R* partialed out. He obtains lower positive correlation coefficients and many negative coefficients in his tables, and attributes this alteration in values not only to a partialling of the effects of *R* but also to the mutually exclusive nature of the scoring system which is employed for main responses. An example of this tendency in the extreme, as pointed out by Glickstein, would be the partial correlation between true-false items, which would have a value of -1.00. Wittenborn (61), in reply, states that the mutually exclusive nature of the scoring categories is not an important consideration since the number of categories is not as small as Glickstein implies. Of greater importance to Wittenborn is his conviction that *R* serves as the whole in a part-whole relationship, rather than as a common third variable, i.e., "the number of responses in the various scoring categories determines *R*, and *R* does not delimit the number of responses in any scoring category" (61, p. 75). For Wittenborn, the partialling of *R* would be the equivalent of partialling the full score on the WAIS from the intercorrelations among subtests.

The question of whether R should be eliminated or partialed from the correlation coefficients of a matrix, like many other questions of the appropriateness of conventional statistical methods in Rorschach methodology, is not limited in implications to the fine points of statistical analysis. It reflects to some extent the subject's tendency to respond to an ambiguous stimulus figure, as distinct from his behavior in a structured test situation in which he is formally requested to respond to a specified number, or even an unlimited number of problems or questions. As an example of the difference, we might imagine that a subject is seated in a small room covered with thousands of randomly assorted cards on each of which is printed a question pertaining to personality, to be answered "yes" or "no." The subject is instructed to continue answering each item he picks up until he becomes bored and restless. The number of responses later to be recorded in a particular scoring category will depend on the universe of items selected by the experimenter and on the response tendencies of the subject; the actual sample of items chosen by the subject, however, will be entirely a matter of chance.

The subject's responsiveness to the ten Rorschach cards would seem to differ on this point. The experimenter, again, supplies the stimulus figures, and the subject continues to respond until he loses interest; but now there are properties of the subject's perceptual behavior which dictate the areas to which he will respond and the determinants which he will utilize. The formula introduced earlier,

Threshold or intensity of response

$$= f \text{ (stimulus) (strength of response tendency)}$$

now becomes a very complex one, since a biased sampling of stimuli as well as the strength of response tendency is involved. It is no longer obvious either that R serves as a common third variable or that R serves as a whole in a part-whole relationship.

Granted that many difficulties in application of the method exist, the potential contribution of factor analysis to Rorschach methodology is not limited to a clarification and suggested revision of the conventional scoring categories. It is conceivable that factor-analytic studies may provide us also with an abstract view of the differences in responsiveness between normal and clinical groups of subjects. Along these lines, Wittenborn has found many similarities in the factorial structure of the Rorschach responses of separate groups of psychiatrically normal and disturbed groups of undergraduates (59, 60). Stotsky has factor-analyzed the responses of schizophrenic patients, eliminating R from the matrix, analyzing location and determinants separately, and utilizing only those variables for which more than half of the subjects gave one or more responses, in order to justify the use of the Pearson correlation coefficient (51). Although no broad generalizations can be made at present from the results of this one study of the responses of schizophrenic patients, such research may eventually help to answer many of our present questions concerning the applicability of the major interpretative hypotheses to a variety of subpopulations.

Now that this analysis of problems in validation has proceeded from a discussion of the verbal-perceptual behavior of the subject to an inspection of highly quantitative methods of analysis of Rorschach test data, a few conclusions are in order. It seems that we are in possession of an instrument which, by the standards of test construction and more rigorous experimental psychology, has not yet been able to justify its inclusion in contemporary psychological science. Its methods are those which have been privately legislated out of existence by many psychologists. The Rorschach test employs subjective report, intuition on the part of the examiner, and a configurational assembly of variables, none of which alone occurs in sufficient quantity to permit a satisfactory demonstration of either reliability or lack of reliability, or to provide evidence for representative sampling of response tendencies within an individual subject or among a group of subjects. The responses which comprise the raw data are themselves influenced by many extraneous variables.

And yet in the wake of this perhaps too painstaking enumeration of what some regard as liabilities and others regard as assets, there remains in the mind of the author a firm conviction that the ink blots do have something meaningful to say about personality which no other method of depth analysis quite succeeds in tapping. This is a conviction, and at our present stage of research can hardly be classified otherwise. This conviction, like that of many other persons who maintain strong loyalties to projective tests, stems from a use of the method in the clinical setting over a period of years. From the author's observations, however, a major shortcoming of the method has been the almost obsessive need on the part of the intuitive interpreter to account for every behavioral fragment in the protocol, as if the commitment to configurational analysis necessarily implied an all-or-none proposition. Such behavior would make it appear that the intuitive interpreter has achieved the impossible goal of eliminating all uninterpretable static from the system, a goal which most objective testers would never hope to reach.

There is little doubt in the author's mind that clinical test data will and possibly should always be interpreted as a configuration, and that the procedure will always involve the element of intuition. But there is considerable disagreement with the opinions of other advocates of the Rorschach method as to what constitutes a proper and reasonable objective for the future. The pressing need in Rorschach methodology seems to this observer to be not so much one of repetition of futile pleas for a larger body of more highly skilled intuitive interpreters, as a thorough experimental analysis of ambiguous perceptual materials and an ultimate resynthesis of more adequate subsets of ink-blot tests. The expectation is not that all undesirable static would be eliminated from the system, but that clarification could be made as to just what is unusable variability and what constitutes reasonably solid material for inference. The accomplishment of such an objective should relieve the Rorschach interpreter of much of his hopeless striving to account for all things at once.

It is a further opinion of this contributor that the many sources of variability inherent in the use of the ten stimulus figures presently available, and in the methods of administering the cards and of interpreting the responses, as discussed throughout this chapter, are sufficient to account for the difficulties in demonstrating the validity of the method as a whole. If it is thus possible to develop an explanation for the unwelcome results of formal experimentation by the processes of logical inference and deduction, it seems unnecessary to consign the negative and contradictory findings of such investigation to the realm of mystery.

It may be apparent to the reader who has a deep faith in the clinical validity of the Rorschach technique that the discussion in this chapter has not included a topical listing of studies which seem to provide evidence for the validity of several Rorschach hypotheses. The intent of the author in writing this chapter was not to place the studies with positive and those with negative results in a delicate balance and, at the conclusion of the compilation, to make a quantitative judgment. The purpose was instead to examine thoroughly the possible underlying reasons for the contradictions in the research literature, and to stick to the position that contradictory evidence is not conclusive evidence, either for or against an argument.

The Rorschach technique is seen in the concluding abstractions of the writer as the symbolic theme of a twentieth-century Prelude,

Chorale, and Fugue.   One may use the method, defend it, advance it, or work for its destruction by any one of these three patterns.

As a participant in the Prelude to a confidently expected future, the researcher may examine all fundamental assumptions, and acknowledge the presence of all relevant and irrelevant variables in Rorschach performance. He may decide that ink-blot methodology, if it is ever to achieve the status of a science, will very likely require a new foundation and new building blocks, chiseled from the vein of pure unrestricted research on experimental ink blot, or even noninkblot materials. The ten Rorschach cards we now use will have a limited life span, as determined by considerations of their current effectiveness relative to that of other available tests, and by the cultural lag involved in the adoption of any newer, more adequate instrument.   Crystallizing this vision of the future into a more perceptible form, the ink-blot test of tomorrow may consist of a number of subtests, both structured and unstructured in nature.

The clinical experimentalist who senses the direction of the Prelude will have a viewpoint different from that expressed by Ainsworth in 1954:

In the meantime [as our knowledge of personality functioning becomes more precise], the Rorschach Technique must be considered a partly finished and continuously developing method, available for investigations into the development and function of the individual personality, and to be brought to a more finished state through use in such investigations (2, p. 492).

Going beyond this position, our methodologist will believe that work on the stimulus materials of the ultimate ink-blot test has not yet begun. Although his research will profit considerably from the findings of previous studies on the ten Rorschach cards, he will not confine his efforts to those stimulus figures.

The voices of the second variation, the Chorale, tell the world of psychological science that the Rorschach technique, as it now exists, will eventually lay claim to its rightful place in the royal circle of scientific acceptability, a place which it deserves, but for which it has not been granted recognition. With a flexible diplomacy, as well as an intensity of conviction, the chanters of the Chorale will continue to strike the word "test" from their communications, thereby disclaiming responsibility for investigating the many contingencies of higher order interpretations. The appeal for recognition is to complexity, to usefulness in the clinical setting, to the intuitive skill of the interpreter, and to the uniqueness of the technique. The methods of research are, with minor concessions to pure experimental investigation, centered in the Rorschach cards themselves.

Finally, the extreme critics, the players of the Fugue, are convinced that they have spelled the end. With periodic bursts of fire followed by skillful retreats into the safety of platitudes concerning the principles of orthodox experimental research, the masters of method contemplate their victory. With little to contribute but verbal destruction, they search the ruins for the prayerful survivors.

What is the current status of the Rorschach technique? It seems to the author that it has no status apart from the methodological orientation of the group that is evaluating it. As a Fugue, it is an endeavor of the past; as a Chorale it is an effort in the timeless present; and as a Prelude it is an exploration, the fruits of which lie largely unknown in the future. By the canons of test analysis, the Rorschach technique as a whole has been shown at present to have neither satisfactory validity nor invalidity. By the vaguely defined canons of interview analysis, it occupies a unique place in the history of clinical investigation. As a part of a pre-science of projective testing, the Rorschach method may pass into oblivion or it may serve as a cornerstone for a future science of perception. It will remain for the man or woman who writes the chapter entitled "Rorschach, one hundred years after," to decide whether ink-blot interpretation has become one of the most powerful methods of understanding human nature—long after the imperialists of direct interrogation have given up all hope of determining the hidden, irreducible meaning of a "yes" response.

BIBLIOGRAPHY

1. Adcock, C. J. A factorial approach to Rorschach interpretation. *J. gen. Psychol.*, 1951, 44, 261–272.
2. Ainsworth, Mary D. Problems of Validation. In: Klopfer, B., Ainsworth, M. D., Klopfer, W. G., and Holt, R. R. *Developments in the Rorschach technique. Vol. I.* Yonkers: World Book Co., 1954.
3. Altus, W. D., and Thompson, Grace M. The Rorschach as a measure of intelligence. *J. consult. Psychol.*, 1949, 13, 341–347.
4. Anastasi, Anne. *Psychological Testing.* New York: The Macmillan Company, 1954.
5. Barron, F. Threshold for perception of human movement in inkblots, and its personality correlates. *Amer. Psychol.*, 1953, 8, 317–318 (abstract).
6. Baughman, E. E. Rorschach scores as a function of examiner difference. *J. proj. Tech.*, 1951, 15, 243–249.

7. Baughman, E. E. A comparative analysis of Rorschach forms with altered stimulus characteristics. *J. proj. Tech.*, 1954, **18**, 151–164.

8. Baughman, E. E. The role of the stimulus in Rorschach responses. *Psychol. Bull.*, 1958, **55**, 121–147.

9. Baughman, E. E. An experimental analysis of the relationship between stimulus structure and behavior on the Rorschach. *J. proj. Tech.*, 1959, **23**, 134–183.

10. Bechtoldt, H. P. Construct validity: a critique. *Amer. Psychol.*, 1959, **14**, 619–629.

11. Beck, S. J. *The six schizophrenias: reaction patterns in children and adults.* New York: The American Orthopsychiatric Association, Inc., 1954.

12. Behn-Rorschach Tafeln. Bern: Hans Huber.

13. Coan, R. A factor analysis of Rorschach determinants. *J. proj. Tech.*, 1956, **20**, 280–287.

14. Consalvi, C., and Canter, A. Rorschach scores as a function of four factors. *J. consult. Psychol.*, 1957, **21**, 47–51.

15. Cox, S. M. A factorial study of the Rorschach responses of normal and maladjusted boys. *J. genet. Psychol.*, 1951, **79**, 95–115.

16. Cronbach, L. J. A validation design for qualitative studies of personality. *J. consult. Psychol.*, 1948, **12**, 365–374.

17. Cronbach, L. J. *Essentials of psychological testing.* New York: Harper, 1949.

18. Cronbach, L. J. Pattern tabulation: a statistical method for analysis of limited patterns of scores, with particular reference to the Rorschach test. *Educ. Psychol. Measmt.*, 1949, **9**, 149–171.

19. Cronbach, L. J. Statistical methods applied to Rorschach scores: a review. *Psychol. Bull.*, 1949, **46**, 393–429.

20. Cronbach, L. J., and Meehl, P. E. Construct validity in psychological tests. *Psychol. Bull.*, 1955, **52**, 281–302.

21. Epstein, S., Nelson, Jane V, and Tanofsky, R. Responses to inkblots as measures of individual differences. *J. consult. Psychol.*, 1957, **21**, 211–215.

22. Fisher, S., and Cleveland, S. E. *Body image and personality.* Princeton: D. Van Nostrand Company, 1958.

23. Glickstein, M. A note on Wittenborn's factor analysis of Rorschach scoring categories. *J. consult. Psychol.*, 1959, **23**, 69–75.

24. Goodenough, Florence L. *Mental testing.* New York: Rinehart, 1949.

25. Guilford, J. P. New standards for test evaluation. *Educ. Psychol. Measmt.*, 1946, **6**, 427–438.

26. Henry, Edith M., and Rotter, J. B. Situational influences on Rorschach responses. *J. consult. Psychol.*, 1956, **20**, 457–462.

27. Holtzman, W. H., and Sells, S. B. Prediction of flying success by clinical analysis of test protocols. *J. abnorm. soc. Psychol.*, 1954, **49**, 485–498.

28. Hsü, E. H. The Rorschach response and factor analysis. *J. gen. Psychol.*, 1947, **37**, 129–138.

29. Kelly, E. L., and Fiske, D. W. *The prediction of performance in clinical psychology.* Ann Arbor: University of Michigan Press, 1951.

30. Klingensmith, S. W. Effects of different methods of structuring the Rorschach inquiry upon determinant scores. *J. clin. Psychol.*, 1957, **13**, 279–282.

31. Korner, Anneliese F.   Theoretical considerations concerning the scope and limitations of projective techniques.   *J. abnorm. soc. Psychol.,* 1950, **45,** 619–627.

32. Levy, D. M., reference in Klopfer, B., and Kelley, D. McG.   *The Rorschach technique.*   Yonkers: World Book Co., 1942.

33. Little, K. B., and Shneidman, E. S.   Congruencies among interpretations of psychological test and anamnestic data.   *Psychol. Monogr.,* 1959, **73,** No. 6 (whole No. 476).

34. Lord, Edith.   Experimentally induced variations in Rorschach performance.   *Psychol. Monogr.,* 1950, **64,** No. 316.

35. Meer, B.   The relative difficulty of the Rorschach cards.   *J. proj. Tech.,* 1955, **19,** 43–53.

36. Merry, Frieda K., and Merry, R. V.   *The first two decades of life* (2nd ed.).   New York: Harper, 1958.

37. Molish, H. B., and Beck, S. J.   Further explorations of the "six schizophrenias": type S-3.   *Amer. J. Orthopsychiat.,* 1958, **28,** 483–505.

38. Morris, C. W.   Foundations of the theory of signs.   In: Neurath, O., Carnap, R., and Morris, C. W. (eds.), *International encyclopedia of unified science. Vol. I.*   Chicago: The University of Chicago Press, 1955, 78–137.

39. Piotrowski, Z. A.   *Perceptanalysis.*   New York: The Macmillan Company, 1957.

40. Rosenzweig, S.   Idiodynamics in personality theory with special reference to projective methods.   *Psychol. Rev.,* 1951, **58,** 213–223.

41. Ruch, F. L.   *Psychology and Life* (5th ed.).   Chicago: Scott, Foresman, and Co., 1958.

42. Rust, R. M.   Some correlates of the movement response.   *J. Pers.,* 1948, **16,** 369–401.

43. Rust, R. M.   The Levy movement cards: EPA round table.   *J. Pers.,* 1948, **17,** 153–156.

44. Sanders, R., and Cleveland, S. E.   The relationship between certain examiner personality variables and subjects' Rorschach scores.   *J. proj. Tech.,* 1953, **17,** 34–50.

45. Sandler, J., and Ackner, B.   Rorschach content analysis: an experimental investigation.   *Brit. J. Med. Psychol.,* 1951, **24,** 180–201.

46. Sarason, S. B.   *The clinical interaction.*   New York: Harper, 1954.

47. Schneider, L. I.   Rorschach validation: some methodological aspects.   *Psychol. Bull.,* 1950, **47,** 493–508.

48. Sen, A.   A study of the Rorschach test.   *Brit. J. educ. Psychol.,* 1949, **19,** 142–143.

49. Singer, J. L., Meltzoff, J., and Goldman, G. D.   Rorschach movement responses following motor inhibition and hyperactivity.   *J. consult. Psychol.,* 1952, **16,** 359–364.

50. Starer, E.   The use of the kaleidoscope as an adjunct to the Rorschach.   *J. consult. Psychol.,* 1956, **20,** 466.

51. Stotsky, B. A.   Factor analysis of Rorschach scores of schizophrenics.   *J. clin. Psychol.,* 1957, **13,** 275–278.

52. Technical recommendations for psychological tests and diagnostic techniques.   *Psychol. Bull. Suppl.,* 1954, 51, **2,** pt. 2, 1–38.

53. Thurstone, L. L. The Rorschach in psychological science. *J. abnorm. soc. Psychol.*, 1948, **43**, 471–475.
54. Vernon, P. E. The Rorschach ink-blot test, I. *Brit. J. Med. Psychol.*, 1933, **13**, 89–118.
55. White, R. W. Interpretation of imaginative productions. In: Hunt, J. McV. (ed.), *Personality and the behavior disorders. Vol. I.* New York: Ronald Press, 1944.
56. Williams, H. L., and Lawrence, J. F. Further investigation of Rorschach determinants subjected to factor analysis. *J. consult. Psychol.*, 1953, **17**, 261–264.
57. Williams, H. L., and Lawrence, J. F. Comparison of the Rorschach and MMPI by means of factor analysis. *J. consult. Psychol.*, 1954, **18**, 193–197.
58. Willner, Allen E. The interpretation of the Rorschach test as a function of interpreter, degree of information, and the subject's personality. *Dissert. Abstr.*, 1957, **17**, 1385–1386.
59. Wittenborn, J. R. A factor analysis of Rorschach scoring categories. *J. consult. Psychol.*, 1950, **14**, 261–267.
60. Wittenborn, J. R. Level of mental health as a factor in the implications of Rorschach scores. *J. consult. Psychol.*, 1950, **14**, 469–472.
61. Wittenborn, J. R. Some comments on confounded correlations among Rorschach scores. *J. consult. Psychol.*, 1959, **23**, 75–77.

APPENDIX

by Laura C. Toomey
and Maria A. Rickers-Ovsiankina

TABULAR COMPARISON OF
RORSCHACH SCORING SYSTEMS

These tables represent a comparison of the basic features of several of the scoring systems that are relatively frequently used in English language writings.

The tables have been prepared to provide the following information:

1. To give the major scoring categories of each system in compact form for quick reference.

2. To show graphically what score in one system corresponds to what score in another system, and to what extent.

3. To demonstrate the general approach of each scoring system in terms of such practical considerations as relative inclusiveness, refinement, clarity, and communicability.

The systems of the following people have been included: Rorschach, Binder, Rapaport and Schafer, Beck, Piotrowski, Hertz, and Klopfer. Binder's scoring is identical with that of Rorschach, except for shading, and with that exception the two systems have been listed as one. The order of presentation is as given above, except in Tables A.2A (Chiaroscuro) and A.4 (Popular-Original), where special features of certain systems made different grouping more logical.

The scores of each system and their definitions are presented in a vertical column, with equivalent scores on the same horizontal level. Where a score is common to two or more systems, the definition extends across the corresponding columns. In general, where vertical lines separate columns, there are significant differences between the systems involved, in categories, in the details of the definitions, or both. Where a score is basically the same for two systems, but minor dif-

TABLE A.1. Locations

RORSCHACH AND BINDER	RAPAPORT AND SCHAFER	BECK	PIOTROWSKI	HERTZ	KLOPFER
DW					
A single detail, more or less clearly perceived, is used as the basis for the interpretation of the whole. Detail used may also be rare or space detail.					
CONFABULATED RESPONSE			Interpretation applies well to particular detail, but not to whole blot.		
W WHOLE					
Response to the whole blot, with no part specifically omitted except white spaces. The entire blot *must* be used.					(1) Entire blot used, or (2) Subject intends to respond to the whole, but inadvertently omits minor part(s).
			Exception: *M* on card III is *W* even when it covers only usual figures.	**W** CUT-OFF WHOLE One or two small parts omitted; subject intends to respond to whole.	**W** CUT-OFF WHOLE Subject uses at least ⅔ of blot and makes a point of omitting certain portions.
			Dr *D* plus some adjacent portions of the blot.		

WHOLE RESPONSE

D

Response to a portion which is relatively large, clearly set off, and/or frequently interpreted.

DETAIL	NORMAL DETAIL	DETAIL	NORMAL DETAIL	NORMAL DETAIL	LARGE USUAL DETAIL
LARGE or USUAL DETAIL					
"Can be determined statistically"; in practice becomes known through experience.	**Dd** — Small but not tiny area, clearly set off from the bulk of the blot.	Statistically determined by frequency of each *D* in each card.	Frequently selected by healthy subjects.	"Frequently perceived" by normal subjects, statistically determined.	Large detail, clearly marked off from rest of blot.
					d SMALL USUAL DETAIL. Small detail clearly marked off from rest of blot.
SMALL or RARE DETAIL					
Dd SMALL DETAIL. An unusual or small detail.	**Dr** — Tiny area, or areas neither clearly set off nor frequently interpreted.	**Dd** RARE DETAIL. Not frequently enough selected to be *D*.	**d** SMALL OR RARE DETAIL. Area rarely selected.	**Dr** RARE DETAIL. Detail which is rarely perceived, as statistically determined.	**dd** TINY DETAIL. Small detail less frequent than d.
	De EDGE DETAIL. Contour part.				**de** EDGE DETAIL **di** INSIDE DETAIL **dr** RARE DETAIL
Do OLIGOPHRENIC DETAIL. Part of human or animal usually seen complete.	**Do** OLIGOPHRENIC DETAIL. Part of any concept usually seen complete.	**Hdx** **Adx** Same as Rorschach's *Do*; scored under Content.	**Do** (After Rorschach.)	**Do** (After Rorschach.)	Large or small detail, not clearly marked off in blot.

443

TABLE A. 1. Locations (Continued)

Rorschach and Binder	Rapaport and Schafer	Beck	Piotrowski	Hertz	Klopfer
s SPACE DETAIL White intermediate figures rather than surrounding black or colored areas.	**s** A relatively large white area in or around the blot.	**Ds** MAJOR WHITE SPACE (1) White areas in cards II, VII, and IX which qualify as *D* on frequency basis; *or* (2) *D* with major or minor white space as unit.	**s** NORMAL SPACE DETAIL White space which is frequently selected by normal subjects.		**s** WHITE SPACE Reversal of figure and ground so that white space is used for principal part of response.
	s A relatively small white area.	**Dds** MINOR WHITE SPACE (1) White area not *Ds*; *or* (2) *Dd* with minor white space as unit.	**d** RARE OR SMALL SPACE DETAIL White space which is rarely selected by normal subjects.		

WHITE SPACE

ferences in definition exist, or the notation for the score is not the same, an incomplete vertical line separates only that part of the material that is not common to the two (e.g., in Table A.2, the *FM* of Piotrowski, Hertz, and Klopfer). Explanations and definitions, as far as possible, are each authors' own.

When an author has given a name to a scoring symbol, it has been included. Names have been assigned to nearly all the scores by everybody except Rapaport and Schafer, who in their writings refer to many of the scores by symbol only. A few "nonscorable" kinds of responses have been mentioned in the tables for reasons of completeness of comparison (in at least one other system, by contrast, they rate a score), and for these, of course, no symbol is given since none is used in actual scoring. For the most part, space limitations precluded illustrating the applications of scoring with actual responses, but in a few places where clarity seemed to demand it, examples have been given.

Table A.1 contains the principal location categories. No attempt has been made to cover the qualitative classifications, such as "fabulized combination" and "contamination," since they are not part of the formal scoring system in the same way as location.

Table A.2 contains the determinant categories other than shading, and Table A.2A covers shading categories. Shading was put into a separate table because the shading scores of one system cannot be compared with the corresponding scores of all the others as can such categories as form and movement.

Table A.3 compares form quality criteria, and Table A.4 covers the popular-original classification. Designation of response content has not been included in the tabulation, because content categories vary widely in range and inclusiveness, and because their names are generally self-explanatory. It is Hertz who has the most comprehensive list of content scores, and she also uses many content subdivisions in her quantitative analysis.

The tables outline the components of the basic scoring only, and no comparison has been made of the ways in which the different authors use summation scores or ratios (such as total number of responses or weighted color sum), or of the different approaches to organization.

Besides their rather obvious function as a convenient reference list, it is hoped that the tables may serve a somewhat broader purpose. For instance, comparison of the classificational criteria employed by different systems may foster insights into the logic underlying the categories, and in some cases might throw new light upon the implicit psychological nature of these categories.

TABLE A.2. Determinants (excluding shading)

Rorschach and Binder	Rapaport and Schafer	Beck	Piotrowski	Hertz	Klopfer
F FORM	Response determined solely by the outline or shape of the blot area.				
				FM ANIMAL MOVEMENT Animal in non-humanlike movement or posture. Involves a feeling of change in muscular tension.	→**FM** TENDENCY TO ANIMAL MOVEMENT Animal movement acknowledged reluctantly, posture in drawing, etc., of animal; animal-like expression in animal; weak movement or weak posture in animal. Includes parts of animals in animal-like motion.

FORM

FM Inanimate object moving or being moved; response determined primarily by definite form.

    Includes unreal figures or masks, animal or human.

mF Inanimate object of indefinite form moving or being moved.

m Inanimate object moving or being moved; no form involved. Includes abstract forces.

→M TENDENCY TO HUMAN MOVEMENT

Human movement or posture conceded reluctantly; human posture in drawing, etc.; humanlike expression on animal; tiny human in landscape.

Includes part of human in motion.

m INANIMATE MOVEMENT

Response involving both (1) "feeling of change in muscular tension" and (2) inanimate object in movement or state in which movement is actively prevented.

INANIMATE MOVEMENT

(Sometimes scored **m**, but generally scored **F**, after Rorschach.)

Includes part of human in motion.

Includes animal in humanlike movement.

FM

WEAK MOVEMENT TENDENCY

Probable *M*-impression admitted under leading questions; usual humans seen as animals in humanlike movement; large part of human in clear movement.

Ms

Human-movement response using relatively small area.

(In rare cases, animals and inanimate objects in motion are scored **m**. Ordinarily a tendency to **M** is noted, but the response is still scored **F**.)

Includes animal in humanlike movement.

TABLE A2. Determinants (excluding shading) (Continued)

RORSCHACH AND BINDER	RAPAPORT AND SCHAFER	BECK	PIOTROWSKI	HERTZ	KLOPFER
MOVEMENT		**M** HUMAN MOVEMENT Human figure in movement or posture, involving feeling of muscular tension on the part of the subject.			
COLOR Color		**FC** FORM-COLOR Interpretation determined primarily by form, secondarily by color.			Colored object of definite form, where color used is that of the object in its natural state.
	FC ARBITRARY ARBITRARY FORM-COLOR Response where subject assigns inappropriate color to a form without rationalizing it as artificial. ("A blue horse.")			**FC ARBIT** ARBITRARY FORM-COLOR (Same as Rapaport and Schafer.)	**F→C** FORCED FORM-COLOR Form-color response where subject "forces" color not that of object naturally; makes some attempt to rationalize color.

	ARBITRARY FORM-COLOR
F/C Same as Rapaport and Schafer.	
FC DENIAL FORM-COLOR DENIAL Color is referred to, but denied or negated.	**Cd** COLOR DENIAL Color which presumably was used is denied. ("Flowers, but not because of the colors.")

F/C

Form-color response where color is used artificially, as "a map of Norway."

FC̄ FORM-COLOR BY DENIAL

Form-color response where inappropriate color is specifically excluded. ("A bear but it's the wrong color.") Not included in calculation of experience balance.

449

TABLE A.2. Determinants (excluding shading) (Continued)

RORSCHACH AND BINDER	RAPAPORT AND SCHAFER	BECK	PIOTROWSKI	HERTZ	KLOPFER
			Cp COLOR PROJECTION Color response to achromatic area (not separate response category and not tabulated with color responses; used as memory aid to facilitate interpreting); e.g., "a blue [colored] bird" to card V, is scored F_{Cp}		

FC sym FORM-COLOR SYMBOLISM Form-color response where color is used symbolically.

Chromatic Color

COLOR

FC'	FY FLAT GREY	Fc'	FCh''	FC' FORM-ACHRO-MATIC COLOR
Response determined primarily by form, secondarily by black, grey or white color.	Response in which form is "dominant," shading as an element in the black-white series is secondary.	Response determined primarily by the form; refers clearly to the dark or black aspects of the blot as dysphoric.	Response determined primarily by form, secondarily by black color.	Response determined primarily by definite form, secondarily by black, grey or white color.
		FCw Response determined primarily by form, secondarily by white color.	**FCh'** Response determined primarily by form, secondarily by grey or white color.	

RORSCHACH AND BINDER	RAPAPORT AND SCHAFER	BECK	PIOTROWSKI	HERTZ	KLOPFER
CF COLOR-FORM		Interpretation determined primarily by color, secondarily by form.			Colored object of vague or indefinite form, with color that of object in its natural state.
					C↔F FORCED COLOR-FORM Color-form response where subject "forces" color not that of the object naturally.
					CF sym COLOR-FORM SYMBOLISM Color-form response where color is used symbolically.

Chromatic Color

FORM

C/F Color-form response where color is used artificially, as "a colored map."			**C/F** ARBITRARY COLOR-FORM Same as Rapaport and Schafer.	
C'F Response determined primarily by black, grey or white color, secondarily by form.	**YF** Response in which shading as values of grey is dominant, form is secondary.	(For practical reasons of simplification, $c'F$ is omitted from this scoring scheme, and all potential $c'F$ are scored as either Fc' or c'.)	**C'F** ACHROMATIC COLOR-FORM Response determined primarily by black, grey or white color, secondarily by form.	
			Ch''F Response determined primarily by black color, secondarily by form.	**Ch'F** Response determined primarily by grey or white color, secondarily by form.

TABLE A.2. Determinants (excluding shading) (Continued)

	RORSCHACH AND BINDER	RAPAPORT AND SCHAFER	BECK	PIOTROWSKI	HERTZ	KLOPFER
C PURE COLOR	Interpretation determined by color, no form being involved.					Scored only where a certain color signifies the same concept in several cards and no attempt is made to relate the concept to other responses in those cards. Ex.: "blood" in isolation, no "animal fighting," etc.
Cn COLOR NAMING	Color is named, with no attempt at interpretation.					
		Scored as a response, since it is so intended, as an answer to "what could this be?"	Scored and tabulated, but not included in sum C.	Color is named, but not included	Scored only when subject intends as interpretation.	Scored only when subject intends as interpretation and gives no other response to same blot.

COLOR
color

COLOR DENOMINATION

Not a scorable response and not so intended by the subject.

COLOR DESCRIPTION

Not a scorable response. Reference to beauty or colorfulness of blot.

C denom COLOR DENOMINATION

Color referred to specifically ("red as you see it in a spectrum"). Infrequently a scorable response.

C des COLOR DESCRIPTION

Colors are described with no attempt at interpretation. Scored only when subject intends as interpretation.

C sym SYMBOLIC CRUDE COLOR

Color stands for an abstract idea.

C sym COLOR SYMBOLISM

TABLE A.2.A. Chiarascuro (shading)

RORSCHACH	BINDER	RAPAPORT AND SCHAFER	PIOTROWSKI	HERTZ	KLOPFER	BECK
F(C)			**Fc**	**Fc** DIFFERENTIATED TEXTURE	DIFFERENTIATED TEXTURE	**FT** FORM-TEXTURE
Response determined primarily by form, secondarily by light-dark nuances of separate shadings.			Interpretation based primarily on form, enriched by light graded (differentiated) shading.	Response determined primarily by definite form, secondarily by surface texture.		
		Shading used to elaborate an *FC* response.		**F(C)**		Also: Rounded effect; surface reflection.
			Includes vista.	Response determined primarily by form, secondarily by light-dark nuances of separate shadings. Includes vista or perspective.	**FK** VISTA	**FV** VISTA
		Also: Shading used to define form within heavily shaded area.			Response involving differentiated depth: a 3-dimensional effect, stressing: one object in front of another.	distance, height, or depth.
Includes vista.						
	FCh	FORM SHADING		**FCh**	**Fk**	**FY** FLAT-GREY
	Response determined primarily by definite form, secondarily by diffuse total "shading impression," which is well integrated with form.			(Same as Rapaport and Schafer.)	3-dimensional expanse projected on a 2-dimensional plane.	Light-determined response, where form is dominant.

FORM SHADING

458

SHADING FORM

	SHADING FORM	UNDIFFERENTIATED TEXTURE		TEXTURE-FORM
	ChF	**cF**		**TF**
	Response determined primarily by general diffuse shading impression with indistinctly perceived form.	Response determined primarily by surface texture and secondarily by form.		Response determined primarily by surface texture and secondarily by form.
Includes texture.				
Form is definite, but shading is undifferentiated.				

Fc	**(C)F**	**ChF**
Highly differentiated texture in indeterminate form.	3-dimensional-effect; shading dominates form.	(Same as Rapaport and Schafer, excluding texture.)

KF UNDIFFERENTIATED DIFFUSION	**kF**	**VF**	**YF**
Response involving diffusion and vague form.	3-dimensions projected on 2; undifferentiated shading and vague form.	Depth or distance dominates form.	Light-determined response, where shading is dominant, form is secondary.

(For practical reasons of simplification, cF is omitted from this scoring scheme, and all potential cF are scored as either Fc or c.)

TABLE A.2.A. Chiarascuro (Shading) (Continued)

RORSCHACH	BINDER	RAPAPORT AND SCHAFER	PIOTROWSKI	HERTZ	KLOPFER	BECK
		(C)F Response in which shading is used to define form rather than "as shading," but form is vague. Also: Shading used in a *CF* response.				

SHADING FORM (Cont.)

Ch — PURE SHADING	**c**	**(C)** / **Ch**	**K** / **k**	**T** — PURE TEXTURE (**V** / **Y**)
Response determined entirely by general diffuse "shading" impression, with no form at all.	Interpretations in which the form is disregarded, but which nevertheless point to a concrete object with a definite physical structure. (Example: "topographical maps," "fog," "summer clouds.") Explicitly excludes responses in which achromatic area is interpreted as dark or black.	**(C)** 3-dimensional effect shading; no form. **Ch** (Same as Rapaport and Schafer excluding texture.)	**K** Diffusion; depth with no form, space-filling light. **k** 3-dimensional object projected on a 2-dimensional plane, with no form at all.	Response determined solely by undifferentiated surface texture, form disregarded. **V** Formless depth distance. **Y** Response determined entirely by grey values, with no form.

TABLE A.3. Form Quality

Rorschach and Binder	Rapaport and Schafer	Beck	Piotrowski	Hertz	Klopfer*
			F+ GOOD FORM		
Form as good as or better than these "given frequently" by normals.	Form responses of acceptable or superior accuracy: (1) can be readily empathized with, or (2) are given frequently by normals.	Established by comparison with tables of responses frequently given by normal subjects and infrequently by mental patients.	Sharply perceived form, which fits blot as well as or better than the percepts of popular responses fit their respective areas.	Sharply perceived form whose contours fit the outline of the blot area: (1) Given frequently by normals, or (2) response resembling established F+, or (3) response quite unlike any in lists, but subjectively judged to fit the blot area.	Form responses above average in accuracy, organization, and/or elaboration.
	F±	**F**	**F±**		**F**
	Basically acceptable (F+) response with some minor inaccuracy.	Response to minute Dd, too infrequent to have established criteria.	Response referring to object which does not have permanent invariable shape, though not formless.		Ordinary, popular, or vague form responses.
	F∓				
	Basically inaccurate (F−) form with				

462

	some saving feature; form responses referring to object with vague shape (cloud, map, etc.).			Form responses where there is marked discrepancy between form qualities of the concept and those of the blot.

F— POOR FORM

Form less good than F+.	Form response of inferior accuracy; strikingly vague or arbitrarily organized response with content that in reality is well articulated.	Established by comparison with tables of responses infrequently given by normal subjects, and frequently by mental patients.	Image of an object with a definite shape, but which does *not* fit its area well; (i.e., less well than popular responses fit their respective areas).	Poorly perceived form.

* In most recent publications, Klopfer outlines a more complex system, which is an expansion of the one given here.

TABLE A.4. Popular—Original

	RORSCHACH AND BINDER	RAPAPORT AND SCHAFER	HERTZ	KLOPFER	BECK	PIOTROWSKI
P POPULAR	Response given by at least one out of three subjects to that blot area.	Response given by at least one out of five subjects to that blot area.	Response given by at least one out of six normal subjects to that blot area.	One of the ten responses representative of the most frequently given, for the whole test.	Response that is *both*: (1) given at least three times as often as the next most frequent response to that location; *and* (2) given by at least 14% of normal subjects.	A list of 13, evidently given by at least 27% of a group of 200 "normal" and "mildly neurotic" adults. Weighted 1, 2, or 3 according to proportion of normative group giving.
(P)		Response approximately but not exactly the same as a popular.	Popular form incorporated in a more elaborated response.	(Same as Rapaport and Schafer.)		
O ORIGINAL	Response given by no more than one out of 100 subjects.				(Beck does not score original responses.)	(After Rorschach.)
	0+ involves good form 0− involves poor form 0 involves no form					

POPULAR

ORIGINAL

464

The selection of a set of scores most suitable for a particular research project should be facilitated by viewing the specific features of each scoring system in the light of the problem under investigation. In fact, in certain cases, the availability of a scoring category might actually prompt a refinement or greater precision in the experimental design.

BIBLIOGRAPHY

Beck, S. J. *Rorschach's test, Vol. I: Basic processes.* New York: Grune and Stratton, 1944.

Hertz, Helen. Binder's shading responses. *Rorschach Res. Exch.*, 1938, **2**, 79–88.

Hertz, Marguerite R. *Rorschach scoring symbols with definitions, scoring formulae, and qualitative notations.* Department of Psychology, Western Reserve University (mimeographed).

Hertz, Marguerite R. *Frequency tables for scoring responses to the Rorschach inkblot test.* Cleveland: Western Reserve University Press, 1951.

Klopfer, B., and Kelley, D. McG. *The Rorschach technique.* Yonkers: World Book Co., 1942.

Klopfer, B., Ainsworth, Mary D., Klopfer, W. G., and Holt, R. R. *Developments in the Rorschach technique, Vol. I: Technique and theory.* Yonkers: World Book Co., 1954.

Klopfer, W. G. The shading responses. *Rorschach Res. Exch.*, 1938, **2**, 76–78.

Piotrowski, Z. A. A comparative table of the main Rorschach symbols. *Psychiat. Quart.*, 1942, **16**, 30–37.

Piotrowski, Z. A. A Rorschach compendium, revised and enlarged. In Brussel, J. A., Hitch, K. S., and Piotrowski, Z. A. *A Rorschach training manual.* Utica, N. Y.: State Hospital Press, 1950, pp. 33–86.

Piotrowski, Z. A. *Perceptanalysis.* New York: Macmillan, 1957.

Rapaport, D., Schafer, R., and Gill, M. *Diagnostic psychological testing, Vol. II.* Chicago: Year Book Publishers, 1945.

Rorschach, H. *Psychodiagnostics.* Bern: Hans Huber; New York: Grune & Stratton, 1942.

Schafer, R. *Psychoanalytic interpretation in Rorschach testing.* New York: Grune & Stratton, 1954.

NAME INDEX*

* Numbers in boldface refer to entries in the bibliography.

467

SUBJECT INDEX

Date Due